CHEF'S
BOOK
OF
FORMULAS,
YIELDS,
AND
SIZES

CHEF'S BOOK OF FORMULAS, YIELDS, AND SIZES

ARNO SCHMIDT

 VAN NOSTRAND REINHOLD
New York

Copyright © 1990 by Van Nostrand Reinhold

Library of Congress Catalog Card Number 89-33711
ISBN 0-442-31835-9

Printed in the United States of America

Van Nostrand Reinhold
115 Fifth Avenue
New York, New York 10003

Van Nostrand Reinhold International Company Limited
11 New Fetter Lane
London EC4P 4EE, England

Van Nostrand Reinhold
480 La Trobe Street
Melbourne, Victoria 3000, Australia

Nelson Canada
1120 Birchmount Road
Scarborough, Ontario
Canada M1K 5G4

16 15 14 13 12 11 10 9 8 7 6 5 4 3 2 1

Library of Congress Cataloging in Publication Data

Schmidt, Arno, 1937-
  Chef's book of formulas, yields, and sizes/Arno Schmidt.
    p. cm.
  Includes index.
  ISBN 0-442-31835-9
  1. Quantity cookery.   I. Title.
TX820.S355 1990
641.5'7—dc20   89-33711
                                                 CIP

PREFACE

All foodservice operators, chefs, caterers, and dietitians are faced with the task and challenge of buying the right amount of food for an estimated number of meals. In order to accomplish this efficiently, they must assess yields realistically. Yields vary greatly. Obviously, serving size determine yields, but so does the accepted amount of trim and waste. The quality and size of the food purchased influence yields as well. In the case of fresh products, the time of year can alter the yield. Cooking methods, care taken during the preparation, and the dishing-out process can also have a bearing on yields.

This book addresses these issues. It mentions, when applicable, the form(s) in which the food is available—such as canned, dehydrated, fresh, or frozen. It lists the season for fresh foods, and the packs and sizes most likely to be purchased by foodservice operators. It lists suggested serving sizes, and the number of servings that are reasonably obtainable from the most common packs and sizes.

All yield calculations are based on at least two average samples, and are always rounded down, to account for spillage, waste, and over-portioning. Meat and fish yields are based on tests done by an experienced butcher. All pieces were well trimmed and acceptable to a fine foodservice operation. A less experienced person might get lower yields than calculated in this book. On the other hand, some operators might accept portions with less trim and consequently get a better yield than indicated.

Since the measuring devices used in kitchens vary greatly, a series of entries listing the sizes and volumes of bottles, cans, scoops, steam-table pans, and the like is also included. To make the book more accessible to foreign-born workers, all measurements are given in both U.S. and metric measurements. An ounce is calculated as 28 grams; a fluid ounce is 0.029 liter. Decimals were rounded off.

In response to current concern about nutrition, the calorie counts for the suggested serving sizes are given when possible. The book also lists formulas for commonly prepared items that are composed of ingredients requiring measurement or scaling for best results. Good examples are dressings and simple bakery items. Yields are always included with these formulas. Since this is a book of formulas, it is assumed that methods for basic preparations are not needed.

To round out the information, important but hard-to-access miscellaneous data are included, from the skirting lengths needed to drape banquet tables, to a simple formula for estimating uniform sizes, to yields of beer kegs.

All entries are listed alphabetically, except certain items that are listed in groups. For example, all beef information is listed under Beef, all clam information appears under Clams. The following is an outline of a standard entry:

ENTRY NAME
Specific Food Type
Further Food Type Differentiation (if necessary)

Season
Pack
Sizes (as packed)
 Kitchen Yields
Cooking recommendations
Waste
Counts (in terms of yield)
Serving size
Calories

This book is based on a lifetime of foodservice experience. It combines easy-to-understand formulas, yields, sizes, and quantities in one volume. It will serve as the most useful, ready reference on the shelves of any operator.

ACKNOWLEDGMENTS

So many friends and colleagues helped me collect the information contained in this book that it is impossible to remember them all. A remark made by a salesman, a question asked by a food server, and even a mistake made by someone in the kitchen have all triggered at different times the curiosity that led to additional information. I thank everyone who has accidentally or consciously helped to shape this book.

Special thanks go to my wife, Margaret, who encouraged me to get a PC at home, and who had the patience to learn the intricacies of the software program. When I needed help, she provided it. Without her, this book would not have been possible.

A

ABALONE

CANNED ABALONE

Imported from several countries. Available in steaks and minced.

Pack:
In water in cans of various sizes; the 1-lb (450 g) can is common.

Kitchen Yields

Serving size:
3 oz (85 g), drained. A 1-lb (450-g) can contains 13 to 14 oz (370 to 400 g) drained abalone, which yields 4 servings.

DRIED ABALONE

Pack:
By weight.

Kitchen Yields

Serving size:
1 oz (28 g).

FRESH ABALONE

Large gastropods with beautiful shells harvested in the tropical and temperate waters of the Pacific Ocean. California law prohibits shipping fresh, frozen, or canned abalone to other states. Most of the abalone available in other states is imported either from Mexico or from the Orient.

Pack:
By piece.

Sizes:
Shell sizes range from 11 in (270 mm) across for the red abalone, to about 3 to 5 in (70 to 120 mm) across for the flat abalone.

Kitchen Yields

Serving size:
4 oz (113 g).
Pound thin and sauté quickly. Serve immediately.

FROZEN ABALONE

Imported from Mexico and other tropical and semitropical countries.

Pack:
3-lb boxes. Other packs are available.

Sizes:
Twelve 4-oz (113-g) pieces. Other sizes are available.

Kitchen Yields

Serving size:
4 oz (113 g).
Pound thin and sauté quickly. Serve immediately.

ACHIOTE

See Mexican Foods.

ACKEE

A tropical fruit about the size of a large plum. Each contains three double-seed kernels. NOTE: The fruit is poisonous until it is ripe and has opened naturally, exposing the kernels.

Season:
Year-round.

Pack:
By count.

Size:
About 4 oz (113 g) each.

Kitchen Yields
Three double-seed kernels to each fruit. About eight double-seed kernels sautéed with seafood may be served as an appetizer.

AGAR-AGAR

A seaweed-based natural thickening agent used for thickening jams and ice cream; normally sold in thin, brittle sticks or in powder; also called *Japanese gelatin.*

Pack:
1-lb (450-g) packages.

Kitchen Yields
Thickening power is about five times greater than that of plain gelatin. It will set in room tempera-

ture and is not affected by acidity to the same extent as gelatin.

Agar-agar thickening power (liquid):
½ oz (14 g) for 20 cups equals 5 qt (4.8 l);
1 oz (28 g) for 40 cups equals 10 qt (9.7 l).

AGAR-AGAR CANDY

Formula
　　1 oz (28 g) agar-agar
　　3 lb (1.4 l) water
　　2 lb, 8 oz (680 g) sugar
　　1 lb, 4 oz (560 g) corn syrup

Boil to 218°F. Then add:

　　1 lb, 4 oz (560 g) corn syrup

Cool to 120°F, and add:

　　½ tb granulated citric acid
　　¾ oz (0.22 l) liquid fruit acid
　　Fruit flavor to taste

Kitchen Yields
5 lb (2.2 kg) mix; about 320 ¼-oz (7-g) candies.

ALFALFA SPROUTS

See Sprouts.

ALLIGATOR MEAT

Available frozen from Florida.

Pack:
By weight, normally 5-lb (2.3-kg) cartons.

Size:
Boneless tail pieces, each about 4 to 6 oz (114 to 170 g).

Kitchen Yields

Serving size:
4 oz (113 g).
The tail pieces are best cut into small medallions of about 2 oz (60 g) each and pounded well.

Trimming waste:
5 percent.

ALMONDS

Almonds used in foodservice are normally purchased shelled. They are available with skin on and blanched (skin removed). The major varieties are California, Carmel, Mission, and Nonpareil.

CALIFORNIA

Size:
18 to 40 kernels per ounce (28 g).

　　Whole, skin on
　　Cross-cut, skin on
　　Halves, skin on
　　Split, skin on
　　Cube-cut, skin on
　　Diced, skin on, available in two sizes
　　Diced, buttered and roasted, skin on

CARMEL

Size:
18 to 40 kernels per ounce (28 g).

　　Whole, skin on
　　Blanched, fine dice
　　Blanched, slivered in two sizes
　　Diced, skin on
　　Chopped pieces, skin on, available in three
　　　sizes

MISSION

Size:
20 to 40 kernels per ounce (28 g).

　　Whole, skin on
　　Whole and broken, skin on
　　Pieces, skin on
　　Slices, skin on, in three sizes
　　Powder, all white

NONPAREIL

Size:
20 to 40 kernels per ounce (28 g).

　　Whole, skin on
　　Whole, blanched
　　Blanched, whole and broken
　　Blanched, split
　　Blanched, sliced
　　Blanched slivers, diced, available in two sizes

Pack:

Six cans, each 5 lb (2.3 kg): raw or blanched almonds.

30-lb (13.5-kg) case: granulated, bleached, or natural almonds.

Six cans, each 5 lb (2.3 kg): salted, blanched, or raw almonds.

Six cans, each 5 lb (2.3 kg): sliced blanched or sliced raw almonds.

10-lb and 25-lb (4.5- and 11.2-kg) cartons of preceding varieties.

Kitchen Yields
1 cup chopped 4½ oz (128 g) = 130 almonds.
1 cup slivered 4 oz (113 g) = 115 almonds.
1 lb (450 g) in shell = 2 cups nutmeats.
1 lb (450 g) nutmeats = 3⅔ cups nutmeats.

Calories:

1 cup chopped = 775 Calories.
1 cup slivered = 690 Calories.
10 to 12 salted almonds, whole = 95 Calories.

ALMOND FILLING FOR BAKING

Formula
2 lb (900 g) almond paste
2 lb (900 g) sugar
2½ lb (11 kg) butter
1 qt (0.94 l) or about 20 whole eggs
Grated lemon peel to taste

Kitchen Yields
For Danish pastry, serving size is 1 oz (28.4 g) per piece; total formula produces 130 pieces.
For coffee cake, serving size is 8 oz (226 g) for each ring; total formula produces 17 rings.

ALMOND PASTE

Sweet almond paste is also called *marzipan.* It is available with either 60 percent unblanched almonds or with 60 percent blanched almonds. Almond paste made with blanched almonds is whiter than paste made with unblanched almonds.

Pack:

Six #10 cans equals 39 lb (17.5 kg).
One #10 can equals 104 oz, or 6½ lb (3 kg).

Kitchen Yields
Use for fillings or for macaroons.

MARZIPAN PASTE FOR MODELING

Formula
One #10 can (3.3 kg) almond paste, warmed
1 lb (450 g) glucose, warmed
3 lb (1.4 kg) confectioners sugar

Kitchen Yields
11 lb (4.9 kg) paste.

SALTED ALMONDS

Pack:

Two hundred ½-oz (14-g) packets; other packs are available.

AMARANTH

A spinachlike vegetable with dark green leaves, available year-round.

Pack:

By weight.

ANISE

Bulb-shaped vegetable with fine, bushy leaves. The flavor is slightly licorice. The vegetable is sometimes confused with the vegetable fennel, but fennel does not form a bulb. Available canned and fresh. Anise seeds are used as a flavoring agent in baked goods and cordials. *See also* Fennel.

CANNED ANISE

Pack:

Various packs are available. It is often marketed as fennel.

FRESH ANISE

Season:

Domestic anise is available from fall to spring and is imported the rest of the year.

Pack:

40- to 50-lb (18- to 22.5-kg) boxes; 10-kg (22-lb) boxes, mostly imports.

Count:
24 bulbs to a box.

Size:
1¾ to 2 lb (780 to 900 g), with greens still attached.
Imported anise is shipped trimmed.

Kitchen Yields
Average size of bulb with most greens removed is
10 oz (280 g).

ANNATTO (ACHIOTE)

See Mexican Foods.

APPLES

Apple products include juice and various forms of
cider. Apples themselves are available canned,
dehydrated, fresh, and frozen. Crab apples are
discussed in a separate entry; *see* Crab Apples.

APPLE CIDER
Cider is available in four forms: *fresh, sweet apple
cider* (cloudy, with a limited shelf life); *pasteurized apple cider* (clear or slightly cloudy, with a
long shelf life unopened; almost indistinguishable
from apple juice); *fermented sweet cider* (may
contain 2 to 3 percent alcohol); and *hard cider*
(fully fermented alcoholic beverage that can be
distilled into apple brandy).

Pack:
1-gal, ½-gal, or 1-qt (3.8-, 1.88-, or 0.94-l) bottles.

Kitchen Yields
Yield varies, depending on use. Pasteurized apple
cider is often substituted for apple juice.

APPLE JUICE
Available canned, in glass bottles, and as frozen
concentrate.

Pack:
Juice, ready to serve, in the following sizes:

> Forty-eight 5½-oz (0.046-liter) cans.
> Twenty-four 10-oz (0.29-l) glass bottles.
> Twelve 46-oz (1.33-l) cans.
> Twelve 1-qt (0.94-l) glass bottles.

> Six 64-oz (1.88-l) bottles.
> Four 1-gal (3.7-l) glass or plastic bottles.

Kitchen Yields

Serving size:
Varies from 6 to 10 oz (0.17 to 0.3 l).

Pack:
Frozen juice concentrate, in the following sizes:

> Six 46-oz (1.3-l) cans.
> Twelve 32-oz (0.94-l) cans.

Kitchen Yields
One part frozen juice mixes with three parts
water.
One 32-oz (0.94-l) can produces 1 gal (3.8 l) juice.
One 32-oz (0.94-l) can produces 21 servings of 6 oz
(0.18 l) each.

CANNED APPLES
Available as rings, slices, pieces, baked whole,
and sauce. Applesauce is available with varying
sugar contents.

APPLE PIECES

Pack:
Six #10 cans. One can contains 93 oz (2.6 kg)
drained apple pieces.

APPLE SAUCE

Pack:
Six #10 cans contain 96 oz (2.6 kg) each.
Twenty-four #303 cans contain 15½ oz (510 g) each.

Kitchen Yields

Serving size:
½ cup, or 4 oz (112 g);
one #10 can contains 24 servings, so
one case contains 144 servings.
One #303 can contains 3½ servings.

Calories:
½ cup: 4 oz (112 g) sweetened = 101 Calories.
½ cup: 4 oz (112 g) unsweetened = 50 Calories.

APPLE SLICES

Pack:
Six #10 cans; twenty-four #2½ cans; twenty-four
#2 cans.

Kitchen Yields
One #10 can contains 96 oz (2.7 kg), drained weight. One #2½ can contains 26 oz (738 g), drained weight. One #2 can contains 18 oz (511 g), drained weight.

BAKED APPLES

Pack:
Six #10 cans of 96 oz (2.7 kg) each.

Kitchen Yields
One #10 can contains 20 apples. Other sizes are available.

SPICED APPLE RINGS

Pack:
10 cans.

Kitchen Yields
One #10 can contains 85 to 90 rings. Other sizes are available.

WHOLE SPICED CRAB APPLES
See also Crab Apples.

Pack:
Six #10 cans.

Kitchen Yields
One #10 can contains 60 to 70 apples.

DEHYDRATED APPLES
Available as rings, wedges, and pie pieces.

Pack:
By weight. Various packs are available.

Kitchen Yields
1 lb (450 g) yields 4⅓ lb (1.9 kg) when cooked.

Serving size:
½ cup; 1 lb (450 g) produces 14 servings.

FRESH APPLES
Apples are generally classified into three categories: eating apples, cooking apples, and all-purpose apples.

Season:
Apples are available year-round. Table A-1 gives more specific information about popular varieties.

Table A-1 Recommended Uses and Seasons of Fresh Apples

Variety	Flavor/Texture	Fresh Salads	Pie	Sauce	Baking	Freezing	Season
Cortland	Crisp, firm	Good	Good	Good	Very good	Good	September to February
Golden Delicious	Sweet, semifirm	Excellent	Excellent	Good	Good	Good	Year-round
Granny Smith	Tart, crisp	Very good	Very good	Very good	Very good	Very good	November to July
Jonathan	Tart, tender	Very good	Very good	Very good	Poor	Very good	September to January
McIntosh	Aromatic, juicy	Excellent	Good	Good	Good	Good	October to April
Newton Pippin	Slightly tart, firm	Very good	Excellent	Excellent	Very good	Excellent	September to June
Red Delicious	Sweet, crisp	Excellent	Fair	Fair	Poor	Fair	Year-round
Rome Beauty	Slightly tart, firm	Good	Very good	Very good	Excellent	Very good	October to June
Winesap	Slightly tart, firm	Excellent	Good	Good	Good	Very good	October to July

Pack:
38 to 42 lb (17.1 to 18.9 kg), loose; 40 to 45 lb (18 to 20.2 kg), with tray packs; 37 to 43 lb (16.6 to 19.3 kg), cell packs; 42 to 52 lb (18.9 to 32.4 kg), bushels.

Counts:
Tray Packs: 48, 56, 64, 72, 80, 88, 100, 113, 125, 138, 150, 163, 175, 198.
Cell Packs: 64, 80, 96, 100, 120, 140, 160, 200, 216.

Sizes:
Apple sizes are listed by diameter. Table A-2 gives sizes in relation to count by carton and by bushel.

Common hotel sizes:
Bakers, 48 to 56 apples to a carton.
Delicious Extra Fancy, 88 apples to a box.

Weights:
Four small apples weigh 1 lb (450 g).
Three medium-size apples weigh 1 lb (450 g).
Two large apples weigh 1 lb (450 g).

Table A-2 Counts and Sizes of Fresh Apples

Cartons		Bushels	
Counts	*Diameter*	*Counts*	*Diameter*
72	3½ in (88.9 mm)		
88	3¼ in (82 mm)	90	3¼ to 3½ in (83 to 89 mm)
100	3⅛ in (80 mm)	100/110	2¾ to 3 in (70 to 76 mm)
113	3 in (76 mm)		
125	2⅞ in (73 mm)		
138	2¾ in (70 mm)	135/145	2¼ to 2¾ in (57 to 70 mm)
150	2⅝ in (67 mm)		
163	2½ in (63 mm)	185/195	2¼ to 2½ in (57 to 63 mm)
		250	2¼ in (57 mm)

Kitchen Yields
1 cup diced apple equals one medium apple; 3 cups diced apple equal 1 lb (450 g) apple.

Pie:
2½ lb (1.1 kg) apple yield one 9-in-diameter pie.
1 bushel apples yields ten 9-in-diameter pies.

Sauce:
1 bushel apples yields 16 to 20 qt (15 to 19 l) apple sauce.

Calories:
One apple, medium, unpeeled, 5.3 oz (150 g), 2¾-in diameter = 90 Calories.
One apple, large, unpeeled, 8 oz (226 g), 3¼ in-diameter = 135 Calories.

FROZEN APPLES
Peeled and sliced Delicious apples are available as Straight Pack and as Flavor Pack. "Flavor Pack" indicates that the apples are mixed with sugar in the ratio of seven parts apple to one part sugar (by weight).

Pack:
Straight Pack sliced apples come in 40-lb (18-kg) tins. Flavor Pack sliced apples come in 30-lb (13.5-kg) tins.

Kitchen Yields

Serving size:
For cooked apples, a serving is ½ cup cooked; so a 30-lb (13.6-kg) Flavor Pack contains 100 servings.

Pie:
40-lb (18.1-kg) Straight Pack yields fruit for thirty-two 9-in-diameter (228-mm-diameter) pies.

FROZEN BAKED APPLES
Frozen baked apples are available ready to serve.

Pack:
Four 6-lb (2.7-kg) boxes, for a total weight of 24 lb (10.8 kg).

Sizes:
3¾ in (95 mm) each. Other sizes are available.

Kitchen Yields
One 6-lb (2.7-kg) box yields 12 baked apples. One case yields 48 servings. Other sizes are available.

APRICOTS

Apricot products include apricot glaze and apricot nectar. Apricots themselves are available canned, dried, fresh, and frozen.

APRICOT GLAZE

This product is a baking glaze used for Danish pastries and other items.

Pack:
Six #10 cans.

Kitchen Yields
One #10 can will glaze 300 large Danish pastries, brushed on.

APRICOT NECTAR

This product consists of sweetened apricot juice; it is available canned.

Pack:
Twelve 46-oz (1.3-l) cans; forty-eight 5½-oz (0.16-l) cans.

Kitchen Yields

Serving size:
5½ oz (0.16 l); one 46-oz (1.3-l) can yields 8 servings.

CANNED APRICOTS

Available in many can sizes and counts. The most common institutional sizes are shown in Table A-3.

Pack:
#10 cans.

Calories:
Halves in heavy syrup: 1 cup or 4½ oz (126 g) = 110 Calories.

DRIED APRICOTS

Pack:
25-lb (11.25-kg) bag; twenty-four 1-lb (450-g) boxes.

Sizes:
From #1 Jumbo, 1⅜ in in diameter, to #6 Standard, $^{13}/_{16}$ in in diameter.

Kitchen Yields
1 lb (450 g) #6 Standard contains 75 to 90 halves, or 3 to 3¼ cups.
1 cup contains 26 to 30 medium uncooked apricots.
1 lb (450 g) yields 3 lb (1.3 kg) cooked apricot.

Serving size:
½ cup. Therefore, 1 lb (450 g) produces 20 servings.

Calories:
Five large, uncooked dried apricots = 60 Calories.
Five medium, uncooked dried apricots = 46 Calories.

FRESH APRICOTS

Season:
June through August; imports during the rest of the year.

Pack:
24-lb (10.8-kg) lugs; 12-lb (5.4-kg) tills; 6-lb (2.7-kg) baskets.

Table A-3 Sizes and Counts of Canned Apricots

Product	Syrup	Weight	Drained Weight	Count
Whole peeled	Light	108 oz (3 kg)	62 oz (1.76 kg)	45 to 55
Halves	Heavy	108 oz (3 kg)	62 oz (1.76 kg)	86 to 108
Halves	Heavy	108 oz (3 kg)	62 oz (1.76 kg)	108 to 130
Halves	Heavy	108 oz (3 kg)	64 oz (1.81 kg)	150 to 175
Halves	Light	106 oz (3 kg)	64 oz (1.81 kg)	86 to 130

The size is determined by the number of fruits arranged in layers. The count on the lowest layer is usually less than that on top layers.

Counts:
6-lb (2.7-kg) basket = 44 pieces 4 × 4
                     = 55 pieces 4 × 5
                     = 65 pieces 5 × 5.
24-lb (10.8-kg) lug = 176 pieces 4 × 4
                    = 220 pieces 4 × 5
                    = 260 pieces 5 × 5.

Sizes:

Extra Extra Jumbo: 6 per lb (450 g).
Extra Jumbo: 8 per lb (450 g).
Jumbo: 10 per lb (450 g).
Large: 12 per lb (450 g).
Medium: 14 per lb (450 g).
Average weight: 8 to 10 per lb (450 g).

Kitchen Yields
3 cups sliced uses 8 to 10 large fruits.
1 cup sliced uses 3 large fruits.

Serving size:
½ cup, sliced; so 1 lb (450 g) medium yields 5 servings.

Calories:
4 oz (110 g) or three large fresh apricots = 55 Calories.

FROZEN APRICOTS
Consist of apricot halves packed in sugar.

Pack:
6½-lb (2.9-kg) cans; 25-lb (11.2-kg) cans; 30-lb (13.5-kg) cans.

Kitchen Yields

Cooking Waste:
20 percent.

Serving size:
½ cup (0.11 l) cooked; one 30-lb (13.5-kg) can yields 100 servings.

Pie:
One 30-lb (13.5-kg) can produces eighteen 9-in-diameter pies.

ARUGULA
See Salad Greens.

ARTICHOKES
Bulb or globe artichokes are available canned, fresh, and frozen. Marinated artichoke hearts are available in jars.

CANNED ARTICHOKES
Available are bottoms, hearts, and pieces in brine.

Pack:
Bottoms: Twenty-four 14-oz (400 g) cans.
Hearts: Twenty-four 14-oz (400 g) cans; six #10 cans.
Pieces: Six #10 cans.
Other packs are available.

Kitchen Yields
Bottoms: One 14-oz (400-g) can may yield a count of 5 to 7, 6 to 9, or 8 to 10.
Hearts: One 14-oz (400-g) can may yield a count of 8 to 10 or of 14 to 16; one #10 can may yield a count of 90 to 100 or of 110 to 120.
Pieces: One #10 can yields a count of 180 to 200.

Serving size:
Bottom: One bottom, filled as garnish.
Hearts: Four to five 120-count pieces, as appetizer; therefore, one #10 can yields 24 to 26 servings, and one case of #10 cans yields 150 servings.

FRESH ARTICHOKES
A vinaigrette marinade for fresh artichokes is described elsewhere; *see* Dressing Formulas.

Season:
There are two crops annually: November through March, and June through October.

Pack:
20- and 25-lb (9- and 11.3-kg) boxes.

Counts:
18, 24, 36, 48, and 60. Small loose artichokes without counts are available by weight. Baby artichokes are also available; *see* Baby Vegetables.

Sizes:

Small:
Less than 2 in (50 mm) across.

Medium:
36 size: 10 oz (283 g) each,
48 size: 8 oz (226 g) each.

Large:
18 size: 20 oz (560 g) each,
24 size: 15 oz (425 g) each.

Kitchen Yields

Serving sizes:
Whole artichoke served by itself as appetizer—18 or 24 size.
Artichoke bottom for stuffing—24 size, with 2½-in (63-mm) diameter when peeled and cleaned.

Calories:
One artichoke, 24 size = 31 Calories.

FROZEN ARTICHOKES
Available as hearts and as quarters.

Pack:
Case of 12 boxes weighing 24 lb (10.8 kg).

Sizes:
Vary; there is no count.

Kitchen Yields
Product is fully cooked; there is no waste.

JERUSALEM ARTICHOKES
See Sunchokes.

MARINATED ARTICHOKE HEARTS
Available imported and from domestic producers.

Pack:
Six ½-gal (1.9-l) jars. Other packs are available.

Count:
85 to 105 pieces per jar.

Kitchen Yields

Serving size:
Appetizer portion is 4 or 5 pieces each; therefore, one jar yields 20 to 22 portions, and one case yields 120 portions.

ASIAN PEARS
See Pears.

ASPARAGUS
Available canned, fresh, and frozen.

CANNED ASPARAGUS
Available are green asparagus and white asparagus in stalks, cuts, and bottom cuts in various sizes. Canned green asparagus has lost importance in foodservice, because fresh and frozen asparagus are readily available.

Inexpensive white asparagus is imported from the Orient. Jumbo-size white asparagus is imported from Europe and is considered a luxury item.

GREEN ASPARAGUS

Pack:
Twenty-four #303 cans; twenty-four #2 cans; six #10 cans.

Counts:
Vary; for this reason the drained weight for each can size is indicated in the kitchen yields.

Kitchen Yields
One #303 can contains 9 to 10 oz (255 to 284 g), drained weight.
One #2 can contains 11½ to 13½ oz (326 to 383 g), drained weight.
One #10 can contains 60 to 64 oz (1.7 to 1.8 kg), drained weight.

Serving size:
½ cup for spears, about six pieces; one #10 can yields 18 servings.
½ cup for pieces; one #10 can yields 18 servings.

INEXPENSIVE WHITE ASPARAGUS

Pack:
Six 64 ½-oz (1.8-kg) cans.

Kitchen Yields
One 64½-oz (1.8-kg) can may yield a count of 80 to 100, 60 to 80, or 40 to 60.

Serving sizes:
Four pieces, as appetizer, from a 40- to 60-count can; then one can yields 10 to 15 servings.
Other serving sizes depend operational needs.

LUXURY WHITE ASPARAGUS

Pack:
Twelve 14½-oz (600-g) jars.

Kitchen Yields
One 14½-oz (600-g) jar contains 10 to 12 pieces.

Serving sizes:
Four pieces, as appetizer; then one jar yields 3 servings.
Other serving sizes depend on operational needs.

Calories:
Four spears totaling 3 oz (85 g) = 18 Calories.

FRESH ASPARAGUS

BABY ASPARAGUS
See Baby Vegetables.

GREEN ASPARAGUS
Fresh green asparagus is very popular. The yield varies greatly, because the stem ends of the stalks get tougher as the season progresses. At the beginning of the season, almost the whole stems can be eaten; toward the end, about half must be discarded.

Season:
Peak is March to June, and again October to November. Green asparagus is available almost year-round. Some asparagus is imported.

Pack:
30-lb (13.5-kg) 12-bunch pyramid crates;
15-lb (6.7-kg) 6-bunch crates;
27-lb (12.1-kg) loose-pack pyramid crates;
13½-lb (6-kg) loose-pack half pyramid crates;
24- to 25-lb (10.8- to 11.2-kg) cartons.
Other packs are also available.
Bunches weigh 1, 2, or 2½ lb (450 g, 900 g, or 1.1 kg).

Sizes:
The names indicating size vary according to growing regions. The most recognized names are:

Colossal, Jumbo, Large, Medium, Small, Pencil (or Grass). Table A-4 lists sizes and counts of different classes of fresh asparagus.

Kitchen Yields
Waste at beginning of season is only 10 percent of weight. At end of season, waste is over 50 percent, because stalks get stringy and tough. Grass or pencil asparagus need not be peeled. The waste factor is very small. The weight of crates and of bunches varies; asparagus should be weighed before quantities are calculated.

Serving sizes:
For appetizer or vegetable course:

Jumbo or Large:
Five to six spears at beginning of season; add one to two spears at end of season.
At beginning of season, one 30-lb (13.5-kg) case yields 50 servings, and a 12-lb (5.4-kg) half-case yields 19 servings.
At end of season, one 30-lb (13.5-kg) case yields 40 servings, and a 12-lb (5.4-kg) half-case yields 16 servings.

Table A-4 Sizes and Counts of Fresh Green Asparagus

Grade or Name	# of Spears per lb (450 gr)	# of Spears per Case
Colossal	7 to 8	30 lb (13.5 kg) = 225 to 235 15 lb (6.75 kg) = 110
Jumbo	8 to 9	30 lb (13.5 kg) = 260 12 lb (5.4 kg) = 100
Large	9 to 10	30 lb (13.5 kg) = 300 12 lb (5.4 kg) = 112
Medium	10 to 12	30 lb (13.5 kg) = 350 15 lb (6.75 kg) = 175
Small	12 to 14	30 lb (13.5 kg) = 390 15 lb (6.75 kg) = 190
Pencil or Grass	14 to 16	30 lb (13.5 kg) = 450 12 lb (6.75 kg) = 180
Grass	26 to 28	30 lb (13.5 kg) = 800

Medium or Small:

Six to seven spears per person at beginning of season; add two spears at end of season.

At beginning of season, one 30-lb (13.5-kg) case yields 52 servings, and a 15-lb (6.7-kg) half-case yields 25 servings.

At the end of season, one 30-lb (13.5-kg) case yields 43 servings, and a 15-lb (6.7-kg) half-case yields 22 servings.

Grass:

Twelve spears per person, regardless of season. One 30-lb (13.5-kg) case yields 65 servings, and a 12-lb (5.4-kg) half-case yields 30 servings.

Serving sizes:

For side order in both restaurant and banquet service:

Jumbo or Large:

Two spears, cut in half (four pieces), at beginning of season; three spears per serving at end of season.

At beginning of season, one 30-lb (13.5-kg) case yields 140 servings, and a 12-lb (5.4-kg) half-case yields 55 servings.

At end of season, one 30-lb (13.5-kg) case yields 90 servings, and a 12-lb (5.4-kg) half-case yields 35 servings.

Medium or Small:

Two and a half spears per serving, cut in half (5 pieces) at beginning of season; four spears per serving at the end of season.

At beginning of season, one 30-lb (13.5-kg) case yields 150 servings, and a 15-lb (6.75-kg) half-case yields 74 servings.

At end of season, one 30-lb (13.5-kg) case yields 94 servings, and a 15-lb (6.75-kg) half-case yields 46 servings.

Grass:

Four to five pieces per person. One 30-lb (13.5-kg) case yields 90 to 100 servings, and a 12-lb (5.4-kg) half-case yields 40 servings.

Calories:

Four medium spears weighing 3½ oz (100 g) = 18 Calories.

WHITE ASPARAGUS

White asparagus is a specialty item. Some supply is imported. Sizes and packs vary greatly. Very thin white asparagus is also available; *see* Baby Vegetables.

Season:

Peak is March to June. Some asparagus is imported in the winter.

Kitchen Yields

Yield varies according to time of year.

1 lb (450 g), as purchased, yields approximately 10 oz (280 g), cooked.

FROZEN ASPARAGUS

Available as spears in various sizes and as cut pieces.

Pack:

Twelve 2½-lb (1.1-kg) boxes. Smaller packs and bulk packs are also available.

Kitchen Yields

One 2½-lb box (1.1-kg) contains 51 jumbo spears packed in one direction, or 80 medium spears randomly packed, or cuts and tips about 1 in (25.4 mm) long—about 18 percent tips.

Serving sizes:

Medium spears:

¼ cup (about four spears); so one 2½-lb (1.1-kg) box yields 18 servings, and one 24-lb (10.8-kg) case yields 216 servings. Four medium spears weigh approximately 2 oz (56 g).

Jumbo spears:

Three spears; so one 2½-lb (1.1-kg) box yields 14 to 16 servings, and one 24-lb (10.8-kg) case yields 160 servings. Three jumbo spears weigh approximately 2⅓ oz (70 g).

Pieces:

½ cup; so one 2½-lb (1.1-kg) box yields 10 servings, and one 24-lb (10.8-kg) case yields 120 servings.

Frozen asparagus equivalent to fresh asparagus:

2½ lb (1.1 kg) frozen = 5 to 5½ lb (2.2 to 2.4 kg) fresh asparagus, as purchased.

Calories:
Four medium spears weighing 2 oz (56 g) = 12 Calories.

ASPIC

Clear meat or fish jelly. Can be made with ready-to-use aspic powder or from scratch.

BEEF ASPIC

Formula
    1 gal and 1 pint (4.2 l) beef stock
    2 lb (900 g) lean ground beef
    8 oz (226 g) mire poix
    1 cup (0.23 l) canned stewed tomatoes
    1 tb peppercorns
    4 oz (112 g) plain gelatin
    salt to taste

Kitchen Yields
1 gal (3.8 l) aspic.

FISH ASPIC

Formula
    1 gal fish stock (3.8 l)
    1 cup (0.235 l) very dry white wine
    8 oz (226 g) mire poix without carrots
    1 tb peppercorns
    2 tb white vinegar
    4 oz (113 g) plain gelatin

Kitchen Yields
1 gal (3.8 l) aspic.

AVOCADOS

Avocados are available fresh and in frozen processed form.

FRESH AVOCADOS
Domestically grown avocados are produced in two areas, California and Florida. Baby (or cocktail) avocados are also available; *see* Baby Vegetables.

Varieties:
The two principal California varieties are Hass, which has a dark green to black, rough and leathery skin (the "alligator pear"), and Fuerte, with a thin, pliable skin. Florida varieties are Booth, Lula, Hill, and Hickson.

Season:
California varieties are harvested year-round. Hass avocados peak from February to October, and Fuerte avocados peak in fall and winter. Florida varieties are harvested from July through February, peaking in October.

    When ordering, specify ripe or green; a ripe specification, however, is no guarantee that fruits are perfectly ripe. Fruit will continue to ripen at kitchen temperature.

Table A-5 Avocado Sizes and Average Yields

Count, Double Carton	Count, Single Carton	Average Weight per Fruit	Average Fresh Pulp per Fruit	Average Fresh Pulp Yield per Double Carton	Average Fresh Pulp Yield per Single Carton
70	35	5¾ oz (160 g)	3½ oz (98 g)	15⅓ lb (6.9 kg)	7½ lb (3.4 kg)
60	30	6¾ oz (190 g)	3⅜ oz (94 g)	12⅓ lb (5.5 kg)	6¼ lb (2.8 kg)
48	24	8½ oz (240 g)	4½ oz (125 g)	13½ lb (6.1 kg)	6¾ lb (3 kg)
40	20	10½ oz (290 g)	5¼ oz (145 g)	13 lb (5.9 kg)	6½ lb (2.9 kg)
36		11 oz (308 g)	6½ oz (182 g)	14¾ lb (6.6 kg)	

Pack:
Flats of 12½ lb (5.6 kg), with one layer fruit.

Count:
9, 12, 14, 16, 18, 20, 24, 30, and 35 fruits per flat.
Lugs of 25 lb (11.2 kg), with two layers of fruit.

Count:
18, 20, 24, 28, 32, 36, 40, 48, 60, 70, 84, and 96
fruits per lug.
Most common sizes used in hotels are 12-, 14-, and
16-count flats. Larger fruits of 1 lb (450 g)
each or more come to the market frequently.
Table A-5 lists information on average sizes and
yields per carton.

Kitchen Yields
One and one-half #36 avocados or one #14
avocado yields 1 cup pulp.
Two #48 avocados or one #12 avocado yields 1
cup diced. Twenty to twenty-four #36 avocados *or*
twenty-three to twenty-six #40 avocados *or* twenty-
eight to thirty-two #48 avocados yields 1 gal pulp.

Calories:
3.5 oz (100 g) edible portion = 177 Calories.
One-half avocado weighing 10½ oz (300 g) whole =
185 Calories.

FROZEN PROCESSED AVOCADO
Frozen processed avocado is available in the
following forms:
  Plain
  Guacamole
  Dip
  Sauce
  Hot'n spicy guacamole
  Western-style guacamole

Table A-6 Pulp Yield of Hass Variety Avocados

Count per Carton	Weight per Fruit	Pulp Yield per Fruit	Pulp Yield per Carton
84	4½ oz (126 g)	3½ oz (98 g)	18¼ lb (8.2 kg)
50	6¾ oz (189 g)	5 oz (140 g)	18¾ lb (8.4 kg)
48	8½ oz (238 g)	6⅓ oz (176 g)	18¾ lb (8.4 kg)
40	10½ oz (294 g)	7¾ oz (217 g)	19½ lb (8.7 kg)

Packs:
Twelve 1-lb (450 g) cans; six #10 cans, 6½ lb
(2.9 kg); one 25-lb (11.25-kg) tub; 100 individual
1-oz (28-g) guacamole packets; eight ½-gal (1.8 l)
avocado sauce.

Kitchen Yields

Serving size:
2 oz (56 g) per sandwich or topping, or 4 oz (112 g)
dip per person. Therefore, one 1-lb can yields 8
servings of topping or 4 servings of dip, and one
#10 can weighing 6½ lb (2.9 kg) yields 50 portions
of topping or 24 portions of dip.

Calories:
Sauce weighing 2 oz (56 g) = 80 Calories.
Pulp weighing 2 oz (56 g) = 100 Calories.
Guacamole weighing 4 oz (113 g) = 108 Calories.

B

BABY VEGETABLES

Many types of fresh baby vegetables are on the market.

BABY ARTICHOKES

Season:
March through May.

Pack:
By weight.

Kitchen Yields
Very little waste. Only the outside leaves are peeled off.

BABY ASPARAGUS

White asparagus is available in this form.

Season:
Available year-round.

Size:
200 pieces per 1 lb (450 g).

Pack:
4-lb (1.8-kg) carton.

Kitchen Yields
No waste; use as is.
4 lb (1.8 kg) = 800 pieces.

Serving size:
10 pieces vegetable, and one carton yields 80 servings.

BABY AVOCADOS

Also known as *cocktail avocados*.

Season:
Available year-round.

Pack:
By weight: 10-lb (4.5-kg) pack is common.

Size:
About 1 in × 3 in (25 mm × 75 mm), oval-shaped.

Kitchen Yields
Fruit is seedless or has soft pit; it can be eaten whole.

BABY BEETS

Available in red and gold varieties.

Season:
Available year-round.

Pack:
Bunches; count varies.

Kitchen Yields
Discard large leaves and serve whole. Do not peel.

BABY BOK CHOY

Season:
Available in fall and winter.

Pack:
Purchase by weight.

Size:
1½ oz (40 g) each, but size can vary.

Kitchen Yields
Vegetable is edible as is. There is no waste.

BABY BRUSSELS SPROUTS

Season:
Fall and winter.

Pack:
By weight.

Kitchen Yields
Very little waste. Count varies greatly. About ten servings per 1 lb (450 g).

BABY CARROTS

Available are long, round, and white baby carrots. They are very sweet.

Season:
Available year-round.

Pack:
Twenty-four bunches per case of 4½ to 5 lbs (2 to 2.2 kg). Also available in cases of twenty 12-oz (340-g) cello packs.

Kitchen Yields
Eight to ten baby carrots to a bunch. Some green top should be left on to increase yield and eye appeal. Vegetable need not be peeled if pur-

chased with green tops on; cello-pack carrots should be peeled.

Serving size:
Three to four pieces, so 24 bunches yields 60 servings. On average, 24 bunches weigh 3 lb (1.3 kg) cleaned, with most green trimmed off.

BABY CAULIFLOWER
Season:
Available in fall and winter.

Pack:
By weight.

Kitchen Yields
Use as is; little waste. Do not trim off greens. Count varies.

BABY CORN
Available in white and yellow varieties. Canned baby corn is also available; *see* Corn.

Season:
Summer.

Pack:
By weight.

Kitchen Yields
Size varies widely. Whole corn can be used; no shucking is necessary.

BABY EGGPLANTS
Available in purple and white varieties. Shape may be round or elongated.

Season:
Year-round; peak is in summer.

Pack:
By weight.

Kitchen Yields
Sizes vary greatly. Common size is five pieces per 1 lb (450 g). Whole vegetables can be used. Baby eggplants are sometimes bitter.

BABY LEEKS
Season:
Available year-round.

Pack:
By weight.

Kitchen Yields
There is no waste. Common sizes are ten to sixteen per 1 lb (450 g).

BABY RADISHES
Black radishes are available in this form.

Season:
Available year-round.

Pack:
Bunches; count varies.

Kitchen Yields
Vegetable can be very pungent. Serve raw as garnish.

BABY SPINACH
Tiny spinach leaves.

Season:
Available year-round.

Size:
About 1 to 2 in (25 to 50 mm) long.

Pack:
By weight.

Kitchen Yields
Product is very light and is often packed in 8-oz (226-g) bags. There is no waste.

BABY SQUASH
Many varieties are available, some with their flowers still intact. In addition to the present general coverage, particular types of baby squash covered under this listing include patty pan, scallop, and zucchini.

Season:
Available year-round.

Pack:
By weight.

Kitchen Yields
There is no waste. Sizes vary according to season and grower.

BABY PATTY PAN SQUASH

Season:
Summer.

Pack:
By weight.

Count:
36 to 39 pieces per 1 lb (450 g).

BABY SCALLOP SQUASH
A cross between zucchini and scallop squash. Available in yellow and green varieties. Not to be confused with ornamental squash.

Season:
From May to October.

Pack:
By weight.

Kitchen Yields
Whole vegetable can be used without cleaning waste. About twenty pieces per 1 lb (450 g).

BABY ZUCCHINI
Often sold with flowers still attached.

Season:
Available year-round; peak is in summer.

Pack:
By weight.

Kitchen Yields
Sizes varies greatly. Average count is fifteen pieces per 1 lb (450 g).

BABY TOMATOES
Available in red and yellow pear-shaped varieties.

Season:
Available year-round. Peak is in summer.

Pack:
By weight or by volume.

Kitchen Yields
About fifteen pieces per 1 pint (0.47 l), but sizes vary.

BACALAO

See Smoked or Cured Fish, under Fish.

BACON

See Pork Products, cured and smoked.

BAGELS

Baked item of Jewish origin. There are two basic varieties:

> *Water bagels:* They have a crisp crust and chewy texture.
> *Egg bagels:* They have a softer texture.

Both varieties are sold in different flavors and with different seed toppings.

Pack:
Available fresh and frozen, normally by the dozen.

Sizes:
Common size is 3 in (85 mm) in diameter.

Weight:
4 oz (112 g).
Miniature bagels for receptions are also available, fresh and frozen.

Kitchen Yields
Bagels are often sold with cream cheese.

Serving size:
2 oz (56 g) cream cheese. A 3-lb (1.3-kg) loaf of cream cheese thus yields 24 servings.

Calories:
One water bagel: 2 oz (56 g) = 165 Calories.
One egg bagel: 2 oz (56 g) = 165 Calories.

BAMBOO SHOOTS

Available canned, packed in water. Fresh bamboo shoots are occasionally available at ethnic markets. The canned product is marketed in slices and whole.

Pack:
Forty-eight 15-oz (420-g) cans; forty-eight 19-oz (532-g) cans; twenty-four #2½ cans; six #10 cans.

Kitchen Yields
One 15-oz (425-g) can contains 8½ oz (240 g), drained weight.

One 19-oz (540-g) can contains 10½ oz (295 g), drained weight.
One #2½ can contains 18 oz (504 g), drained weight.
One #10 can contains 65 oz (1.8 kg), drained weight.
One #2½ can yields about 3 cups sliced; and one #10 can yields about 11 cups sliced.

BANANAS
Available dehydrated, fresh, and as processed pulp.

DEHYDRATED BANANAS
Toasted chips.

Pack:
By weight.

Kitchen Yields
Used as snacks.

FRESH BANANAS
Bananas are shipped green and are ripened with ethylene gas. US#1 is normally purchased for foodservice. Many varieties and sizes are available in ethnic food markets.

Season:
Available year-round.

Pack:
40-lb (18-kg) cartons.

Sizes:
100 to 150 count. The 150-count size is called Petite. Average count is 115 bananas per carton.

Kitchen Yields
1 lb (450 g) yields 12 oz (340 g) peeled.
One medium banana yields 1 cup sliced and weighs 4¼ oz (120 g).
One peeled medium banana weighs 4¼ oz (120 g).

Calories:
One peeled medium banana weighing 4¼ oz (120 g) = 100 Calories.

FINGER BANANAS (MANZANITA BANANAS)
Small bananas are often called *finger bananas*.

Season:
Year-round. Peak is in summer.

Pack:
By weight.

Size:
1 hand = 12 to 14 oz (340 to 400 g).

Count:
10 to 12 bananas.

PROCESSED BANANAS
Available in drums, polyester bags, and cans.

Pack:
Six #10 cans; individual 5-gal (19-l) bags; individual 55-gal (208-l) drum.

Kitchen Yields
One #10 can contains 13 cups (3 l) or 7½ lb (3.3 kg) purée. This is equivalent to the pulp of 30 medium-size bananas. Therefore, six #10 cans contain 45 lb (20.2 kg) purée — equivalent to the pulp of 180 medium bananas.
One 5-gal (37.6-l) bag contains 40 lb purée — equivalent to the pulp of 375 medium bananas.

BARLEY

Dry barley is used in soups and stews.

Pack:
Twenty-four 1-lb (450-g) boxes. Larger packs are available.

Kitchen Yields
1 cup dry barley weighs 2½ cups (0.27 l).
1 cup uncooked barley weighs 7 oz (220 g); ½ cup uncooked barley provides garnish for 1¼ gal (7.7 l) soup.

Calories:
1 cup, weighing 7 oz (220 g), uncooked = 700 Calories.

BASIL

See Herbs & Spices.

BAY LEAVES

See Herbs & Spices.

BEAN CURD (TOFU)

Bean curd, commonly called *tofu* (its Japanese name), is a soybean product with a custardlike consistency. It is available in many shapes and flavors. Plain tofu is also called *Chinese-style tofu.* Bean curd is sold moist in squares of various sizes. Keep refrigerated in brine.

Pack:
Twelve 20-oz (570-g) tubs.
Many other packs are available.

Kitchen Yields
Serving size depends on application.

Calories:
4 oz (113 g) = 114 Calories.

BEANS

Beans are classified as immature and mature. Immature beans—for example, string beans, lima beans, and flageolet beans—are still green when harvested. Mature beans—for example, kidney beans and navy beans—are dry when harvested.

Both immature and mature beans are available canned, fresh, and frozen. Mature beans are also available dried. The Beans entry listings include canned, dehydrated (dried), fresh, and frozen beans.

CANNED BEANS

FLAGEOLET BEANS
Available imported from France, they are green and resemble small lima beans.

Pack:
Twenty-four 15-oz (426-g) cans.

Kitchen Yields

Serving size:
½ cup (0.11 l) drained.
One 15-oz (426-g) can yields 4 servings.

GARBANZO BEANS
Also called *chick-peas.* Garbanzos are often classified as peas. They are a popular component of salad bars and are the main ingredient of the Arab dip hummus.

Pack:
Six #10 cans.

Kitchen Yields

Serving size:
½ cup (0.11 l) drained. One #10 can contains 72 oz (2 kg), drained weight, and yields 22 servings.

GREEN BEANS
The most suitable variety for canning is Blue Lake. Canned green beans are available whole, cut across, and cut lengthwise. This last cut is referred to as *French style.* Green bean purée is also available.

Pack:
Six #10 cans, for most varieties. Twenty-four #303 cans for green bean purée.

Sizes:
Extra large, large, medium, and small, for both whole and cut beans. French-style beans are not graded by size.

Kitchen Yields

Green Beans:

Serving Size:
½ cup (0.11 l) drained. One #10 can, drained, weighs between 61 and 66 oz (1.7 and 1.8 kg); a #10 can yields 16 servings.

Green Bean Purée:

Serving size:
½ cup, or 4 oz (0.11 l). One #303 can yields 2 cups, or four servings.

Calories:
½ cup = 10 Calories.

KIDNEY BEANS
Kidney beans are identified with Mexican dishes, especially chili con carne. They are also used as a salad ingredient. Available are light red and dark red beans. A mixture of three beans as salad is

also available. Pinto beans belong to the broad group of kidney beans.

Pack:
Six #10 cans. Other packs are available.

Kitchen Yields

Serving size:
½ cup, or 4 oz (112 g) drained. One #10 can has drained weight of about 80 oz (2.2 kg). A #10 can yields 19 servings, so a case of six #10 cans yields 114 servings.

Calories:
½ cup weighing 4 oz (112 g) = 115 Calories.

LIMA BEANS

Pack:
Six #10 cans. Other packs are available.

Sizes:
Tiny, small, medium, and large.

Kitchen Yields

Serving size:
½ cup, or 4 oz (112 g) drained. One #10 can weighs 70 oz (2 kg), drained, and yields 17 servings. One case of six #10 cans yields 102 servings.

Calories:
½ cup = 123 Calories.

NAVY BEANS
Available "baked," with meat (such as pork or frankfurters) or without meat. The flavor choices are molasses and tomato sauce. Plain navy beans, flavored only with salt, are also available.

Pack:
Six #10 cans. Other packs are available.

Kitchen Yields

Serving size:
1 cup (0.23 l) with sauce. One #10 can yields 12 servings, so one case of six #10 cans yields 72 servings.
NOTE: Product is served with its sauce, so yield is higher than for a drained product.

Calories:
1 cup baked, with meat and sweet sauce = 384 Calories.
1 cup baked, with pork and tomato sauce = 310 Calories.

WAX BEANS
Available whole and cut.

Pack:
Six #10 cans.

Kitchen Yields

Serving size:
½ cup (0.11 l) drained. One #10 can weighs 62 oz (1.76 kg), drained, and yields 15 servings; so one case of six #10 cans yields 90 servings.

Calories:
½ cup = 15 Calories.

DRIED BEANS

BLACK TURTLE BEANS
A staple in South America, often served with rice. The popular black bean soup is made with black turtle beans.

Pack:
Twenty-four 1-lb (450-g) boxes; individual 25-lb (11.25-kg) bags.

Kitchen Yields
1 lb (450 g) dry measure is equivalent to 2⅓ cups (0.5 l); 1 cup (0.22 l) dry measure is equivalent to 2 cups (0.47 l) cooked beans.

Serving size:
½ cup (0.11 l) cooked beans; therefore, 1 lb (450 g) yields 9 servings.

Calories:
½ cup cooked beans = 95 Calories.

FAVA BEANS
Large, flat, light brown beans, good in salads and in stews.

Pack:
Twenty-four 1-lb (450-g) boxes; individual 25-lb (11.25-kg) bags.

Kitchen Yields

1 lb (450 g) dry measure is equivalent to 2 cups (0.47 l).

1 cup (0.22 l) dry measure is equivalent to 2¼ cups (0.52 l) cooked beans.

Serving size:

½ cup cooked beans; therefore, 1 lb (450 g) yields 9 servings.

Calories:

½ cup cooked beans = 95 Calories.

FLAGEOLET BEANS

Pack:

Twenty-four 1-lb (450-g) boxes; individual 25-lb (11.25-kg) bags.

Kitchen Yields

1 cup, or 8 oz (225 g), dry is equivalent to 2½ cups (0.58 l) cooked.

1 lb (450 g) dry measure is equivalent to 2 cups (0.47 l) cooked.

Serving size:

½ cup (0.11 l) cooked beans; so 1 lb (450 g) dry is equivalent to 5 cups (1.17 l) cooked, and 5 cups cooked yields 10 servings.

Calories:

½ cup cooked beans = 95 Calories.

GARBANZO BEANS

Also called *chick-peas.*

Pack:

Twenty-four 1-lb (450-g) boxes; individual 25-lb (11.25-kg) bags.

Kitchen Yields

1 cup, or 8 oz (225 g), dry is equivalent to 2½ cups (0.58 l) cooked.

Serving size:

½ cup (0.11 l) cooked beans; so 1 lb (450 g) dry is equivalent to 5 cups (1.17 l) cooked, and 5 cups cooked yields 10 servings.

Calories:

½ cup cooked beans = 100 Calories.

KIDNEY BEANS

Popular in bean salads and in other dishes. In Mexican cooking, the beans are used for refried beans, called *frijoles refritos. See* Mexican Foods. Pinto beans are also used for refried beans.

Pack:

Twenty-four 1-lb (450-g) boxes; individual 25-lb (11.25-kg) bags.

Kitchen Yields

1 cup, or 8 oz (225 g), dry is equivalent to 2½ cups (0.58 l) cooked.

Serving size:

½ cup (0.11 l) cooked beans; so 1 lb (450 g) dry is equivalent to 5 cups (1.17 l) cooked, and 5 cups cooked yields 10 servings.

Calories:

½ cup cooked beans = 100 Calories.

NOTE: The calorie content of refried beans depends on the amount of fat used.

LIMA BEANS

White, kidney-shaped beans.

Sizes:

Baby and Large.

Packs:

Twenty-four 1-lb (450-g) boxes; individual 25-lb (11.25-kg) bags.

Kitchen Yields

1 cup, or 8 oz (225 g), dry is equivalent to 2½ cups (0.58 l) cooked.

Serving size:

½ cup (0.11 l) cooked beans; so 1 lb (450 g) dry is equivalent to 5 cups (1.17 l) cooked, and 5 cups cooked yields 10 servings.

Calories:

½ cup cooked beans = 95 Calories.

MUNG BEANS

A staple in China and India, mung beans are available whole, skinned, and split. They are also used in the form of fresh bean sprouts; *see* Sprouts.

Pack:

By weight.

Kitchen Yields

1 cup dry is equivalent to 2½ cups (0.58 l) cooked.

Serving size:
½ cup (0.11 l) cooked beans; so 1 lb (450 g) yields
5½ servings.

NAVY BEANS
Small white bean, often called *Boston bean.* The
traditional bean for Boston baked beans.

Pack:
Twenty-four 1-lb (450-g) boxes; individual 25-lb
(11.25-kg) bags.

Kitchen Yields

Serving size:
1 cup (0.23 l) baked beans with sauce; 1 cup, or 8
oz (225 g), dry yields 3 servings, and 1 lb (450 g)
dry yields 6 servings.

Calories:
1 cup cooked, drained, plain beans = 216 Calories.
1 cup cooked, with pork and tomato sauce = 360
Calories.

PINTO BEANS
Related to the pink beans of Arizona and New
Mexico. Pinto beans are also used in Mexican
cooking for refried beans.

Pack:
Twenty-four 1-lb (450-g) boxes; individual 25-lb
(11.25-kg) bags.

Kitchen Yields
1 cup, or 8 oz (225 g), dry is equivalent to 2¼ cups
(0.58 l) cooked.

Serving size:
½ cup (0.11 l) cooked beans; so 2¼ cups (0.58 l)
cooked yield 5 servings. In addition, 1 lb (450 g)
dry is equivalent to 5 cups (1.17 l) cooked, and 5
cups cooked yields 10 servings.

Calories:
½ cup cooked beans = 95 Calories.

FRESH BEANS

FAVA BEANS

Season:
Summer and fall.

Pack:
By weight.

Kitchen Yields
Yield varies as a result of uneven quality. Buying
fresh is not recommended.

GARBANZO BEANS
Also called *chick-peas.* Available shelled.

Season:
Late summer and fall.

Pack:
Twelve 11-oz (309-g) bags, shelled.

Kitchen Yields
No cleaning waste.

Serving size:
½ cup (0.11 l).
One 11-oz (309-g) bag yields 2 cups cooked beans,
which are equivalent to 4 servings.

GREEN BEANS
Fresh green beans are also called *bush* or *snap
beans.* They get stale and dry rapidly. A good
indication of freshness is if they snap when
broken.

Season:
Available year-round. Peaks are in summer and
fall.

Pack:
26- to 31-lb (11.7- to 13.9-kg) bushel baskets or
cartons.

Count:
Varies: Length of beans is no indication of quality,
but thickness is. Good-quality beans are thin.

Kitchen Yields

Serving size:
½ cup (0.11 l) cooked and cut beans. Trimming
loss is about 12 to 15 percent. Therefore, 1 lb
(450 g) yields 14 oz (400 g) cleaned or approximately 2½ cups, cooked and cut; this is equivalent
to 5 servings. Thus, 1 bushel weighing 30 lb
(13.5 kg) yields 150 servings.

Calories:
½ cup of cooked beans weighing 2¼ oz (63 g) = 14 Calories.

HARICOTS VERTS
French name for green beans. Very tiny beans, usually imported, are marketed under this name.

Season:
Imported year-round; available domestic May to July.

Pack:
8⅞-lb (4-kg) case. Other packs are available.

Kitchen Yields
When merchandise is fresh, there is little cleaning waste.

Serving size:
2 oz (56 g); one case yields 70 servings.

LIMA BEANS
Fresh lima beans are seldom used in foodservice.

Season:
July to December.

Pack:
Whole:
26- to 31-lb (11.7- to 13.9-kg) hampers. Other packs are available.

Shelled:
Twelve 11-oz (312-g) bags.

Kitchen Yields

Serving size:
½ cup (0.11 l) cooked beans; 1 lb (450 g) in pod is equivalent to 6 oz (170 g) shelled, or 2 servings; 26 lb (11.2 kg) in pod is equivalent to 9¾ lb (4.3 kg) shelled, or 52 servings.
One 11-oz (308-g) bag (shelled) yields 3½ servings, and twelve bags (shelled), 132 oz (3.7 kg) yield 44 servings.

Calories:
½ cup cooked beans = 85 Calories.

PINTO BEANS
Available already shelled.

Season:
July to December.

Pack:
Twelve 11-oz (312-g) bags.

Kitchen Yields

Serving size:
½ cup (0.11 l) cooked beans; 11 oz (308 g) yields 3½ servings, and twelve bags, 132 oz (3.7 kg), yield 44 servings.

Calories:
½ cup cooked beans = 85 Calories.

WAX BEANS

Season:
Year-round, peak is in summer and fall.

Pack:
26- to 31-lb (11.7- to 13.9-kg) bushels.

Kitchen Yields

Serving size:
½ cup (0.11 l) cooked beans; 1 lb (450 g) beans as purchased is equivalent to 14 oz (400 g) cleaned; and 14 oz (400 g) cleaned are equivalent to 11¼ oz (320 g) cooked, which yield 2½ cups.
1 lb (450 g) as purchased yields 5 servings, and 1 bushel weighing 30 lb (13.5 kg) yields 150 portions.

Calories:
½ cup whole cooked beans = 14 Calories.

FROZEN BEANS
BUTTER BEANS

Pack:
Twelve 3-lb (1.3-kg) boxes.

Kitchen Yields

Serving size:
3½ oz (98 g) raw; ½ cup cooked; one 2½-lb (1.1-kg) box yields 11 servings, so a 36-lb case (16.2-kg) yields 132 servings.

Calories:
½ cup weighing 3½ oz (98 g) = 26 Calories.

GARBANZO BEANS

Pack:
Twelve 2½-lb (1.1-kg) boxes; twelve 3-lb (1.3-kg) boxes.

Kitchen Yields

Serving size:
3½ oz (98 g) raw; ½ cup (0.11 l) cooked; one 2½-lb (1.1-kg) box contains 11 servings, and one 3-lb (1.3-kg) box contains 13 servings.
One case of 2½-lb (1.1-kg) boxes yields 132 servings, and 1 case of 3-lb (1.3-kg) boxes yields 156 servings.

GREEN BEANS
Blue Lake variety is preferred for frozen beans. Available forms include regular cut, french cut, and whole in various sizes. Most varieties are available frozen in block and IQF.

Pack:
Twelve 2½-lb (1.1-kg) boxes; 30-lb (13.5-kg) IQF loose pack.

Kitchen Yields

Serving size:
½ cup (0.11 l) cooked; one 2½-lb (1.1-kg) box contains 12 servings, so a 30-lb (13.5-kg) case contains 140 servings.

Calories:
½ cup cooked = 15 Calories.

ITALIAN BEANS

Pack:
Twelve 2½-lb (1.1-kg) boxes.

Kitchen Yields
2½ lb (1.1 kg) frozen is equivalent to 3 lb (1.3 kg) fresh.

Serving size:
½ cup (0.11 l) cooked; one 2½-lb (1.1-kg) box contains 12 servings, so a 30-lb (13.5-kg) case contains 140 servings.

LIMA BEANS
Two varieties are marketed, Baby and Fordhook. Baby lima beans are small, have thin skins, and are bright green. Fordhook lima beans are large,

plump, and have a thicker skin than baby lima beans. They also have about 20 percent fewer calories than baby lima beans.

Pack:
Twelve 2½-lb (1.1-kg) boxes.

Kitchen Yields
2½-lb (1.1-kg) frozen lima beans is equivalent to 6½ lb (2.9 kg) fresh beans in pod.

Serving size:
½ cup (0.11 l) cooked Fordhooks or baby lima beans. One 2½-lb (1.3-kg) box Fordhooks contains 13 servings, while one 2½-lb (1.3-kg) box baby lima beans contains 12 servings.

Calories:
½ cup, or 3 oz (85 g), Fordhooks, cooked and drained = 85 Calories.
½ cup, or 3⅛ oz (90 g), baby limas, cooked and drained = 90 Calories.

WAX BEANS (CUT)

Pack:
Twelve 2-lb (0.9-kg) boxes; twelve 2½-lb (1.1-kg) boxes.
Other packs are available.

Kitchen Yields

Serving size:
½ cup (0.11 l). One 2-lb (0.9-kg) box contains 10 servings, and one case contains 120 servings. One 2½-lb (1.1-kg) box contains 13 servings, and one case contains 150 servings.

Calories:
½ cup (0.11 l) cooked = 15 Calories.

BEAN SPROUTS

See Sprouts.

BEAR

Available are frozen hind legs and loins.

Average sizes:

Hind legs:
8 to 10 lb (3.6 to 4.5 kg).

Loins:
6 to 7 lb (2.7 to 3.1 kg), bone in.

Kitchen Yields
Basically the same as well-done beef.

BEEF

Beef is graded by the USDA at request of the packer. The grades of interest to foodservice operators are Prime, Choice, Select (formerly Good), and Standard. Much ungraded beef reaches the market and is sold under brand names. Weight is one criterion of the grading process, and a number of cuts are available only in grades of Prime or Choice in a specific weight range. Other grading criteria are marbling and configuration (which determines yield). There is increased demand for leaner beef, and the grading criterion involving marbling is undergoing periodic revision.

Most beef shipped is packed in Cryovac wrapping and boxed. Fresh beef is about 10 days old when it reaches the market. It can be used without additional aging. Some purveyors dry-age strips and ribs on request. Black Angus is a particular breed of cattle.

Besides containing a description of the various cuts, the following subentries include the *Meat Buyers Guide* (MBG) numbers, for further identification.

LARGER CUTS OF BEEF

BLADE MEAT, MBG #109B
Also called *deckel meat,* this boneless cut is situated over the shoulder end of the primal rib and is removed when the rib is prepared for roasting.

Pack:
By weight.

Size:
2½ lb (1.1 kg).

Best use:
Stew meat.

Kitchen Yields
Trimming loss of 5 percent.
Cooking shrinkage 40 percent by weight.

BONES, MARROW
Marrow bones are from the round and are very hard. They are purchased primarily to extract the marrow. There is little flavor in the bones.

Pack:
By weight.

Kitchen Yields
50 lb (22.6 kg) bones yield 10 to 12 lb (4.5 to 5.4 kg) marrow.
NOTE: Specify 2-in center-cut bones, not knuckle bones.

BONES, SHIN AND BACK
The best bones for making brown stock are back bones or neck bones.

Pack:
By weight.

Kitchen Yields
50 lb (22.6 kg) bones make 5½ gal (20.9 l) brown stock; 50 lb (22.6 kg) bones make 3 gal (11.4 l) brown sauce.

BOTTOM ROUND, GOOSE NECK, MBG #170
Muscle inside the leg, called the *round*. This piece consists of the outside round and the eye round. It also contains the heel muscle, which can only be used for stew. If this piece cannot be used, specify #170A.

Weight range:
18 to 29 lb (8.1 to 13 kg).

Best size:
26 to 29 lb (11.7 to 13 kg).

Best uses:
Roasts, stews, braised steaks.

Sample Kitchen Yields

Purchased weight:

Choice:
22 lb (9.9 kg).

Waste and trim:

Fat:
1 lb (450 g).

Usable trim:
3½ lb (1.5 kg).

Usable meat:
17½ lb (7.8 kg), or 13½ lb (6 kg) roasted whole. One piece yields forty 6-oz (170-g) steaks for braising, and 2½ lb (1.1 kg) of additional trim.

BOTTOM SIRLOIN BUTT, MBG #185
Tender muscle at the end of the short loin.

Weight range:
4 to 10 lb (1.8 to 4.5 kg).

Best weight:
8 lb (3.6 kg).

Best uses:
Whole roasts, steaks, cut in julienne and sautéed.

Sample Kitchen Yields

Purchased weight:

Choice:
8 lb (3.6 kg).

Waste and trim:

Fat:
8 oz (225 g).

Usable trim:
8 oz (225 g).

Usable meat:
7 lb (3.1 kg).
One piece yields fifteen 6-oz (170-g) steaks and 22 oz (0.6 kg) julienne meat.

BRISKET, FRESH, MBG #120
This piece has the deckel meat already removed; however, it is still a rather wasteful piece.

Weight range:
6 to 12 lb (2.7 to 5.4 kg).

Best size:
10 to 12 lb (4.5 to 5.4 kg).

Best uses:
For boiling or braising.

Sample Kitchen Yields

Purchased weight:

Choice:
12 lb (5.4 kg).

Cooked weight:
Boiled, tender: 8½ lb (3.8 kg).

Fat trim after cooking:
2¼ lb (1 kg).

Usable cooked meat:
6¼ lb (2.8 kg).

Serving size:
5 oz (140 g) for main course. Therefore, a 12-lb (5.4 kg) cooked piece yields 19 servings.

CHUCK ROLL, MBG #116A
Boneless, netted muscle from the inside of the shoulder. Tender and juicy meat for braising; can be fatty and fall apart after cooking. Portion size is hard to control, because muscle configuration is uneven.

Weight range:
13 to 25 lb (5.8 to 11.2 kg).

Best weight:
13 to 15 lb (5.8 to 6.7 kg).

Best uses:
For braising or roasting.

Sample Kitchen Yields

Purchased weight:

Choice:
14 lb (6.3 kg).

Weight after braising:
9½ lb (4.2 kg).

Serving size:
4 oz (113 g). When cut manually, one piece yields 35 total servings. A machine-cut yield might be smaller because of scraps.

CHUCK, BONELESS SQUARE-CUT, MBG #115
Boneless, whole shoulder. The shoulder clod, a large outside muscle weighing between 13 and 18 lb (5.8 to 8.1 kg), should be removed and used for braising. If this piece is not needed, Chuck, MBG #116, without clod, should be specified. The chuck meat is best used as ground meat.

The fat content of ground meat should be approximately 20 percent of weight. It is best to weigh trimmings and lean before grinding. A fat-testing machine is inexpensive and easy to use.

Weight range:
55 to 90 lb (24.7 to 40.5 kg).

Best size:
65 to 85 lb (29.2 to 38.2 kg).

Best uses:
Ground meat; clod for roasting or braising.

Sample Kitchen Yield

Purchased weight:

Choice:
75 lb (33.7 kg).

Weight:
After clod has been removed, 59 lb (26.5 kg).

Waste and trim:
5½ lb (2.4 kg).

Usable ground meat:
53.5 lb (24 kg).

Serving size:
4 oz (113 g) hamburger patty.
6 oz (168 g) hamburger steak.
8 oz (225 g) chopped steak.
Thus, total yield is: 214 hamburger patties,
142 hamburger steaks, or
106 chopped steaks.

CLARIFICATION MEAT
When butchering is done in-house, the trimmings from tenderloins and other cuts can be used. They should be ground through the largest-diameter plate of the meat grinder. Meat purchased for clarification should be as lean as possible. Shin meat is best for this purpose.

Kitchen Yields
20 lb (9 kg) meat cooked with 10 gal (38 l) stock yields 8 gal (30 l) consommé.
Formula for beef consommé is given under Soups.

DECKEL MEAT
See Blade Meat under this same subheading.

EYE ROUND, MBG #171C
Muscle inside the bottom round. It is dry, but evenly shaped. Piece is often used for pot roast or for braised steaks.

Weight range:
3 to 6 lb (1.3 to 2.7 kg).

Best weight:
5 to 6 lb (2.2 to 2.7 kg).

Best uses:
Braised whole or braised steaks.

Sample Kitchen Yields

Purchased weight:

Choice:
6 lb (2.7 kg).

Waste and trim:

Fat:
6 oz (170 g).

Usable trim:
6 oz (170 g).

Usable meat:
5 lb 4 oz (2.3 kg).

Serving size:
4 oz whole braised. Thus, the total yield is 20 servings. If the round is cut into 6-oz (170-g) braising steaks, total yield is 12 servings.

FILET TIPS
Also called *tails,* they are the pieces left after the filet mignon is cut.

Pack:
By weight.

Weight range:
6 to 7 oz (170 to 200 g) each.

Best use:
Cut in strips or small slices and sautéed quickly to order.

Sample Kitchen Yields
10 lb (4.5 kg) yield 9 lb (4 kg) usable meat.

Waste fat:
10 percent.

Serving size:
4 to 6 oz (113 to 170 g); 9 lb of usable meat provides 27 servings of 5 oz (140 g) each.

FLANK STEAKS, MBG #193
Skinned flat muscle from the belly.

Weight ranges:
1 to 1½ lb (0.4 to 0.6 kg);
2 to 2¾ lb (0.9 to 1.2 kg).

Best size:
2 to 2½ lb (0.9 to 1.2 kg).

Best use:
London broil.

Sample Kitchen Yields

Purchased weight:
2½ lb (1.1 kg).

Waste fat:
3 oz (85 g).

Usable meat:
2 lb 5 oz (1 kg).
When cooked medium rare, shrinkage is about 6 oz (170 g).

Serving size:
5 oz (140 g) cooked meat; thus, total yield of one piece is 6 servings.

GOOSENECK BOTTOM ROUND
See Bottom Round under this same subheading.

HAMBURGER MEAT, MBG #136
Fat content may be specified; most common is 80 percent lean and 20 percent fat. The cut may be specified as well, and the buyer can select from various quality levels; sirloin and chuck are considered the best. Ground meat oxidizes and turns brown quickly after grinding.

Ground meat is available fresh and frozen. Frozen meat loses its juices after cooking.

Pack:
Normally, 10-lb (4.5-kg) bags.

Kitchen Yields
Shrinkage varies according to fat content and to how well the meat is cooked. Average shrinkage is one-third by weight when meat is cooked to well-done stage.

KNUCKLE, MBG #167
This tender piece is cut from the leg above the knee.

Weight range:
8 to 15 lb (3.6 to 6.7 kg).

Best size:
14 to 15 lb (6.3 to 6.7 kg).

Best use:
Pot roast and stew.

Sample Kitchen Yields

Purchased weight:

Choice:
10 lb (4.5 kg).

Waste and trim:

Skin and fat:
1½ lb (0.61 kg).

Usable trim:
8 oz (226 g).

Usable meat:
8 lb (3.6 kg).

Serving size:
4 oz (113 g) cooked. Thus, a knuckle braised whole yields 23 servings. For stew, the serving size is 4½ oz (127 g) cooked meat, and a knuckle yields 19 servings.

KNUCKLE, MBG #167A
Same pieces as #167, but with fat trimmed off. It is referred to as *peeled knuckle.*

Weight range:
6 to 11 lb (2.7 to 4.9 kg).

Best size:
8 to 11 lb (3.6 to 4.9 kg).

Best uses:
Pot roast, stew, roasted whole, kebab, and tartar steak.

Sample Kitchen Yields
Refer to knuckle, MBG #167.

OXTAILS

Make sure pieces are cut at the joints, not random-cut with meat saw, because bone splinters will cook free and are a potential eating hazard.

Weight range:
1½ to 2 lb (0.6 to 0.9 kg).

Best size:
1½ to 2 lb (0.6 to 0.9 kg).

Best use:
Stew and soup.

Sample Kitchen Yields

Purchased weight:
10 lb (4.5 kg).

Waste fat:
6 oz (170 g).
NOTE: Only larger center pieces can be used as stew. Smaller pieces should be used for soup only.

Usable meat:
For stewing, 7 lb 10 oz (3.3 kg); for soup, 2 lb (0.9 kg).

Serving size:
10 oz (280 g) raw meat, or two to four pieces. Total yield as purchased is 12 servings. For soup, 5 lb (2.2 kg) of tail tips yield 1 gal (3.8 l) clear oxtail consommé.

RIB-EYE ROLL, MBG #112

This is the muscle part of the rib, boneless and completely trimmed.

Weight range:
5 to 12 lb (2.2 to 5.4 kg).

Best weight range:
8 to 10 lb (3.6 to 4.5 kg).

Best uses:
Roast whole or cut into rib-eye steaks.

Sample Kitchen Yields

Purchased weight:
9 lb (4 kg).

Cooked weight:
8 lb (3.6 kg) medium rare.

Waste and trim:
¼ lb (113 g) after cooking.

Serving size:
8 oz (226 g) servings, 16 steaks weighing each 9 oz (255 g).

RIB, OVEN-PREPARED, MBG #107

Prime rib with short ribs and aitch bone removed, but with blade meat still attached.

Weight range:
17 to 28 lb (7.6 to 12.6 kg).

Best size:
20 to 22 lb (9 to 9.9 kg).

Best uses:
Prime rib and standing prime rib.

Sample Kitchen Yields

Oven-prepared Rib, #107, has the blade bone and the muscles above and below attached. Oven-ready rib, #109, has the blade bone and muscles removed; these pieces weigh about 3 to 4 lb (1.3 to 1.8 kg). This is important to remember when comparing prices.

Purchased weight:
20 lb (9 kg).

Cooked weight:
16 lb (7.2 kg).
NOTE: When cooked in slow roasting oven, cooking loss can be as low as 10 percent of weight.

Waste and trim:
2½ lb (1.1 kg) after cooking.

Bones:
2¼ lb (1 kg).

Usable cooked meat:
11¼ lb (5 kg).

Serving size:
For à la carte, 10 oz (340 g) without bones; thus, one piece (providing both end cuts are sold) yields 18 total servings. Banquet serving size is 9 oz (255 g) cooked weight, medium and boneless. One piece yields 20 total servings. Buffet serving size is 6 oz (170 g) cooked weight. One medium and boneless piece yields 30 total servings.

RIB, OVEN-READY, MBG #109
Prime rib with rib bones in, but aitch bone removed.

Weight range:
14 to 24 lb (6.3 to 9.9 kg).

Best sizes:
18 to 20 lb (8.1 to 9 kg) and 20 to 22 lb (9 to 9.9 kg).

Best uses:
Prime rib, and standing prime rib.

Kitchen Yields
Yield depends on shrinkage during the roasting process. Normal roasting time is 3½ hours at 325°F. Low-temperature roasting increases yield. *See* Rib, MBG #107, for yield information.

RIB, PRIMAL, MBG #103
Whole rib, with short ribs still attached. Few operators purchase the Primal Rib #103, because it is a heavy, unwieldy piece of meat.

Weight range:
24 to 40 lb (10.8 to 18 kg).

Best size:
33 to 40 lb (14.8 to 18 kg).

Best use:
Roast prime rib.

Kitchen Yields
One #103 rib weighing 38 lb (17.1 kg) yields one #109 Rib weighing 22 lb (9.9 kg).

RIB, ROAST-READY AND BONELESS, MBG #110
This is a popular specification for banquet operations because the meat needs little trim after roasting.

Weight range:
11 to 19 lb (4.9 to 8.5 kg).

Best weight:
13 to 16 lb (5.8 to 7.2 kg).

Best use:
Roasted whole.

Sample Kitchen Yields

Purchased weight:
16 lb (7.2 kg).

Cooked weight:
14 lb (6.3 kg).

Waste and trim:
1 lb (450 g) after cooking.

Usable cooked meat:
13 lb (5.8 kg).

Serving size:
For à la carte, 10 oz (340 g) cooked weight, medium; thus one rib roast yields 20 total servings. Banquet serving size is 8½ oz (240 g) cooked weight, medium (outside cuts are counted as sold); one rib roast yields 24 total servings. Buffet serving size is 6 oz (170 g) cooked weight, medium; thus, one rib roast yields 34 total servings, providing both end cuts are used.

ROUND, CHICAGO, MBG #158
Untrimmed Primal Round, with aitch bone and shin attached. This heavy piece needs considerable butchering before it can be used. Roasting time is about 6 hours at 325°F.

Weight range:
60 to 100 lb (27.1 to 45 kg).

Best weight:
80 to 95 lb (36 to 42.7 kg).

Sample Kitchen Yields

Purchased weight:

Choice:
80 lb (36 kg).

Waste and trim:

Fat:
8 lb (3.6 kg).

Usable scraps:
6 lb (2.7 kg).

Aitch and knuckle bones:
9 lb (4 kg).
NOTE: Center bone remains.

Roasting weight:
57 lb (25.6 kg), with handle attached.

Serving size:
Roasted whole, this piece yields 150 5-oz (140-g) servings on main-course buffet, when other items are served, or 220 3½-oz (100-g) servings for cocktail reception, when other items are served.

ROUND, STEAMSHIP, MBG #160
Partially boneless round.

Weight range:
47 to 80 lb (21.2 to 36 kg).

Best weight:
60 to 70 lb (27 to 31.5 kg).

Best use:
Roast whole as steamship round.

Sample Kitchen Yields
Trimming waste before roasting is about 5 percent, because the bone must be trimmed and some fat removed. *See also* Round, Chicago under this same heading.

SHIN MEAT

Weight:
Purchased by weight.

Best uses:
Clarification for consommé, and as stew meat.

Kitchen Yields
When ordering, specify trimmed or untrimmed. If pieces are to be used for consommé, only the superfluous fat has to be removed. Trimming loss is about 35 percent.

Trimming loss:
For stew meat, 20 percent by weight; 50 lb (22.5 kg) shin meat as purchased yields 40 lb (18 kg) usable meat.

Serving size:
For stew, 4 oz cooked; thus, 40 lb (18 kg) meat yields 100 servings.

SHORT RIBS, THREE BONES, MBG #123
Ready to use; no further trim required.

Weight:
1 lb (450 g) each.

Best uses:
Boiling and braising.

Sample Kitchen Yields

Serving size:
One 11-oz (312-g) piece, cooked weight.

SIRLOIN BUTT, MBG #182
The boneless end piece of the loin, with some of the fat, flap piece, and connecting tissues removed. When split, it is separated into the Top Sirloin Butt, MBG #184, and the Bottom Sirloin Butt, MBG #185.

Weight range:
11 to 22 lb (4.9 to 9.9 kg).

Best weight:
18 to 22 lb (8.1 to 9.9 kg).

Best uses:
Steaks, split and roasted, cut in julienne and sautéed if meat is Choice grade and aged.

Kitchen Yields
It is better to purchase either Top Sirloin Butt, #184, or Bottom Sirloin Butt, #185, than MBG #182. See these subheadings for information on yields.

STRIP LOIN, MBG #179
Short-cut strip loin, bone in.

Weight range:
10 to 20 lb (4.5 to 9 kg).

Best weight:
17 to 20 lb (7.6 to 9 kg).

Best uses:
Roast whole or cut into NY-cut shell steaks.

Sample Kitchen Yields
NOTE: In strip loin purchasing, the length of flank (which is basically worthless and must be trimmed off) determines usable yield. MBG #175 has a 4-in flank, MBG #177 has a 3-in flank, and MBG #179 has the shortest—only a 2-in flank—all measured at the sirloin end.

Grade and age also influence yield. Prime strips are fattier than Choice. Yield of Prime strips can be as much as 20 percent less than yield of Choice strips. Aged meat requires more trim, but weighs less on account of the drying-out process it undergoes during aging.

STRIP LOIN, MBG #180
This is the #179 loin, with bones removed.

Weight range:
8 to 15 lb (3.6 to 6.7 kg).

Best weight:
10 to 12 lb (4.5 to 5.4 kg).

Best uses:
Steaks and roasted whole.

Sample Kitchen Yields
See the comments about kitchen yields under Strip Loin, MBG #179.

Purchased weight:

Choice #180:
10 lb (4.5 kg).

Waste and trim:

Fat:
1 lb (450 g).

Usable scraps:
4 oz (112 g).

Usable meat:
8 lb 12 oz (3.9 kg).

Serving sizes:
Roasted, 6 oz (170 g) cooked meat, medium; thus, one piece yields 20 servings.
Cut into 10-oz (280-g) steaks, one piece yields 12 servings; the nerve end piece is not used.

Purchased weight:
16½ lb (7.4 kg) Choice, aged.

Trimmed meat:
5 lb 5 oz (2.3 kg).

End steak (nerve end):
1 lb 13 oz (0.8 kg).

Bones:
2½ lb (1.1 kg).

Usable scraps for chopped meat:
5 oz (140 g).

Waste fat and sinews:
6 lb 9 oz (2.9 kg).

Serving size:
12-oz (336-g) steaks, well trimmed, yield 7 steaks.

TENDERLOIN, MBG #189
Often referred to as *filet:* full tenderloin with all fat still attached.

Weight range:
5 to 8½ lb (2.2 to 3.8 kg).

Best size:
7 to 8½ lb (3.1 to 3.8 kg).

Best uses:
Roast tenderloin, chateaubriand, filet mignon.

Sample Kitchen Yields

Purchased weight:
7½ lb (3.3 kg).

Waste and trim:

Fat:
3¼ lb (1.5 kg).

Usable meat:

Defatted, side muscle on:
4¼ lb (1.9 kg).

Trimmed for roasting, side muscle on, head on:
3¾ lb (1.2 kg).

Usable scrap:
8 oz (224 g).

Serving sizes:
Roasted whole, 5 oz (140 g) cooked meat; one piece yields 8 to 9 servings. When the piece is cut into filet mignon, with side muscle on and head partly used, the following serving sizes and yields are obtained:

6 oz (170 g) = 8 each,   7 oz (200 g) = 7 each,
8 oz (227 g) = 6 each,   9 oz (255 g) = 5 each.

Usable tenderloin tips are 10 oz (280 g) to 12 oz (336 g).

TENDERLOIN, MBG #190
Also referred to as *filet.* This piece is defatted, with silver skin, wedge fat, and side strip muscle still attached.

Weight range:
3 to 6 lb (1.3 to 2.7 kg).

Best size:
5½ to 6 lb (2.2 to 2.7 kg).

Best uses:
Roasting and filet mignon.

Sample Kitchen Yields

Purchased weight:
5 lb 2 oz (2.3 kg).

Usable meat:

Filet mignon, center cut:
44 oz (1.1 kg).

Tenderloin, head and tips:
18 oz (504 g).

Ground meat:
4 oz (112 g).

Waste fat and skin:
1 lb (450 g).

TENDERLOIN, SHORT, MBG #192
When tenderloin is removed from the short loin, it has no butt, or head. The piece is normally sold with natural fat on.

Weight range:
2 to 5 lb (0.9 to 2.2 kg).

Best weight:
4 to 5 lb (1.8 to 2.2 kg).

Best use:
Filet mignon.

Sample Kitchen Yields
The piece is awkward to use, because it yields only three or four servings of filet mignon; the rest consists of tenderloin tips and fat.

TONGUE, FRESH

Weight:
4 to 5 lb (1.8 to 2.2 kg).

Kitchen Yields

Serving size:
5 oz (141 g); 1 lb (450 g) as purchased produces 9 oz (255 g) cooked and trimmed; therefore, 4½ lb

(2 kg) tongue produces 2 lb 9 oz (1.1 kg) cooked and trimmed, or 8 to 9 servings.

TOP ROUND, MBG #168
Also called *inside round,* it is a large muscle, available with aitch bone in or boneless.

Weight range:
14 to 23 lb (6.3 to 10.3 kg).

Best weight:
21 to 23 lb (9.4 to 10.3 kg).

Best uses:
Roasted whole or split, pot roast, stew, ground.

Sample Kitchen Yields
Specify boneless round. For roasting whole, purchase smaller rounds, in the 15- to 18-lb (6.7- to 8.1-kg) range, or purchase 21- to 23-lb (9.4- to 10.3-kg) rounds split and netted.

Purchased weight:
17 lb (7.6 kg), boneless.

Waste and trim:

Fat:
8 oz (226 g).

Scraps and trim:
12 oz (340 g).

Roasted weight:
12 lb 4 oz (3.5 kg).

Serving size:
For a sandwich, 4 oz (113 g); therefore, one round yields 46 servings.

TOP SIRLOIN BUTT, MBG #184

Weight range:
7 to 15 lb (3.1 to 6.7 kg).

Best weight:
12 to 15 lb (5.4 to 6.7 kg).

Best uses:
Steaks, roast, ground meat, cut in julienne and sautéed if meat is Choice grade and aged.

Sample Kitchen Yields

Purchased weight:

Choice:
14 lb (6.3 kg).

Waste and trim:

Fat:
4 lb (1.8 kg).

Usable scraps:
12 oz (220 g).

Usable meat:
9 lb 4 oz (4.1 kg).

POPULAR BEEF DISHES

BRACIOLE
Braciole are stuffed and braised Italian rouladen. The same cuts of meat can also be used for German beef rouladen.

Best cuts:
Bottom Round, MBG #170; or Top Round, MBG # 168.

Best weights:

Bottom Round:
26 to 29 lb (11.7 to 13 kg).

Top Round:
21 to 23 lb (9.4 to 10.3 kg).

Eye Round:
5 to 7 lb (2.2 to 3.1 kg).

Kitchen Yields

Serving size:
5 oz (140 g) raw weight; cooked weight depends on weight of stuffing. For untrimmed Top Round, 22 lb (9.9 kg) yields 60 steaks. For Bottom Round, 27 lb (12.1 kg) yields 75 steaks. For Eye Round, 6 lb (2.7 kg) yields 16 steaks.
NOTE: Pieces must be pounded flat in order to achieve yield.

BRAISED STEAK

Best cuts:
Top Round, MBG #168; Bottom Round, MBG #170; or Eye Round, MBG #171C.

Best weights:

Top Round:
21 to 23 lb (9.4 to 10.3 kg).

Bottom Round:
26 to 29 lb (11.7 to 13 kg).

Eye Round:
5 to 7 lb (2.2 to 3.1 kg).

Kitchen Yields

Serving size:
6 to 7 oz (170 to 200 g), raw; 4 to 5 oz (113 to 142 g) cooked.
For untrimmed Top Round, 22 lb (9.9 kg) yields 40 steaks.
For Bottom Round, 27 lb (12.1 kg) yields 50 steaks.
For Eye Round, 6 lb (2.7 kg) yields 12 steaks.

Calories:
5 oz (142 g) cooked steak = 408 Calories.

BRISKET, BARBECUED

Purchase:
Fresh Brisket, MBG #120.

Best size:
10 to 12 lb (4.5 to 5.4 kg).

Kitchen Yields
1 lb (450 g) as purchased produces 6½ oz (182 g) cooked and lean meat.

Serving size:
4 oz (112 g) cooked and lean; 11 lb (4.9 kg) brisket produces 4 lb 7 oz (2 kg) cooked and well-trimmed meat, so one brisket yields 17 servings.

Calories:
4 oz (112 g) cooked = 220 Calories.

BRISKET, BOILED

Purchase:
Fresh brisket, MBG #120.

Best size:
11 to 14 lb (4.9 to 6.3 kg).

Kitchen Yields
1 lb (450 g) as purchased produces 9 oz, cooked and trimmed.

Serving size:
4 oz (140 g), cooked and lean; 12 lb (5.4 kg) brisket produces 6½ lb (3 kg) cooked and well-trimmed, so one brisket yields 22 servings.

Calories:
4 oz (113 g) lean and fat = 326 Calories.

CHATEAUBRIAND
Large tenderloin steak, for two or more servings.
Roast tenderloin of beef is often referred to as
chateaubriand.

Best cut:
Tenderloin, fat on, MBG #189.

Kitchen Yields
Meat tastes better if some fat is left on during the
broiling and roasting process and is peeled away
at service. Normally, the head of the tenderloin is
used for chateaubriand.

Serving size:
10 oz (280 g), including fat, per person.

CHOPPED STEAK
Purchase the following cuts, if meat is ground in
house. (They are listed in order of preference.)

• Boneless Square-Cut Chuck, MBG #115

Best weight:
65 to 85 lb (29.2 to 38.2 kg).

• Top Sirloin Butt, MBG #184

Best weight:
12 to 15 lb (5.4 to 6.7 kg).

• Blade Meat, MBG #109B

Best weight:
By weight.

• Top Round, MBG #168

Best weight:
14 to 15 lb (6.3 to 6.7 kg).

Kitchen Yields

Serving size:

Raw weight:
7 to 8 oz (200 to 227 g). The following weights
and numbers of servings can be obtained for
different cuts of beef:

> Boneless, untrimmed chuck: 75 lb (33.7 kg)
> yields 120 chopped steaks.

Top sirloin: 12 lb (5.4 kg) yields 20 chopped
steaks.
Blade meat: 40 lb (18 kg) yields 78 to 80
chopped steaks.
Top round: 15 lb (6.7 kg) yields 30 chopped
steaks.

KEBAB
Also spelled *kebob.*

Best cuts:
Tenderloin tips (pack by weight, 6 to 7 oz; 170 to
200 g); Top Sirloin Butt, MBG #184 (best weight
12 to 15 lb; 5.4 to 6.7 kg); Knuckle, MBG #167A
(best weight 8 to 11 lb; 3.6 to 4.9 kg); or Strip Loin,
MBG #180 (best weight 10 lb; 4.5 kg).

Kitchen Yields

Serving sizes:
5 oz (140 g) for main course; 1½ oz (42 g) for hors
d'oeuvres (meat only).

> For untrimmed Tenderloin Tips, 50 lb (22.5
> kg) yields 140 main-course orders or 480
> hors d'oeuvres.
> For untrimmed Top Sirloin Butt, 14 lb (6.3
> kg) yields main-course orders or 110 hors
> d'oeuvres.
> For untrimmed Knuckle, 10 lb (4.5 kg) yields
> 28 main-course orders or 95 hors d'oeuvres
> orders.
> For Strip Loin, MBG #180, 10 lb (4.5 kg)
> yields 26 main-course orders or 86 hors
> d'oeuvres orders.

LONDON BROIL

Best cuts:
Flank Steaks, MBG #193 (purchase 2 to 2½ lb; 0.9
to 1.2 kg), Strip Loin, MBG #180 (purchase one
10-lb or 4.5-kg piece), Strip Loin, nerve-end cuts
(best weights are 22 to 24 oz; 625 to 680 g), or Top
Sirloin Butt, MBG #184 (purchase 12 to 15 lb; 5.4
to 6.7 kg).

Kitchen Yields

Serving size:
5 oz (140 g) cooked medium rare.

> For flank steak, 2 lb (0.9 kg) yields 5
> servings.

For strip loin, MBG #180, 10 lb (4.5 kg)
yield 20 servings, when cut on machine
for banquets.

For strip loin, nerve-end cuts, 22 to 24 oz (625
to 680 g) yield 3½ servings.

For untrimmed top sirloin butt, seamed into
3 pieces, 14 lb (6.3 kg) yield 25 to 26
servings.

Calories:
5 oz (140 g), Choice grade, cooked medium
rare = 287 Calories.

NEW YORK-CUT SIRLOIN STEAK
Also called *strip steak* or *sirloin steak*.

Purchase:
Strip Loin, MBG #179, bone in—17 to 20 lb (7.6
to 9 kg) or 14 to 16 lb (6.3 to 7.2 kg)—or Strip
Loin, MBG #180, boneless—10 to 12 lb (4.5 to
5.4 kg).

Kitchen Yields

Serving sizes:

Bone in:
8 to 16 oz (227 to 450 g).

Boneless:
7 to 16 oz (200 to 450 g).
For strip loin, MBA #179, 15 lb (6.7 kg) yield 20
steaks, bone in, of 10 oz (280 g) each or 15 steaks,
bone in, of 14 oz (400 g) each. The same piece can
alternatively yield 12 steaks, boneless, of 10 oz
(280 g) each or 8 steaks, boneless, of 14 oz
(400 g) each.
NOTE: Nerve ends are used as steaks.
For strip loin, MBA #180, 10 lb (4.5 kg) yield 11
steaks, boneless, of 12 oz (340 g) each or 15
steaks, boneless, of 8 oz (227 g) each.
NOTE: Nerve ends are used as steaks.

POT ROAST

Best cuts and sizes:
Knuckle, MBG #167 (purchase one 14- to 15-lb
(6.3- to 6.7-kg) piece), Gooseneck Bottom Round,
MBG #170 (purchase one 26- to 29-lb or 11.7- to
13-kg piece), Top Round, MBG #168 (purchase
one 21- to 23-lb or 9.4- to 10.3-kg piece), Chuck
Roll, MBG #116A (purchase one 13- to 15-lb or

5.8- to 6.7-kg piece), or Eye Round, MBG #171C
(purchase one 5- to 6-lb; 2.2- to 2.7-kg piece).

Kitchen Yields
NOTE: Yield varies according to trim and fatness
of meat.

Serving size:
4 oz (112 g) cooked meat.

One 14-lb (6.3-kg) Knuckle yields 24 to 28
servings.

One 27-lb (12.1-kg) Gooseneck Bottom Round
yields 55 servings.

One 21-lb (9.4-kg) boneless Top Round yields
40 to 45 servings.

One 15-lb (6.7-kg) netted Chuck Roll yields
35 to 40 servings.

One 6-lb (2.7-kg) Eye Round yields 18 to 20
servings.

Pot Roast Formula
10 lb (4.5 kg) meat, trimmed, lean
1 cup (0.22 l) oil
16 oz (450 g) mire poix
2 cups (0.47 l) tomato purée
2 to 2¼ qt (1.8 to 2.1 l) cooking liquid
1 pt (0.47 l) dry red wine
4 oz (113 g) corn starch

Kitchen Yields

Serving size:
4 oz (113 g) cooked meat, plus 1½ to 2 oz (0.04 to
0.06 l) sauce. Therefore, 10 lb (4.5 kg) trimmed
meat yield 30 servings.

Calories:
4 oz (113 g) meat, plus 1½ oz (0.04 l) gravy = 376
Calories.

PRIME RIB

Purchase:
Oven-ready Rib, MBG #109, or boneless Roast-
ready Rib, MBG #110. The Roast-ready Rib is a
popular specification for banquet operation because
the meat needs little trim after roasting.

Best weights:
For Oven-ready Rib, 18 to 20 lb (8.1 to 9 kg) or 20
to 22 lb (9.9 kg); for Roast-ready Rib, 14 to 15 lb
(6.3 to 6.7 kg).

Kitchen Yields

Serving sizes:
10 oz (280 g) without bone. À la carte 8 oz (224 g) without bones in banquet.

> One 19-lb (8.5 kg) Oven-ready Rib, MBG #109, yields 20 servings on banquet or 16 à la carte servings.
> NOTE: Yield calculated if both ouside cuts are sold.
> One boneless 14-lb (6.3-kg) Roast-ready Rib, MBG #110, yields 20 servings on banquet or 30 servings on buffet.

RIBS, BARBECUED

Best size:
1½ to 2 lb (0.6 to 0.9 kg).

Kitchen Yields
Shrinkage is 50 percent.

Serving size:
1 lb (450 g) cooked, bone in; 25 lb (11.2 kg) ribs yield 12 servings.

ROUND ROAST

Purchase:
Top Round, MBG #168—21 to 23 lb (9.4 to 10.3 kg).

Kitchen Yields

Serving sizes:
For cold sandwiches, 4 oz (113 g); for hot main course, 5 to 6 oz (142 to 170 g).
One 18-lb (8.1-kg) trimmed, oven-ready Top Round, produces 14 lb (6.3 kg) roasted medium-rare meat. This yields 50 servings of cold sandwiches or 38 servings as hot main course.

Calories:
4 oz (113 g) lean meat = 180 Calories.

SIRLOIN ROAST

Purchase:
Loin, bone in, MBG #179—17 to 20 lb (7.6 to 9 kg) or 14 to 16 lb (6.3 to 7.2 kg)—or Strip Loin MBG #180—10 to 12 lb (4.5 to 5.4 kg).

Kitchen Yields

Serving sizes:
For main course, 7 oz (200 g) consisting of 2 slices or 1 thick slice; for buffet, 3½ oz (100 g) consisting of 1 slice.

> One Strip Loin, MBG #179, weighing 18 lb (8.1 kg) as purchased, yields 20 servings main course of 2 slices each or 38 buffet servings.
> One Strip Loin, MBG #179, weighing 16 lb (7.2 kg) as purchased, yields 18 main-course servings of 2 slices each or 34 buffet servings.
> One Strip Loin, MBG #180, weighing 10 lb (4.5 kg) as purchased, yields 20 main-course servings of 2 slices each or 38 buffet servings.

TARTAR STEAK

Purchase:
Peeled Knuckle, MBG #167A (10 lb; 4.5 kg), Bottom Sirloin Ball Tip, MBG #185B (3 lb; 1.3 kg), or Tenderloin, MBG #190A (4 lb 10 oz; 2 kg).

Kitchen Yields

Serving sizes:
6 oz (170 g) as main course, ½ oz (14 g) for each canapé, or 1½ oz (42 g) on buffets with other choices.

> One 10-lb (4.5-kg) peeled knuckle provides 7 lb (3.1 kg) clean meat. This yields 18 main-course servings, 220 canapés, or 75 buffet servings.
> One 3-lb (1.3-kg) bottom sirloin ball tip provides 2½ lb (1.1 kg) clean meat. This yields 6½ main-course servings, 80 canapés, or 26 buffet servings.
> One 4-lb-10-oz (2-kg) tenderloin provides 3 lb 6 oz (1.5 kg) clean meat. This yields 9 main-course servings, 108 canapés, or 36 buffet servings.

TENDERLOIN ROAST

Purchase:
Tenderloin, with fat, MBG #189—7 to 8½ lb (3.1 to 3.8 kg)—or Tenderloin, trimmed, MBG #190—5½ to 6 lb (2.2 to 2.7 kg).

Kitchen Yields

Serving sizes:
For main course, 2 slices totaling 5 oz (142 g); for buffet, 1½ slices totaling 3 oz (85 g).

> One Tenderloin, MBG #189, weighing 7½ lb (3.3 kg) as purchased, yields 9 servings main course or 12 servings buffet.
> One Tenderloin, MBG #190, weighing 5½ lb (2.2 kg) as purchased, yields 9 servings main course or 12 servings buffet.
> One trimmed, oven-ready Tenderloin, weighing 4 lb (1.8 kg), yields 9 servings main course or 10 servings buffet.

PORTION CUTS OF BEEF
This list includes descriptions of commonly available portion cuts. Additional cuts may be available locally. When ordering, specify frozen or fresh.

Pack:
Varies according to product. All items may be obtained either by count or by weight.

BOTTOM ROUND STEAKS
Rather dry steaks, available in many sizes. Suitable for braising.

Sizes:
From 4 to 24 oz (85 to 680 g), in 2-oz (56-g) increments.

Kitchen Yields

Serving sizes:
4 oz (113 g) for buffets; 6 or 8 oz (170 or 226 g) for lunch; 8 or 10 oz (226 or 280 g) for dinner. Use the 24-oz (680-g) piece as Pot Roast; cut on bias, this will yield about 3 portions.

BRAISING STEAKS
Sizes:
4, 6, and 8 oz (113, 170, and 226 g).

Kitchen Yields

Serving sizes:
4 oz (85 g) for buffets; 6 or 8 oz (170 or 226 g) for main course.

CHOPPED STEAKS AND HAMBURGERS
Sizes:
From 1 to 10 oz.

Kitchen Yields

Serving sizes:
Varies according to operation. For hamburgers, average size ranges from 3 to 6 oz (98 to 170 g), and typical size is 4 oz (113 g). Thus, 10 lb (4.5 kg) hamburger yield forty 4-oz (113-g) patties, and 50 lb (22.5 kg) yield two hundred 4-oz (113-g) patties.

Calories:
One 4-oz (113-g) patty, with 20 percent fat content = 324 Calories.

CUBED STEAKS
Inexpensive boneless steaks, mechanically tenderized for broiling.

Sizes:
3, 4, 6, and 8 oz (85, 113, 170, and 226 g).

Kitchen Yields
Cooked to order for sandwiches.

PORTERHOUSE STEAKS
Bone-in steak cut from the short loin, basically the same as a T-bone steak. Available with different trim.

Sizes:
From 10 to 24 oz (280 to 680 g) in 2-oz (56-g) increments.

Kitchen Yields
When ordering steaks, make sure to specify trim clearly.

Serving size:
12 to 16 oz (340 to 450 g) for 1 serving; 20 or 24 oz (568 or 680 g) for 2 servings.

RIB-EYE STEAKS
Boneless steaks cut from the eye of the prime rib. Available with the tail (also called the *lip*) left on, or as rib-eye roll steaks with the lip removed. Suitable for broiling.

Sizes:
4, 6, 8, 10, and 12 oz (113, 170, 226, 280, and 340 g).

Kitchen Yields

Serving sizes:
6 or 8 oz (170 or 226 g) for lunch; 8, 10, or 12 oz (226, 280, or 340 g) for dinner.

RIB STEAKS, BONE IN
Trimmed steaks with bone, cut from the prime rib. Suitable for broiling, and great for outdoor barbecues.

Sizes:
8, 10, 12, 14, 16, and 18 oz (226, 280, 340, 400, 450, and 510 g).

Kitchen Yields

Serving sizes:
8 or 10 oz (226 or 280 g) for lunch; 14 or 16 oz (400 or 450 g) for dinner.

STRIP LOIN STEAKS
Also called *sirloin steak* or *New York-cut steak.* Available with bone in or with bone removed. The length of flank left on steaks varies and should be clearly specified.

Sizes:
For bone-in steaks, 6, 8, 10 12, 14, 16, 18, and 20 oz (170, 226, 280, 340, 450, 511, and 568 g); for boneless steaks, 8, 10, 12, 14, 16, 18, 20, and 24 oz (226, 280, 340, 450, 511, 568, and 680 g).

Kitchen Yields
Make sure the flank length is well specified when ordering. Intermediate size has about 3-in (75-mm) flank, when measured from the eye.

Serving sizes:
For bone-in steaks, 6 or 8 oz (170 or 226 g) for breakfast, 10 or 12 oz (280 or 340 g) for lunch, 14 or 16 oz (340 or 450 g) for dinner, or 20 oz (568 g) for steak for two. For boneless steaks, 8 oz (226 g) for breakfast, 10 or 12 oz (280 or 340 g) for lunch, 14 or 16 oz (340 or 450 g) for dinner, or 20 or 24 oz (568 or 680 g) for steak for two.

Calories:
One 10-oz (280-g) boneless strip loin steak, lean = 650 Calories.

TENDERLOIN STEAKS
A number of types of trim are available:

> Fat on and side muscle on
> Defatted, with side muscle on
> Silver skin on and side muscle removed
> Both silver skin and side muscle removed

Sizes:
For most types of trim, 3 to 14 oz (85 to 400 g).

Kitchen Yields
Make sure to specify trim and fat cover clearly when ordering steaks.

Serving sizes:
3 or 4 oz (85 or 113 g) for breakfast or buffet; 6 or 8 oz (170 or 226 g) for restaurant or banquet service; 10, 12, or 14 oz (280, 340, and 400 g) steakhouse sizes.

TOP ROUND STEAKS
Suitable for braising, such as Swiss steaks.

Sizes:
3, 4, 6, 8, 10, or 12 oz (85, 113, 170, 226, 280, and 340 g).

Kitchen Yields

Serving sizes:
3 or 4 oz (85 or 113 g) for buffets; 6 or 8 oz (170 or 226 g) for lunch; 8 or 10 oz (226 or 280 g) for dinner.

TOP SIRLOIN BUTT STEAKS
Juicy, tender steaks for broiling. Center cuts are more uniform in shape and have a better trim than end pieces.

Sizes:
4 to 24 oz (113 to 680 g), in 2-oz (56-g) increments.

Kitchen Yields

Serving sizes:
4 to 6 oz (113 to 170 g) for breakfast or lunch; 8 to 12 oz (226 to 340 g) for dinner. When used as sliced steak, one 18-oz (511-g) piece yields 3 servings, and one 24-oz (680-g) piece yields 4½ servings.

SMOKED AND CURED BEEF PRODUCTS

BUENDNERFLEISCH

Also called *viande de grison*. Air-dried beef, available imported or domestically produced. Use like prosciutto ham.

Weight:
5 lb (2.2 kg) average.

Kitchen Yields
The product is boneless, and there is little waste.

Serving size:
1 oz. One 5-lb piece yields 75 servings.

CHIPPED BEEF

Pack:
3 lb (1.3 kg), loose in boxes; 4, 5, and 6 oz (113, 140, and 170 g) in individual bags.

Kitchen Yields

Serving size:
4 oz (113 g).

Calories:
4 oz (113 g), without sauce = 232 Calories.

CORNED BEEF

Available canned, cooked, and raw. Many different cuts and trims are on the market.

Brisket, Cooked
Fully cooked briskets, with most fat removed. First-cut is a better-trimmed piece.

Weight ranges:

Whole brisket:
5 to 8 lb (2.2 to 3.6 kg).

First-cut:
3 to 5 lb (1.3 to 2.2 kg).

Kitchen Yields
Whole cooked brisket has trimming waste of 5 percent. First-cut brisket is fully trimmed and has minimal waste.

Brisket, Uncooked, Deli Trim and Flat-cut
Some fat has been removed from deli trim briskets. Flat-cut briskets are split along the natural seam separating the two muscles in the brisket.

Weight ranges:

Deli trim:
8 to 13 lb (3.6 to 5.8 kg).

Flat-cut:
3 to 4½ lb (1.3 to 2 kg).

Kitchen Yields
1 lb (450 g) as purchased yields 9 oz (250 g) cooked, trimmed meat.
One 10-lb (4.5-kg) brisket produces 5½ lb (2.5 kg) cooked meat.

Brisket, Uncooked, Regular Trim
Raw corned briskets are often delivered packed in brine, making it difficult to verify their real weight. The cooking and trimming losses are large.

Weight range:
12 to 14 lb (5.4 to 6.3 kg).

Kitchen Yields
1 lb (450 g) as purchased is equivalent to 7 oz (200 g) cooked, trimmed meat.

Serving sizes:
5 oz (140 g) as hot deli sandwich; 5 oz (140 g) as main course, served with cabbage.
One 13-lb (5.8-kg) brisket, as purchased (drained but wet), produces 5½ lb (1.3 kg) lean, trimmed cooked meat. One brisket yields 17 servings for sandwiches or main course.

Usable trimmings:
8 oz (227 g) from a 13-lb (5.8-kg) brisket, usable for hash.

Corned Beef, Canned

Pack:
Six #10 cans, weighing 6 lb (2.7 kg) each. Other packs are available.

Calories:
4 oz (113 g) = 246 Calories.

Corned Beef Hash
Ground, cooked, corned beef, mixed with diced cooked potatoes.

Pack:
Six #10 cans, weighing 6 lb (2.7 kg) each. Other packs are available.

Kitchen Yields

Serving sizes:

1¼ cup, or 9 oz (250 g), for restaurant serving; ¾ cup, or 5½ oz (156 g) for buffet serving.
One #10 can yields 10 restaurant servings or 17 buffet servings.

Calories:

1¼ cup, weighing 9 oz (250 g) = 483 Calories.

ROUNDS, ROASTED AND COOKED
Fully cooked rounds are available fresh or frozen; they are normally shipped in vacuum bags.

Weight ranges:

Flat rounds:
5 to 8 lb (2.2 to 3.6 kg).

Bottom round halves:
5 to 8 lb (2.2 to 3.6 kg).

Eye rounds:
4 to 7 lb (1.8 to 3.1 kg).
Portion packs are available in various sizes.

Kitchen Yields

There is little trimming waste, and the meat is ready for use.

Calories:

5 oz (140 g) = 300 Calories.

ROUNDS, CORNED
Available with small bone attached or boneless. Bottom rounds are more likely than top rounds to be corned.

Weight range:

35 to 45 lb (15.7 to 20.2 kg).

Kitchen Yields

Bone weight:

About 6 percent of weight.

Cooking loss:

35 percent is average.

Trimming loss:

5 percent of cooked weight.
One 40 lb (18 kg) round with bone yields 23 lb 12 oz (10.6 kg) cooked, trimmed meat.

GYROS
See Gyros.

PASTRAMI
Pastrami is cured, smoked beef that has been rolled in crush coriander seeds. Genuine pastrami is made from the plate, but pastrami made from other beef cuts is also produced. Plate pastrami must be steamed before use. Most other cuts are fully cooked.

Weights:

Plate pieces:
2 to 4 lb (0.9 to 1.8 kg).

Round pieces:
2 to 6 lb (0.9 to 2.7 kg).
Other sizes are available.

Kitchen Yields

Serving size:

4½ oz (127 g) for sandwich.

Cooking loss:

18 to 20 percent of weight for plate pastrami.

Trimming loss:

5 to 10 percent for plate pastrami; 5 percent for cooked round pastrami.
3 lb plate pastrami, as purchased are equivalent to 2 lb 8 oz (1.2 kg) cooked and yield 8 servings (sandwiches); 5 lb cooked Round pastrami yield 16 servings (sandwiches).

ROAST BEEF
Fully cooked products are normally frozen. Many ready-to-eat products are poached in pouches with seasonings and caramel color. Oven-roasted products are roasted in pouches; some are dry-roasted. Some products are identified by USDA grade, normally Choice.
Many different cuts are available. The most popular are the following:

Bottom Round, no heel
Eye Round
Top Round, whole
Top Round, split
Prime Rib

Weight:
Vary, depending on cuts.

Kitchen Yields

Pouch weight:
2 oz (56 g).

Residual juices:
Up to 5 oz (142 g).

Trimming waste:
5 percent. Trim varies, depending on manufacturer.

Calories:
4 oz (113 g) lean roast round = 225 Calories.

SALAMI, BEEF

Size:
5 to 6 lb (2.2 to 2.7 kg).

Kitchen Yields
Trimming waste, end pieces, and wrapping account for 3 percent of purchased weight.

Serving size:
3 oz (85 g) for sandwiches. One 5½-lb (2.4-kg) salami yields 28 sandwiches.

Calories:
One 4-oz (113-g) slice = 180 Calories.

TONGUE, SMOKED, RAW

Size:
4 to 5 lb (1.8 to 2.2 kg).

Kitchen Yields

Cooking and trimming loss:
50 percent of weight. Therefore, 1 lb (450 g) as purchased produces 8 oz (226 g) cooked and trimmed.

Serving size:
3 oz (85 g) for sandwich, so 5 lb (2.2 kg) as purchased yields 13 servings.

BEEF CONSOMMÉ

See Soups.

BEER

Keg Sizes:
1 barrel = 31 gal (117.8 l).
½ barrel (one standard keg) = 15½ gal (58.9 l).

Table B-1 Serving Yields for Beer (in Glasses per Keg)

Type of Glass	Size	1-in (25-mm) head	Number of Servings 3/4-in (19.5-mm) head	1/2-in (12.7-mm) head
Pitcher	60 oz (1.7 l)	41		
	40 oz (1.1 l)	62		
Schooner	10 oz (0.29 l)	330	293	256
	12 oz (0.35 l)	256	214	198
Sham pilsner	8 oz (0.235 l)	345	317	283
	10 oz (0.29 l)	264	248	233
	12 oz (0.35 l)	214	203	188
Footed pilsner	10 oz (0.29 l)	248	233	220
	12 oz (0.35 l)	208	198	184
Stein	10 oz (0.29 l)	248	233	220
	14 oz (0.40 l)	170	165	158
Paper cup	10 oz (0.29 l)	265	245	225
	12 oz (0.34 l)	245	220	205
	14 oz (0.40 l)	195	180	170

½ barrel (one standard keg) = 165 bottles, 12-oz (0.34-l).

Table B-1 shows serving yields from a keg of beer, based on type of glass and thickness of head.

Calories:
One 12-oz (0.34-l) bottle = 150 Calories.

BEER BATTER

Formula
six 12-oz (0.34-l) cans beer
3 cups (0.7 l) warm water
½ cup (0.17 l) oil
8 cups, or 46 oz (1.3 kg), flour
3 tb salt

Kitchen Yields
The preceding formula produces 1 gal (3.8 l) beer batter.

BEETS

Available canned and fresh.

CANNED BEETS
Canned beets are available whole, diced, sliced, and in shoestrings, in various sizes.

Pack:
Six #10 cans.

Kitchen Yields

• Diced Beets

Serving size:
½ cup (drained) (0.11 l), and one #10 can yields 23 servings.

• Sliced Beets

Serving size:
½ cup (drained) (0.11 l), and one #10 can yields 22 servings.

• Whole Beets

Count:
Each #10 can contains 250 to 300 extra tiny beets, 175 to 250 tiny beets, 174 to 125 small beets, 75 to 124 medium beets, or fewer than 74 large beets. Counts vary slightly from one packer to another.

Serving size:
4 to 5 small beets; therefore, one #10 can yields 30 to 35 servings.

Calories:
½ cup whole, small (drained) = 30 Calories.
½ cup diced or sliced (drained) = 35 Calories.

FRESH BEETS
Sold with and without leaves. Leaves may be cooked separately; they resemble chard. Baby beets are also available; *see* Baby Vegetables.

Season:
Available year-round.

Pack:
25- and 50-lb (11.2- and 22.5-kg) bags, without leaves; 43- to 47-lb (19.3- to 21.1-kg) cartons containing 24 bunches, with leaves still attached.

Count:
None established; sizes vary.

Kitchen Yields
1 lb (450 g) beets without leaves is equivalent to 2 cups or 12 oz (340 g) beets, cooked and sliced.

Calories:
½ cup diced or sliced (drained) = 35 Calories.
½ cup greens, leaves, and stems, cooked (drained) = 20 Calories.

BELGIAN ENDIVE

Available canned and fresh.

CANNED BELGIAN ENDIVE

Pack:
Twenty-four 15-oz (426-g) cans.

Kitchen Yields

Serving size:
One piece, as hot vegetable. One 15-oz (426-g) can yields 3 to 4 servings.

FRESH BELGIAN ENDIVE

Imported vegetable, most often used as salad but can also be braised, grilled, or sautéed.

Season:
Fall until spring.

Pack:
10-lb (4.5-kg) boxes.

Count:
Varies, but approximately 50 pieces per box.

Weight per stalk:
3⅓ oz (94 g), average.

Kitchen Yields
Very little waste. One stalk has 8 to 9 leaves; 2 lb (0.9 kg) endive yield 90 leaves.

Serving size:
4 oz (113 g) for salad, cut up; therefore, one box yields 40 servings.

BELL PEPPERS

See Sweet Peppers, under Peppers.

BIBB LETTUCE

See Lettuce.

BISCUITS

Formula 1
    1½ lb (675 g) bread flour
    1½ lb (675 g) pastry flour
    4 oz (112 g) baking powder
    6 oz (170 g) sugar
    8 oz (224 g) shortening
    1 oz (28 g) salt
    5 eggs
    3 cups (0.7 l) milk

Kitchen Yields

Scaling size:
1½ oz (42 g). The total mix yields 65 pieces.

Formula 2
    4½ lb (2 kg) patent flour
    8 oz (224 g) baking powder
    8 oz (224 g) sugar
    1½ lb (670 g) shortening
    12 eggs
    1 qt (0.94 l) milk

Kitchen Yields

Scaling size:
1 oz (226 g). The total mix yields 160 pieces.

Calories:
One biscuit, 2 in (5 cm) in diameter, or 1 oz (28 g) = 105 Calories.

BITTER MELON

See Squash.

BLACKBERRIES

Available fresh. Canned and frozen blackberries are available in small quantities. Domestic blackberries are also called *bushberries*.

Season:
Late spring to fall for domestic production. Imports available in winter.

Pack:
Flats or trays with 12 half-pints (0.23 l).

Kitchen Yields

Count:
½ pint (0.235 l) contains 45 to 50 berries.

Serving sizes:
½ pint yields 1½ servings for breakfast or dessert, so one flat yields 18 servings; ½ pint yields 3 servings as garnish with desserts and ice cream, so one flat yields 36 servings.
There is no waste when merchandise is fresh.

Calories:
¾ cup berries, weighing 5 oz (145 g) = 65 Calories.

BLACK-EYED PEAS

See Peas.

BLACK MISSION FIGS

See Figs.

BLACK RADISHES

See Radishes.

BLINTZES

Thin pancakes, baked on one side only and then filled with cottage cheese or fruit; served with sour cream and fruit sauce. Used in Jewish cooking.

Formula

    2½ cups, or 14 oz (400 g), flour
    10 eggs
    1 qt + 1 cup (1.16 l) milk
    ¼ cup (0.06 l) oil

Kitchen Yield
The preceding formula yields forty 6-in (150-mm) blintzes.

Formula for Cottage Cheese Filling

    5 lb (2.2 kg) cottage cheese
    8 egg yolks
    1 lb (450 g) sugar
    4 grated lemon rinds

Kitchen Yield
The preceding formula provides filling for forty blintzes.

BLUEBERRIES

Available canned, fresh, and frozen.

CANNED BLUEBERRIES

Pack:
Six #10 cans; twenty-four #300 cans. Other packs are available.

Kitchen Yields

Serving size:
½ cup fruit and juice. One #10 can yields 24 servings fruit and juice or 9 cups drained fruit.

FRESH BLUEBERRIES
Most blueberries sold on the commercial market are cultivated. The juice of blueberries is white. Huckleberries resemble blueberries but have purple-colored juice.

Season:
June to September. Peak is in summer. Imports are available in winter.

Pack:
Flats of twelve 1-pint (0.47-l) cartons; flats of eight 1-qt (0.94-l) cartons; 5-lb (2.3-kg) bulk cartons.

Kitchen Yields
There is basically no cleaning waste.

Serving size:
½ cup (0.11 l); 1 pint contains 2 cups blueberries, so 1 pint yields 4 servings. Therefore, one flat of 12 pints yields 48 servings, and one flat of 8 qt yields 64 servings.
One 5-lb bulk carton yields 30 servings.
1 cup dry blueberries weighs 5½ oz (150 g).
For blueberry pie, 3½ cups, or 20 oz (560 g), blueberries fill one 9-in pie.
For blueberry muffins, add 3½ cups, or 20 oz (560 g), blueberries to 80 oz batter; yield is 48 muffins formed by using a 2-oz (#16) scoop.

Calories:
½ cup blueberries = 35 Calories.

FROZEN BLUEBERRIES
Available IQF.

Pack:
Twelve 1-lb (450-g) polybags, for total weight of 12 lb (5.4 kg); six 3-lb (1.4-kg) polybags for total weight of 18 lb (8.1 kg); individual 25-lb (11.2-kg) cans; individual 30-lb (13.5-kg) cartons.

Kitchen Yields

Serving size:
½ cup (0.11 l); 1 lb (450 g) yields 3½ servings, and one 25-lb (11.2-kg) can yields 90 servings.

BOAR

Wild boar meat is available from farm-raised animals.

Pack:

Fresh Ham, bone in:
8 to 12 lb (3.6 to 5.4 kg).

Loins:
10 lb (4.5 kg).

Kitchen Yields
Difficult to estimate, because fatness of meat
varies greatly.

BOILING ONIONS

See Onions.

BOK CHOY

See Chinese Foods.

BONIATO

See Sweet Potatoes & Yams.

BOTTLE SIZES

This entry presents listings of champagne, liquor,
and wine bottle sizes.

Champagne Bottle Sizes:
   Split = 6.4 fl oz (0.87 l).
   Half-bottle = 12.8 fl oz (0.375 l).
   Fifth = 25.6 fl oz (0.75 l).
   Magnum = 2 fifths: 51.2 fl oz (1.5 l).
   Jeroboam = 4 fifths: 102.4 fl oz (3 l).
   Rehoboam = 6 fifths: 153.6 fl oz (4.5 l).
   Salmanazar = 12 fifths: 307 fl oz (9 l).
   Balthazar = 16 fifths: 409 fl oz (12 l).
   Nebuchadnezzar = 20 fifths: 512 fl oz (15 l).
   Sovereign = 34.6 fifths: 885.7 fl oz (26 l).

Liquor Bottle Sizes:
   Half-pint = 8 fl oz (0.235 l).
   Pint = 16 fl oz (0.47 l).
   Fifth = 25.6 fl oz (0.75 l).
   Liter = 34.1 fl oz (1.0 l).
   Quart = 32 fl oz (0.94 l).
   Half-gallon = 64 fl oz (1.9 l).

Wine Bottle Sizes:
   Half-bottle = 12.8 fl oz (0.37 l).
   Fifth = 25.6 fl oz (0.75 l).
   Liter = 34.1 fl oz (1.0 l).
   One-and-a-half liter = 51 fl oz (1.5 l).
   Half-gallon = 64 fl oz (1.88 l).
   Gallon = 128 fl oz (3.76 l).
   Magnum = 2 fifths: 51.2 fl oz (1.5 l).
   Double magnum = 4 fifths: 102.4 fl oz (3 l).
   Jeroboam = 6 fifths: 153.6 fl oz (4.5 l).
   Imperial = 8 fifths: 204.8 fl oz (6 l).

The fifth, which contains 25.6 oz (0.75 l), is the
most common wine bottle size.

Liquor Serving Yields:
Approximate number of drinks per bottle of
liquor are listed in Table B-2.

Table B-2 Drink Yields for Liquors (per Bottle)

	Number of Drinks					
Drink Size	*Half-pint* *8 oz (0.235 l)*	*Pint* *16 oz (0.47 l)*	*Fifth* *25.6 oz (0.75 l)*	*Quart* *32 oz (0.94 l)*	*Liter* *34.1 oz (1 l)*	*Half-Gallon* *64 oz (1.9 l)*
⅞ oz (0.025 l)	9	18	30	37	40	74
1 oz (0.029 l)	8	16	25	32	34	64
1⅛ oz (0.033 l)	7	14	22	28	30	56
1¼ oz (0.036 l)	6½	13	20½	26	27	52
1½ oz (0.043 l)	5½	11	17	21½	23	43

Table B-3 Drink Yields for Wines (per Bottle)

				Number of Drinks		
Serving Size	Half-bottle 12.8 oz (0.37 l)	Fifth 25.6 oz (0.75 l)	Liter 34.1 oz (1 l)	One-and-a-half liter 51 oz (1.5 l)	Half-gallon 64 oz (1.88 l)	Gallon 128 oz (3.76 l)
4 oz (0.12 l)	3	6	8	12	15	30
5 oz (0.14 l)	2	5	6	10	12	25
6 oz (0.17 l)	2	4	5½	8½	10½	21

Wine Serving Yields:
Approximate number of glasses per bottle of wine are listed in Table B-3.

Common Serving Sizes:
4 oz (0.1 l) for champagne and sparkling wine and for dessert wines (often sold in half-bottles); 5 oz (0.15 l) for white wines; and 6 oz (0.17 l) for red wine.

Banquet Serving Sizes:
6 glasses per bottle for champagne toast; 2 bottles of white wine for table of 10 covers; 2 bottles of red wine for a table of 10 covers.

BOYSENBERRY

Boysenberries are shaped like raspberries, but are longer and slightly larger. Their color is red.

Season:
Late summer.

Pack:
Flats of twelve ½-pint (0.23-l) containers.

Kitchen Yields

Serving size:
⅔ half-pint; therefore, one flat yields 18 portions. One ½-pint—8 fl oz (0.22 l)—weighs 5 oz (140 g). Four ½-pints (0.9 l) weigh 1¼ lb (560 g).

Calories:
⅔ half-pint (0.15 l) berries = 55 Calories.

BRAZIL NUTS

Available shelled.

Pack:
By weight.

Kitchen Yields
1 lb (450 g) is equivalent to 3¼ cups (0.75 l).

Calories:
6 to 8 large kernels weighing 1 oz (28 g) total = 185 Calories.

BREAD

Breads are available in countless varieties and sizes. Listed are common sizes for cocktail, commercial, and noncommercial loaves. Bread crumbs are also covered by this entry.

BREAD CRUMBS

Weights:
1 cup dry crumbs weighs 3½ oz (100 g).
1 cup soft white crumbs weighs 1⅝ oz (45 g).

Kitchen Yields
For soft white bread crumbs, 1 lb white bread, crust removed, yields 7 cups (315 g); 5 lb white bread, crust removed, yield 56 oz (1.6 kg).

Calories:
1 cup dry crumbs weighing 3½ oz (100 g) = 390 Calories.
1 cup soft crumbs weighing 1⅝ oz (45 g) = 120 Calories.

BREAD DOUGH

BREADBASKET DOUGH
Baskets can also be made with noodle dough.

Formula
 2½ lb (1.1 kg) bread flour
 1 egg
 1 oz (28 g) shortening
 1 oz (28 g) oil
 1 pint = 16 oz (0.47 l) cold water

BREAD DOUGH FOR BASIC HARD ROLLS
This dough can also be used for decorative bread-baskets.

Formula
5 lb (2.2 kg) bread flour
2 oz (56 g) salt
2 oz (56 g) sugar
2 oz (56 g) shortening
2 oz (56 g) egg whites
3 lb (1.4 kg) water
3 oz (85 g) yeast

Baking instructions:
Set oven to 400°F; steam for the first 10 minutes.

Kitchen Yields
1 lb (450 g) dough yields 1 dozen rolls; the total mix from the preceding formula yields 8½ dozen rolls.
Alternatively, 1 lb (450 g) dough yields 3 French flutes.

Calories:
One 1¼-oz (35-g) roll = 110 Calories.

BREAD DOUGH SHRINKAGE
Shrinking loss of yeast dough in baking is approximately 11 percent.

Kitchen Yields
Shrinkage is 2 oz (57 g) for each 1 lb (450 g) of product; thus, 18 oz (500 g) dough yields 1 lb (450 g) bread.

COCKTAIL LOAVES

Flavors:
Rye, pumpernickel, or marble.

Weights and counts:
8 oz (225 g) contains 30 to 32 slices.
12 oz (336 g) contains 42 slices.

COMMERCIAL SANDWICH LOAVES

Flavors:
White, whole wheat, or square rye.

Sizes:
Commercial loaves are classified by the size of the slice, as detailed in Table B-4.

Table B-4 Weights and Sizes of Commercial Bread Loaves

Size Number	Weight	Number of Normal Slices	Size of Slice
#2	2 lb (0.9 kg)	32	3½ × 3½ in (89 × 89 mm)
#3	3 lb (1.3 kg)	32	3¾ × 3¾ in (95 × 95 mm)
#4	4 lb (1.8 kg)	32	4¼ × 4¼ in (107 × 107 mm)

Table B-5 Weights and Sizes of Noncommercial Bread Loaves

Variety	Weight of Loaf	Number of Slices	Loaves per 100 Slices
Raisin Bread	1 lb (450 g)	18	5¾
	2 lb (900 g)	36	2¾
Rye Bread	1 lb (450 g)	23	4½
	1½ lb (675 g)	28	3¾
	2 lb (900 g)	33	3
White Bread	1 lb (450 g)	16	6¼
	1¼ lb (560 g)	19	5½
	1½ lb (675 g)	24	4¼
	2 lb (900 g)	28	3¾
	2 lb (900 g)	36	2¾

Thickness of slice:

Normal:
8/16 in (12.7 mm), or 32 slices per loaf.

Thin:
7/16 in (11 mm), or 34 slices per loaf.

Extra thin:
6/16 in (10 mm), or 40 slices per loaf.
Bread is available sliced lengthwise for canapés or finger sandwiches. Length of such a loaf is 18 in (450 mm), and one loaf yields 11 or 12 slices.

NONCOMMERCIAL SANDWICH LOAVES

Flavors:
Raisin, rye, and white.

Sizes:

Table B-5 gives weight and slice information for noncommercial loaves.

Kitchen Yields of Commercial Bread Loaves

One loaf sliced horizontally yields 60 double finger sandwiches.

One loaf sliced horizontally yields 420 canapés.

One horizontal slice yields 12 toast croustades (2¾ in × 1¾ in); therefore, one #3 loaf sliced horizontally yields 132 toast croustades.

Weight:

1 cup fresh cubes of white bread weigh 1⅛ oz (31 g). One #2 loaf yields 12 to 13 cups.

Calories:

#2 loaf, one slice = 75 Calories.

1 cup of white cubes, 1⅛ oz (31 g) = 80 Calories.

BREADFRUIT

Large roundish fruit, belonging to the same family as figs. There are seedless and seeded breadfruit varieties. The unripe fruit has a slightly unpleasant aroma, but this disappears when the fruit becomes fully ripe.

Season:

May until February.

Pack:

By count.

Size:

Varies greatly, but normally is 8 to 12 in (20 to 30 cm) long; best size is 3 to 3½ lb (1.3 to 1.5 kg) each.

Weight:

2 to 9 lb (1 to 4 kg).

Kitchen Yields

Best size:

3 to 3½ lb (1.3 to 1.5 kg).

Serving size:

⅙ breadfruit; therefore, one breadfruit yields 6 servings as vegetable garnish.

BRINE

For preserving meat, the following formula should be used in making brine.

Formula for Meat Brine

14 oz (400 g) salt
4 oz (113 g) sugar
1½ oz (63 g) saltpeter
2 oz (56 g) pickling spice
1 gal (3.8 l) water

For smoking fish, the following formula should be used in making brine.

Formula for Fish Brine

2½ gal (11.4 l) water
1 cup, or 8 oz (226 g), salt
¼ cup, or 2 oz (56 g), sugar

Soak thin fillets for 30 minutes; soak thick pieces overnight. Air-dry in refrigerator before smoking.

BROCCOLI

Available fresh and frozen.

FRESH BROCCOLI

Fresh broccoli is available in a broad range of packs. The stem length of the spears is crucial in calculating yield. For whole broccoli, the edible part extends about 6 in down from the top; the rest is stem, which can only be used in soups and purées.

Season:

Available year-round, with no discernible peak months. Lower supply in summer.

Pack:

Table B-6 lists data about different broccoli packs that are available.

Kitchen Yields

Serving size:

3½ oz (100 g) cleaned vegetable.

One 1¼-lb (560-g) bunch provides 13 oz (360 g) usable product, or about 4 servings; thus, 34 lb (15 kg), or 25 small bunches, as purchased, yields 22

Table B-6 Pack Information for Fresh Broccoli

Pack and Weight	Number of Bunches	Weight per Bunch, or Count	Size of Spears
Full carton 42 lb (19 kg)	18	2¼ to 2½ lb (1 to 1.10 kg)	8 to 9 in (200 to 230 mm)
Half cartons 20 to 23 lb (9 to 10.3 kg)	14 to 18	1¼ to 1½ lb (560 to 675 g)	8 to 9 in (200 to 230 mm)
Carton spears 21 lb (9.45 kg)	loose pack	57	6 in (150 mm)
Carton spears 15 lb (7.75 kg)	loose pack	no count	3 to 4 in (75 to 100 mm)
Carton florets 9 lb (4.1 kg)	loose pack	no count	1 to 2¾ in (25 to 70 mm)
Carton buds 9 lb (4 kg)	three 3-lb bags	80 pieces per 1 lb (450 g) 720 pieces per case	
Carton buds 12 lb (5.4 kg)	four 3-lb bags	80 pieces per 1 lb (450 g) 960 pieces per case	
Carton buds 18 lb (8.1 kg)	six 3-lb bags	80 pieces per 1 lb (450 g) 1,440 pieces per case	

lb (10 kg) cleaned vegetable or about 100 servings. Similarly, one 42-lb (19-kg) carton yields about 130 servings.

Calories:
One 3½-oz (100-g) serving, cooked = 30 Calories. 1 cup, or 5½ oz (150 g) cooked = 45 Calories.

FROZEN BROCCOLI
Available as spears and as cut or chopped pieces.

Pack:
Twelve 2½-lb (1.1-kg) boxes; one 30-lb (13.5-kg) case, loose. IQF.

Kitchen Yields

Serving size:
½ cup cooked spears. One 2½-lb (1.1-kg) box yields 10 servings, so ten boxes yield 100 servings;

one case of loose spears yields 120 servings. For chopped pieces, serving size is ½ cup, so one 2½-lb (1.1-kg) box yields 10 servings.

Calories:
½ cup cooked = 22 Calories.

BROCCOLI RABE

Also called *rapini* or *broccoli rappe*. It is a leafy, bitter vegetable.

Season:
November to March.

Pack:
By weight or in bunches.

Kitchen Yields

Cleaning loss is about 20 percent by weight, when the stem ends are discarded. Cooking loss is about 30 percent.

Serving size:

½ cup (0.232 l). 1 lb (450 g) as purchased yields 8 oz (224 g) cooked, or about 1½ cups.

BROWN RICE

See Rice.

BRUSSELS SPROUTS

Available fresh and frozen.

FRESH BRUSSELS SPROUTS

Individual sizes vary. Baby Brussels sprouts are available in fall and winter; *see* Baby Vegetables.

Season:

Available year-round. Peak from August to March. Low supply from May to July.

Pack:

Twelve 1-pint (0.47-l) containers, weighing 9 lb (4.1 kg) total; twelve 10-oz (280-g) containers, weighing 7½ lb (3.4 kg) total; individual 25-lb (11.15-kg) cartons, loose.

Kitchen Yield

12 oz (340 g) as purchased produces 9 oz (255 g) ready to cook.

Serving size:

½ cup (0.11 l), or 3 oz (85 g) cooked; thus; 1 pint (0.47 l) as purchased yields 4 servings, and 10 oz (280 g) as purchased yields 2½ servings.

Count:

Varies greatly.

1 cup, or 7 oz (200 g), raw contains 7 to 8 sprouts; 1 pint (0.47 l) contains 25 to 30 pieces medium; and one 10-oz (280-g) container holds 20 to 25 pieces medium.

Trimming waste:

By weight, about 20 to 25 percent.

Calories:

½ cup cooked, drained = 38 Calories.

FROZEN BRUSSELS SPROUTS

Frozen Brussels sprouts are graded by size.

Pack:

Twelve 2-lb (0.9-kg) packages; twelve 2½-lb (1.1-kg) packages; one 30-lb (13.6-kg) case, IQF.

Sizes:

Medium:
60 to 80 pieces per 1 lb (450 g).

Small:
100 + pieces per 1 lb (450 g).

Kitchen Yields

Serving size:

½ cup (0.11 l); one 2½-lb (1.1-kg) package yields 13 servings; one 2-lb (0.9-kg) package yields 10 servings; and one 30-lb (13.6-kg) case IQF yields 150 servings.

3½ pints (1.17 l) fresh Brussels sprouts are equivalent to 2 lb (0.9 kg) frozen Brussels sprouts.

Calories:

½ cup, weighing 3½ oz (100 g) cooked, drained = 45 Calories.

BUFFALO

Most available cuts:

Prime Ribs:
18 to 24 lb (8.1 to 10.8 kg).

Rounds:
35 to 50 lb (15.7 to 22.5 kg).

Full Loins, bone in:
18 to 30 lb (8.1 to 13.5 kg).

Kitchen Yields

Trim varies greatly among purveyors. Use beef yield information after trim has been confirmed. Meat itself is generally leaner than beef. Ribs and loins can be roasted; rounds should be braised.

BURDOCK (GOBO)

See Japanese Foods.

BUTTER

Butter is made from pasteurized cream. It can be purchased salted or unsalted. USDA AA and A grades are usually used in foodservice.

Pack:

Solids:
1-lb (450-g) prints, 36 to a case.

Reddies:
12- and 15-lb (5.4- and 6.7-kg) cases, with varying counts; 30-lb cases of six 5-lb (2.25-kg) cartons.

Quarters:
36-lb (16.2-kg) cases with 144 ¼-lb (113-g) sticks.

Cups:
8-lb (3.6-kg) cases with 90 1.4-oz (40-g) cups.

Tubs:
24-, 7-, and 5-lb (10.8-, 3.1-, and 2.2-kg) whipped tubs.

Bulk:
68-lb (30.6-kg) box, domestic; 56-lb (25.2-kg) box, imported; 64- or 50-lb (28.8- or 22.5-kg) solid cubes.
Butter is also available mixed with margarine.

Kitchen Yields

Butter pat counts:
1 lb (450 g) yields 60, 72, 90, or 108 pats.

Butter chip weights:
60 count are ¼ oz (7.5 g) each.
72 count are ⅕ oz (5.6 g) each.
90 count are ⅙ oz (4.6 g) each.
108 count are ⅛ oz (4.1 g) each.
1 lb (450 g) butter comprises 4 sticks or 2 cups;
1 lb (450 g) whipped butter comprises 6 sticks or 3 cups.
1 lb (450 g) butter is equivalent to 10 oz (340 g) melted, clear fat; 3 cups (0.47 l) melted, clear fat is equivalent to 2½ lb (1.1 kg) butter.

Calories:
1 lb (450 g, or 4 sticks) regular butter = 3,260 Calories.
1 stick (113 g, or ½ cup) regular butter = 815 Calories.
1 tb (14 g, or ⅛ stick) regular butter = 100 Calories.
1 pat (1 in^2; 90 per 1 lb) regular butter = 35 Calories.
1 lb (450 g, or 6 sticks) whipped butter = 3,240 Calories.
1 stick (76 g or ½ cup) whipped butter = 540 Calories.
1 tb (9 g, or ⅛ stick) whipped butter = 65 Calories.
1 pat (120 count per 1 lb) whipped butter = 25 Calories.

BUTTER COOKIES

See Cookies.

C

CABBAGE

Many varieties of cabbage are available.

BOK CHOY (CHINESE CABBAGE)

White vegetable in the cabbage family. Baby bok choy is also available; *see* Baby Vegetables.

Season:
Year-round.

Pack:

Half crate:
30 to 40 lb (13.5 to 18.0 kg).

Full crate:
65 to 70 lb (29.5 to 31.7 kg).

Size:
16 in (400 mm) long.

Kitchen Yields
1 lb as purchased produces 14 oz (400 g) ready to cook.

Serving size:
¾ cup raw pieces or 1 lb (450 g) yields 5 servings.

Calories:
½ cup, weighing 3 oz (85 g) cooked and drained = 5 Calories.

CELERY CABBAGE

Celerylike stalks.

Season:
Year-round.

Pack:

Half crate:
30 to 40 lb (13.6 to 18 kg).

Full crate:
65 to 70 lb (29.2 to 31.5 kg).

Size:
16 in (400 mm) long.

Kitchen Yields
Little cleaning waste and little shrinkage.

Calories:
½ cup, weighing 3 oz (85 g) cooked and drained = 5 Calories.

GREEN CABBAGE

Fresh green cabbage is available whole, sliced, and as ready-to-use coleslaw mix. The most important varieties are Domestic and Danish. Domestic is a spring variety; Danish is a firm winter cabbage.

Season:
Available year-round. Early cabbage is marketed from December to May. Domestic variety is available in spring, and Danish variety in winter.

Pack:
40-, 50-, and 60-lb (18-, 22.5-, and 27-kg) cartons.

Sizes:

Early cabbage; mostly Domestic:

Small:
Under 1½ lb (0.6 kg).

Medium:
1½ to 3 lb (0.6 to 1.3 kg).

Large:
Over 3 lb (1.3 kg).

Late cabbage; Domestic and Danish:

Small:
Under 2 lb (0.9 kg).

Medium:
2 to 5 lb (0.9 to 2.2 kg).

Large:
Over 5 lb (2.2 kg).
For sliced cabbage and coleslaw mix, pack is two 10-lb (4.5-kg) bags.

Kitchen Yields
1 lb (450 g) as purchased produces 12 oz (340 g) ready to cook or to marinate for coleslaw.

Serving sizes:
For cole slaw, 1 cup, or 2½ oz (70 g) raw cabbage; thus, 10 lb (4.5 kg) as purchased yields 50 servings.
NOTE: Cabbage will shed liquid when mixed with dressing and will shrink when stored overnight. For cooked chopped cabbage, serving size is ½

cup cooked; 1 lb (450 g) yields 4 servings, so 10 lb (4.5 kg) as purchased yields 40 servings.

Calories:
1 cup: 2½ oz (70 g) raw, coarsely shredded = 12 Calories.
½ cup cooked, drained = 5 Calories.

RED CABBAGE
Available canned, whole, and as sliced red cabbage as coleslaw addition.

CANNED RED CABBAGE

Pack:
Six #10 cans.

Kitchen Yields

Serving size:
½ cup; one #10 can yields 24 servings.

FRESH RED CABBAGE

Season:
Available year-round.

Pack:
40-, 50-, and 60-lb (18-, 22.5-, and 27-kg) cartons. For coleslaw, sliced red cabbage is packed as four 5-lb (2.3-kg) bags.

Kitchen Yields
Same yields as green cabbage.

Calories:
1 cup, or 2½ oz (70 g), raw and shredded = 12 Calories.

SAUERKRAUT
See Sauerkraut.

SAVOY CABBAGE
Curly, soft cabbage — edible only when cooked.

Season:
Late summer until spring.

Pack:
40, 50, and 60 lb (18, 22.5, and 27 kg).

Kitchen Yields
1 lb (450 g) as purchased produces 13 oz (364 g) shredded; 1 cup shredded weighs 2½ oz.

Serving size:
½ cup cooked; 1 lb (450 g) as purchased yields 5 servings.

Calories:
½ cup cooked, plain = 15 Calories.

CACTUS FRUIT (TUNA)
See Mexican Foods.

CACTUS LEAVES (NOPALES)
See Mexican Foods.

CAKE
Refer to Table C-1 for information on scaling.

CALABASA (CUBAN SQUASH)
See Squash.

CALYMIRNA FIGS
See Figs.

Table C-1 Cake Scaling Guide

Size of Cake	Scaling Weight
6-in round	12 oz (336 g)
7-in round	1 lb (450 g)
8-in round	1½ lb (672 g)
10-in round	2 lb (0.9 kg)
12-in round	3 lb (1.3 kg)
14-in round	4 lb (1.8 kg)
17- by 24-in sheet	6 lb (2.7 kg)
8-in round angel food	13 oz (364 g)

CANTALOUPE

See Melons.

CAN SIZES

There are many different can sizes on the market. Table C-2 is a listing of the most common can sizes in institutional foodservice; their approximate sizes in fluid ounces, cups, and liters; and the number of cans per case. The weight of cans varies greatly, depending on the density of the contents.

TRANSPOSING CAN SIZES

Filling one #10 can requires approximately three #3 cans, five #2 cans, or two and one-quarter #3 cylinder cans.

NOTE: These transposition figures does not take count (number of pieces) into consideration.

Case equivalents:
Twenty-four #303 cans = Nineteen #2 cans.
Twenty-four #2 cans = Fourteen #3 cans.
Eighteen #3 cans = Six #10 cans.
Twelve #10 cans = Thirty-six #3 cans.

CAPE GOOSEBERRY

The berry is enclosed in a papery pod, resembling a Chinese lantern. Fruit is light green or orange when ripe.

Season:
Winter.

Pack:
Sold by weight.

Size:
1½ to 2 in (45 to 50 mm) across.

Kitchen Yields
Use berry, with pod, as exotic garnish on fruit displays.

CAPERS

Available pickled in vinegar or salted. All varieties are imported. Non Pareil is the preferred variety.

Table C-2 Can Names, Volumes, and Counts

Can Name	Volume in Fluid Ounces	Volume in Cups	Volume in Liters	Number per Case
#1 picnic	10½	1¼	0.308	24 or 48
#211 cylinder	12	1½	0.348	24, 36, or 48
#300	13½	1¾	0.391	24, 36, or 48
#303	15½	2	0.449	12, 24, or 36
#2	20	2½	0.580	12 or 24
#2½	28½	3½	0.826	12 or 24
#3	33½	4¼	0.971	12 or 24
#3 cylinder	46	5¾	1.334	12
#5	56	7	1.624	12
#10	103½	13	3.001	6
Gallon	128	16	3.712	6

Pack:
Four 1-gal (3.8-l) jars. Other packs are available.

CARAMEL FOR DIPPING FRUITS

Formula
    2 lb sugar (900 g)
    10 oz glucose (280 g)
    1½ cups water (0.34 l)
    Boil to 310°F

Kitchen Yields
Provides caramel for approximately 50 orange sections or 40 large strawberries.

CARDONI

Also spelled *cardoon,* this vegetable looks like celery, but is a member of the thistle family. It must be cooked before use.

Season:
Fall and winter.

Pack:
By weight.

Kitchen Yields

Trimming loss:
30 percent by weight.

CAROB

Also known as *St. John's bread.* Pods, normally available dried, contain twelve hard seeds. The pods are very hard when dried.

Pack:
Sold by weight, often in 10-lb (4.5-kg) cartons.

Size:
About 8 in (20 cm) long.

CARROTS

Available canned, fresh, and frozen.

CANNED CARROTS
Available whole, diced, sliced, and shoestring-style in various sizes; also available mixed with peas. Carrot purée is manufactured, too. Whole carrots are often imported.

Pack:

Domestic whole carrots:
Six #10 cans.

Imported whole carrots:
Six 5-lb-10-oz (3-kg) cans.

Diced or sliced carrots:
Six #10 cans.

Carrot purée:
Twenty-four #303 cans.

Kitchen Yields

• Domestic Whole Carrots

One #10 can weighs 69 oz (1.9 kg), drained.

Counts:

Small: 180 to 225.
Tiny: 260 to 320.
Extra: 350 to 425.

• Imported Whole Carrots

One can weighs 62 oz (1.7 kg), drained.

Counts:

Small: 180 to 220.
Tiny: 250 to 310.
Extra: 320 to 400.

Common foodservice size is 250 to 320 count.

Serving size:
2 oz (56 g), about 6 whole small carrots; therefore, one #10 can yields 30 servings, one case of six #10 cans yields 180 servings, and four #10 cans yield 120 servings.

• Diced or Sliced Carrots

One #10 can weighs 72 oz (2 kg), drained.

Serving size:
½ cup diced or sliced carrots; one #10 can yields 25 servings

• Carrot Purée

One #303 can weighs 15½ oz and contains 2 cups (0.47 l).

Serving size:
½ cup; one #303 can yields 4 servings.

Calories:
2 oz (56 g) whole, plain = 16 Calories.
2 tb strained purée weighing 1 oz (28 g) = 10 Calories.

FRESH CARROTS

Fresh carrots are available with and without top greens. They are also available peeled, shredded, and cut into sticks. All store well.

There are many carrot varieties. Size and shape are important to foodservice operators. Even-shaped carrots, regardless of size, are easier to peel and involve less waste. The shapes can range from long and slender to round. Smaller carrots are more tender than large carrots. Baby carrots can be either immature carrots of standard varieties, or more mature carrots of miniature varieties; *see* Baby Vegetables. Belgian carrots are a special miniature variety. The color of all carrots may range from light yellow to dark orange.

Season:
Year-round. Peak from late fall to spring.

Sizes:

Large or Jumbo:
1½ to 2½ in (53 to 88 mm) in diameter, and 7 to 12 in (188 to 304 mm) long.

Medium:
¾ to 1½ in (19 to 53 mm) in diameter, and 7 to 9 in (177 to 228 mm) long.

Pack:

Carrots without tops:
50-lb (22.5-kg) bags or boxes; 1-, 2-, and 3-lb (0.45-, 0.9-, and 1.3-kg) bags.

Carrots with tops:
23- to 27-lb (10.3- to 12.1-kg) crate of 24 bunches.

Shredded carrots:
Four 5-lb (2.3-kg) bags.

Sticks, random pack:
Four 5-lb (2.2-kg) bags.

Sticks, precision pack:
Two 9-lb (4.0-kg) bags.

Kitchen Yields
1 lb (450 g) as purchased produces 14 oz (400 g) cleaned and peeled, and 12 oz (340 g) cooked.
1 lb (450 g) cello pack contains 10 to 12 thin carrots each.
1 lb (450 g) cleaned carrots, grated, yields 3 cups (0.7 l).

Serving size:
½ cup shredded raw carrots; thus, 1 lb (450 g) as purchased yields 6 servings.
Serving size for sliced, cooked carrots is ½ cup; and 1 lb (450 g) as purchased yields 4 servings.

Calories:
One raw, whole carrot weighing 2½ oz (70 g) = 30 Calories.
1 cup raw, grated carrots weighing 4 oz (112 g) = 45 Calories.
½ cup cooked, drained carrots weighing 3 oz (84 g) = 28 Calories.

FROZEN CARROTS

Available whole, petite whole, diced, sliced, and shoestring-style in various sizes.

Pack:
Twelve 2-lb (0.9-kg) packages; individual 20-lb (9.0-kg) cartons.
Whole carrots are IQF.

Kitchen Yields
4 lb (1.8 kg) fresh carrots are equivalent to one 2-lb (0.9-kg) package frozen carrots.

Serving size:
½ cup (0.1 l); one package yields 10 servings, and one case yields 120 servings.

Calories:
½ cup = 30 Calories.

CASINO BUTTER

Formula

½ cup (0.11 l) chopped garlic
½ cup (0.11 l) chopped shallots
2 cups (0.47 l) diced green pepper
2 cups (0.47 l) diced red pimientos
1 cup (0.22 l) oil

Sauté, and mix with the following:

10 lb (4.5 kg) butter
Salt and pepper to taste

Kitchen Yields

The preceding formula produces 1¼ gal (4.75 l); ½ gal (1.9 l) provides casino butter for 150 little neck clams, so the total mix provides casino butter for 375 little neck clams.

CATSUP

See Tomatoes.

CATTAIL SHOOTS

Wetland plant with edible shoots.

Season:

March to May.

CAUL FAT

Netlike fat layer that keeps the intestines in place. Most caul sold to foodservice is from pigs. Caul is used to wrap pâtés, meat loaves, and other soft ground-meat products to provide moisture during the cooking process and to preserve product shape.

Pack:

By weight.

Kitchen Yields

Caul is available fresh or frozen. It should be kept in ice water until used. Yield varies.

CAULIFLOWER

Available fresh and frozen.

FRESH CAULIFLOWER

Cauliflower is available whole and cut into florets. Baby cauliflower is available in fall and winter; *see* Baby Vegetables.

Season:

Year-round, with slightly greater supplies from October through January.

Pack:

Whole heads:
16- to 23-lb (7.2- to 10.3-kg) cartons, with 9, 12, or 16 heads per carton.

Florets:
6-lb (2.7-kg) cartons containing two 3-lb (1.3-kg) bags of florets; 12-lb (5.4-kg) cartons containing four 3-lb (1.3-kg) bags of florets.

Kitchen Yields

One head as purchased weighs 2 to 2½ lb (0.9 to 1.1 kg). Smaller sizes are also available. One 2½-lb (1.1-kg) head produces 22 oz (616 g) florets; thus, 1 lb (450 g) as purchased produces 9 oz (252 g) ready to cook, or 7½ oz (210 g) cooked.

Serving size:

4 oz raw, or ½ cup cooked; therefore, one large head yields 5 to 6 servings raw, or 5 servings cooked; and a 21-lb (9-kg) carton with 9 heads yields 50 servings raw, or 45 servings cooked.

Calories:

4 oz (112 g) raw florets = 30 Calories.
½ cup cooked = 18 Calories.

FROZEN CAULIFLOWER

Frozen as small florets, about 1 to 2½ in (25 to 63 mm) in length. Available in block and IQF.

Pack:

Twelve 2-lb (0.9-kg) packaged blocks; twelve 2-lb (0.9-kg) bags IQF; 30-lb (13.6-kg) boxes IQF.

Kitchen Yields

One 2-lb (0.9-kg) package is equivalent to 4 to 4½ lb (1.8 to 2 kg) fresh.

Serving size:
½ cup (0.1 l) cooked; therefore, one package yields 10 servings.

Calories:
½ cup cooked = 18 Calories.

CAVIAR

Caviar is fish roe. The most esteemed is sturgeon roe, but other fish roe is also popular. Caviar is available fresh and pasteurized. The word *malossol,* often found on caviar tins, means "lightly salted" in Russian.

BELUGA STURGEON CAVIAR
Beluga is the largest species of sturgeon; almost all are caught in the Caspian Sea, which is bordered by the Soviet Union and Iran. Beluga sturgeon produces the largest eggs, and this type is the most expensive caviar.

Season:
Fresh and pasteurized beluga caviar is available year-round.

Pack:
Beluga caviar is imported in original tins, which are then repacked. Original 2-kg tin (Russian pack) is equivalent to 4 lb 4 oz. The Iranian pack is equivalent to 3 lb 14 oz (1.8 kg); originally the weight is expressed in troy ounces. Other packs begin as small as 1 oz (28.4 g). Smaller packs are often pasteurized.

Kitchen Yields
1 oz (28 g) is equivalent to 1½ level tb or 1 heaped tb.

Serving size:
1 oz (28.4 g) or more; this is sufficient to make 3 canapés. Therefore, 7 oz (200 g) yields 21 canapés. NOTE: Caviar should always be weighed before use to ensure exact portion size.

LUMPFISH CAVIAR
Available black or red, this is less expensive than beluga caviar; it is often dyed black.

Pack:
Thirty-six 2-oz (56-g) jars; twenty-four 3½-oz (100-g) jars; twelve 7-oz (200-g) jars; twelve 12-oz (240-g) jars.
Use is the same as with other types of caviar.

OSETRA STURGEON CAVIAR
Medium-size eggs from a medium-size species of sturgeon. Pack varies. Use is the same as with beluga caviar.

PRESSED CAVIAR
Imported sturgeon caviar of lesser quality that has been pressed before shipment. The flavor is very concentrated and much acclaimed by connoisseurs. Not available pasteurized.

Pack:
By weight.

SALMON CAVIAR
Available in various grades of quality and in various egg sizes, ranging in color from dark red to golden yellow.

Pack:
2-, 4-, 7-, and 12-oz (56-, 113-, 200-, and 240-g) jars. Other packs are available.

Kitchen Yields
1 oz (56 g) contains an average of 110 large eggs.

SEVRUGA STURGEON CAVIAR
Roe of a small sturgeon found in the United States and in some other countries. The eggs are small but can be of excellent quality. Pack varies. Use is the same as with beluga caviar.

WHITEFISH CAVIAR
Domestic or imported caviar of small individual size.

Pack:
Jars of various sizes.

CELERIAC (KNOB CELERY)

Large round root with white flesh. It can be used raw in salads or cooked as a vegetable. Available canned or fresh, with or without green tops.

CANNED CELERIAC

Available imported in slices and shoestring-style.

Pack:
9-lb (4-kg) cans. Other packs are available.

Kitchen Yields

Serving size:
Varies. One 9-lb (4 kg) contains 4 lb 13 oz (2.1 kg) celeriac drained weight.
NOTE: Drained weight varies according to packer.

FRESH CELERIAC

Season:
Fall and winter.

Pack:
½ bushel or in bunches.

Count:
Count varies because the vegetable may be sold either with greens on or trimmed.

Size:
2½ to 4 in (63 to 100 mm) across.

Kitchen Yields

Trimming waste:
About 25 percent after greens have been removed.

CELERY

Available canned, fresh, and frozen. Knob celery is called *celeriac; see* Celeriac. *See also* Cardoni, and (under Cabbage) Celery Cabbage.

CANNED CELERY

Canned celery is available as stalks or as hearts.

Pack:
Twenty-four 28-oz (795-g) cans. Drained weight of each can is 15 oz (426 g).

Kitchen Yields

One can yields 2½ to 3 portions, and one case yields 60 to 68 portions

FRESH CELERY

Available whole (trimmed), as hearts, as sticks, and diced. Green celery of the Pascal variety is the most widely available variety on the market. There is no pronounced season. Celery is sized. Golden celery is yellowish white because it has been covered with soil during the growing process. It is a specialty item.

Packs:

Whole trimmed:
55- or 56-lb (24.7- or 25.2-kg) cartons or crates of 18, 24, 30, 36, and 48 whole pieces each.

Hearts:
25- to 28-lb (11.2- to 12.6-kg) cartons, with bag counts of 12, 18, or 24.

Sticks, cut and trimmed:
Four 5-lb (2.2-kg) bags.

Diced:
Four 5-lb (2.2-kg) bags.

Kitchen Yields

1 lb (450 g) as purchased produces 12 oz (340 g) ready to use.

Serving size:
For raw celery, ½ cup (0.1 l) chopped or diced; 1 lb (450 g) as purchased yields 4½ servings. For cooked celery, ½ cup (0.1 l) diced and cooked; 1 lb (450 g) as purchased yields 4 servings.

Formula for Blue Cheese Stuffing for Celery
        10 lb (4.5 kg) blue cheese, crumbled
        5 lb (2.3 kg) cream cheese
        1 lb (450 g) butter
        1 pint (0.47 l) heavy cream, whipped

Kitchen Yields
The preceding formula yields 2¼ gal (8.3 l) stuffing.

Calories:
½ cup diced celery = 5 Calories.
One stalk, 8 × 1½ in (200 × 38 mm), or ½ oz (42 g) = 5 Calories.

FROZEN CELERY
Available diced.

Pack:
20-lb (9-kg) packages of diced celery.

Kitchen Yields
Use the same as precooked fresh celery. There is no waste.

CEREALS

DRY CEREALS
Many varieties are available. Most cereals are available both in self-serve bowls and in regular boxes. Bulk packs are available for dispenser and kitchen use.

Pack:
Cases of 70 or 96 individual boxes each, with weight varying according to product; cases of 4 bags, with weight varying according to product. Corn-flake crumbs are packed in six 5-lb (2.2-kg) containers or in individual 50-lb (22.5-kg) cases.

Kitchen Yields

Milk per serving:
½ pint (0.23 l); therefore, 100 servings require 6 gal and 1 qt (23.5 l) milk.

Calories:
Vary according to product and serving size. Generally between 40 and 110 Calories per serving in individual box or bowl. Refer to label for precise information.

HOT CEREALS

CORNMEAL

Pack:
1-lb (450-g) packages.

Kitchen Yields
1 lb dry measure equals 3 cups.

Serving size:
¾ cup (0.17 l).
2 cups cornmeal boiled with 10 cups or 5 pints (2.3 l) water yield 15 servings; 1 lb (450 g) boiled with 15 cups or 7½ pints (3.5 l) water yields 23 servings.

Calories:
¾ cup (0.174 l), cooked in water = 80 Calories.

CREAM OF WHEAT

Pack:
1-lb (450-g) packages.

Kitchen Yields
1 lb dry measure equals 3 cups.

Serving size:
2 cups cream of wheat boiled with 10 cups or 5 pints (2.3 l) water yield 15 servings; 1 lb (450 g) cream of wheat boiled with 15 cups water yields 23 servings.

Calories:
¾ cup (0.17 l) cereal, cooked in water = 100 Calories.

ROLLED OATS

Pack:
1-lb (450-g) packages.

Kitchen Yields
1 lb (450 g) dry measure equals 5 cups.

Serving size:
¾ cup (0.17 l).
2 cups oats boiled with 5 cups or 2½ pints (1.2 l) water yield 8 servings; 1 lb (450 g) boiled with 12½ cups or 6¼ pints (2.9 l) water yields 20 servings.

Calories:
¾ cup (0.17 l) oatmeal cooked in water = 106 Calories.

CHAMPAGNE GRAPES

Tiny red grapes, grown especially to be used for garnish in small bunches. Sold in individual bunches and also in bulk.

Pack:
5-lb (2.2-kg) lugs.

Kitchen Yields

Serving size:
2-oz (56-g) bunches; thus, one 5-lb (2.2-kg) lug yields 40 servings.

CHARD

See Swiss Chard.

CHAYOTE (MIRLITON)

See Squash.

CHEESE

There are many varieties of cheeses and brands on the market. Following are descriptions of the most widely used and readily available cheese varieties.

AMERICAN PASTEURIZED PROCESS CHEESE
Available unsliced, sliced vertically, and sliced horizontally. Available yellow and white, regular and light (low-calorie) in both colors. Used for hot or cold sandwiches and cooking.

Pack:
Six 3-lb (1.3-kg) loaves; six 5-lb (2.2-kg) loaves; individual 10-lb (4.5-kg) loaves; four 5-lb (2.2-kg) loaves, with individual slices wrapped in plastic; four 5-lb (2.2-kg) loaves, with ribbon-cut horizontal slices; individual 40-lb (18-kg) blocks.

Needs ripening:
No.

Kitchen Yields
1 lb (450 g) produces 5 cups (1.1 l) grated cheese. One 3-lb (1.3-kg) loaf yields 65 slices, and one 5-lb (2.2-kg) loaf yields 110 slices. Average weight of one slice is ¾ oz (21 g).

Serving size:
3 oz (85 g), or four slices; therefore, one 3-lb (1.3-kg) loaf yields 16 servings, and one 5-lb (2.2-kg) loaf yields 27 servings.

Calories:
One ¾-oz (21-g) slice regular cheese = 71 Calories.
1 oz (28 g) regular cheese = 95 Calories.
One 3-oz (85-g) serving regular cheese = 285 Calories.
One ¾-oz (21-g) slice light cheese = 53 Calories.
1 oz (28 g) light cheese = 70 Calories.
One 3-oz (85-g) serving light cheese = 210 Calories.

AMERICAN PASTEURIZED PROCESS CHEESE SPREAD
Available with different flavoring ingredients, such as wine and herbs. Texture is smooth.

Pack:
1-lb (450-g) tubs. Other packs are available.

Needs ripening:
No.

Kitchen Yields

Serving size:
2 oz (56 g), as spread; one 1-lb (450-g) tub yields 8 servings.

Calories:
1 oz (28 g) = 82 Calories.
2 oz (56 g) = 164 Calories.

ASIAGO
Available in Mild, Semifirm, Medium, and Aged forms. Use for finger food, grating, or hot sandwiches.

Packs:
12-lb (5.4-kg) half-moons; 22-lb (9.9-kg) daisies; 24-lb (10.8-kg) wheels.

Needs ripening:
No.

Kitchen Yields

Serving size:
2 oz (56 g).

BAKERS CHEESE
Cream cheese-type cheese, used mostly in baking.

Packs:
3-lb (1.3-kg) loaves; 10-lb (4.5-kg) tubs.

Needs ripening:
No.

Kitchen Yields

Serving size:
Varies depending on recipe.

BEL PAESE
Rather soft, white cheese with wax coating, available domestic and imported. Good cheese for cheese platters and banquets.

Pack:
Approximately 5-lb (2.2-kg) wheels.

Needs ripening:
No.

Kitchen Yields

Serving size:
3½ oz (100 g) restaurant portion; thus, one 5-lb (2.2-kg) wheel yields 20 servings, and one-third wheel yields 10 banquet servings.

BLUE CHEESE

BLEU DE BRESSE
One of many blue cheese varieties made in France. Crumbly, hard to cut. Nice cheese for cheese platters because it is small, has mild flavor, and is not smelly.

Pack:
8-oz (220-g) packages.

Needs ripening:
No.

Kitchen Yields

Serving size:
3 oz (122 g).

CRUMBLED BLUE
Domestic blue cheese in soft-textured, crumbled pieces. Used for dressing and stuffing.

Pack:
20-, 25-, and 50-lb (9-, 11.2-, and 22.5-kg) bags. Other packs are available.

Needs ripening:
No.

Kitchen Yields

Serving size:
1 oz (28 g) added to dressing.

Calories:
1 oz (28 g) = 100 Calories.

DANISH BLUE
Texture is semifirm to crumbly and has no rind, so the whole cheese can be used.

Pack:
One 5- to 5½-lb (2.2- to 2.5-kg) wheel; three 7½-lb (3.4-kg) wheels.

Needs ripening:
No.

Kitchen Yields

Serving size:
3½ oz (100 g); one 5-lb (2.2-kg) wheel yields 22 servings.

Calories:
3½ oz (100 g) = 350 Calories.

GORGONZOLA
See Gorgonzola as a primary subheading under Cheese.

INDIVIDUALLY PACKAGED BLUE CHEESE
Available domestic and imported.

Weights:
From 1¼ oz (35 g) up.

Needs ripening:
No.

Kitchen Yields

Serving size:
2 oz (56 g), as snack.

Calories:
2 oz (56 g) = 200 Calories.

ROQUEFORT
See Roquefort as a primary subheading of Cheese.

STILTON
See Stilton as a primary subheading of Cheese.

WISCONSIN BLUE
Texture is semifirm to crumbly.

Pack:
Individual 6-lb (2.7-kg) wheels.

Needs ripening:
No.

Kitchen Yields

Serving size:
3½ oz (100 g); therefore, one 6-lb (2.7-kg) wheel yields 26 servings.

Calories:
3½ oz (100 g) = 350 Calories.

BOURSIN
Delicate French cheese with high fat content.

Pack:
5-oz (142-g) packages.

Texture:
Soft.

Needs ripening:
Yes.

Kitchen Yields

Serving size:
2½ oz (70 g); therefore, 1 package yields 2 servings.

BRICK
Texture is semisoft and waxy. Good cheese for cutting into cubes.

Packs:
5-, 10-, and 40-lb (2.2-, 4.5-, and 18-kg) blocks.

Needs ripening:
No.

Kitchen Yields

Serving size:
4 oz (112 g), for receptions; one 10-lb (4.5-kg) block yields 38 servings.

BRIE
One of the most popular soft dessert cheeses. Available domestically made or imported from various countries. The cheese may be flavored, as with herbs or peppercorns. Texture is firm when unripe, soft and runny when ripe. The fat content varies; about 60 percent is normal.

Packs:
8-oz (228-g), 2-lb (0.9-kg), 2.2-lb (1-kg), and 4.4-lb (2-kg) wheels.

Needs ripening:
Yes.

Kitchen Yields

Serving sizes:
In restaurant, one-eighth of a 2.2-lb (0.9 kg) imported wheel, or 4⅓ oz (122 g); one-eighth of a 2-lb (0.9-kg) domestic wheel, or 4 oz (113 g). In sandwich, one-twelfth of a domestic or imported wheel, or approximately 2½ oz (70 g).
For canapés, one 4.4-lb (2-kg) wheel yields cheese for 200 canapés.

Calories:
2½ oz (70 g) = 312 Calories.
NOTE: Calories vary depending on fat content.

BUCHERON
Soft-textured French goat cheese.

Pack:
3¾-lb (1.7-kg) logs.

Needs ripening:
Little.

Kitchen Yields

Serving size:
2½ oz (70 g); therefore, one 3¾-lb (1.7 kg) log yields 23 servings.

CAMEMBERT
Available domestic and imported. Texture is firm when unripe, soft and runny when ripe.

Pack:
8-oz (228-g) wheels. Individual packs are available in many sizes.

Needs ripening:
Yes.

Kitchen Yields

Serving size:
One 1⅓-oz (37-g) wedge; one 8-oz (228-g) wheel yields six wedges.

Calories:
One 1⅓-oz (37-g) wedge = 166 Calories.
2 oz (56 g) = 250 Calories.

CANTAL
Hard-textured French cheese. Good cheese for cheese boards.

Packs:
40- to 120-lb (18- to 54-kg) wheels.

Needs ripening:
No.

Kitchen Yields

Serving size:
3 oz (85 g) in restaurant; therefore, one 40-lb (18-kg) wheel yields 200 servings.

CHEDDAR
Domestic yellow or white cheese, available sharp and mild. Often covered with colored wax. Texture is firm to semisoft (for some grated cheddars). Grated cheddar is ready to use for cheese sauces and soups, or to sprinkle on food to be baked; there is no waste. The moisture content of block cheddar varies greatly depending on age and brand. This influences weights and slicing characteristics.

Packs:

Cylindrical, longhorn:
13 lb (5.8 kg).

Rectangular:
5, 10, and 40 lb (2.2, 4.5, and 18 kg).

Wheel:
12, 22, and 75 lb (5.4, 9.9, and 33.7 kg).

Grated:
Six 5-lb (2.2-kg) bags.

Needs ripening:
No.

Kitchen Yields

Serving sizes:
3 oz (85 g), in restaurant; 1½ oz (42 g), with apple pie.
1 cup shredded weighs 4 oz (112 g), on average.

Calories:
3 oz (85 g) = 345 Calories.
1- × 1- × 1-in cube weighing ⅝ oz (17 g) = 71 Calories.
1 cup shredded, weighing 4 oz (112 g) = 460 Calories.

CHEVRE
Soft-textured goat-milk cheese made domestically in various states; also available imported. Some imported cheeses are covered with a thin layer of ground cinders, which is edible. Cheese is available in different shapes, the most practical of which is the log shape.

Weights:
3 to 11 oz (85 to 320 g).

Need ripening:
No.

Kitchen Yields

Serving size:
2 oz (56 g) for salads; one 11-oz (320 g) log yields 5 servings, or 16 slices for canapés.

COLBY
Type of cheddar cheese, sold in same sizes. Good for shredding.

Kitchen Yields
See Cheddar.

COLD-PACK CHEESE SPREADS
Spreads are available in a number of flavors. These soft, versatile products are used for making canapés, dips, and sandwiches.

Packs:
5-lb (2.2-kg) tub; 10-lb (4.5-kg) tub; 30-lb (13.5-kg) tub.

Needs ripening:
No.

Kitchen Yields
Varies depending on use. There is no waste.

COTTAGE CHEESE
This soft-textured product is available creamed and in different-size curds. Fat content also varies.

Pack:
5-lb (2.2-kg) tubs. Many other sizes are available.

Needs ripening:
No.

Kitchen Yields

Serving size:
½ cup for fruit salad; 5 lb (2.2 kg) yields 19 servings.

Calories:

Creamed:
½ cup, or 4 oz (112 g), 4 percent fat = 118 Calories.
2 percent fat = 103 Calories.
1 percent fat = 83 Calories.

Dry curd:
½ cup, or 2½ oz (70 g), 0.5 percent = 63 Calories.

COULOMMIERS
Soft-textured French cheese.

Pack:
1 lb (450 g), in wooden boxes.

Needs ripening:
Yes.

Kitchen Yields

Serving size:
2 oz (56 g); therefore, 1 lb (450 g) yields 8 servings.

CREAM CHEESE
Soft-textured cheese, available from domestic producers.

Packs:
1-oz (28-g) individual packs; 3-oz (85-g) individual packs; 8-oz (226-g) individual packs; 3-lb (1.3-kg) loaves, 18-lb (8.1-kg) cartons; 30-lb (13-kg) blocks.

Needs ripening:
No.

Kitchen Yields

Serving size:
2 oz (56 g) with smoked salmon.

Calories:
3 oz (85 g) = 300 Calories.
2 oz (56 g) = 200 Calories.
1 oz (28 g) = 100 Calories.

CREME FRAICHE
Texture is soft and creamy, like sour cream.

Pack:
Twelve 10-oz (228-g) tubs; 3-lb (1.3-kg) tubs; 5-lb (2.2-kg) tubs.

Needs ripening:
No.

Kitchen Yields

Serving size:
Varies according to recipe.

EDAM CHEESE
Ball- or round-shaped firm-textured cheese, most often covered with red or yellow wax. Attractive cheese for platters. Rounds may be hollowed out and filled with cubed cheese for display.

Weights:
Individual packs; 2 lb (0.9 kg); 4 lb (1.8 kg).

Needs ripening:
No.

Kitchen Yields

Serving size:
2 oz (56 g); thus, 4 lb (1.8 kg) yields 29 servings.

FETA
Domestic or imported white cheese, usually made with goat or sheep milk, sometimes made with cow milk. Popular in salads and in cooking. Feta cheese is slightly salty and has a slightly crumbly texture. The cheese is shipped in brine. There is no rind.

Pack:
8-lb (3.6-kg) tubs, net weight; 28-lb (12.6-kg) tubs, net weight.

Needs ripening:
No.

Kitchen Yields
There is little waste.

Serving size:
3 oz (85 g) for Greek salad; thus, an 8-lb (3.6-kg) tub yields 40 servings.

FONTINA
Domestic and Italian import, with semisoft and buttery texture. Good cheese for cheese boards or for fruit baskets. Little smell.

Pack:
18-lb (8.1-kg) wheel.

Needs ripening:
No.

Kitchen Yields

Serving size:
2 oz (56 g); one wheel yields 140 servings.

GORGONZOLA

Blue cheese imported from Italy or made domestically. Texture is firm but crumbly and can be hard to portion. Gorgonzola can be salty. It is wrapped in foil.

Pack:
4- to 7-lb (1.8- to 3.1-kg) wheels.

Needs ripening:
No.

Kitchen Yields
There is little waste.

Serving size:
4 oz (112 g) as dessert cheese.

GOUDA

Cheese that resembles Edam. Texture is firm to hard. Available imported and domestic. The domestic product is also available smoked. Good cheese for buffet displays. Baby Gouda is sometimes covered with red wax, as Edam often is.

Pack:

Imported:
Twelve 8-oz (226-g) 170 Baby Gouda; 8-lb (3.6-kg) wheel.

Domestic:

Circular:
2-lb (0.9-kg) balls.

Rectangular:
5-lb (2.2-kg)loaf; 8-lb (3.6-kg) block.

Wheel:
11-lb (4.9-kg) wheel.

Needs ripening:
No.

Kitchen Yields

Serving size:
2 oz (56 g); 2 lb (0.9 kg) yields 14 servings.

GRAPE CHEESE

White, buttery cheese made in France. The outside is covered with the seeds and skins of black grapes. The rind should be served with the cheese, although it is not intended to be eaten.

Weight:
4 lb (1.8 kg).

Needs ripening:
No.

Kitchen Yields

Serving size:
3 oz; thus, 4 lb (1.8 kg) yields 20 servings.

GRATED CHEESE

Grated cheese is available made from imported or domestic hard cheeses. It is often a blend of various cheeses; the most common varieties used are Parmesan and Romano, because they do not melt when exposed to heat. *See also* Parmesan and Romano as primary subheadings of Cheese.

Texture of grated cheese is dry. Fresh cheese should be kept refrigerated. It is best to get a number of samples from different purveyors and select the one best suited for the operation. The least expensive cheese might not provide satisfactory yield and flavor.

Packs:
1 lb (450 g); 20 lb (9 kg), and larger.

Needs ripening:
No.

Kitchen Yields
1 cup is equivalent to 4 oz (112 g).
4 tb is equivalent to 1 oz (28 g).
1 tb is equivalent to 7 g.

Calories:
1 cup, or 4 oz (100 g) = 448 Calories.
1 oz (28 g) = 112 Calories.
1 tb (7 g) = 28 Calories.

GRUYÈRE
Version of Swiss cheese, originally made in the village of Gruyère in Switzerland. Texture is firm, with small holes. Available imported from Switzerland and France; also domestically made.

Packs:
40-lb (18-kg) wheel; 6-lb (2.7-kg) loaf.

Needs ripening:
No.

Kitchen Yields
When Gruyère is purchased in wedges with rind still attached, waste is about 5 percent.

LIEDERKRANZ
Soft-textured American cheese made originally in New York state.

Pack:
8-oz (224-g) packages.

Needs ripening:
Yes.

Kitchen Yields
There is no waste.

Serving size:
2 oz (56 g).

MASCARPONE
Soft-textured cream cheese of Italian origin. Available imported from Italy and domestic. Use for Italian desserts.

Pack:
1.1-lb (1-kg) tubs.

Needs ripening:
No; use fresh.

Kitchen Yields
There is no waste.

MONTEREY JACK
Firm, cheddar-type cheese, often used in Mexican cooking.

Packs:

Cylindrical longhorn:
13-lb (5.8-kg) blocks.

Rectangular:
5- and 10-lb (2.2- and 4.5-kg) pints.

Needs ripening:
No.

Kitchen Yields
This cheese has a thin rind; there is little waste.

MOZZARELLA
The types of Mozarella covered here are cured and fresh. *See also* String Cheese as a separate heading under Cheese.

CURED MOZZARELLA
Cheese mostly used for pizza, but also for sandwiches.

Pack:

Rectangular:
5- to 6-lb (2.2- to 2.7-kg) loaves; 20-lb (9-kg) loaves; 40-lb (18-kg) blocks.

Sausage shape:
12-lb (5.4-kg) packs.

Shredded:
Available in various packs.

Needs ripening:
No.

Kitchen Yields

Serving size:
For pizza, 1 lb (450 g) supplies cheese for one large pizza, and 10 to 12 oz (280 to 340 g) supplies cheese for one medium pizza. Therefore, one 30-lb (13.5-kg) box of mozzarella supplies cheese for 30 large pizzas and 40 medium pizzas.

Calories:

Whole Milk:
16 oz (450 g) = 1440 Calories.
1 oz (28 g) = 90 Calories.

Part Skim Milk:
4 oz (112 g) = 320 Calories.
1 oz (28 g) = 80 Calories.

FRESH MOZZARELLA
Fresh mozzarella is a soft-textured cheese that is packed in brine. It is an excellent cheese to use for appetizers.

Pack:
3-lb (1.4-kg) tub containing 114 $\frac{1}{3}$-oz (9-g) ciliegine (small balls); 3-lb (1.4-kg) tub containing thirty-two 1½-oz (42-g) bocconcino (bite size); 3-lb (1.4-kg) tub containing twelve 4-oz (112-g) pieces; 6-lb (2.7-kg) tub containing six 16-oz (453-g) pieces.

Needs ripening:
No.

Kitchen Yields

Serving size:
$\frac{1}{3}$ oz (9 g) ciliegine for receptions; 4 oz (112 g) for appetizer.

MUENSTER CHEESE
This firm white cheese was originally made in Alsace, France. It is available imported and domestic. Muenster is a good cheese for sandwiches and slices well on machine. The rind is very thin and edible; do not remove it.

Packs:

Imported:
½ to 2 lb (0.22 to 0.9 kg).

Domestic:

Cylindrical longhorn:
10 to 11 lb (4.5 to 4.9 kg).

Rectangular:
5, 10, and 40 lb (2.2, 4.5, and 18 kg).

Wheel:
5 lb (2.2 kg).

Needs ripening:
No.

Kitchen Yields

Serving size:
3 oz (85 g), for sandwiches. One 5-lb (2.2-kg) loaf yields 25 servings.

PARMESAN
Italian cheese with rather a hard texture that makes it difficult to cut. It can be eaten as a dessert cheese but most commonly is used for grating. Parmesan is made also domestically. Available whole and grated.

Pack:

Whole wheels:
80-lb (36-kg) wheel; 40-lb (18-kg) half wheel; 20-lb (9-kg) quarter wheel; 10-lb (4.5-kg) eighth wheel. Other sizes are available.

Grated:
5-lb (2.2-kg) bags; 1-lb (450-g) bags.

Needs ripening:
No.

Kitchen Yield
When buying cheese for grating, buy it already cut into chunks. NOTE: Yields vary according to age of cheese.

Serving size:
2 oz as dessert cheese.

> 20 lb (9 kg) ¼ wheel with rind produces 74 cups grated cheese.
> 1 cup grated cheese weighs 4 oz (112 g).
> 4 tb grated cheese weighs 1 oz (28 g).
> 1 tb grated cheese weighs 7 g.

PONT-L'EVEQUE
Soft-textured cheese imported from France.

Pack:
10-oz (228-g) square boxes.

Needs ripening:
Yes.

Kitchen Yields
There is no waste.

Serving size:
2 oz (56 g); thus, 10 oz (228 g) yields 5 servings.

PORT DU SALUT
Firm to semifirm cheese with a thin rind. Good cheese for buffets and platters.

Pack:
3½- to 4-lb (1.5- to 1.8-kg) wheels.

Needs ripening:
No.

Kitchen Yields
There is little waste.

Serving size:
$\frac{1}{16}$ wedge of one wheel—about 4 oz (113 g).

PROVOLONE

This cheese has a firm, smooth texture and somewhat smoky flavor. It is a good cheese to use for sandwiches and buffets and it is easy to slice on machine.

Pack:

Rectangular:
20-, 40-, and 50-lb (9-, 18-, and 22.5-kg) blocks.

Round:
12-lb (5.4-kg) balls.

Sausage shape:
12-, 25-, and 50-lb (5.4-, 11.2-, and 22.5-kg) pieces.

Wheel:
6-lb (2.7-kg) half-moons.

Needs ripening:
No.

Kitchen Yields

Serving size:
3 oz (85 g), for sandwiches; 12 lb (5.4 kg) yields cheese for 60 sandwiches.

Calories:
3 oz (85 g) = 300 Calories.
1 oz (28 g) = 100 Calories.

REBLOCHON

Soft and buttery French cheese.

Pack:
1-lb (450-g) round loaves.

Needs ripening:
No.

Kitchen Yields

Serving size:
2 oz (56 g); thus, 1 lb (450 g) yields 8 servings.

RICOTTA CHEESE

Soft cheese that resembles cream cheese. Available made with skim milk or with whole milk. Excellent cheese for baking (as in lasagna), and also good with fruit salad.

Pack:
3-lb (1.3-kg) tubs; 5-lb (2.2-kg) tubs; 10-lb (4.5-kg) tubs; 20-lb (9-kg) boxes; 30-lb (13.5-kg) bags.

Needs ripening:
No; use as fresh as possible.

Kitchen Yields

Serving size:
Varies according to use.

Calories:

Whole milk:
1 cup, weighing 8½ oz (240 g) = 428 Calories.

Skim milk:
1 cup weighing 8½ oz (240 g) = 340 Calories.

ROMANO

Hard cheese used for grating. Sometimes blended with Parmesan or other grated cheeses.

Pack:
10 lb (4.5 kg).

Needs ripening:
No.

Kitchen Yields
1 cup grated weighs 4 oz (112 g).
4 tb grated weighs 1 oz (28 g).
1 tb grated weighs (7 g).

Calories:
4 oz (112 g) = 440 Calories.

ROQUEFORT

French blue cheese made with sheep milk. Roquefort has a crumbly texture and is hard to cut into portions. The cheese gives excellent flavor to dressing. When the name *Roquefort dressing* is used on the menu, only genuine Roquefort cheese may be used. The cheese is wrapped in foil, and there is no rind.

Packs:
5-lb (2.2-kg) wheel; 6-lb (2.7-kg) wheel. Individual packs are available.

Needs ripening:
No.

Kitchen Yields

Serving size:
1½ oz for dressing; thus, one 5-lb (2.2-kg) wheel yields 50 servings.

SAINT PAULIN
A buttery cheese imported from France. It cuts easily and is good to serve on cheese platters and buffets. The cheese has a thin rind.

Pack:
4-lb (1.8-kg) loaf.

Needs ripening:
No.

Kitchen Yields

Serving size:
3 oz (85 g); thus, one 4-lb (1.8-kg) loaf yields 20 servings.

STILTON
English blue cheese that is salty and difficult to cut. Stilton is attractive on buffets.

Pack:
12-lb (5.4-kg) wheel; 14-lb (6.3-kg) wheel.

Needs ripening:
No.

Kitchen Yields
When Stilton is old, the yield is reduced, because the crusty rind cannot be used.

Serving size:
2 oz (56 g); 12 lb (5.4 kg) yields 75 servings.

STRING CHEESE
A form of Mozzarella cheese available in sticks and twists. The texture is stringy. Individual portions are handy for cheese baskets.

Pack:
Sticks of 1 oz (28 g) each; twists of 6 to 10 oz (170 to 280 g) each.

Needs ripening:
No.

Kitchen Yields
There is no waste.

SWISS CHEESE

DOMESTIC SWISS CHEESE
Domestic Swiss has a firm texture and slices well on machine. Many packs are available.

Packs:

Loaves without rind:
4 × 4 in (101 × 101 mm), weighing 6 to 8 lb (2.7 to 3.6 kg); 4 × 8 in (101 × 202 mm), weighing 9 to 15 lb (4 to 6.7 kg); 90-, 100-, and 200-lb (40-, 45-, and 80-kg) blocks.

Wheels with rind:
175 lb (18.7 kg).

Baby Swiss:
3- to 5-lb (1.3- to 2.2-kg) wheels.

Needs ripening:
No.

Kitchen Yields
Cheese purchased in loaves has no rind and, therefore, very little waste. Cheese purchased in wheels has about 5 percent trimming waste.

Serving size:
3 oz (85 g) for sandwiches; therefore, one 8-lb (3.6-kg) loaf, 4 × 4 in, yields cheese for 40 sandwiches.

Calories:
3 oz (85 g) = 315 Calories.

IMPORTED SWISS CHEESE
The genuine Swiss cheese is imported from the Emmenthal Valley in Switzerland; such cheese is labeled *Switzerland Swiss.* Swiss cheese is also imported from other countries, especially from Austria, Norway, and Finland. *See also* Gruyère as a separate heading under Cheese.

Packs:
Loaves without rinds, 4×7 in (101×175 mm), weighing 10 to 14 lb (4.5 to 6.3 kg).

Needs ripening:
No.

Kitchen Yields
When imported Swiss is purchased as a wedge with the rind on, waste is about 5 percent. Loaves have little cutting waste.

Serving size:
3 oz (85 g) for sandwiches; thus, one 10-lb (4.5-kg) loaf, 4×4 in, yields cheese for 50 sandwiches.

Calories:
3 oz (85 g) = 315 Calories.
1 oz (28 g) = 105 Calories.

CHEESECAKE

Formula
Combine the following ingredients:

12 lb (5.4 kg) bakers cheese
3 lb (1.4 kg) cream cheese
7¾ lb (3.5 kg) sugar
3 lb (1.4 kg) softened butter
2¼ qt (2.1 l) egg yolks
1½ lb (675 g) patent flour
12 oz (340 g) cornstarch
8½ qt (8 l) sour cream

In a separate bowl, whip egg whites, then fold in sugar.

2¼ qt (2.1 l) egg whites
1¼ lb (560 g) sugar

Combine egg whites with batter.

Kitchen Yields

Scale:
2 lb (900 g) for 8-in (200-mm) molds.
3 lb (1.3 kg) for 10-in (254-mm) molds.

Number of cheesecakes:
Twenty-three 8-in (200-mm) cakes.
Fifteen 10-in (254-mm) cakes.

CHERIMOYA

This fruit resembles a large, closed pinecone. It has large black seeds and custardlike flesh.

Season:
November to May.

Pack:
By piece.

Sizes:
3½ to 5 in (7 to 12 cm) across.

Kitchen Yields
Use in fruit displays, or make sorbet with fruit pulp.

Calories:
4-oz (112-g) edible fruit pulp = 130 Calories.

CHERRIES

The most general division of cherries is into the classifications *sweet* and *tart or sour.*

SWEET CHERRIES
Sweet cherries are available candied, canned, fresh, frozen, and maraschino.

CANDIED CHERRIES
Used in baking.

Pack:
By weight.

CANNED CHERRIES
Available pitted and with pit in. The two major varieties are Royal Ann, which is light-colored, and Bing, which is dark-colored. Available in various syrup densities.

Pack:
Six #10 cans, with drained weight of 64 to 70 oz (1.8 to 2 kg); twenty-four #2½ cans, with drained weight of 18 oz (504 g); twenty-four #2 cans, with drained weight of 12½ oz (350 g). Other packs are available.

Counts:
Table C-3 identifies counts for various cherry sizes and can sizes.

Table C-3 Cherry Counts for Different Can Sizes

	#2 Can	*#2½ Can*	*#10 Can*
Cherries	35 to 40	50 to 60	210 to 235
	36 to 39	65 to 70	240 to 260
	54 to 64	80 to 90	290 to 335
	64 to 75	90 to 103	335 to 390
	90 to 95	130 to 135	480 to 540

Kitchen Yields
One #10 can contains 10 cups drained fruit.

Serving size:
½ cup fruit and juice as desserts, so one #10 can yields 22 servings; 2 oz (56 g) for dessert sauce, so one #10 can yields 30 servings.

Calories:
½ cup, fruit and juice, in medium syrup = 105 Calories.

FRESH CHERRIES
The principal varieties are as follows:

Bing:	Dark red, large, firm, and juicy
Lambert:	Dark red, heart-shaped, slightly smaller than Bing
Vans:	Resembles Bing
Rainers:	Light-colored— cream to golden
Black Republican:	Very dark, medium size
Royal Ann:	Light yellow with pink blush

Cherries do not continue to ripen once off the tree; they just decay.

Season:
May to July; imports available in winter.

Pack:
12-lb (5.4-kg) flats; 18-lb (8.1-kg) California lugs; 20-lb (9-kg) lugs.

Kitchen Yield

Count:
Depends on weather and on variety. Typically, 1 lb (450 g) Bing cherries consists of 60 to 150 fruits, while 1 lb (450 g) other varieties consists of 280 to 290 fruits.

Serving size:
½ cup (heaping) cherries, with pits; 1 lb (450 g) yields 5 servings. With pits in, 3½ oz (100 g) comprises 20 medium cherries or 15 large cherries.
1 qt (0.9 l) whole cherries yields 1 lb (450 g) pitted fruit.

Calories:
3½ oz (100 g), with pits in = 70 Calories.

FROZEN CHERRIES
Available pitted, IQF, and in a solid-pack vacuum pack.

Pack:
40-lb (18.1 kg) pack of pitted, IQF cherries; 37-lb (16.6-kg) vacuum pack, solid block.

Kitchen Yields
40 lb (18.1 kg) yield filling for twenty-four 9-in (225-mm) pies.

MARASCHINO CHERRIES
Preserved cherries, available red and green, with and without stem. Maraschino cherries are always pitted.

Pack:
½-gal (1.8-l) jars; 1-gal (3.8-l) jars.
Other packs are available.

Count:
Table C-4 lists the count per gallon of maraschino cherries.

Table C-4 Maraschino Cherries per Gallon

	Whole with Stems	*Whole without Stems*
Medium	450	600
Large	350	500
Extra large	200	400

SOUR OR TART CHERRIES.

Tart or sour cherries are marketed primarily in canned and frozen forms or as pie filling. Dry cherries are available as a specialty item. Principal varieties are Montmorency, Early Richmond, and English Morello.

CANNED SOUR CHERRIES

Available pitted and with pit in. Packed in syrup or in water.

Pack:
Six #10 cans; six #10 cans pie filling.

Kitchen Yields

One #10 can yields filling for four 9-in (225-mm) pies.

Calories:
1 cup, or 8 oz (0.235 l), pitted, water-packed cherries = 105 Calories.

DRIED SOUR CHERRIES

Pack:
By weight.

Kitchen Yields

Available pitted and with pit in. The product has little foodservice importance.

FRESH SOUR CHERRIES

Specialty item; very little reaches the market fresh.

Season:
July.

Pack:
By weight.

Kitchen Yields

1 lb (450 g) is equivalent to 2½ cups (0.58 l).

FROZEN SOUR CHERRIES

Available pitted and mixed with sugar at a ratio of 5 lb (2.2 kg) sugar to 25 lb (11.2 kg) cherries.

Pack:
30-lb (13.5-kg) tins.

Kitchen Yields

Serving size:
½ cup (0.11 l); one 30-lb (13.5-kg) can yields 90 servings, or filling for eighteen 9-in (225-mm) pies.

CHESTNUTS

Available canned, dried, fresh, and glazed. For information on water chestnuts, *see* Water Chestnuts.

CANNED CHESTNUTS

Available whole and as purée. Chestnut purée can be obtained in either sweetened or natural form.

Pack:

Whole chestnuts:
Twenty-four 15½-oz (440-g) cans; twelve 31-oz (880-g) cans.

Unsweetened purée:
Twenty-four 15½-oz (440-g) cans; twelve 31-oz (880-g) cans.

Sweetened purée:
Twenty-four 17-oz (482-g) cans.

Kitchen Yields

Whole chestnuts:
One 15½-oz (440-g) can contains 10 oz (280 g), drained weight; one 31-oz (880-g) can contains 20½ oz (580 g), drained weight.
Serving size depends on application.

DRIED CHESTNUTS

Available whole and as flour. Dried whole chestnuts double in weight after soaking and boiling.

Pack:
25-lb (11.2-kg) bags.

Kitchen Yields

Serving size depends on application.

FRESH CHESTNUTS

Season:
Winter.

Pack:
By weight.

Kitchen Yields

Old or improperly stored chestnuts can be moldy or empty. Check before buying.

Peeling loss:
50 percent of raw weight.

GLAZED CHESTNUTS
Often called *marrons glacés,* these are whole, candied chestnuts. Use as candy or as garnish on desserts.

Pack:
5-oz (142-g) tin; 7¾-oz (220-g) tin; 14-oz (440-g) tin.

Kitchen Yields
One 5-oz (142-g) tin contains 7 glazed chestnuts; one 7¾-oz (220-g) tin contains 11 glazed chestnuts; and one 14-oz (400-g) tin contains 20 glazed chestnuts. Count varies.

CHICKEN

Major subheadings under this entry include Breeds and Varieties, Fresh Chicken Parts, Frozen Chicken Parts, and Processed Chicken Products.

BREEDS AND VARIETIES
Many breeds and varieties of chicken are available; most of these are marketed fresh and whole. Whole chickens are sold with the weight of gizzards included; the gizzards represent approximately 6 percent of weight. The yellow color of chicken is often achieved by mixing marigold petals in the feed before slaughter. Color is not necessarily an indication of quality.

Industry terms:

Dressed poultry:
Picked clean; head and feet still attached; not eviscerated.

Read-to-cook-poultry:
Picked clean and singed; head and feet removed; eviscerated.

BABY CHICKEN
Also called *squab chicken,* or *poussin* in French.

Pack:
By weight and by piece.

Sizes:

Bone in:
14 to 16 oz (400 to 450 g).

Boneless:
14 oz (400 g) or less.

Kitchen Yields

Serving size:
One bird.

BROILER
Available in a number of sizes.

Pack:
By weight and by piece, packed in ice.

Sizes:
2, 2¼, or 2½ lb (0.9, 1.0, or 1.2 kg). Most common size is 2½ lb (1.1 kg).

Serving size:
½ broiler per person.

Calories:
3½ oz (100 g) cooked meat, skinless = 136 Calories.

CAPON
Capon is a castrated male bird. The meat is tender.

Pack:
By weight and by piece.

Sizes:
3 to 7 lb (1.3 to 3.1 kg).

Kitchen Yields

Serving size:
5 oz (140 g) boneless meat. One 5-lb (2.2-kg) bird weighs 3¼ lb (1.5 kg) cooked and yields 2 lb 4 oz (1 kg) cooked meat; this is equivalent to 5 servings, in slices, plus some leftover pieces for salad.

CORNISH HEN
Young chicken of the Cornish chicken breed. Available boned or bone in. NOTE: Leg bones are normally not removed.

Pack:
By weight and by piece.

Sizes:

Boned:
14 to 16 oz (400 to 450 g).

Bone in:
16 to 20 oz (450 to 570 g).

Kitchen Yields

Serving size:
One bird, usually stuffed. Purchase 14-oz (400-g) birds.

FOWL
Mature chicken, used for boiling.

Pack:
By weight and by the piece, packed in ice.

Sizes:
4½ to 5 lb (2 to 2.2 kg); 5 to 5½ lb (2.2 to 2.4 kg).

Kitchen Yields

One 5-lb (2.2-kg) bird yields 2 lb (0.9 kg) cooked meat.

Calories:
3½ oz (100 g) cooked meat, skinless = 185 Calories.

FREE-RANGE CHICKEN
Free-range chickens are birds not confined to cages. They are more flavorful than caged chickens.

Average size:
3 to 3½ lb (1.3 to 1.5 kg).

Kitchen Yields

About 10 percent less than a roaster of the same size.

FRYER
Medium-size chicken.

Pack:
By weight and by piece.

Sizes:
2¾, 3, or 3¼ lb (1.2, 1.3, or 1.5 kg).

Kitchen Yields

Breakdown of parts, raw weight, for a 3-lb (1.35-kg) chicken: two 9-oz (250-g) breasts; two 8-oz (224-g) legs; two 2-oz (56-g) wings; 7-oz (200-g) neck, backbone; 3-oz (84-g) gizzard.

Calories:
3½ oz (100 g) cooked light meat, skinless = 163 Calories.

3½ oz (100 g) cooked dark meat, skinless = 175 Calories.

ROASTER
Large chicken. The 3½-lb (1.5-kg) size is often cut into parts.

Pack:
By weight and by piece.

Sizes:
3½, or 4, or 4½ lb (1.5, 1.8, or 2.0 kg).

Kitchen Yields

Breakdown of parts, raw weights:
One 3½-lb (1.56-kg) roaster yields one 22-oz (616-g) double breast, two 10-oz (280-g) legs, and 10-oz (280-g) back, wings, and bones, with 4-oz gizzard and neck.

FRESH CHICKEN PARTS

BREAST
Available as either single or double breast. Single breast is available with bone in or boned. Boned and skinless double breast is often marketed as *chicken cutlet.* The term *French-cut double breast* refers to a breast with wings and back removed.

Pack:
By weight and by piece.

Sizes:
10-oz (283-g) single breast, bone in, skin on; 8-oz (226-g) single breast, boneless, skin on; 16- to 18-oz (450- to 511-g) French-cut double breast.

CUTLETS
Boneless and skinless breast, normally sold as double breast.

Pack:
By weight.

Sizes:
Pieces range from 4 to 14 oz (113 to 400 g).

Kitchen Yields

Specify size when ordering. Trimming waste is 5 percent or less, depending on how uniformly pieces must be cut. Trimming waste can be cooked and used in chicken salad or in other applications.

Serving size:
7 oz (200 g) for grilled main course; 6 oz (170 g) for breaded main course.

Cooking loss:
30 percent. Thus, 45 lb (20.2 kg) uncooked yields 31½ lb (14.1 kg) cooked.

Calories:
3½ oz (100 g) cooked meat, skinless = 126 Calories.

GIZZARDS
Hearts and stomachs are available by weight.

LEGS

Pack:
By weight and by piece.

Sizes:
6, 8, and 10 oz (170, 226, and 280 g), bone in.

Kitchen Yields

Serving size:
8-oz (226-g) leg for broiling; 6-oz (170-g) leg for stuffing; 10-oz (280-g) leg for cutting into six tidbits.
NOTE: When ordering, specify back removed.

LIVERS
Available by weight.

Pack:
5-lb (2.2-kg) tubs.

Formula for Chopped Chicken Liver
    10 lb (4.5 kg) chicken livers, cleaned
    4 lb (1.8 kg) peeled onions
    3 lb (1.3 kg) chicken fat
    24 hard-boiled eggs
    Salt to taste

Sauté onions in chicken fat before grinding together with broiled livers.

Kitchen Yields

Serving sizes:
6 oz (170 g) as appetizer; 3 oz (85 g) on buffet. Total mix yields 17 lb (7.6 kg), which is equivalent to 45 servings as appetizer or 90 servings on buffet.

NECKS AND BACKS
Sold fresh or frozen, with little difference in quality. Used for sauces and stocks.

Pack:
Sold by weight—normally, 5-lb (2.3-kg) bags.

Kitchen Yields
10 lb (4.5 kg) bones produces 2 gal (7.6 l) chicken stock, and 100 lb (45 kg) bones produces 20 gal (76 l) chicken stock.
NOTE: Boil bones no longer than 1 hour.

FROZEN CHICKEN PARTS
Most frozen chicken parts are machine cut, with bones left in. Many different sizes and packs are available.

Parts with backbone:

Quarters:
8.7 oz (250 g); 60 pieces per pack.

Halves:
17.9 oz (508 g); 30 pieces per pack.

Pieces:
4 or 4½ oz (113 or 127 g); 96 or 108 pieces per pack.

Segments:

Breast halves:
6.4 oz (180 g); 48 pieces per pack.

Thighs:
3.6 oz (102 g); 96 pieces per pack.

Drumsticks:
2.6 oz (74 g); 112 pieces per pack.

Whole legs:
6.5 oz (184 g); 50 pieces per pack.

Drumettes:
1.4 oz (40 g); 175 pieces per pack.

Wings:
2.5 oz (71 g); 96 pieces per pack.

PROCESSED CHICKEN PRODUCTS

CANNED CHICKEN STOCK
Chicken stock is the most frequently used canned product in foodservice.

Sizes:
46-oz (1.3-l) cans.

FROZEN CHICKEN PRODUCTS
Numerous processed chicken products are on the market. Some are fully cooked; others are ready to cook.

Breaded boneless products:

Nuggets:
½ to 1¼ oz (14 to 35 g).

Patties:
2½ to 4 oz (70 to 113 g).

Breast filets:
3 oz (85 g) and larger.

Tenders:
1.2 oz (34 g) and larger.

Bone-in breaded segments:

Breast halves:
8 oz (226 g) and larger.

Drumsticks:
3.9 oz (110 g) and larger.

Thighs:
6.9 oz (196 g) and larger.

Wings:
3.3 oz (93 g) and larger.

Drumettes:
1.6 oz (45 g) and larger.

Breaded pieces:
5 oz (140 g) per piece, average weight.

Other:

Nonbreaded, marinated, bone-in breasts:
4 and 6 oz (113 and 170 g), packed IQF, ready for broiling.

Cooked, boneless white meat:
one 10-lb (4.5-kg) bag, IQF.

Cooked, boneless white and dark meat:
one 10 lb (4.5 kg) bag, IQF.

SMOKED CHICKEN PRODUCTS
Available whole or in parts.

Pack:

Whole capon:
4 to 5 lb (1.8 to 2.2 kg) each.

Chicken:
1¾ to 2 lb (0.8 to 0.9 kg) each.

Rock Cornish:
18 to 21 oz (0.5 to 0.6 kg) each.

Chicken breasts:
8 oz (224 g) average.

Kitchen Yields
According to application.

STUFFED BREASTS
Stuffed breasts are available with various stuffings. Some products are fully boneless; others have the wing bone still attached. Most products are prebrowned.

Packs:
Twenty-four 7- or 8-oz (200- or 226-g) breasts, bone in; twenty-four 6-oz (170-g) breasts, boneless.

CHICK-PEAS (GARBANZOS)

See Beans.

CHILIES

See Mexican Foods.

CHILI POWDER

See Herbs & Spices.

CHILI SAUCE

A variety of tomato catsup. *See* Tomatoes.

CHINESE FOODS

ABALONE
See Abalone.

BAMBOO SHOOTS
See Bamboo Shoots.

BEAN CURD (TOFU)
See Bean Curd.

BEANS

FERMENTED BLACK BEANS

Pack:
Bottles, cans, or plastic bags.

Kitchen Yields
Use as a vegetable or as a condiment in sauces.

LONG BEANS
Available year-round.

Pack:
Purchase by weight; often sold in bundles.

Size:
1 to 3 ft (30 cm to 90 cm).

Kitchen Yields
There is little waste.

BEAN SPROUTS
See Sprouts.

BECHE-DE-MER (DRIED)
Cucumber-shaped holothurian; also called *sea cucumber.*

Pack:
Dried only; available by weight.

Kitchen Yields

Common size:
8 in (200 mm) long. Product will triple in size after soaking and cooking.

BIRD'S NEST
Available dried as a clean whole and as bits. Whole nests are the more expensive form. Soak and add to soups.

Pack:
6-oz (170-g) packages.

Kitchen Yields
1½ oz (42 g) yields 1 qt (0.47 l) soup.

BITTER MELON
See Squash.

BOK CHOY (CHINESE CABBAGE)
See Cabbage.

CELERY CABBAGE
See Cabbage.

CELLOPHANE NOODLES
Transparent noodles made of mung bean flour.

Pack:
8-oz (224-g) packages.

Kitchen Yields
Boil about 1 minute, or fry raw. Noodles will expand. NOTE: Some noodles need scalding with boiling water only.

Serving size:
3 oz (85 g) as base for meat.

CHINESE EGGPLANT
White outside and inside.

Season:
Year-round.

Pack:
By weight.

Size:
6 to 8 in (150 to 200 mm) long.

CHINESE PARSLEY
See Cilantro under Herbs & Spices.

CHINESE TURNIP
Long white root resembling a white radish. It has a strong taste and is used as a cooked vegetable. Also available salted and dried.

Season:
Year-round.

Pack:
By weight.

Kitchen Yields

Size:
8 to 12 in (200 to 250 mm).

CUTTLEFISH (DRIED)
Dried small squid.

Pack:
By weight.

Size:
6 to 8 in (150 to 200 mm).

DUCK SAUCE
See Hoisin Sauce in this section.

EGGROLL WRAPPER

Pack:
Twelve 1-lb (450-g) packages containing 14 wrappers each.

Size:
6 in (150 mm) square.

Kitchen Yields
One wrapper is used per eggroll. To seal the wrapper properly, make a paste with water and flour.

GALANGAL
These aromatic roots are also called Siamese Ginger.

Pack:
Available dried in slices, fresh, and powdered.

Kitchen Yields
The dried root can be reconstituted by soaking it in water.

GARLIC CHIVES
Long chives with strong garlic smell.

Season:
Year-round, peak in spring.

Pack:
Sold in bunches of various size.

Size:
12 to 16 in (300 to 400 mm) long.

Kitchen Yields
Use the same as other chives.

GINGER
See Ginger Root.

GREEN TEA
Tea made from leaves that have undergone incomplete fermentation prior to drying. Green tea is popular throughout China and Japan.

Kitchen Yields
1¾ oz (50 g) dry leaves yields 30 cups brewed tea.

HOISIN SAUCE
Often called *duck sauce,* this is a thick, slightly sweet sauce. It is used as condiment.

Pack:
Cans or bottles.

JELLYFISH (DRIED)
Available dried—normally whole, but sometimes shredded.

Pack:
Individual jellyfish, sold by weight.

Size:
25 in (900 mm) square.

LEMON GRASS
A tropical grass resembling leeks. The lower white part is edible.

Pack:
Available dried, fresh, and powdered.

Kitchen Yields
The dried form can be reconstituted by soaking it in water.

LILY FLOWERS
Dried flower petals.

Pack:
By ounce, in cellophane bags.

LILY ROOT
See Lotus Root under this same general heading.

LITCHIS
See Lychees.

LO BOK (CHINESE RADISH)
Radish similar to Daikon.

LONGANS
Fruit resembling lychees. Available pitted and dried, or canned.

LOTUS ROOT
Available fresh, canned, or dried.

Pack:
Fresh bulb sold by weight.
Dried root sold by weight.
Canned slices packed in water.

Size:
4×8 in (100×200 mm) fresh bulb.

LYCHEE NUTS
See Lychees.

100-YEAR-OLD EGG
Duck egg artificially aged through application of a black, salty crust. Several varieties are available. Ready to eat.

Pack:
Sold individually or by the dozen.

OYSTER SAUCE
Condiment sauce.

Pack:
Bottles and cans in various sizes.

OYSTERS (DRIED)
Available raw or cooked.

Pack:
1-lb (450-g) bags.

Kitchen Yields

Size:
About 2 in (50 mm) long. Soak raw dried oyster for 12 to 24 hours, to remove sand.

RICE
Special high-gluten rice is grown under various brand names.

Pack:
50- and 100-lb (22.5- and 45.0-kg) cotton bags.

Kitchen Yields

Serving size:
½ cup cooked; 1.6 oz (45 g) raw. 10 lb yields 160 servings.

SCALLOPS (DRIED)

Pack:
By weight.

Size:
Pieces or shreds.

SESAME OIL
Yellow flavoring oil.

Pack:
Bottles in various sizes.

SHARK FINS (DRIED)
Dried cartilage from the fin of sharks. Also available canned.

Pack:
By weight.

Size:
Shaped like thin spaghetti. Length is an indication of quality; best fins are 5 in (127 mm) long.

Kitchen Yields
1 oz (28 g) dried shark fin is sufficient for 1 qt (0.47 l) soup.

SHRIMP CHIPS
Popular snack items, available in many colors. Dried chips puff up when fried.

Pack:
By weight.

Kitchen Yields
Chips triple in size when fried.

SHRIMP (DRIED)
Small dried shrimp, available in various sizes. Very strong seafood smell.

Pack:
By weight, in bags.

Sizes:
½ to 2 in (12 to 50 mm) long.

SHRIMP PASTE
Thick paste used as condiment.

Pack:
8-oz (227-g) jars.

TARO ROOT
See Taro Root.

TEA
See Green Tea under this same general heading.

TOFU
See Bean Curd.

WATER CHESTNUTS
See Water Chestnuts.

WINTER MELON
See Squash.

WONTON WRAPPERS
1-lb (450-g) package.

Kitchen Yields
One 1-lb (450-g) package contains 60 skins. To seal the wrapper properly, make a paste with water and flour.

CHIVES

Chives are available dried, fresh, and frozen. Garlic chives are a special type used in Oriental cooking; see *Chinese Foods.*

DRIED CHIVES

Pack:
Various packs are available.

FRESH CHIVES
Available year-round, cut or potted.

Pack:
Bunches in various sizes.

Kitchen Yields
Size of bunches vary greatly; they are smallest in early spring.
3½ average bunches are equivalent to 1½ cups cut and weigh 2 oz (56 g).

FROZEN CHIVES

Pack:
4-oz (113-g) packs.

CHOCOLATE

The primary division in chocolate is between bitter chocolate and sweet chocolate.

BITTER CHOCOLATE

Pack:
5- and 10-lb (2.2- and 4.5-kg) blocks.

Calories:
1 oz (28 g) = 145 Calories.

Formula for Chocolate for Modeling
3 lb (1.3 kg) melted dark baking chocolate
1 lb (450 g) corn syrup
1 tb (14 g) warm water

SWEET CHOCOLATE

Pack:
5- and 10-lb (2.2- and 4.5-kg) blocks.

Calories:
1 oz (28 g) = 145 Calories.

Chocolate Mousse Formula 1
1½ qt (1.4 l) egg whites, whipped
1 pt (0.47 l) water

Add to egg whites:

3 lb (1.3 kg) sugar boiled in water to 235°F

Fold in:

8 lb (3.6 kg) sweet chocolate melted and cooled to 80°F

Again fold in:

3 qt (2.8 l) heavy cream, whipped

Kitchen Yield

Serving size:
5 oz (0.14 l). The total mix yields 120 servings.

Chocolate Mousse Formula 2
Boil together:

5 lb (2.25 kg) sugar
1 pint (0.47 l) water, heated to 235°F

Blend in:

8 lb (3.6 kg) sweet chocolate, melted and cooled to 80°F
2 qt, or 96 egg yolks
4 lb (1.8 kg) sweet butter
6 oz (170 g) unflavored gelatin
3 qt (2.8 l) heavy cream, whipped

Kitchen Yield

Serving size:
5 oz (0.14 l). The total mix yields 100 servings.

CILANTRO

See Herbs & Spices.

CLAMS

Clams can be classified as Atlantic or Pacific hard-shell or soft-shell varieties. Canned clams, clam juice, and breaded clams are considered separately, as processed clam products.

ATLANTIC HARD-SHELL CLAMS
Atlantic hard-shell clams are available canned, fresh in shell, shucked fresh, and shucked frozen.

Also known as *quahogs,* these clams are classified by size.

CHERRYSTONES
Cherrystones are medium-size clams, normally served raw on the half shell or baked. On account of scarcity, size and count vary. Many operators purchase clams by the piece.

Season:
Available year-round. Scarce when inclement weather makes clamming difficult.

Pack:
Bushels or cartons.

Count:
275 to 300.

Kitchen Yields
Normal portion is six clams on the half shell. Therefore, 1 bushel yields 45 to 50 portions.

CHOWDER CLAMS
Chowder clams are available canned, shucked, and whole.

SHUCKED CHOWDER CLAMS
Available fresh-shucked with juice, either whole or chopped.

Pack:
1-gal (3.8-l) container.

Kitchen Yields
No waste.
1 gal (3.8 l) shucked clams provides clams for 5 gal (19 l) clam chowder.

Calories:
3 oz (85 g) raw clams (shucked) = 65 Calories.

WHOLE CHOWDER CLAMS
Large clams that are used for making chowder.

Season:
Available year-round. Scarce during severe winters.

Pack:
Bushels or cartons.

Count:
150 to 175.

Kitchen Yields
1 bushel whole clams provides clams for 4 gal (15.2 l) clam chowder.

Calories:
3 oz (85 g) raw whole clams = 65 Calories.

LITTLE NECKS
Formula for butter sauce for Little Neck Clams Casino is given elsewhere; *see* Casino Butter.

Pack:
Bushels or cartons.

Count:
500 to 550.

Kitchen Yields

Serving size:
On the half shell, nine clams; therefore, 1 bushel yields 50 to 55 servings.

Calories:
3 oz (85 g) raw clams = 65 Calories.

ATLANTIC SOFT-SHELL CLAMS
Also called *steamer clams* or *piss clams,* these clams are steamed and served whole with clam broth and melted butter. The shells are soft and easy to crush. The clams are often sandy.

Season:
Available year-round, but scarcity develops during severe winters.

Pack:
42- to 46-lb (18.9- to 20.7-kg) bushel baskets or cartons.

Sizes:
Small, medium, and large; but soft-shell clams are seldom graded. Medium-size clams are 2 to 4 in (50 to 100 mm) in length.

Count:
550 to 600; count varies according to individual clam size.

Kitchen Yields
About 20 percent loss because of crushed clams is possible.

Serving size:
14 to 18 clams, weighing approximately 15 oz (420 g) total; 1 bushel yields 25 to 32 servings.

PACIFIC HARD-SHELL CLAMS
BUTTER CLAMS

Pack:
By weight; often in 80-lb (36-kg) sacks.

Kitchen Yields
Clams are seldom sorted by size, although minimum sizes are established by state authorities.

LITTLE NECKS
Formula for butter sauce for Little Neck Clams Casino is given elsewhere; *see* Casino Butter.

Pack:
By weight; often in 80-lb (36-kg) sacks.

Kitchen Yields
Clams are seldom sorted by size, although minimum sizes are established by state authorities.

PISMO CLAMS
Large clam, used for making chowders.

Kitchen Yields
Clams are seldom sorted by size, although minimum sizes are established by state authorities.

GEODUCK CLAMS
Very large clam harvested along the Pacific coast, especially in Puget Sound. The meat is often breaded and fried or grilled. Geoduck clams are a popular selection in sushi bars; they are available canned, fresh, frozen, and smoked.

Pack:
By the piece.

Size:
3 lb (1.3 kg), on average.

Kitchen Yields
Cleaning loss is about 50 percent by weight, without shell.

PACIFIC SOFT-SHELL CLAMS
ATLANTIC SOFT-SHELL CLAMS
This clam has been introduced along the Pacific coast from the Atlantic.

Pack:
By weight; often in 50-lb (22.5-kg) sacks.

Kitchen Yields
Clams are seldom sorted by size, although minimum sizes are established by state authorities.

RAZOR CLAMS
This clam is normally minced for use in chowders.

Kitchen Yields

Size:
3½ to 4 in (87 to 100 mm) in length.

PROCESSED CLAM PRODUCTS

CANNED CLAMS
The clams used for canning are called *skimmer clams;* they are also known as *beach clams, giant clams,* and *sea clams.* They are normally available chopped and are used for chowders and fritters.

Pack:
Twelve 5-lb (2.2-kg) cans; twelve 51-oz (1.4-kg) cans. Other packs are available.

Kitchen Yields
One 5-lb (2.2-kg) can contains 38 oz (1.1 kg) clams, drained weight.
One 51-oz (1.4-kg) can contains 24 oz (680 g) clams, drained weight.

Calories:
3 oz (85 g) drained meat = 45 Calories.

CLAM JUICE
Clam juice is available plain or mixed with tomato juice.

Pack:
Twelve 46-oz (1.3-l) cans; twelve 16-oz, or 1-pint (0.47 l) bottles; twelve 8-oz, or ½-pint (0.235-l) bottles.

Kitchen Yields

Serving size:
4 oz (0.11 l).

FROZEN, BREADED SOFT-SHELL CLAMS
Pack:
Twelve 2-lb (0.9-kg) boxes.

Kitchen Yields

Serving size:
6 oz (170 g).

COCONUT

Coconut is available fresh and in a multitude of processed forms.

FRESH COCONUT

Available year-round, with peak supply during winter.

Pack:
50-lb (22.5-kg) burlap bags, or loose by the piece.

Sizes:
Bald 24s; bald 30s; and husk 12s.

Weights:
Balds range from 26 to 33 oz (0.75 to 0.93 g).

Kitchen Yields
Balds have the outer husk removed to expose the underlying hard shell. Waste is about 50 percent, by weight, depending on the amount of liquid left in the nut.

Calories:
1 cup fresh, shredded coconut weighing 4 oz (112 g) = 373 Calories.

PROCESSED COCONUT PRODUCTS

CANNED COCONUT JUICE
This homogenized coconut liquid with sugar added is available for kitchen uses and for bar drinks.

Pack:
Case of twenty-four 15-oz (0.43-l) cans; case of twelve 57.5-oz (1.66-l) cans; case of twenty-four 13-oz (0.37-l) bottles; case of twelve 32-oz (0.93-l) bottles.

Kitchen Yields
One 15-oz (0.43-l) can contains 1⅛ cups. Use in dessert sauces, custards, curries, and other preparations.

SHREDDED DRIED COCONUT

Available as short, medium, and angel hair, usually sugared. Shredded coconut without sugar is also available.

Pack:
10-, 25-, and 50-lb (4.5-, 11.2-, and 22.5-kg) bags; 1-lb (450-g) boxes.

Coconut Custard Cream Pie Formula
> 5 qt (4.7 l) milk
> 2 lb (0.9 kg) sugar
> 30 whole eggs
> 20 oz (568 g) shredded dried coconut
> 5 oz (142 g) melted butter
> Vanilla to taste

Kitchen Yields
Ten 9-in (225-mm) pies.
NOTE: Pie shells must be prebaked.

COFFEE

All coffees are blends. Even when a specific country or region is listed on the label, the quantity proportions of beans from different farms and from different harvest years are not specified. Since the information available to the operator is incomplete, the integrity and experience of the purveyor is the only guarantee for receiving coffee of consistent quality.

The expected strength and flavor of coffee varies from region to region in the country. Coffee companies adjust their products in response to their market. The flavor differences depend on the bean blend, the degree of roasting, and the fineness of the grind. All coffees are available whole or ground to different degrees of fineness. Different pieces of equipment require different grinds.

DECAFFEINATED COFFEE

Coffee may be naturally or chemically decaffeinated.

Packs:
Same as regular coffee.

Kitchen Yields
Same as regular coffee.

ESPRESSO COFFEE

Packs:
1-lb (450-g) bags. Other packs are available.

Kitchen Yields

Serving size:
3-oz (0.09-l) cup; ½ oz (14 g) coffee = 1 cup; 1 lb (450 g) yields 30 to 35 cups.

INSTANT COFFEE

Packs:
Four trays of 100 single-service packets; 1,000-piece random pack.

REGULAR COFFEE

Ground coffee is available packed in vacuum-seal packages premeasured to be used with specific equipment.

Pack:
1 lb (450 g) each. Many other packs are available.

Kitchen Yields

Serving size:
6 oz (0.17 l); 1 gal yields 20 cups.
A small coffee maker's capacity is 2 qt (1.8 l), or 8 to 10 cups. The amount of coffee is needed is 2 oz (57 g) for weak coffee or 3 oz (85 g) for strong coffee.

Large-urn water ratio:
1 lb (450 g) coffee should be combined with 2½ gal (9.5 l) water, yielding 40 cups; thus, 5 lb (2.2 kg) coffee yield 200 servings.

SPECIALTY COFFEES

BLUE MOUNTAIN COFFEE
This coffee is grown in Jamaica. Production is limited, and the price is high.

KONA COFFEE
This coffee is grown in Hawaii. Production is limited, and the price is high.

COLLARD GREENS

Collard greens are available canned, fresh, and frozen.

CANNED COLLARD GREENS
Available chopped.

Pack:
Six #10 cans.

Kitchen Yields
One #10 can contains 62 oz (1.7 kg), drained weight.

Serving size:
½ cup, drained. One #10 can yields 18 servings, so one case yields 108 servings.

Calories:
½ cup (0.11 l) drained greens = 32 Calories.

FRESH COLLARD GREENS
Collard greens are grown mainly in the southern states. There are four basic varieties.

> *Georgia:* Large, crumpled blue-green leaves
> *Vates:* Thick green leaves with short stems
> *Morries Heading:* Broad, medium-size leaves with short stems
> *Louisiana Sweet:* Large, thick leaves with short stems

Season:
Available year-round. Peak supply is in winter, and low production occurs from June to August.

Pack:
By weight.

Kitchen Yields
1 lb (450 g) as purchased produces 11 oz (320 g) ready to cook.

Serving size:
½ cup; 1 lb (450 g) as purchased yields 3½ servings.

Calories:
½ cup cooked, drained leaves = 35 Calories.

FROZEN COLLARD GREENS
Available chopped.

Pack:
Twelve 3-lb (1.3-kg) boxes.

Kitchen Yields

Serving size:
½ cup. One 3-lb (1.3-kg) package yields 12 servings, so one case yields 144 servings.

Calories:
½ cup = 33 Calories.

CONCHES

Large gastropod of tropical and temperate seas. It is normally sold freshly caught and removed from its shell, frozen raw, or frozen cooked.

Pack:
5-lb (2.3-kg) cartons.

Kitchen Yields
About 30 percent trimming waste from raw product. Cooked product also has some cleaning waste unless purchased chopped.
3½ lb (1.5 kg) cleaned conch yield 3 gal (11.4 l) chowder.

COOKIES

Entries under this head include formulas for butter and butter-and-shortening cookies, and information on prepackaged frozen cookie dough.

BUTTER COOKIES
The weight of butter cookies varies greatly.

Formula
> 6½ lb (3 kg) butter
> 4½ lb (2 kg) sugar
> 1½ qt (0.7 l) heavy cream
> 4½ lb (2 kg) patent flour
> 4½ lb (2 kg) cake flour
> Salt, vanilla, and lemon to taste

Kitchen Yields

Serving size:
1 oz; yield from the total mix produced by the preceding formula is 350 pieces.

Average count:
1 lb (450 g) yields 25 ready-to-serve cookies.

Banquet quantities are 1½ lb (675 g) for each table of ten.

BUTTER-AND-SHORTENING COOKIES
This is the basic cookie dough from which a multitude of varieties can be produced.

Formula
3 lb (1.35 kg) butter
3 lb (1.35 kg) shortening
4½ lb (2 kg) sugar
1½ qt (1.4 l) heavy cream
4½ lb (2 kg) patent flour
5 lb (2.3 kg) cake flour
Salt, vanilla, and lemon to taste

Kitchen Yields
Scale the preceding formula into 360 cookies, each weighing 1 oz (28 g).

FROZEN COOKIE DOUGH
Frozen cookie dough is available from many manufacturers.

Pack:
Four 6-lb (2.7-kg) buckets.

Kitchen Yields
One 6-lb (2.7-kg) bucket yields ninety-six 1-oz (28-g) cookies, uncooked.

CORIANDER

See Herbs & Spices.

CORN

Corn is available fresh, canned, and frozen.

CANNED CORN
Canned corn is available as cut corn, creamed corn, and whole baby corn. Also available as vacuum-packed cut corn.

Pack:
Six #10 cans cut or creamed corn weighing 105 oz (2.9 kg) each; six #10 cans whole baby corn weighing 103 oz (2.9 kg) each. Other packs are also available.

Kitchen Yields
One #10 can cut corn contains 70 oz (2 kg) corn, drained weight.
One #10 can creamed corn contains 100 oz (2.8 kg) corn.
One #10 can whole baby corn contains 53 oz (1.5 kg) corn, drained weight.

Serving size:
For cut corn, ½ cup, or 3 oz (85 g); thus, one #10 can yields 20 servings, and one case cut corn yields 120 servings. For creamed corn, ½ cup, or 4½ oz (127 g); thus, one #10 can yields 22 servings, and one case yields 132 servings. For whole baby corn, one #10 can contains 300 pieces, on average, although count varies; six pieces of whole baby corn weigh, on average, 1 oz (28 g).

Calories:
½ cup, or 3 oz (85 g), cut corn = 65 Calories.
½ cup 4½ oz (127 g) creamed corn = 76 Calories.
½ cup whole kernel, vacuum pack = 88 Calories.

FRESH CORN
CORN ON THE COB
Many local varieties of corn are on the market. In foodservice, the basic distinction is between yellow and white sweet hybrid corn. Baby corn is available in summer; *see* Baby Vegetables. A well-developed ear of corn has twelve to fourteen even rows of kernels. Corn loses quality rapidly after picking although chilling helps to prevent flavor loss.

Season:
Available year-round. Peaks are from May to August in Florida and from July to September in other parts of the country.

Pack:
45- to 50-lb (20.2- to 22.5-kg) cartons; 35-lb (15.7-kg) bushels containing 42 to 48 ears each.

Counts:
54, 60, and 66 ears per 50-lb (22.6-kg) carton.

Kitchen Yields
Serving size:
One ear.
Two 60-size ears yield 1 cup (0.235 l) fresh corn kernels.

Calories:
One 5 × 1¾-in (127 × 45-mm) ear weighing 6 oz (168 g) = 70 Calories.

FROZEN CORN
Frozen corn is available whole on the cob and shucked.

CORN ON THE COB
Available IQF fully cooked.

Packs:
30-lb (13.6-kg) cases, or slightly smaller cases.

Counts:
48 whole ears or 96 half ears.

Kitchen Yields
Product is fully cooked and ready to use.

Calories:
One 6-in (152-mm) ear weighing 9 oz (225 g) = 120 Calories.

CORN KERNELS
Available cut or cream style; also available as succotash.

Pack:

Cut Corn:
Twelve 2½-lb (1.1-kg) boxes; individual 20-lb (9.1-kg) carton.

Cream-style Corn:
Twelve 4-lb (1.8-kg) boxes.

Kitchen Yields

Serving size:
For cut corn, ½ cup or 3 oz (85 g); thus, one 2½-lb (1.1-kg) package yields 12 servings, and one case yields 140 servings. For creamed corn, ½ cup, or 4½ oz (127 g); thus, one 2½-lb (1.1-kg) package yields 9 servings, and one case yields 108 servings.

Calories:
½ cup cut corn, weighing 3 oz (85 g) = 65 Calories.
½ cup creamed corn weighing 4½ oz (127 g) = 55 Calories.

CORN KERNELS MIXED WITH RED AND GREEN PEPPERS
Also called *succotash.*

Pack:
Twelve boxes, each 2½ lb (1.1 kg).

Kitchen Yields

Serving size:
½ cup, or 3 oz (85 g); so one 2½-lb (1.1-kg) package yields 12 servings; and one case yields 140 servings.

CORN BREAD
Formula
    5 lb (2.2 kg) cornmeal
    3 lb (1.3 kg) pastry flour
    ½ lb (22 g) sugar
    4 oz (112 g) baking powder
    4 oz (112 g) salt
    3½ qt (3.3 l) milk
    24 whole eggs
    1½ lb (675 g) melted butter

Kitchen Yields
Two 18- by 24-in sheet pans, or 72 pieces, each 3 by 4 in.

CORN HUSKS

See Mexican Foods.

CORNMEAL

See Cereals, under Hot Cereals.

CORN MUFFINS
Formula
    2 lb (0.9 kg) cornmeal
    3 lb (1.3 kg) pastry flour
    3 pints (1.4 l) milk
    8 whole eggs
    1¼ lb (560 g) butter
    2 lb (0.9 kg) sugar
    3 oz (84 g) baking powder
    1 oz (28 g) salt

Kitchen Yields
Scale muffins 2 oz each; the preceding formula yields 8 dozen muffins.

CORNSTARCH

Kitchen Yields

Thickening power:
1 cup cornstarch is equivalent to 2 cups flour.

COURGETTES

French and British term for zucchini. *See* Squash.

COUSCOUS

North African wheat product, consisting of small semolina kernels. Small, medium, and large kernels available. Product is imported. Most products are instant.

Pack:
17½-oz (500-g) boxes. Large packs are available.

Kitchen Yields
1 cup dry measure is equivalent to 7 oz (200 g) raw; 1¼ cups or 8¾ oz (250 g) raw yield 3¾ (0.87 l) cups cooked; 1 cup, or 7 oz (200 g) raw yields 3 cups (0.7 l) cooked.

Couscous Formula
1½ cup (250 g) couscous
2½ (0.58 l) cups boiling water or stock
2 oz (56 g) fat

Sauté couscous in fat; mix with boiling liquid; let stand 10 minutes; bake in oven, or steam 10 minutes.

Kitchen Yields
The preceding formula yields 3¾ cups cooked couscous.

Serving size:
½ cup (0.1 l) cooked; therefore, the preceding formula yields 7 servings.

CRAB APPLES

Crab apples are small ornamental apples, available fresh and canned.

Season:
Fall.

Kitchen Yields
Use as decoration.

CRAB MEAT SUBSTITUTES

Products based on Surimi (Japanese fish cakes) technology. They are available in shapes resembling lobster tails, crab claws, and shrimp, among others. The most popular products resemble king crab meat. Various brand names are used. Some products are shipped frozen; others are shipped refrigerated.

Pack:

Frozen:
Six 5-lb (2.3-kg) blocks IQF, consisting of 64 whole-leg, 5-in (127-mm) pieces, 384 bite-size, ¾-in (19-mm) pieces, or random chunks of ¼ to ½ in (6.3 to 12.7 mm). Or six 3-lb (1.4-kg) blocks, IQF, consisting of 16 pieces per 1 lb imitation shrimp, 16 per box 3-oz (85-g) imitation lobster tails, or 16 per box 2-oz (56-g) split legs. Or twelve 2.5-lb (1.1-kg) boxes, consisting of chunky leg and flaky body-style meat.

Refrigerated:
Twelve 8-oz (225-g) packages of whole leg meat, chunks (cut legs), or flakes.

Kitchen Yields

Serving size:
5 oz (142 g) random chunks for cocktail; therefore, one 5-lb (2.3-kg) box yields 16 servings.

Calories:
4 oz (113 g) imitation shrimp (four pieces) = 118 Calories.
3 oz (85 g) imitation lobster tail (one piece) = 80 Calories.

CRABS

ALASKAN KING CRAB
King crab is caught in the Bering Sea off Alaska. It is always marketed cooked and is available canned and frozen. The foodservice industry primarily uses frozen king crab meat. Only male crabs are processed, and they can weigh up to 12 lb (5.4 kg).

Season:
Available year-round. The actual fishing season is from September to December.

Pack:

Whole king crab:
Available for buffet displays. Sold by weight.

Merus leg meat:
Six 5-lb (2.25-kg) packages whole, unsplit leg meat.

Fancy meat:
Six 5-lb (2.25-kg) blocks, consisting of 25 to 35 percent merus leg meat, 20 to 25 percent broken leg and claw meat, 40 to 50 percent white shoulder meat, and 10 percent or less shreds.

Split legs:
Twelve 12-oz (340-g) bags.

Fancy legs and claws:
One 25-lb (11.2-kg) carton, layer-packed, with minimum leg length of 16 in (406 mm), minimum leg weight of 8 oz (227 g), 32 to 45 legs per carton, and 5 to 8 claws per carton.

Standard legs and claws:
One 20-lb (9-kg) carton, loose-packed, with minimum leg length of 16 in (406 mm), minimum leg weight of 7 oz (200 g), 24 to 36 legs per carton, and 8 to 12 claws per carton.

Crab claws with arms:
One 25-lb (11.2-kg) carton containing extra-large, large, or small claws. Extra-large claws come 35 to 50 per carton and weigh 8 to 10 oz (227 to 280 g) each. Large claws come 50 to 80 per carton and weigh 5 to 8 oz (140 to 227 g) each. Small claws come 75 to 125 per carton and weigh 3 to 5 oz (85 to 140 g) each.

Kitchen Yields
One 5-lb (2.25-kg) frozen block yields 4½ lb (2 kg) crab, thawed and drained.

Serving sizes:
For cocktail, 4 oz (113 g), so one 5-lb (2.2-kg) block yields 18 servings. For crab Newburg, ⅔ cup, or 6½ oz (180 g); two 5-lb (2.2-kg) blocks produce enough crab for 1 gal, which is equivalent to 20 servings.

Calories:
3½ oz (100 g) edible meat = 100 Calories.

ALASKAN SNOW CRAB
Available frozen in blocks or cans, and canned. Foodservice uses mostly frozen products.

Pack:

Fancy snow crab meat:
Six 5-lb (2.2-kg) frozen blocks consisting of 45 percent red meat, 34 to 45 percent white meat, and 10 to 20 percent shreds.

Tin-pack fancy crab meat:
Six 5-lb (2.2-kg) cans, frozen, consisting of 30 percent whole leg meat and 70 percent broken leg and shoulder meat.

Tin-pack whole leg meat:
Six 5-lb (2.3-kg) cans, frozen, consisting of 75 percent red meat and 25 percent white meat.

Cocktail claws:
Twelve 2-lb (0.9-kg) bags of crabs (available with shell removed above the pincers), in sizes of 7 to 12, 12 to 16, or 16 to 20 per 1 lb (450 g).

Kitchen Yields
One 5-lb (2.3-kg) frozen block yields 4½ lb (2 kg) thawed meat.

BLUE CRAB
Blue crab is the common crab found along the Eastern Seaboard from Maine to Texas. They are available live, frozen whole, and in pieces canned, fresh, or pasteurized. When the crabs molt and the new shell is soft, they are marketed as soft-shell crabs.

BLUE CRAB MEAT
Lump crab meat is available in tins—fresh, frozen, or pasteurized. The size of the pieces is an important element of quality. The meat should be reasonably free of shell and should contain little roe. Cans should be opened as they are used, and the meat should not be handled. Good-quality crab meat should be wrapped in paper inside the can.

Pack:
1-lb (450-g) tins.

Kitchen Yields
1-lb (450-g) tin of canned crab meat contains 14 oz (400 g) meat, drained.

Serving sizes:

For salad, 7 oz (200 g); thus, one 1-lb (450-g) tin yields crab for 2 servings of salad. For cocktail, 5 oz (142 g); thus, one 1-lb (450-g) tin yields 2½ to 3 servings.

NOTE: Crab meat is very perishable.

SOFT-SHELL CRAB

Blue crab caught after molting while the new shell is still soft. Soft-shell crabs are harvested in the Chesapeake Bay and along the Atlantic coast. They are available live and frozen. Trapping molting crabs is prohibited on the Pacific coast.

Season:

April to July, depending on weather.

Pack:

Sold by the dozen live, in flats lined with seaweed.

Sizes:

Hotel Prime:
3 to 3½ in (76 to 89 mm) across.

Large Medium:
3½ to 4 in (89 to 100 mm).

Prime:
4½ to 5 in (114 to 127 mm).

Large Prime:
5 to 5½ in (127 to 140 mm).

Jumbo:
Over 5½ in (140 mm).

Kitchen Yields

Soft-shell crabs are small when the season starts.

Serving size:

4 small crabs, 3 prime crabs, or 2 large crabs as main course when sauteed or broiled; 1 large crab as main course when breaded and fried.

WHOLE BLUE CRAB

Whole blue crabs are marketed live or frozen.

Season:

May to August.

Pack:

Live by weight. Weight per crab varies.

DUNGENESS CRAB

Dungeness crabs are caught commercially from Alaska to southern California. Only male crabs of a specific size can be taken. Dungeness crabs are available fresh whole, frozen whole, and as picked crab meat frozen and canned.

Season:

From May to September in Alaska and the Pacific Northwest.

Pack:

Whole, with average weight of 2 to 2¼ lb (0.9 to 1 kg); clusters (half crabs); individual cut legs; cocktail claws; picked crab meat in 5-lb (2.3-kg) boxes.

Sizes:

22 to 24 lb (9.9 to 10.8 kg) per dozen, cooked whole.

Kitchen Yields

Varies depending on application.

Calories:

3½ oz (100 g) edible meat = 100 Calories.

OYSTER CRAB

Tiny crab, normally dusted with flour and fried. Available frozen.

Pack:

14-oz (400-g) tins.

Kitchen Yields

About 5 oz (142 g) per serving. Oyster crabs are often served combined with fried whitebaits (*see* Fish).

RED CRAB

An underutilized species, this deep-sea crab is trapped off the coast of New England. Most of the annual harvest is canned.

Size:

1 to 2 lb (450 to 900 g) for whole crab.

STONE CRAB

Caught off the coast of Florida and normally shipped whole. Only the claws are eaten.

Season:
October to April.

Pack:
Whole crabs are sold by weight or in bushels. Claws are sold in 1-lb (450-g) cans, fresh or frozen.

Kitchen Yields

Size:
About 3 whole, raw crabs per 1 lb (450 g).

CRANBERRIES

Cranberries are available canned, fresh, and frozen.

CANNED CRANBERRY SAUCE

Available strained and whole, with different flavors added.

Pack:
Six #10 cans, for all varieties. Smaller packs are available.

Kitchen Yields
One serving as garnish with turkey equals ⅓ cup (116 l); therefore, one #10 can yields 36 servings, and four #10 cans yield 100 servings; one case of 6 #10 cans yields 200 servings.

Calories:
⅓ cup (140 g) sweetened, strained sauce = 133 Calories.

FRESH CRANBERRIES

Season:
Late fall and winter.

Pack:
Twenty-four 1-lb (450-g) cello packs. Bulk packs are available.

Kitchen Yields
10 lb (4.5 kg) yields 12 qt (11.3 l) whole sauce or 10 qt (9.4 l) strained sauce.

Cranberry Sauce Formula
>   10 lb (4.5 kg) cranberries
>   20 lb (9.4 kg) sugar
>   5 qt (4.7 l) water

CRANBERRY JUICE

Available plain and mixed with other fruit juices.

Pack:
Forty-eight 6-oz (0.176-l) bottles; twelve 1-qt (0.94-l) glass jars; four 1-gal (3.8-l) jugs.

Kitchen Yields

Serving size:
6 oz (0.176 l); therefore, 1 qt (0.94 l) yields 5 servings, and 1 gal (3.8 l) yields 21 servings.

Calories:
6 oz (0.176 l) sweetened juice = 123 Calories.

CRAYFISH

Crayfish are available as fresh tail meat, as frozen tail meat, frozen whole, and live.

FRESH CRAYFISH TAILS

Available shelled, with fat on or washed. Shelf life is shorter with fat on.

Pack:
8-oz (226-g) or larger plastic bags.
Shelf life with fat on is about 2 weeks; shelf life washed is about 1 month.

Count:
None established.

FROZEN CRAYFISH TAILS

Available cooked and washed (with fat removed).

Packs:
8-oz (226-g), 16-oz (450-g), and other sizes of bags; IQF 8-oz (226-g) to 15-lb (6.8-kg) boxes.
Shelf life for frozen crayfish tails is 12 months.

Kitchen Yields
There is no established count. Approximate weight for tails broken out is ⅙ oz (5 g) each.

FROZEN WHOLE CRAYFISH

Frozen whole crayfish are available raw and cooked. Whole cooked crayfish are available flavored, such as with dill or with Cajun flavoring.

Pack:
For both cooked and raw frozen whole crayfish, 8⅞-oz, 17½-oz, and 35-oz (250-g, 500-g, and 1-kg) boxes. Count varies.

LIVE CRAYFISH
Available live from Louisiana, both wild and pond-raised.

Season:
March to June for wild crayfish; November to April for pond-raised crayfish.

Pack:
Sold live by weight, often in 30-lb (13.6-kg) boxes.

Count:
1 lb (450 g) comprises 12 to 15 crayfish.

Kitchen Yields
Counts are not reliable. Approximate size is ½ in (12 mm). Weight is about 1 oz (28 g) each.

Serving sizes:
35 to 40 whole crayfish per person when clients break out the meat themselves; 10 tails for appetizer with pasta; 25 tails for main course with pasta (plus 1 whole crayfish for decoration).

Do not buy any size smaller than 15 pieces per 1 lb. Crayfish suffocate easily. Make sure boxes are not filled too high and are kept refrigerated. Crayfish are freshwater animals and should be kept wet.

SOFT-SHELL CRAYFISH
Pond-raised crayfish are harvested at the time of molting. Available fresh locally, and frozen.

FRESH

Season:
Harvested from December to July.

Pack:
By weight.

Sizes:

Jumbo Premium:
20 or more per lb (450 g). Average weight is 23 g each.

Extra Large Premium:
20 to 25 per lb (450 g). Average weight is 18 to 23 g each.

Large Premium:
25 to 30 per lb (450 g). Average weight is 15 to 18 g each.

Medium Premium:
30 to 35 per lb (145 g). Average weight is 13 to 15 g each.

Soft Fryers:
Miscellaneous sizes, including those with claws missing.

Kitchen Yields
Between 70 and 90 percent of the animal is usable, depending on the amount of processing.

FROZEN
Available stuffed and breaded, fully dressed, and ready to cook.

Season:
Available year-round.

Pack and sizes:

Giants:
3½ in (89 mm) long and more. A master carton contains eight 2-dozen trays.

Big daddies:
3 to 3½ in (76 to 89 mm) A master carton contains eight 3-dozen trays.

CREAM

Types considered under this general heading are coffee or light cream, heavy cream, imitation sour cream, and sour cream.

COFFEE OR LIGHT CREAM
Coffee or light cream is approximately 18 percent fat.

Pack:
1-pint (0.47-l), 1-qt (0.94-l), and 5-gal (3.8-l) containers; individual packs. 24 qt. per case.

Kitchen Yields

Serving size:
¾ to 1 oz (0.022 to 0.029 l) per person with coffee.

Calories:
1 cup (0.235 l) light cream = 470 Calories.
1 tb (0.015 l) light cream = 30 Calories.

HEAVY CREAM
Heavy cream is approximately 36 percent fat.

Pack:
½-pint (0.235-l) and 1-qt (0.47-l) containers.

Kitchen Yield
Cream doubles in volume when whipped. Thus, 1 cup (0.235 l) unwhipped cream yields 1 pint (0.47 l) whipped cream, and 1 qt (0.94 l) unwhipped cream yields 2 qt (1.9 l) whipped cream.

Calories:
1 cup (0.235 l) as purchased = 820 Calories.

IMITATION SOUR CREAM
Sour dressing is an imitation sour cream made with nonfat dry milk.

Calories:
1 tb (12 g) = 20 Calories.

SOUR CREAM

Pack:
5-qt (4.7-l) tubs. Smaller packs are available.

Kitchen Yields

Serving size:
3 oz (85 g), with baked potato; thus, one 5-qt tub yields 50 servings.

Calories:
1 cup (0.235 l) = 495 Calories.
3 oz (85 g) = 180 Calories.

CREAM PUFF PASTE
See Pâté à Chou.

CRÊPES (THIN PANCAKES)

Formula
> 2 lb (900 g) cake flour
> 10 eggs
> 1 qt (0.94 l) milk
> 1 qt (0.94 l) light cream

Kitchen Yields
The preceding formula yields fifty 4-in (100-mm) crêpes.

CROISSANTS

Frozen croissants are available prebaked and ready to bake.
Ready-to-bake croissants are available filled and unfilled.

Sizes:

Plain:
1.3 oz (34 g) for bread baskets; 2.4 oz (68 g) for single servings; 3.5 oz (100 g) for entrées.

With sweet fillings:
2.8 to 3.9 oz (80 to 110 g).

With meat, cheese, or vegetable fillings:
5.3 oz (150 g).

CUCUMBERS

Cucumbers are classified as Hothouse (or Greenhouse) Cucumbers, Pickling (or Kirby) Cucumbers, and Slicing Cucumbers. Hothouse Cucumbers have almost no seeds and are burpless. They are often grown hydroponically.
   Cucumbers are often dipped in wax, which is harmless, before shipment.

HOTHOUSE CUCUMBERS
Hydroponically grown and virtually seedless.

Season:
Available year-round.

Pack:
By weight or by piece. Usually 12 cucumbers per case.

Average weight:
1 lb (450 g).

Kitchen Yields
For canapé bases, one cucumber yields 26 slices cut on a machine set at #30.

PICKLING (KIRBY) CUCUMBERS

Season:
Summer until early winter.

Pack:
By weight.

Size:
4 oz (226 g) average.

SLICING CUCUMBERS

Season:
Available year-round, with peak in May and June.

Pack:
26- to 28-lb (11.7- to 12.6-kg) cartons with 24 cucumbers each; 30- to 32-lb (13.5- to 14.4-kg) cartons with 35 or 40 cucumbers each; 50- to 55-lb (22.5- to 24.7-kg) cartons with 60, 70, 80, or 90 cucumbers each.

Kitchen Yields
1 lb (450 g) as purchased yields 15 oz (426 g) pared, or 11 oz (312 g) peeled with seeds removed.

Serving size:
½ cup unpared, sliced cucumber; 1 lb (450 g) yields 4 servings.

Calories:
6 to 8 slices, with peel, weighing 1 oz (28 g) = 5 Calories.

CURRANTS

BLACK CURRANTS
Aromatic black berries, available in late summer but seldom available fresh because the bulk of the harvest is processed. Black currants are the basic ingredient in the manufacture of Cassis.

Pack:
1 pint (0.47 l).

Size:
About ½ in (1.3 cm) in diameter or smaller.

Kitchen Yields
Currants are sold in small clusters that can be used whole as garnishes on fruit plates.

Calories:
4 oz (112 g) = 45 Calories.

RED CURRANTS
Red berries growing in clusters; tart when not completely ripe. Red currants are available in summer but rare because most of the harvest is used to produce jelly.

Pack:
1 pint (0.47 l).

Size:
½ in (1.3 cm) in diameter, or smaller.

Calories:
4 oz (112 g) = 45 Calories.

WHITE CURRANTS
Available in late summer, they are seldom found on the commercial market.

CUSTARD

CUSTARD SAUCE
Custard sauce is poured over fruit desserts such as raspberries.

Formula
> 1 qt (0.94 l) milk
> 1 tb cornstarch
> 6 oz (170 g) sugar
> 7 egg yolks
> Flavoring to taste

Kitchen Yields

Serving size:
2 oz (0.05 l), as sauce for dessert. The preceding formula yields 50 servings.

EGG CUSTARD

Egg custard is a light puddinglike dessert. Storage should be as brief as possible and must be carefully monitored to avoid spoilage.

Formula

    1 qt (0.94 l) hot milk
    1 cup, or 8 oz (224 g), sugar
    7 to 8 whole eggs
    Flavor to taste

Kitchen Yields

Serving size:
4½ oz (120 g). The preceding formula yields 10 servings.

D

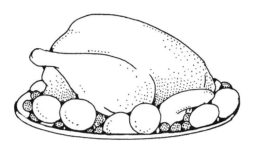

DAIKON

See Japanese Foods.

DAIRY PRODUCTS

See specific product names, such as Cream, Cheese, and Milk.

DANDELION GREENS

Used as a salad ingredient or as a separate cooked vegetable.

Season:
Year-round, with peak supply during April and May.

Pack:
By weight; often packed in bunches.

Kitchen Yields
When these greens are used for salads, cleaning waste is about 20 percent.

Serving sizes:
Varies for salad. As a vegetable, one ½ cup. One lb (450 g) as purchased yields 2½ to 3 cups (0.58 to 0.7 l) cooked.

Calories:
½ cup, or 2½ oz (70 g) of cooked, drained greens = 23 Calories.

DANISH PASTRIES

Items considered under this general heading include dough, cheese filling, and whole pastries. *See also* Apricot Glaze, under Apricots, and Prune Paste.

DANISH PASTRY DOUGH

Formula
> 2 lb (0.9 kg) sugar
> 4 qt (3.7 l) milk
> 2 lb (0.9 kg) yeast
> 4 qt (3.7 l) whole eggs
> 4 lb (1.8 kg) butter
> 20 lb (9 kg) patent flour
> 4 lb (1.8 kg) cake flour
> ¼ cup (50 g) salt
> Lemon flavor and nutmeg to taste

Make dough and let rest. Then fold in:

> 12 lb (5.4 kg) sweet butter

Kitchen Yield

Miniature Danish:
Scale 1½ oz (40 g) each before filling. The preceding formula yields 50 dozen pieces of pastry.

Breakfast Danish for baskets:
Scale 2 oz (55 g) each before filling. The preceding formula yields 37 dozen pieces of pastry.

Large Danish:
Scale 3½ oz (100 g) each before filling. The preceding formula yields 22 dozen pieces of pastry.

DANISH PASTRY FILLING

Formula
> 16 lb (7.2 kg) bakers cheese
> 6 lb (2.7 kg) sugar
> 32 eggs
> 1 lb (450 g) cake flour
> Lemon or vanilla flavor to taste

Kitchen Yields

Serving size:
1½ oz (42 g) for regular pastry; the total mix from the preceding formula yields filling for 260 pieces of Danish pastry.

WHOLE DANISH PASTRIES

Quantities needed:
For breakfast parties, two 2-oz pieces per person.

Calories:
One round, commercial-quality, 4¼-in (112-mm), 2⅓-oz (65-g) pieces = 275 Calories.

DATES

Domestically, the date industry is centered in Indio, California. Several varieties are grown. Medjool dates are extra-large dates. Dates are shipped fresh or dried, pitted or with pit in.

DRIED DATES

Types available:
Whole dates, pitted and unpitted; pieces without pits; macerated dates (ground, chopped, and broken pieces); slab dates (ground, chopped, and broken pieces in slab form). Both domestic and imported dates are available.

Pack:
15-lb (6.7-kg) cartons of whole pitted dates; 30-lb (13.5-kg) cartons of date pieces; 40-lb (18-kg) cartons of macerated dates; 50-lb (22.5-kg) cartons of slab dates.
Sizes and counts vary.

Kitchen Yields
1 lb (450 g) whole, dried dates with pits yields 2½ cups (0.5 l).
6¼ oz (177 g) with pits yield 1 cup chopped dates (0.325 l).
Ten pitted dates weigh 3 oz (85 g).

Calories:
1 cup chopped dates weighing 6¼ oz (175 g) = 490 Calories.

FRESH DATES
Fresh dates are available in some markets during the fall but are seldom available nationally.

Season:
Fall.

Calories:
Ten whole, pitted dates weighing 2⅞ oz (80 g) = 220 Calories.
1 cup chopped dates weighing 6½ oz (180 g) = 460 Calories.

DILL

See Herbs & Spices.

DOUGH

See entries for individual baked products, such as Biscuits, Bread, and Danish Pastry. For modeling dough, *see* Salt Dough.

DRESSING FORMULAS

COCKTAIL SAUCE

Formula
1 qt (0.94 l) tomato purée
One #10 can (3 l) chili sauce
One #10 can (3 l) catsup
1 pint (0.47 l) grated horseradish in vinegar
1 cup (0.232 l) lemon juice
1 oz (0.029 l) tabasco sauce
2 oz (56 g) salt
4 oz (112 g) sugar

Kitchen Yield
The preceding formula makes 2 gal (7.5 l) sauce.

Serving size:
2 oz. The total mix from the preceding formula yields 125 servings.

FRENCH DRESSING

Formula
1 gal (3.8 l) oil
½ gal (1.9 l) cider vinegar
½ gal (1.9 l) wine vinegar
1 cup (0.22 l) prepared mustard
1 cup (0.22 l) dry mustard
1 cup (0.22 l) sugar
½ cup (0.12 l) crushed peppercorns
½ cup (0.12 l) salt

Kitchen Yields
The preceding formula makes 2 gal (7.6 l) dressing.

Serving size:
1 oz. The total mix from the preceding formula yields 250 servings.

GREEN GODDESS DRESSING

Formula
    1 gal (3.8 l) mayonnaise
    ½ gal (1.9 l) sour cream
    1 qt (0.9 l) chopped parsley
    1 qt (0.9 l) chopped, uncooked spinach
    1 pint (0.47 l) chopped chives
    One 28-oz (780-g) can anchovy fillets with oil
    ¼ cup chopped garlic
    ¼ cup lemon juice
    1 cup (0.22 l) tarragon vinegar

Purée in food processor.

Kitchen Yields
The preceding formula makes 2¼ gal (8.5 l)
dressing.

Serving size:
2 oz (56 g). The total mix from the preceding
formula yields 140 servings.

RUSSIAN DRESSING

Formula
    3 qt (2.8 l) mayonnaise
    1 qt + 1 cup (1.1 l) cocktail sauce, canned or
        prepared (see above recipe)
    1 pint (0.47 l) cooked chopped eggs
    1 cup (0.23 l) lemon juice

Kitchen Yields
The preceding formula makes 1 gal (3.7 l) dressing.

Serving size:
1½ oz (42 g). The total mix from the preceding
formula yields 85 servings.

THOUSAND ISLAND DRESSING

Formula
    1 gal (3.8 l) mayonnaise
    ½ gal (1.9 l) cocktail sauce
    ½ gal (1.9 l) whipped cream, 36 percent
    1 qt (0.9 l) chopped dill pickle relish
    1 qt (0.9 l) cooked, chopped beets, drained
    1 cup (0.23 l) lemon juice

Kitchen Yields
The preceding formula makes 2½ gal (9.5 l)
dressing.

Serving size:
1½ oz (42 g). The preceding formula yields 200
servings.

VINAIGRETTE MARINADE
This marinade is used for marinating artichokes
or mushrooms.

Formula
    1 qt (0.9 l) dry white wine
    1 pint (0.47 l) wine vinegar
    2 qt (1.8 l) olive oil
    1 tb chopped garlic
    2 tb thyme
    1 cup (0.23 l) lemon juice
    1 cup (0.23 l) chopped onions
    ½ cup (0.11 l) prepared mustard
    3 tb crushed peppercorns

Kitchen Yields
The preceding formula makes 1 gal (3.8 l) marinade.

DUCK

Duck is available fresh or frozen, as well as in
various processed forms. *Duckling* is a term used
for young duck. Virtually all ducks coming to the
market are young and have been raised under
controlled conditions.

FRESH OR FROZEN DUCKLING
Most ducklings are shipped frozen, but fresh
ducklings are also available in some markets. The
most common breeds are Barberie, Mallard, and
Peking. Various other breeds also reach the
market.

BARBERIE DUCKLING
Bred from Muscovy stock, this duckling is often
sold as breast only, to be grilled and served
medium rare. Barberie ducklings are leaner than
other breeds.

BARBERIE DUCKLING BREASTS

Pack:

Boneless breast (male):
Six 27- to 38-oz (0.75- to 1-kg) double breasts.

Bone Breast (Female):
Twelve 19- to 23-oz (0.53- to 0.64 g) double breasts.

Kitchen Yields
Male (drake) double breasts yield 5 to 6 servings; female (hen) double breasts yield 2 to 3 servings. Duckling breasts are best served medium rare.

BARBERIE DUCKLING LEGS

Pack:
36 per case.

Sizes:
5- to 7-oz (140 to 200 g) hen legs; 10 to 12 oz (280 to 340 g) drake legs.

Kitchen Yields
One drake leg constitutes 1 main-course serving. One hen leg constitutes 1 appetizer serving.

WHOLE BARBERIE DUCKLING

Pack:
22- to 32-lb (9.9- to 12.8-kg) case of four drakes; 21- to 30-lb (9.45- to 13.5-kg) case of six hens.

Sizes:
Drakes:
6 to 8 lb (2.7 to 3.6 kg), on average.

Hens:
3.5 to 6 lb (1.5 to 2.7 kg), on average.
Weights include gizzards, necks, and hearts.

Kitchen Yields

Servings:
Medium-sized Drake:
5 to 6 servings, using breast only.

Medium-sized Hen:
2, using breast only.

MALLARD DUCKLING
Farm-raised gamy birds. Leaner than Peking ducklings.

Pack:
10 to 12 birds per carton.

Average sizes:
1¾ to 2¾ lb (0.8 to 1.2 kg).

Kitchen Yields
When serving half a duckling per person, purchase larger sizes.

Serving size:
One half duckling, including legs, as a main course.

PEKING DUCKLING
The prevalent domesticated variety of duck is the Peking duck. All ducklings, regardless of whether they are fresh or frozen, are shipped cleaned and eviscerated.

PEKING DUCKLING BREAST
Boneless duckling breasts.

Pack:
Twelve breasts per bag, and 4 bags per master carton.

Sizes:
10 to 12 oz (280 to 340 g); 12 to 14 oz (340 to 400 g); 16 to 18 oz (450 to 510 g)

Kitchen Yields
The breasts are boneless. They should be served well-done.

Serving size:
One 12- to 14-oz (340- to 400-g) breast.
One 12-oz (340-g) raw breast yields 8 oz (224 g) cooked.

Calories:
8 oz (224 g) cooked breast = 640 Calories.

PEKING DUCKLING LEGS

Pack:
36 legs per case.

Size:
6 to 8 oz (170 to 226 g), bone in.

Kitchen Yields

Serving size:
2 legs per portion. Thus, one case contains 18 portions.

WHOLE PEKING DUCKLING
Available fresh or frozen. Long Island, New York, was once a major producer of these ducklings.

Pack:
Six ducklings in various weight ranges.

Sizes:
4 to 4½ lb (1.8 to 2 kg); 4½ to 5 lb (2 to 2.2 kg); 5 to 6 lb (2.2 to 2.7 kg).

Kitchen Yields
Purchase at least the 4½-lb (2-kg) size when serving portions of half a duckling per person. Purchase the 6-lb (2.7-kg) size when serving portions of one-quarter duckling per person.

PROCESSED DUCKLING
Various processed duckling products are available.

BREADED DUCKLING STRIPS (FROZEN, RAW)
Lightly breaded with almonds.

Pack:
5-lb (2.3-kg) box.

Size:
1- to 1½-oz (28- to 42-g) strips.

Kitchen Yields
About 65 pieces per box. Use as hors d'oeuvres or as appetizer.

IQF DUCKLING MEAT
Boneless, uncooked leg meat; mostly skinless.

Pack:
5-lb (2.2-kg) box.

Kitchen Yields

Serving size:
5 oz (142 g), stir-fried.

ROASTED DUCKLING HALF
Fully cooked product; available boneless or with bone in.

Pack:
12 boneless halves; 10 bone-in halves.

Size:
11 to 13 oz (312 to 370 g), boneless; 14 oz (400 g), boneless, with sauce; 15 to 17 oz (426 to 480 g), bone in.

Kitchen Yields
Product is ready to use. There is no waste.

SKINLESS, MARINATED DUCKLING BREAST (UNCOOKED)
Available plain or marinated in teriyaki, vinaigrette, or green peppercorns.

Packs and sizes:
Thirty-two 4-oz (113-g) portion per case; sixteen 6-oz (170-g) portions per case; sixteen 8-oz (226-g) portions per case.

Kitchen Yields

Serving sizes:
4 oz (113 g) as appetizer; two 6-oz (170-g) breast, or one 8-oz (224-g) breast as a main course.

SMOKED DUCK
Available whole.

Weight:
3½ to 5 lb (1.5 to 2.2 kg).

DULSE

See Seaweed.

DUMPLINGS

Formula
    1 lb (450 g) cake flour
    4 tsp baking powder
    1 tsp salt
    14 oz (400 g or 0.4 l) milk

Kitchen Yields
Thirty 1-oz (56-g) dumplings.

E

EGGS

FRESH EGGS
Freshness, grade, and size are the important considerations in purchasing and using shell eggs. Eggs are graded by the USDA or by the individual state. Almost all foodservice facilities use grade A eggs. *See also* Quail Eggs.

Pack:
One case contains 30 dozen shell eggs; one-half case contains 15 dozen shell eggs; one layer containers 2½ dozen (or 30) shell eggs.

Market Sizes:
Table E-1 lists available sizes of fresh eggs, together with their unit weight.

Size conversions:
Table E-2 lists size substitutions for recipes that call for eggs.

Kitchen Yields

Serving sizes:
For individual servings of scrambled eggs or omelette, 3 eggs; therefore, one case eggs yields 120 individual servings, two layers broken eggs yield 20 individual portions, and one-half case broken eggs yields 60 individual portions. For banquet service of scrambled eggs or omelette, 2½ eggs per person; therefore, one case eggs yields 144 banquet servings; two layers eggs yield 24 banquet portions; and one-half case eggs yields 60 banquet portions.

Quantities:
For chopped, boiled eggs, 1 cup is equivalent to 4 large eggs.
For sliced eggs, 1 egg yields 6 slices.
For egg whites, 1 cup beaten is equivalent to ½ cup unbeaten whites.

Volume conversions:
The following equivalencies exist between volume measures and numbers of large eggs.

Whole eggs:
1 cup = 8 oz (0.235 l) = 5 eggs.
1 pint = 16 oz (0.47 l) = 10 eggs.
1 qt = 32 oz (0.94 l) = 20 eggs.
1 gal = 128 oz (3.8 l) = 80 eggs (2⅔ layers).

Egg yolks:
1 cup = 8 oz (0.235 l) = 11 to 12 yolks.
1 pint = 16 oz (0.47 l) = 24 yolks (2 dozen).
1 qt = 32 oz (0.94 l) = 46 to 48 yolks (4 dozen).
1 gal = 128 oz (3.8 l) = 190 yolks (16 dozen).

Egg whites:
1 cup = 8 oz (0.235 l) = 7½ egg whites.
1 pint = 16 oz (0.47 l) = 15 egg whites.
1 qt = 32 oz (0.94 l) = 30 egg whites.
1 gal = 128 oz (3.8 l) = 120 egg whites (11 dozen).

Calories:
One raw 1¾-oz (50-g) large egg = 80 Calories.
One raw ⅝-oz (17-g) large egg yolk = 65 Calories.
One raw 1¹/₁₆-oz (33-g) large egg white = 15 Calories.
One hard-cooked 1¾-oz (50-g) large egg = 80 Calories.
One large egg, fried in butter = 85 Calories.
Two large eggs, fried in butter = 170 Calories.
Three-large-egg plain omelette = 270 Calories.

Table E-1 Sizes and Minimum Weights of Fresh Eggs

Size	Minimum Weight by Dozen	Minimum Weight per Case
Jumbo	30 oz (840 g)	56 lb (25.2 kg)
Extra large	27 oz (756 g)	50½ lb (22.7 kg)
Large	24 oz (672 g)	45 lb (20.2 kg)
Medium	21 oz (590 g)	39½ lb (17.8 kg)
Small	18 oz (504 g)	34 lb (15.3 kg)
Peewee	15 oz (420 g)	28 lb (12.6 kg)

Table E-2 Eggs Size Substitution Chart

Jumbo	Extra Large	Medium	Small
2	2	2	3
5	6	7	8
10	12	13	15
21	24	27	28
44	50	56	62

FROZEN SHELLED EGGS

Frozen shelled eggs are available as whole eggs, yolks only, egg whites only, and whole eggs with extra yolks. Frozen eggs yolks mixed with sugar are also available.

Pack:
30-lb (13.5-kg) can; 15-lb (6.75-kg) can.

Weight conversions:
The following equivalencies exist for large eggs without sugar.

Whole eggs:
One 30-lb (13.5-kg) can = 300 eggs (25 dozen or 10 layers).
One 15-lb (6.75-kg) can = 150 eggs (12½ dozen or 5 layers).

Egg yolks:
One 30-lb (13.5-kg) can = 675 yolks.
One 15-lb (6.75-kg) can = 338 yolks.

Egg whites:
One 30-lb (13.5-kg) can = 540 egg whites.
One 15-lb (6.75-kg) can = 270 egg whites.
The following equivalencies exist for frozen egg yolks mixed with sugar.
One 30-lb (13.5-kg) can = 608 yolks and 3 lb (1.35 kg) sugar.
One 15-lb (6.75-kg) can = 304 yolks and 1.5 lb (675 g) sugar.
1 cup = 8 oz (0.235 l) = 10 yolks and ⅔ oz (22 g) sugar.

Table E-3 Conversion Amounts for Dehydrated Eggs, Water, and Fresh Eggs

Large Eggs	Dried Whole Sifted	Water
6	3 oz (85 g): 1 cup	1 cup (0.23 l)
12	6 oz (170 g): 2 cups	2 cups (0.47 l)
24	12 oz (340 g): 1 qt	1 qt (0.94 l)
50	25 oz (700 g): 2 qt + ⅓ cup	2 qt + ⅓ cup: (1.95 l)
100	51 oz (1.43 kg): 1 gal + ⅔ cup	1 gal + ⅔ cup: (3.95 l)

OTHER EGG PRODUCTS

Eggs can be purchased hard-boiled, dehydrated, and in various ready-to-use mixes. Table E-3 identifies conversion amounts for dehydrated eggs plus water and for large fresh eggs.

SUBSTITUTES FOR EGG

Egg substitutes are commercial products made with egg whites and cholesterol-free additives. Products can be used for omelette and scrambled eggs.

Pack:
Twelve 2-lb (0.9-kg) cartons; twenty-four 1-lb (450-g) cartons.

Kitchen Yields

Quantities:
¼ cup, or 2 oz (0.56 g) is equivalent to 1 egg.
1 cup, or 8 oz (0.226 g) is equivalent to 4 eggs.
1 pint, or 1 lb (450 g) is equivalent to 8 eggs.

Calories:
½ cup, or 4 oz (112 g), egg substitute = 60 Calories.

EGGPLANTS

Eggplants are grown in many states and are always in good supply because the seasons overlap in the various growing areas. Baby eggplants are also available; *see* Baby Vegetables. Chinese and Japanese species are marketed, too; *see* Chinese Foods and Japanese Foods.

Season:
Available year-round.

Pack:
20- to 22-lb (9- to 9.9-kg) lugs containing 24 eggplants; 30- to 34-lb (13.5- to 15.3-kg) bushels containing 30 to 35 eggplants.

Weight:
About 15 oz (420 g) each.

Kitchen Yields
Size and shape are important for best yield. Best size is 3 in (76 mm) in diameter and 6 in (152 mm) long.

One eggplant produces 2 cups diced pieces or 22 cross slices, each ¼ in (6 mm) thick; 1 cup diced eggplant weighs 6 oz (170 g).

Calories:
4 oz (112 g) = 28 Calories.

EGGROLL WRAPPERS

See Chinese Foods.

ELDERBERRIES, ELDER BLOSSOMS

Shrub with clusters of fragrant blossoms, which mature into purple, rather acidic berries.

Season:
Blossoms in spring, berries in fall.

Kitchen Yields
Berries make excellent stewed fruit, pie, and jelly and can be fermented into wine. Blossoms can be dipped in batter and deep-fried.

ELEPHANT GARLIC

See Garlic.

ENDIVE

See Belgian Endive.

ESCARGOTS

Most commonly available canned and imported. Much is imported from Asia and is sometimes repacked in France. Large snails are of the Asian Achatina variety, and small snails are of the French Petit Gris variety. Petit Gris are also cultivated in California. Clean, empty shells are sold separately.

Pack:

Giant:
4½-oz (127-g) packs with 12 snails each.
18-oz (511-g) packs with 60 snails each.

Extra Large:
4½-oz (127-g) packs with 18 snails each.
9-oz (255-g) packs with 36 snails each.
18-oz (511-g) packs with 72 snails each.

Very Large:
4½-oz (127-g) packs with 24 snails each.
9-oz (255-g) packs with 48 snails each.
18-oz (511-g) packs with 96 snails each.

Petit Gris:
7½-oz (213-g) packs with 36 snails each.

Extra Large Shells:
Two 864-piece packs = 1,728-piece case.

Very Large Shells:
Two 1,152-piece packs = 2,304-piece case.
Other packs are available.

F

FENNEL

Fennel is often confused with cultivated anise, which forms a bulb. Some wild fennel reaches the market in some parts of the United States. *See also* Anise.

Kitchen Yields

The stalks are used as either a raw or cooked vegetable. The seeds are used in flavoring stocks and baked goods.

FIDDLEHEADS

These items, which are eaten as a cooked green vegetable, are available canned, fresh, and frozen. Fiddleheads are the tightly curled tips of young fern fronds. Only the tips of ostrich ferns (one of many fern species) should be used.

CANNED FIDDLEHEADS

The supply is small and mostly appears in retail packs.

FRESH FIDDLEHEADS

Season:
Middle of April until June.

Pack:
By weight.

Kitchen Yields

There is basically no waste. Only the thin brown skin must be removed.

Serving size:
3 oz (85 g); 1 lb (450 g) as purchased yields 5 servings.

FROZEN FIDDLEHEADS

Only a small quantity in retail pack reaches the market. There is no waste.

FIGS

Figs are available canned, dried, and fresh.

CANNED FIGS

Available whole, whole split, and broken in syrup of various densities. Kadota is the most commonly used variety for canning.

Packs:
Six #10 cans; twenty-four #2½ cans; twenty-four #2 cans; twenty-four #303 cans.

Drained weights:
#10 can weighs 63 oz (1.8 kg); #2½ weighs 18 oz (510 g); #2 can weighs 12½ oz (355 g); #303 weighs 10 oz (284 g).

Count:
#10 can contains 70 to 90 whole figs, or 8 cups drained fruit.

Kitchen Yields

Serving size:
Four fruits; thus, one #10 can yields 18 to 22 servings, and one case of #10 cans yields approximately 110 to 130 servings.

Calories:
Four fruits, or 4¾ oz (130 g) with syrup = 100 Calories.

DRIED FIGS

A number of varieties are on the market. Adriatic, Calymirna, and Kadota figs are light to dark brown; Mission figs are dark purple to black. Figs are often imported for specific ethnic consumers.

Pack:
By weight.

Size:
Available whole, loose, and chopped for baking.

Count:
1 lb (450 g) is equivalent to 30 average-size figs.

Kitchen Yields

1 lb (450 g) dried figs produces 2¼ lb (1 kg) cooked figs.

FRESH FIGS

The important varieties are Calymirna (a green fig when ripe) and Black Mission. Fresh figs are highly perishable.

Season:
June to October.

Pack:
3¾-lb (1.7 kg) flats containing 30 figs each; 5-lb (2.2 kg) flats containing 56 figs each.

Weight:
1½ oz (42 g) each and larger

Kitchen Yields
Calymirna figs are often peeled for service. The peeling loss is about 20 percent.

Calories:
Three fresh fruits, weighing about 4½ oz (126 g) = 258 Calories.

FILBERTS

Filberts, also called *hazelnuts,* are available shelled and in the shell, but they are almost always purchased shelled. They can be obtained peeled or with skin on, whole or chopped.

Pack:
By weight. Often sold in vacuum cans or in boxes.

Kitchen Yields
1 cup, or 4 oz (112 g), chopped uses 80 kernels.
1 lb (450 g) in shell yields 1⅓ cups nutmeat.
1 lb (450 g) nutmeat is equivalent to 3½ cups.

Calories:
1 cup, or 4 oz (112 g) = 730 Calories.

FILO

FILO SHEETS
Filo sheets (also called *phyllo sheets* or *strudel leaves*) are shipped frozen and should be defrosted in the refrigerator for best results. Available as sheets and as kataife (shredded dough).

Sizes:
Standard size is 14 × 8 in (355 × 100 mm); other widely available sizes are 12 × 17 in (304 × 430 mm) and 9 × 13 in (230 × 330 mm). Other sizes are available in bulk.

Thickness:
#4 (thinnest) to #10 (thickest).

Pack:
Case of 12, 16, 24, or 30 packages, each weighing 1 lb (450 g).

Kitchen Yields
The number of filo sheets obtained per package is approximate because some will break during handling.

Counts:

#4 (thinnest):
twenty-six 12 × 17 in (300 × 430 mm) sheets.

#7 (medium):
twenty-two 14 × 18 in (355 × 460 mm) sheets;
eighteen 17 × 14 in (430 × 355 mm) sheets;
twenty 12 × 17 in (300 × 430 mm) sheets.

#10 (thickest):
eighteen 12 × 17 in (300 × 430 mm) sheets.
It is difficult to calculate a yield for kataife, because it is shredded dough, and its use varies.

FILO DOUGH (STRUDEL DOUGH)
Formula
    1½ lb (0.675 g) bread flour
    1½ oz (42 g) oil
    2 eggs
    1½ cups (0.35 l) warm water

FISH

Fish are categorized as canned, fresh or frozen, frozen or prepared products, and smoked or cured.

CANNED FISH
ANCHOVIES
Available packed in oil as flat fillets or as rolled fillets with caper in center. Also available salted. Anchovy paste is marketed in tubes. Practically all anchovy products are imported.

Pack:
Twenty-four 28-oz (795-g) cans of flat fillets;
twenty-four 13-oz (370-g) cans of flat fillets;

forty-eight 2-oz (56.8-g) cans of flat fillets; forty-eight 2-oz (56.8-g) of rolled fillets. Salt-packed anchovies are packed by weight.

Drained weight:
About 20 percent of a tin of anchovies is oil.

Kitchen Yields
Salt-packed anchovies can be rinsed and packed in oil. They can be used as a less expensive substitute for oil-packed anchovies. Anchovies packed in olive oil are more expensive than those packed in other oils. Fillets are approximately the same size in all larger cans, and they are slightly smaller in the smaller cans.

GEFILTE FISH
Fish dumpling, normally made with carp. A traditional item in Jewish cookery. Gefilte fish is available in jars, packed in its own jellied broth. For gefilte fish formula, *see* Frozen or Prepared Fish products.

Pack:
Six 1-qt (0.94-l) jars.

Kitchen Yields
About 18 to 22 per 1 qt.

Serving size:
Two pieces per person as appetizer.

HERRING
See Smoked and Cured Fish, under this same general entry.

MACKEREL
Available whole or as fillet, smoked or plain, packed in oil.

Pack:
15-oz (426-g) cans. Other sizes are available.

Kitchen Yields
One 15-oz (420-g) can contains 12½ oz (350 g) mackerel, drained.

Serving size:
2 oz as appetizer.

SALMON
Most canned salmon is produced in Alaska. There are five species of Alaskan salmon, each with its own color, texture, and cost. Most canned salmon is packed in brine. Some specialty packs of smoked or flavored salmon packed in oil are available, but they have little commercial distribution.

Varieties:

Red sockeye salmon:
Meat is deep red and firm; used in salads.

Pink salmon:
Pale color; less expensive than red sockeye.

King or chinook salmon:
Color ranges from deep red to white; meat is rich in oils and excellent for salads.

Coho or silver salmon:
Orange-red flesh; all-purpose use.

Chum or keta salmon:
Pale-colored, coarse-textured meat; this is the least expensive variety.

Packs:
Forty-eight 3¾-oz (105-g) cans; forty-eight 7¾-oz (220-g) cans; twenty-four 15½-oz (440-g) cans; six 4-lb (1.8-kg) cans.

Drained weights:
Good-quality salmon is solid-packed. Drained weights are about 10 percent less than net weights.

Kitchen Yields
For individual servings, use 3¾-oz (105-g) cans. For salads, use red sockeye salmon in the larger cans. One serving of salmon salad uses 4 oz (112 g) fish.

Calories:
3¾ oz (105 g) king salmon = 188 Calories.
red sockeye = 161 Calories.
coho or silver = 150 Calories.
pink salmon = 130 Calories.
chum or keta = 133 Calories.

SARDINES
Most products are packed in oil, but specialty packs such as sardines in tomato sauce or in mustard sauce are available. Distinction is made between skin-on sardines and skinless and boneless

sardines. The bone structure is very soft, and all canned sardines can be eaten in their entirety.

Much product is imported from Portugal, and other countries are also major producers. There is some domestic production. The quality of the packing oil is important; better sardines are packed in olive oil. Brisling, also called *silt* or *small sardines,* are normally imported from Norway and are packed in oil.

Pack:
Twenty-four 15-oz (420-g) oval cans, usually packed in California; forty-eight 12-oz (340-g) cans, usually packed in Maine; one hundred 7-oz (198-g) cans; one hundred 3¾-oz (105-g) cans.

Drained weights:
One 15-oz (426-g) can weighs 11½ oz (326 g); one 12-oz (340-g) can weighs 10¾ oz (305 g).

Count:
Varies greatly. Brisling number about eight fish per 3¾-oz (105-g) can.

Kitchen Yields
The size of fish varies greatly. Domestic products normally use smaller fish. Portuguese sardines are considered to be of high quality.

Serving size:
2 oz as appetizer or on sandwich. Serving size is most often determined by piece size.

Calories:
3¾ oz (105 g) canned, packed in oil, drained = 218 Calories.

TUNA
Available packed in oil or in water. The cans are labeled *light meat, dark meat,* or *mixed meat.* Canned tuna is manufactured from a number of different species. Albacore tuna has the lightest meat. Bonito is not considered tuna and cannot be labeled as such. Some canned tuna, most often packed in water, is imported from Asia. High-quality tuna packed in olive oil is imported from Mediterranean countries.

Product varieties:
Prime Fillet—Solid Pack or Fancy Pack:
Meat from the loin; should be used for cold plates.

Chunk Style:
Mixture of pieces; up to 50 percent can be less than ½ in (12 mm) in size. This pack should be used for salads.

Flaked Tuna:
Mixture of small pieces. Can be used for salad, especially in sandwiches.

Grated Tuna:
Almost granular, but not pasty. Can be used as sandwich filling.

Pack:
Forty-eight 3½-oz (100-g) cans; forty-eight 6½- or 7-oz (184- or 200-g) cans; forty-eight 8-oz (224-g) cans; twenty-four 9¼-oz (260-g) cans; twenty-four 13-oz (370-g) cans; twelve 42-oz (1.2-kg) cans; six 66½-oz (1.9-kg) cans.

Drained weights:
One 66½-oz (1.9-kg) can weighs 60 oz (1.7 kg); one 7-oz (200-g) can weighs 6 oz (68 g).

Kitchen Yields
For salads mixed with mayonnaise, buy tuna packed in water. For chunk tuna salad plate, use only tuna packed in oil.

Serving sizes:
One 3½-oz can for single salad plate; 3 oz for tuna salad sandwich, mixed with celery and mayonnaise. One 66½-oz (1.9-kg) can yields 20 servings for sandwiches.

Calories:
One 3½-oz (100-g) can tuna, packed in oil, drained = 170 Calories.
1 cup, or 7 oz (200 g) tuna salad made with celery and mayonnaise = 350 Calories.

FRESH OR FROZEN FISH
Fresh and frozen fish can be purchased with the following specifications:

Round: not eviscerated; seldom marketed.
Drawn: also called *gutted;* entrails removed.
Dressed: scaled and eviscerated, with head and fins removed.
Fillets: meat cut away lengthwise from fish's spine.

Steaks: Cut cross-sectionally across fish's spine, including bones and skin.

Both fresh and frozen fillets are marketed with skin on or with skin removed. Sometimes, some bones are still attached. When comparing prices, buyer should inquire how fillets are dressed.

ANCHOVIES
Small quantities of anchovies are available from the Mediterranean and from the Pacific.

Season:
Available year-round.

Pack:
By weight.

Count:
Varies; often 12 to 18 fish per 1 lb (450 g).

Kitchen Yields
The fish spoils very rapidly; its shelf life is less than 48 hours.

BASS

BLACK SEA BASS
Harvested along the Atlantic coast.

Season:
Available year-round, with peak in spring.

Average size:
1½ lb (680 g).

Kitchen Yields
Purchase in fillets; spines are very sharp. Waste is about 50 percent.

STRIPED BASS
Nearly extinct on the Atlantic coast and protected by a complete ban on commercial fishing, this once very popular fish is currently unavailable wild. Farm-raised striped bass has come onto the market to fill the void.

Season:
Available year-round, with peaks in late fall and early spring.

Sizes:
1 to 1¼ lb (450 to 560 g) dressed, farm-raised; 6 to 8 lb (2.7 to 3.6 kg); 8 to 10 lb (3.6 to 4.5 kg).

Kitchen Yields
Purchase whole fish to ensure freshness. Striped bass may be served as fillet for appetizer or for main course; whole poached bass may be used as buffet centerpiece.

Serving sizes:
For appetizer, 3 oz (85 g); for main course, 7 oz (200 g).

Waste:
About 40 percent. From drawn fish.

Best size:
For filleting purchase 6- to 8-lb (2.7- to 3.6-kg) whole fish. One 7-lb (3.2-kg) fish yields 4 lb (1.8 kg) fillet, and 4-lb (1.8-kg) fillet yields 20 appetizer servings or 8 main-course servings. For buffet service, purchase 8- to 10-lb (3.6- to 4.5-kg) whole fish. One such fish yields 35 servings when served with other items.

Farm-raised fish:
One 1¼-lb (560-g) bass yields two 6-oz (170-g) fillets.

WHITE BASS
Related to the Mexican *corvina,* the fish is not a true bass. Available whole and as fillets.

Season:
Summer.

Average size:
10 lb (4.5 kg).

Kitchen Yields
Excellent fish, resembling weakfish. Purchase fillets.

BLUEFISH
Popular and abundant Atlantic coast commercial and sport fish. Available whole and in fillets. Large fish can be oily and tough.

Season:
Summer.

Average size:
For food service: 2 lb (0.9 kg) or more.

Kitchen Yields
2- to 2½-lb (0.9- to 1.1-kg) dressed fish yields 2 servings each 8 oz (224 g)

Calories:
8 oz (226 g), baked with ½ oz (12 g) butter = 360 Calories.

BLOWFISH

Also called *chicken of the seas,* this fish is harvested in the Atlantic.

Season:
Summer.

Average sizes:
Skinned tail pieces, 4 to 8 oz (112 to 226 g).

Kitchen Yields
Purchase skinned tail pieces only. Cook whole.

BONITO

This member of the mackerel family resembles tuna. It is found along the Atlantic coast. Most of the catch is canned. Fresh fish should be soaked in brine and acidulated water to lessen the strong taste. Weights range from 5 to 12 lb (2.3 to 5.4 kg).

Season:
Available June to October.

Kitchen Yields
Normally sold in fillets. Yield depends on trim of fillet.

BRILL

Also called *barbue,* this is an imported flatfish resembling flounder. It is sometimes imported whole.

Pack:
10-kg (22.2-lb) crates.

Average size:
Varies; normally 2 to 4 lb (0.9 to 1.8 kg).

BUTTERFISH

Small, thin fish of little commercial distribution, also called whiting or California pompano. Available on both the Atlantic and the Pacific coasts.

Season:
Summer.

Average sizes:

Whole Atlantic fish:
From 4 to 12 oz (113 to 340 g).

Pacific fillets: From 4 oz to 6 oz (112 to 168 g).

Kitchen Yields
Use whole fish for pan-frying.

CARP

Bony freshwater fish with little commercial importance in the United States. Used in making gefilte fish, a fish dumpling, and popular in central Europe. Large fish can taste muddy.

Season:
Winter and early spring.

Average sizes:
3 to 5 lb (1.4 to 2.2 kg).

Kitchen Yields
Red-flesh fish, very bony with large head and large belly cavity. Some species have scales; others do not. Purchase scaled and in fillet.

Waste factor:
Purchased whole, 60 percent; purchased in fillets, 20 percent.

CATFISH

Most catfish are freshwater fish, although at least one species of sea catfish is also marketed. The most popular commercial species is the channel catfish. Most production is farmed in southern states. Catfish is normally sold in fillets. *See also* Blackened Catfish, under Frozen or Prepared Fish Products.

Average size:
For whole fish, 15 to 20 lb (6.8 to 9.0 kg).

Pack:
IQF frozen fillets with and without nuggets (small flank under head): 3 to 5 oz (85 to 140 g); 5 to 7 oz (140 to 200 g); 7 to 9 oz (200 to 252 g); 9 to 11 oz (252 to 308 g). IQF fillet strips, nuggets, and steaks are also available in various sizes.

Kitchen Yields

Serving size:
5 to 7 oz (140 to 200 g) breaded; 7 to 9 oz (200 to 225 g) blackened.

COD
Popular fish, without scales, harvested in both the Atlantic and the Pacific Oceans. Atlantic and Pacific cod are closely related species, and little distinction is made between them on the market. Most cod is processed into fish products and frozen fillets. Immature cod is called *scrod*.

Season:
Available year-round. Peak occurs from March to September.

Average sizes:
Up to 20 lb (9.1 kg).

Trade sizes:

Scrod:
1½ to 2 lb (675 to 900 g).
2 to 4 lb (0.9 to 1.8 kg).

Market:
2½ to 8 lb (1.13 to 3.6 kg).

Large:
8 to 20 lb (3.6 to 9 kg).

Frozen fillets:
4, 5, 6, 7, and 8 oz (113, 141, 170, 200, and 226 g).

Kitchen Yield
About 50 percent waste, when whole fish is cut in fillets. Fresh cod fillets, with skin still on, are available in some markets. Skin should be left on for broiling. When buying frozen fillets, make sure they are IQF or layer-packed.

Serving sizes:
5-oz (140-g) fillet in institutions; 7-oz (200-g) fillet in restaurants.
5-lb (2.3-kg) market cod yields 2½-lb (1.1-kg) fillet, and 2½-lb (1.1-kg) fillet yields 6 servings.

COD CHEEKS
New England specialty, available frozen.

Pack:
By weight.

Size:
Little nuggets about 1 oz (28.4 g) each.

Kitchen Yield
No waste; use as sold.

COD TONGUES
New England specialty, available frozen.

Pack:
By weight.

Size:
Varies; usually about 1½ to 2 oz (42 to 56 g).

SALTED COD
See Bacalao, under Smoked or Cured Fish.

SCROD
See Scrod, under this same heading.

CROAKER
Small pan fish from the Atlantic coast.

Season:
March to October.

Average sizes:
½ to 2 lb (224 to 900 g).

Kitchen Yields
Purchase 2-lb (900-g) fish for fillets. One fish yields 2 servings.

CUSK
Also known as *deep-sea whitefish,* cusk is a deep-water flatfish, harvested along the New England coast. The fish has a white, delicate flesh.

Season:
February to July.

Average sizes:
Scrod:
1½ to 3 lb (0.675 to 1.3 kg).

Medium:
3 to 7 lb (1.3 to 3.1 kg).

Large:
7 to 15 lb (3.1 to 6.7 kg).

Jumbo:
15 lb (6.7 kg) and larger.

Kitchen Yields
About 60 percent waste when cut into fillets.

DAB (PLAICE)
Flatfish, found in both the Atlantic and Pacific Oceans.

Season:
Available year-round.

Average sizes:
Small: Under 2 lb (0.9 kg).
Large: 2 lb (0.9 kg) and larger.

Kitchen Yields
Fish is most often used for pan-frying whole.

Serving size:
One 1-lb (450-g) whole fish per person.

DOLPHIN
See Mahi Mahi, under this same heading.

EEL
Elongated, snakelike fatty fish that lives in both freshwater and saltwater. Most production is smoked.

Season:
Available year-round. Peak is in November and December.

Average size:
From 3 lb (1.4 kg) up, with head and skin removed.

Kitchen Yields
When eel is cut into fillets, waste is only 15 percent.

BABY EEL
Baby eel is a specialty of Spain and is available frozen year-round. The tiny fish are fried in olive oil and eaten whole.

Season:
Early spring, fresh.

Kitchen Yields
Use whole; there is no waste.

ENGLISH OR DOVER SOLE
Imported flatfish of excellent quality, available fresh or frozen. It is normally imported whole, with skin, head, and fins still attached. Flatfish of lesser quality is harvested under the name *Dover sole* in the Pacific. The English sole found in fine restaurants on the Atlantic coast is an imported fish not directly related to the English sole marketed on the Pacific coast. *See also* Sole.

Sizes:
10 to 12 oz (280 to 340 g); 12 to 16 oz (340 to 450 g); 16 to 20 oz (450 to 570 g); 20 to 24 oz (570 to 680 g); 24 to 28 oz (680 to 800 g); 28 oz (800 g) and larger.

Pack:
Fresh fish: 25-lb (11.2-kg) cases.
Frozen fish: 50-lb (22.5-kg) cases.

Kitchen Yields
Fish is normally served whole, one fish per serving. Some operations feature the 23-oz (650-g) fish for 2 servings. Fish gives best yield when filleted after cooking.

Waste:
About 30 percent, when head, fins, and skin are removed.

Best size:
For restaurant use, 19 oz (540 g) or larger. If fish is to be filleted raw, buy very large fish. Yield is very low, approximately 30 percent.

FLOUNDER
Both winter flounder and summer flounder (also called *fluke*) belong to the large family of flatfish. There are a number of distinct subspecies, marketed under many local names. *See also* English or Dover Sole and Sole under this same heading. The fish is found on both the Atlantic and Pacific coasts, and the following varieties are often found.

> *Atlantic Coast:* Blackback or winter flounder (also called *lemon sole*), fluke or summer flounder, yellowtail flounder.
> *Pacific Coast:* Rex, petrale sole, English or Dover sole, sand sole, and rock sole.

The name *sole* is often used interchangeably with *flounder.* Most flounder is purchased as fresh or frozen fillets under the name *fillet of sole.* Much of this is imported. Stuffed flounder is also marketed; *see* Frozen or Prepared Fish Products. There are noticeable differences in texture and flavor among the different species, but the market often does not indicate which species is being offered. There is much confusion regarding names.

Season:
Available year-round, but larger supply in summer.

Average sizes:
Whole fish: ½ to 6 lb (0.224 to 2.7 kg).
Fillets: 3 oz (84 g) and larger.

Kitchen Yields

Best sizes:
For pan-frying, use ¾- to 1-lb (336- to 450-g) whole fish. For filleting, use 5- to 6-lb (2.2- to 2.7-kg) whole fish.

Boning Yield:
When fillets are cut, waste from gutted fish is 50 percent.

Calories:
7 oz (200 g) steamed = 200 Calories.

GAR
See Needlefish, under this same heading.

GROUPER
Grouper are related to sea bass and may be found in the Atlantic Ocean from Brazil to Virginia.

Season:
Available year-round. Peak is from April to December.

Sizes:
5 to 15 lb (2.2 to 6.7 kg); 2 to 3 ft (0.2 to 0.9 m) long.

HADDOCK
Scaleless bottom fish found in the North Atlantic Ocean. Although most of the catch is filleted and frozen, a large volume is processed into frozen fish sticks and related products. Haddock and cod are related but distinct species; however, the names are often used interchangeably. *See also* Scrod, under this same heading.

Season:
Available year-round.

Average size:
For whole fish, 1½ to 6 lb (675 g to 2.7 kg).

Pack:
For IQF fillets, 5-lb (2.2-kg) cartons.

Fillet sizes:
6, 8, or 10 oz (170, 224, or 280 g).

Kitchen Yields

Serving sizes:
6 to 7 oz (170 to 200 g) for broiling; 4 to 5 oz (112 to 140 g) for frying.

Waste:
About 55 percent when fish is cut into fillets and skin is left on.

Best size:
For whole fish, 5 to 6 lb (2.2 to 2.7 kg). One 5½-lb (2.5-kg) whole fish yields 2 lb 7 oz (1.1 kg) fillet, which provides 6 servings broiled or 8 servings fried.

Calories:
6 oz breaded haddock, fried = 280 Calories.

HAKE
Codlike bottom fish harvested in both the Atlantic and Pacific oceans. Most production is processed. The meat is white and lean.

Season:
June to September.

Sizes:
From ½ to 6 lb (224 g to 2.7 kg).

Kitchen Yields
Buy fresh fillets only. Size depends on application.

HALIBUT
Large flatfish found in both the Atlantic and Pacific Oceans. Halibut is graded according to size.

Season:
Available year-round. Peak is from March to August.

Sizes:

Chicken:
5 to 10 lb (2.2 to 4.5 kg).

Medium:
10 to 60 lb (4.5 to 27 kg).

Large:
60 to 80 lb (27 to 36 kg).

Whales:
80 lb (36 kg) and larger.
Boneless fillets are called *fletches* and are available fresh or frozen, in many sizes. Steaks are normally sold bone-in, with skin on, under the following trade names:

>*Full moon:* crosscut.
>*Half-moon:* half crosscut.
>*Loin cut:* almost boneless cut.
>*Regular cut:* cut from full moon cut.
>*Roast:* tail cut, with the most bones per weight of any cut.

Pack:
For steaks, 5-, 10-, and 15-lb (2.3-, 4.5-, and 6.8-kg) cartons; for fletches, per weight.

Steak sizes:
4 to 6 oz (112 to 170 g); 6 to 8 oz (170 to 224 g); 8 to 10 oz (224 to 280 g).
NOTE: All steak varieties are not available in all sizes.

Kitchen Yields
Whole halibut is shipped dressed and with head removed.

Waste factor:
For fresh fish, 40 percent when fish is cut into fillets and skin is removed. For frozen fish, 42 percent, because fish is glazed with ice.

Calories:
7-oz (200-g) fletch = 200 Calories.

HERRING
Herring is a small fish abundant in both the Atlantic and Pacific Oceans. Fresh herring is seldom marketed. Most is canned or pickled; *see* Smoked or Cured Fish, under this same general entry. Herring roe is a delicacy in Japan and is

exported fresh from Washington state and Alaska during a limited season.

JOHN DORY
See St. Peter Fish, under this same heading.

LOTTE
See Monkfish, under this same heading.

MACKEREL
Mackerel are related to tuna and are found along both the Atlantic and Pacific coasts. Three species are commercially important: Spanish mackerel (the smallest of the three), Boston mackerel, and King Mackerel (the largest).

Season:
Spanish mackerel is available year-round; Boston mackerel is available from early summer to December; king mackerel is available from November to March.

Market sizes:

Spanish mackerel:
1½ to 4 lb (675 g to 1.8 kg).

Boston mackerel:
½ to 2½ lb (0.224 to 1.1 kg).

King mackerel:
5 to 30 lb (2.2 to 13.5 kg).

Kitchen Yields
About 50 percent waste when cut into fillets.

Serving size:
One 1¼-lb (560-g) fish yields 2 servings for broiling or sautéing.

MAHI MAHI
Also known as *dolphin,* this fish is not related to the sea mammal called *dolphin.* Most is harvested in the Pacific and sold under the name *Hawaiian mahi mahi.* Available fresh or frozen.

Season:
Available year-round.

Sizes:
Up to 50 lb (22.5 kg).

Pack:
Sold as fillet, with skin on.

Kitchen Yields
Fish must be skinned. Waste is about 10 percent
by weight if fish is purchased as fillet.

MONKFISH
Also known as *angler fish* or by its French name,
lotte. Harvested in the Atlantic.

Season:
Available year-round.

Average sizes:
1- to 2-lb (450- to 900-g) fillets.

Kitchen Yields
Trimming waste when fillets are purchased is 10
percent.

Serving size:
6 oz (170 g), two pieces per serving, as main
course; thus, 2 lb (900 g) yields 5 servings.

MULLET
Popular fish in southern states, harvested in the
Atlantic and off the southern California coast.
Available as whole fresh fish and as fresh and
frozen fillets.

Season:
Available year-round. Peak is in September.

Average size:

Small:
1 to 2 lb (450 to 900 g).

Medium:
2 to 3 lb (0.9 to 1.3 kg).

Large:
Over 3 lb (1.3 kg).

Kitchen Yields
About 50 percent waste when fish is cut into
fillets. Purchase fillets when possible. Fillets have
some bones left in.

NEEDLEFISH
This fish lives in temperate and tropical oceans. It
has an elongated snout resembling that of a pike
or gar. Good eating fish, but seldom found on the
market. The bones can have a slightly green tint.

Size:
Up to 10 ft (3 m) long.

Kitchen Yields
About 55 percent waste.

OCEAN PERCH
Small Atlantic Ocean food fish, available mostly
in fillets. Imported frozen fillets are available.

Average size:

For whole fish:
½ to 2 lb (224 to 900 g).

Season:
Early summer.

Kitchen Yields
Purchase fillets, which weigh 3 oz (85 g) or more.
Good buy for buffets and inexpensive meals.

ORANGE ROUGHY
Fish with firm, white flesh, imported as fillets
from the subantarctic waters around New Zealand.

Pack:

Frozen fillets:
22-lb (10-kg) box.

Fresh fillets:
35-lb (15.7-kg) box.

Sizes:
2 to 4 oz (56 to 112 g); 6 to 8 oz (170 to 224 g); 8 oz
(224 g) and larger.

Kitchen Yields
Use as is; there is no waste.

Calories:
6 oz (170 g) = 270 Calories.

PIKE (NORTHERN PIKE OR MUSKELLUNGE)
Fine freshwater fish, but of little commercial
importance.

Season:
Summer.

Average sizes:
1 to 2 lb (450 to 900 g).

Kitchen Yields
Fish has scales and is bony. Pike is excellent in fish
mousse. Buy fillets.

PLAICE
See Dab, under this same heading.

POLLACK
Harvested off the coast of Alaska and in the Atlantic, pollack is also known as *Boston bluefish* or *Alaska snow cod.* The fish resembles haddock in taste and texture, but with meatier and firmer flesh. *See also* Scrod, under this same heading.

Season:
Available year-round. Peak is in late Fall.

Average Size:

Alaskan pollack:
1 lb (450 g), 16 in (406 mm).

Atlantic pollack:
4 to 12 lb (1.8 to 5.4 kg), 2 to 3 ft (0.6 to 0.9 m).

Pack:

Alaskan pollack:
3- to 10-oz (85- to 280-g) frozen fillets.

Calories:
7 oz (200 g) = 185 Calories.

POMPANO
Very delicate fish harvested off the Florida coast. Some imports are available. Marketed whole, as fresh fillets and as frozen fillets.

Season:
Available year-round. Peak is from March to May.

Average sizes:
Whole, 1½ to 4 lb (0.67 to 1.8 kg). Fillets, 6 oz to 1¾ lb (170 to 784 g).

Kitchen Yields
Fish is expensive.

Best size:
For cutting fillets, 1¾ lb (800 g). One 1¾-lb (800-g) fish yields two 6-oz (170-g) fillets.

RED FISH
Abundant in the Gulf of Mexico and the South Atlantic.

Season:
Available year-round, with winter as a peak season.

Sizes:
1½ to 3 lb (0.6 to 1.3 kg); 3 to 8 lb (1.3 to 3.6 kg).

Kitchen Yields
Serve as a fillet. Scale, but leave skin on. Waste is about 50 percent.

RED SNAPPER
Popular fish harvested in the Gulf of Mexico and in other tropical waters. Available whole or in fillets, fresh or frozen. Frozen fillets are often imported.

Season:
Available year-round. Peak is in summer.

Sizes:

Whole small:
under 2 lb (900 g)

Whole medium:
2 to 5 lb (0.9 to 2.3 kg).

Whole large:
5 to 8 lb (2.3 to 3.6 kg) and larger.

Fillets:
3½ oz (100 g) and larger.

Kitchen Yields
About 55 percent waste, because head is very large.

Serving size:
For broiling with skin on, 6 oz (170 g). One 1¾-lb (790-g) whole fish yields 2 servings.
Buy 6- to 8-lb (2.7- to 3.6-kg) fish for cutting fillets. One 7-lb (3.2-kg) fish yields 3-lb 3-oz (1.5-kg) fillet, which provides 8 servings. Larger fish give slightly better yields, but they can be dry and tough.

ROCKFISH
Found along the Pacific coast in many varieties. Mostly available as fresh or frozen fillets. The four most important commercial varieties are the following:

> *Orange rockfish:* Up to 30 in (760 mm) long.
> *Yellowtail rockfish:* Up to 26 in (660 mm) long.
> *Bocaccio:* Up to 40 in (1 m) long.
> *Red Rockfish:* Up to 3 ft (900 mm) long. This fish resembles red snapper and is often sold

as such, although it is not related to the genuine red snapper of the Atlantic.

Kitchen Yields
Buy 3- to 4-lb (1.4- to 1.8-kg) fillets.

SABLEFISH
A fatty fish also known as *black cod,* but not related to the Atlantic cod, sablefish is found along the Pacific coast from Alaska to California. Much of the sablefish catch is smoked.

Average Sizes:
8 lb (3.6 kg), 30 in (0.76 m) long.

Season:
Late summer and fall.

Calories:
One 7-oz (200-g) fresh fish = 400 Calories.

ST. PETER FISH
Also known as *St. Pierre fish*, this is a cultivated fish, originally cultivated in the Sea of Galilee. It is available whole and in fillets. *John Dory* is the British name for a related saltwater fish.

Average size:
1½ to 2 lb (0.6 to 0.9 kg).

Kitchen Yields
One fish yields two fillets, or two servings.

SALMON
Salmon is also available canned and smoked. *See* Canned Fish and Smoked or Cured Fish under this same general entry. Most fresh salmon comes from Alaska and the Pacific Northwest. Canada is a big producer of Atlantic salmon, but most of the production is smoked. Fresh pond-raised salmon is imported from Norway. Because salmon can successfully be raised in ponds, it is now available year-round.

Alaskan salmon species:
King or chinook salmon: Fish with high oil content and (usually) very red flesh. It is often smoked. White king salmon has pale flesh and is often kippered. Size is up to 20 lb (9 kg).

Sockeye salmon: Salmon with very red flesh. Excellent for broiling. Weight ranges from 4 to 12 lb (1.8 to 5.4 kg).

Silver or coho salmon: Fish with orange-red flesh, often smoked. Average weight is about 6 lb (2.7 kg).

Pink salmon: Most abundant Alaska salmon, often sold whole, but most production is canned. Average weight is about 2 to 3 lb (0.9 to 1.4 kg).

Chum or keta salmon: Lightest-colored and leanest salmon. Most production is canned. Weight ranges from 4 to 13 lb (1.8 to 5.8 kg).

Mini salmon: Hatchery-raised fish; normally sold frozen, boneless, with head on.

Season:
Farm-raised salmon is available year-round, but there are distinct seasons for fresh wild salmon:

King or chinook salmon: May to October.
Sockeye salmon: June to July.
Silver or coho salmon: June to September.
Pink salmon: June to November.
Chum or keta salmon: August to October.
Atlantic salmon: June to September.

Pack:

Whole Salmon:
Headless, dressed, 6 to 8 lb (2.7 to 3.6 kg).
Headless, dressed, 8 to 10 lb (3.6 to 4.5 kg).
Other sizes are available.

Fillets:
Boneless, skin on, imported from Norway; 22- to 26-lb (10- to 12-kg) cartons consisting of ten 2½-lb (1.1-kg) sides each.

Loins:
Skinless, boneless pieces, individually wrapped, imported from Norway; sizes vary.

Steaks:
Cross-cut, with bone in and skin on; 8 oz (226 g) each. Other sizes are available.

Mini Salmon:
8- to 10-oz (226- to 280-g) fish, boneless, with head and tail on, packed 10 to the box in 5-lb (2.2-kg) boxes; six boxes make up a 30-lb (13.5-kg) master carton.

Kitchen Yields

Waste:

About 30 percent when fish is purchased with head on; about 20 percent when fish is purchased headless.

One 7-lb (3.1-kg) fish, with head on, produces 5-lb (2.3-kg) fillet, with skin on. One 10-lb (4.5-kg) fish, with head off produces 8-lb (3.6-kg) fillet, with skin on.

Serving sizes:

5 to 7 oz (140 to 200 g) for boneless fillet, with skin on for broiling; 7 oz (200 g) for boneless fillet to be eaten cold, with skin removed after poaching; 5 oz (140 g) for boneless fillet to be poached and served with a sauce.

Calories:

All figures are for 5-oz (140-g) boneless fillet:

> King or chinook = 270 Calories.
> Sockeye = 230 Calories.
> Silver or coho = 172 Calories.
> Pink = 190 Calories.
> Chum or keta = 171 Calories.

SALMON TROUT (LAKE TROUT)

Delicate freshwater fish, with pale pink to gray flesh. Salmon trout is harvested in the Great Lakes.

Season:

Peak is in summer. Small catch is available in winter.

Trade sizes:

2 to 4 lb (0.9 to 1.8 kg); 4 to 8 lb (1.8 to 3.6 kg).

Kitchen Yields

Buy whole and cut into fillets. Waste is about 50 percent. Leave skin on for broiling or pan-frying; remove skin for poaching.

SARDINES

Maine sardines belong to the herring family. Relatively little is sold fresh; most is canned.

Average size:

3 to 4 in (76 to 100 mm) long; 6 to 9 pieces per 1 lb (450 g).

Season:

Winter.

Kitchen Yields

Serving size:

4 pieces with bones removed, fried whole.

SCROD

Scrod is immature cod, haddock, or pollack.

Season:

Available year-round. Peak is in late fall and winter.

Average size:

Boston scrod:
New York market: 1½ to 2 lb (675 to 900 g).
Boston market: 2 to 4 lb (0.9 to 1.8 kg).

SEA BASS

See Bass, under this same heading.

SEA TROUT

Also called *speckled trout* or *spotted sea trout*, a popular game fish in the Gulf states. Lean and delicate, it spoils rapidly.

Season:

Available year-round.

Average size:

1 to 5 lb (450 g to 2.2 kg).

Kitchen Yields

Purchase fillets.

SHAD

This fatty fish is remotely related to the herring. Shad is found on both the Atlantic and Pacific coasts. The mature fish returns for spawning to the freshwater stream where it was hatched. Both shad fillets and shad roe are marketed. The fish's erratic bone structure is difficult to remove, and for this reason shad is marketed as boneless fillets. The fillets are sold as two fillets wrapped in paper. Roe is marketed by the pair.

Season:

Early spring until mid-June, depending on weather.

Average sizes:

Shad fillets, individual:
8 to 10 oz (226 to 284 g) each.

Shad fillet pairs:
16 to 20 oz (450 to 570 g).

Roe pairs:
6 to 8 oz (170 to 224 g); 8 to 10 oz (224 to 280 g); 12 to 14 oz (340 to 400 g).

Kitchen Yields
The customer is normally given a choice of ordering shad fillet only, shad and roe, or roe only.

Serving sizes:
Shad fillet only:
7 to 8 oz (200 to 227 g).

Shad and roe:
5 oz (140 g) shad, 4 oz (113 g) roe.

Roe only:
8 to 10 oz (227 to 280 g) per pair.

One pair shad fillets yields approximately four servings when served with roe; one pair roe yield two portions when served with fillets, or one portion when served alone.

SHARK
There are many different species of shark, only a few of which reach the commercial market. Sharks are harvested in both the Atlantic and Pacific oceans. Mako Shark is a well-recognized food fish.

Season:
Available year-round.

Average size:
Varies greatly.

Kitchen Yields
Shark skin is very tough and leathery and must be removed before cooking. Bones (actually cartilage) are very soft. Purchase fillets only.

SKATE
Also called *ray,* this relative of the shark renders excellent meat. The wings only are used.

Season:
Available year-round.

Average sizes:
16 oz to 24 oz (450 to 670 g). The pieces are sold skinned, but the thin, secondary skin should be removed before preparation.

Kitchen Yields
One wing yields 2 main-course servings.

SMELTS
Small fish related to salmon that are capable of living in both freshwater and saltwater. Smelts are harvested in the Atlantic Ocean, the Pacific Ocean, and in many lakes, including the Great Lakes.

Season:
Late winter and early spring.

Average sizes:
1½ to 1¾ oz (40 to 50 g), 7 to 8 in (177 to 200 mm) long.

Kitchen Yields
1 lb (450 g) smelts yields 8 to 11 pieces, and 1 serving, fried, consists of 4 to 5 pieces.

SOLE
Flatfish, considered the best eating fish. Species of sole are caught on both the Atlantic and Pacific coasts. The names *sole* and *flounder* are often used interchangeably, but they cover a number of distinct but closely related species. *See also* Flounder and English or Dover Sole under this same heading. Most production is sold as fresh or frozen fillets. Much is imported. Domestically harvested species include the following:

> *Atlantic sole species:* gray sole and lemon sole, also called *winter flounder* or *blackback* when weighing less than 3½ lb (1.5 kg).
> *Pacific sole species:* petrale sole, brill sole, and English sole (often called *lemon sole,* but a different species from the Atlantic lemon sole).

Season:
Available year-round.

Average sizes:

Whole fish:
1 to 6 lb (450 g to 2.7 kg).

Fillets:
6 to 8 oz (170 to 224 g).
8 to 10 oz (224 to 280 g).

Kitchen Yields

Waste:
About 50 percent when fish is cut into boneless fillets.

Serving size:
For poaching, 7 oz.
Buy 5- to 6-lb (2.3- to 2.7-kg) fish when planning to cut fillets. One 5½-lb (2.5-kg) whole fish produces 2-lb-14-oz (1.3-kg) fillet, which yields 6 to 7 portions.

STURGEON
Harvested in both the Atlantic and Pacific oceans, the fish lives in saltwater and spawns in freshwater rivers. Lake sturgeon live in freshwater. Sturgeon is known primarily as the producer of caviar and as an excellent smoked fish.

Much sturgeon is frozen and imported from caviar-producing countries and from Canada for smoking. Sturgeon species are distinguished in the caviar trade, but little distinction is made when purchasing sturgeon meat. Sturgeon has no bones, only soft cartilage, but skin is tough and must be removed. The spine marrow is called *vesiga* and can be used in fish soups and coulibiac. *See* Vesiga.

Season:
Spring and summer.

Size:
From 5 to 500 lb (2.3 kg to 225 kg).

Kitchen Yields

Waste:
About 30 percent when buying whole fish.

Best size:
Buy 8- to 10-lb (3.6- to 4.5-kg) fish with head removed or 8- to 10-lb (3.6- to 4.5-kg) sturgeon saddle.

SWORDFISH
Large fish found in warm waters in both the Atlantic and Pacific oceans. Available fresh in pieces and frozen in steaks.

Season:
June to October, imports available year-round.

Average sizes:
From 100 to 200 lb (45 to 90 kg).

Pack:
Sold by weight, bone in, skin on.

Kitchen Yields
Purchase by weight and cut in kitchen. Specify center cut, with no belly flap. Skin is usually left on. Tail pieces have a high ratio of bones to meat. Flap pieces left on the cut can reduce yield per pound by as much as 25 percent. Heavy pieces give better yield. Frozen swordfish steaks are available in many sizes. They are usually dry.

Serving sizes:
3 oz for appetizer; 8 oz for thick steak.
One 20-lb center cut, with no belly flaps, yields 17 lb usable meat.

TILEFISH
Atlantic coast fish with firm flesh and good flavor.

Season:
Summer.

Average sizes:
2 to 6 lb (0.9 to 2.6 kg).

Kitchen Yields
Purchase fillets. Best size is 1½ lb (675 g).

TROUT

FRESHWATER TROUT
The best-known species is the rainbow trout. Most commercial production is hatchery-grown. Fresh trout are available in many states. The whole fish is always sold gutted, with head and tail attached; it is also available boned and as fillets. Live trout is available in selected markets. The fish can be kept alive in a fish tank, but it needs clean, cold freshwater that contains sufficient oxygen.

Season:
Available year-round. Peak in summer. Frozen trout is readily available at all times.

Sizes:
From 5 oz (140 g) up.

Kitchen Yields

Serving size:
For stuffed trout as appetizer, 5 oz (140 g). For main course, single service, 7- to 9-oz (200- to 252-g) or 9- to 11-oz (252- to 308-g) whole fish. For main course, double service, 20-oz (570-g) whole fish.

Waste factor:
For filleting, 45 percent.
For filleting, buy 28-oz (800-g) or larger whole fish.

LAKE TROUT
See Salmon Trout, under this same heading.

SEA TROUT
See Weakfish, under this same heading.

TUNA

Fresh tuna has become widely accepted as a fresh-food fish in fine restaurants. It is often cooked rare, like a steak. Fresh tuna is one of the most important fish varieties used in sushi bars. The flesh of all species is dark but lightens during cooking. Four species are available:

> *Albacore.* Fish with light-colored flesh. Weights range from 10 to 60 lb (4.5 to 27 kg).
> *Yellowfin.* Fish with light-colored flesh. Weights range from 40 to 100 lb (18 to 45 kg).
> *Bluefin.* Also called *horse mackerel.* Weights range from 15 to 18 lb (6.7 to 36 kg).
> *Skipjack.* The smallest of the four tuna species. Weights range from 4 to 24 lb (1.8 to 10.8 kg).

Bonito is a member of the mackerel family and is not classified as genuine tuna. It is very similar in taste and flesh to tuna, but only after it has been soaked in brine to lessen the strong flavor. It is not suitable for serving raw, as in sushi, or as undercooked steak. Weights range from 5 to 12 lb (2.3 to 5.4 kg). *See* Bonito, under this same heading.

Season:
Fresh tuna is available year-round, but supply peaks in summer.

Kitchen Yields

Fillets are generally the best buy. Make sure to specify loin fillets. Tuna should be undercooked, and consequently the portion size is small.

Serving size:
5 oz (140 g).

TURBOT

Turbot, imported from Europe, is an elegant flatfish; it should not to be confused with the lower-quality Pacific turbot. The fish is usually available frozen, but occasionally is freshly flown in for the luxury market. In either case, it is available whole.

Pack:
22.2- to 26.6-lb (10- to 12-kg) cases.

Sizes:
With head on, 6 to 9 lb (2.7 to 4 kg), 9 to 12 lb (4 to 5.4 kg), 12 to 15 lb (5.4 to 6.7 kg), and 15 lb (6.7 kg) and larger.

Kitchen Yield

The fish is normally sold eviscerated, with head on. It has a very large head and heavy bones. Best size to buy is the 9- to 12-lb (4- to 5.4-kg) fish.

Waste:
When turbot is cut into steaks, with skin on and bone in, 40 percent; when it is cut into boneless fillets, with skin off, 60 percent.
One 10-lb (4.5-kg) fish yields 4-lb (1.8-kg) fillet.

WEAKFISH

Weakfish is also called *gray sea trout.* It is a member of the drum family and is harvested off the Atlantic coast.

Season:
Summer.

Average size:
1 to 3 lb (0.45 to 1.4 kg).

Kitchen Yields

Purchase largest whole fish available, and cut fillets. There is about 45 percent waste.

WHITEBAITS

Tiny fish that are dusted with flour and fried. Available fresh or frozen IQF or in block.

Pack:
By weight.

Kitchen Yields
Serve whole. About 10 to 15 percent loss occurs as a result of sorting out impurities.

WHITEFISH
A freshwater fish harvested mainly from the Great Lakes. Cisco and lake herring are related.

Season:
Summer.

Average weights:
2 to 6 lb (0.9 to 2.7 kg).

Kitchen Yields
Best weight is 4 lb (1.8 kg). Waste is about 45 percent. Fish should be scaled and skin left on.

WHITING
Inexpensive fish with limited application in the hospitality industry. Harvested off the coast of New England.

Season:
Summer.

Average size:
1 to 4 lb (0.45 to 1.8 kg).

FROZEN OR PREPARED FISH PRODUCTS
There are numerous ready-to-cook fish products on the market. This section mentions a few of these. Size and pack of product vary from manufacturer to manufacturer.

BLACKENED CATFISH
Fully seasoned ready-to-bake blackened catfish is available.

Pack:
10-lb (4.5-kg) cartons.

Size:
6- or 8-oz (170- or 224-g) fillets.

Count:
Twenty-seven 6-oz (170-g) fillets; twenty 8-oz (224-g) fillets.

COD PRODUCTS
Many products, either plain or breaded, are on the market.

Sizes:
3 to 6 oz (85 to 170 g).

Pack:
Varies.

FISH MOUSSE

Formula
> 8 lb (3.6 kg) solid fish, such as halibut, sole, pike, or salmon
> 20 egg whites, or 2½ cups (0.6 l)
> 3½ qt (3.1 l) heavy cream
> Salt and pepper to taste

Fish should be fresh. If frozen fish is used, the amount of egg whites should be increased. It is advisable to mix frozen fish with about 30 percent fresh scallops, in order to improve the binding of the mixture.

Kitchen Yields
The preceding formula yields sixty 4-oz (112-g) appetizer servings or forty 6-oz (170-g) main-course servings.

FISH STICKS
Fish portions, usually made of cod, haddock, or pollack. Available breaded or batter-dipped, raw or precooked, in different shapes and sizes. Fish sticks contain at least 60 percent fish, by weight.

Pack:
Varies. 2-lb (0.9-kg) boxes are common.

Sizes:
1½ to 5 oz (43 to 140 g).

Kitchen Yields
There is no waste.

Serving size:
Approximately 4 to 6 oz (113 to 170 g).

Calories:
4 oz (113 g) = 200 Calories.

GEFILTE FISH
For canned gefilte fish, *see* Canned Fish.

Formula

    2 lb (0.9 kg) whitefish fillets, skinless
    2 lb (0.9 kg) carp fillets, skinless
    2 lb (0.9 kg) pike fillets, skinless
    6 eggs
    1 cup matzo meal
    3 tb salt
    1 tb sugar
    1 tb ground white pepper
    1 cup chopped onion
    Fish stock (made with fish bones, sliced
       carrots, sliced onions, salt, pepper, and
       allspice)

Kitchen Yields

The preceding formula produces fifty 2-oz (56-g) pieces, raw weight.

Serving size:

2 pieces, as an appetizer.

STUFFED FLOUNDER

Available with many varieties of stuffing and in many sizes.

Sizes:

6 to 10 oz (170 to 280 g).

Pack:

Varies.

SMOKED OR CURED FISH

Smoked or otherwise cured fish is shipped freshly smoked, frozen, dried, or canned.

BACALAO

Bacalao, also called *salt cod* or *stockfish,* is salted and air-dried fish, sold split or in fíllets. Most is imported from Europe or Canada. Available with skin on or off.

Pack:

Sold by weight.

Kitchen Yields

Soak overnight. Size will roughly double in volume.

Serving size:

3 oz (85 g) dried product.

BLOATERS

Fat herring, salted and smoked.

CHUBS

Name given to many small fresh- or saltwater fish species. In gastronomy, the name *chub* usually refers to smoked small whitefish.

Average size:

Whole fish:
4 to 6 oz (113 to 170 g).

FINNAN HADDIE

Smoked haddock, available in fillets fresh or frozen. Some product is cured and colored, but not smoked, and has inferior flavor.

Pack:

By weight. Often sold in 15-lb (6.8-kg) cases.

Kitchen Yields

Poach in milk/water mixture to reduce saltiness.

Serving sizes:

4 oz (113 g) for breakfast; 6 oz (170 g) for luncheon dishes.

Trimming waste:

About 5 percent or less.

GRAVELAX

Swedish pickled salmon, made most often on premises.

Pickling Formula

    2 cups salt
    1 cup sugar
    ¼ cup crushed juniper berries
    ¼ cup crushed peppercorns
    2 cups coarsely chopped dill (including
       stems)

Kitchen Yields

The mixture produced by the preceding formula is sufficient to pickle two 3-lb (1.3-kg) fillets, with skin on.

Serving sizes:

For appetizer, 2½ oz (70 g); thus, one side (skin-on fillet) yields 18 servings. For buffet, 1 oz (28 g); thus, one side yields 45 servings.

HERRING SPECIALTIES

Many varieties of cured, smoked, and preserved herring specialties are on the market, including the following:

> *Bismark herring:* Marinated fillets, available in plain marinade and in sour cream.
>
> *Brat herring:* Herring fillets or whole herrings dipped in flour, fried, pickled, and canned.
>
> *Buekling:* Smoked whole herring.
>
> *Digby chick:* Smoked fillets.
>
> *Matjes herring:* Marinated fillets from young herrings.
>
> *Fresh matjes herring:* Available in June, this Dutch specialty herring is lightly cured in brine and then is shipped by air in boneless fillets ready to eat.
>
> *Kippered herring:* Butterflied smoked herring, served grilled, usually with scrambled eggs. When customer demand is low, purchase the canned product.
>
> *Rollmops:* Herring fillet rolls filled with onions, pickle, and sauerkraut, marinated in vinegar and spices.
>
> *Herring in sour cream:* Available in fillets and bite size; specify boneless pieces.
>
> *Schmaltz herring:* Fat, skinless marinated herring pieces.
>
> *Sill:* Swedish name for various herring specialties.
>
> *Sprat:* Small herring that can be smoked or pickled.

See also Bloaters and Sprats under this same heading.

Pack:
Varies. Most products are packed in 1-qt (0.94-l) or 1-gal (3.8-l) glass jars or plastic buckets.

Sizes and counts:
Vary greatly, according to product.

LOX

Cured salmon from large, fatty fish, sold sliced or whole. Sliced lox is often frozen or canned. The name *lox* is sometimes used erroneously for smoked salmon.

Pack:
Four 3-lb (1.4-kg) trays of sliced fish.

Sizes:

Weight of average slice:
About ½ oz (14 g).

Kitchen Yields
When lox is purchased sliced, there is no waste. When it is purchased whole, yield is the same as for smoked salmon, if the fatty belly part is used.

Serving size:
For buffet service, with scrambled eggs and bagels, 3 slices per serving, totaling 1½ oz (40 g).

SMOKED EEL

Available whole, with head on or off. Skin is normally left on. Skinless fillets are also available canned.

Size:
3 lb (1.3 kg) and larger.

Kitchen Yields
Buy the 4- to 5-lb (1.8- to 2.2-kg) size. Larger eels are fatty.

Waste:
About 25 percent when fish is purchased with head on.

SMOKED MACKEREL

Smoked mackerel is available whole, in fillets, and canned.

Pack:
Varies.

Sizes:

Whole Mackerel:
8 to 10 oz (224 to 280 g).

Mackerel Fillets:
4 to 5 oz (113 to 140 g), two fillets per pack.

Kitchen Yields
Serve as is.

SMOKED SABLEFISH

The fish, which is considered kosher, is sold cured, smoked, and sprinkled with paprika.

Pack:
By weight.

Size:
Best size is 2- to 3-lb (0.9- to 1.4-kg) fillets.

Kitchen Yield
Little waste; skin only must be discarded. About 5 percent trimming waste.

Serving size:
2 oz (56 g).

SMOKED SALMON
Smoked salmon is available in many sizes, quality levels, and packs. It is marketed whole with skin on, and presliced with and without skin. Some products are imported. *See also* Gravelax and Lox, under this same heading.

Average sizes:

Canadian nova, sides:
3½ lb (1.5 kg).

Canadian nova, presliced:
2 to 3 lb (0.9 to 1.3 kg).

Gaspe nova, sides:
4 to 6 lb (1.8 to 2.7 kg).

Irish salmon, sides:
3 to 3½ lb (1.3 to 1.5 kg).

Norwegian salmon, presliced:
3 lb (1.3 kg), 2.2 lb (1 kg).

Pacific nova, sides, headless:
4 to 10 lb (1.8 to 4.5 kg).

Scotch salmon, sides, headless:
2¼ to 3 lb (1 to 1.3 kg).

Scotch salmon, presliced:
1½ lb (675 g).

Kitchen Yields
Trimming waste from whole sides is about 15 percent. Skin weight is about 5 percent, not included in the preceding waste estimate. Usable scraps such as end pieces account for 5 percent of total weight after slicing.

Serving sizes:
3 oz (85 g) for appetizer; 2 oz (56 g) for buffet; ⅓ oz (10 g) each for canapés. One side weighing 8 lb (3.6 kg), as purchased, yields 30 appetizer servings, 45 buffet servings, or 280 pieces for canapés.

Larger sides have better yield than do smaller sides.

SMOKED SHAD
Boneless smoked shad is a spring specialty.

Pack:
By weight. Fillet size is about 8 oz (224 g).

Kitchen Yields

Serving size:
4 oz (113 g).

SMOKED STURGEON
This elegant fish is considered kosher.

Pack:
By weight. Average weight is 3 to 5 lb (1.3 to 2.2 kg).

Kitchen Yields
Order #1, center cut. The pieces should be without cartilage. Skin is often left on. Some pieces have the belly flap left on, reducing the yield per pound. Trim loss is about 10 percent. Slice on machine; smoked sturgeon is not available presliced.

Serving size:
3 oz (85 g) for appetizer; thus, one 4-lb (1.8-kg) piece yields 18 appetizer servings.

SMOKED TROUT
Available whole, with head on, and in boneless fillets. Product is sometimes frozen.

Pack:
Sold by piece. Two 2-oz (56-g) fillets: Tray pack is available. Two each, total 4 oz (112 g).

Sizes:

Whole fish:
6 to 8 oz (170 to 220 g);
8 to 10 oz (220 to 280 g).

Kitchen Yields
Serving size:
Half trout, for appetizer.

SMOKED WHITEFISH
Available whole, with head on. The fish is considered kosher. *See also* Chubs under this same heading.

Pack:
By weight.

Size:
1½ to 2½ lb (0.67 to 1.1 kg). Other sizes are available.

Kitchen Yields
Fish must be boned, with head and skin removed. Waste is about 50 percent.

Serving size:
6 oz, cleaned for salad plate, as main course; one 2-lb (0.9-kg) fish yields 2½ servings.

SPRATS
Small smoked herring, sold whole as a specialty item.

FLOUR

Table F-1 identifies unsifted and sifted weights for different volumes of flour. The chart is based on bread flour; cake flour is slightly lighter.

FLOWERS

Many varieties of edible flowers come onto the market.

ACACIA
Dip acacia blossoms in batter and fry as a dessert.

Season:
Spring.

BORAGE
Tiny blue star-shaped flowers that taste like cucumbers. Use in salads and soups.

Table F-1 Converting Flour Volume to Weight

Volume	Weight Unsifted	Weight Sifted
1 cup	6 oz (170 g)	4¼ oz (120 g)
1 pint	12 oz (340 g)	10 oz (285 g)
1 qt	1½ lb (675 g)	1 lb 2 oz (510 g)
1 gal	6 lb (2.7 kg)	4½ lb (2 kg)

Season:
Available year-round.

Pack:
100, 300, and 600 blooms.

CALENDULA
Large full cushion of petals in yellow or orange. Use whole or sprinkle the petals.

Season:
Available year-round.

Pack:
100, 300, and 600 blooms.

CHAMOMILE
Fresh or dried blossoms and leaves are used as tea.

Season:
Available year-round.

CHRYSANTHEMUM
Use chrysanthemums in hot dishes as garnish, or in salads.

Season:
Fall.

CLOVER
Clover blossoms can be used in salads, teas, and compound butters.

Season:
Summer.

DAISY
Daisy flowers can be used to flavor wine.

Season:
Summer.

DANDELION
Dandelion blossoms and leaves are used in wine and salads.

Season:
Spring and summer.

ELDER
Elder blossoms may be dipped in batter and fried as a dessert.

Season:
Spring.

FUCHSIA
Frilly blooms in pinks, whites, and blues. Flowers keep well. Use as a garnish.

Season:
Available year-round.

Pack:
100, 300, and 600 blooms.

JASMINE
Flower essence used with desserts.

Season:
Available year-round.

LILAC
Used for candied flowers and water ice.

Season:
Spring.

MARIGOLD
Flower petals are used as a flavoring agent in meat dishes and desserts.

Season:
Available year-round.

NASTURTIUM
Bright red, yellow, and orange flowers with peppery taste; mix in salad. Leaves (available in May) may also be used in salads, and buds may be pickled.

Season:
Spring.

Pack:
100, 300, and 600 blooms.

ORANGE
Orange flowers may be used in ice cream and other desserts.

Season:
Available year-round.

ORCHIDS
Wanda orchids are used in salads, desserts, and as a drink garnish.

Season:
Available year-round.

PANSY
Round blooms in beautiful colors. Keep well. Use as garnish.

Season:
Available year-round.

Pack:
100, 300, and 600 blooms.

ROSELLE (JELLY OKRA)
This flower is used to make jelly.

Season:
Spring and summer.

ROSES
Flower petals are used for jelly, as candied dessert, or in flavored water. Rose fruit, called *rose hips,* are used for jelly and tea.

SQUASH
Squash flowers can be put in salads and used to make fritters or can be stuffed.

Season:
Available year-round.

TIGER LILY
Used fresh and dried in Oriental cooking.

Season:
Spring.

VIOLET
Violets are used in making candied petals, flavored water, water ice, and syrup.

Season:
Spring.

WOODRUFF
Used to flavor wine or tea.

Season:
Spring.

ZUCCHINI

Zucchini blossoms can be used to make fritters or can be stuffed.

Season:
Available year-round.

FOIE GRAS

Fatty goose or duckling liver. Available canned, fresh, and frozen in many varieties and many levels of quality.

CANNED FOIE GRAS

Numerous canned products are on the market, with distinct quality and price differences. Some products must be refrigerated for storage; all must be refrigerated for service. The following terminology is most often used to describe the products:

> *Terrine:* Whole liver poached in a ceramic container and studded with truffles. Available in the decorated container that the product was cooked in, or canned. Terrines are considered the top-of-the-line products.
> *Whole liver:* Canned whole liver in natural shape, without truffle center.
> *Block:* Whole liver with truffle center; most often packed in tunnel-shaped cans.
> *Parfait:* Puréed liver, often with truffle center; most often packed in tunnel-shaped cans.
> *Pâté:* Large chunks of liver baked in crust and filled with aspic jelly. The name pâté is also used often for products without crust.
> *Purée or mousse:* Liver product to which a binder such as eggs or gelatin has been added.
> *Roulade:* Purée or mousse packed in a cylindrical can, often with truffle center.
> *Liver pâté:* Canned liver product made of pork and other livers, to which a small percentage of foie gras has been added.

Pack:

Terrine:
Packed in ceramic container, with net weight of 7 oz (200 g), 3.7 oz (105 g), 3.5 oz (100 g), 2.25 oz (67 g), or 1.5 oz (43 g).

Whole liver:
28 oz (888 g), net.

Block:
Packed in tunnel-shaped can, weighing 10⅞ oz (309 g) or 7⅜ oz (209 g), net. Large slice, 15 oz (640 g) or 5 oz (142 g), net.

Purée:
10⅞ oz (309 g), net.

Roulade:
Packed in tall, cylindrical tin, 11¼ oz (320 g), net.

Liver pâté:
34½ oz (980 g), 14 oz (400 g), or 7 oz (200 g), net.

Kitchen Yields

Serving size:
Individual-serving terrine is 1½ oz (43 g) or 2.25 oz (67 g). For block foie gras, one 15-oz (640-g) can yields 20 to 22 large slices, and one 5-oz (142-g) can yields 6 to 7 large slices.

FRESH FOIE GRAS

Domestic foie gras of excellent quality is produced in a number of states and is available shipped by air. Imported livers, precooked and cryovac-packed, with a shelf life of 3 to 4 weeks, are available around Christmas. The size and weight of fresh livers determines their grade. The largest livers are the best.

Season:
Fall and winter. Some growers ship fresh liver year-round.

Pack and grades:

Domestic livers:
Grade A = 14 to 22 oz (400 to 625 g).
Grade B = 11 to 13 oz (312 to 370 g).
Grade C = 7 to 10 oz (200 to 284 g).

Imported livers:
9 to 10 oz (256 to 284 g), precooked.

Kitchen Yields

Use the largest livers for slicing and cooking to order, or for making terrines. Livers should always be cooked pink. Use smaller livers and liver trimmings for making pâtés.

Serving size:
3 oz (85 g) raw, or two slices, as appetizer; one 18-oz (512-g) liver yields 4 to 5 portions, with some usable trimmings left over.

FROZEN FOIE GRAS
Liver freezes well for short-term storage, and some "fresh livers" are shipped frozen to prevent spoilage. Pâtés and other prepared products do not freeze well.

FRAISE DES BOIS

French name for wild strawberry. *See* Strawberries.

FROGS

Usually only the legs are sold, although Oriental markets sell the whole frogs live. Legs are sold fresh or frozen, fully cleaned, normally in pairs. Some shippers do not trim the spine close to the legs, thereby inflating weight and reducing yield. Most product is imported, and quality varies greatly.

Sizes:
6 to 8 pairs per 1 lb (450 g); 8 to 10 pairs per 1 lb (450 g); 10 to 12 pairs per 1 lb (450 g).

Kitchen Yields
Large frog legs can be tough and dry.

Serving sizes:
For dinner, 1 lb (450 g) untrimmed yields 2 servings. For receptions, buy the 12 pieces per 1 lb size.

FRYING BATTER

See Beer Batter.

G

GALAX LEAVES

Round, tough leaves about 2½ in (63 mm) across, green or reddish brown, used for garnishing fruits. Order from florist.

Pack:
Bunches of 24 leaves each.

Kitchen Yields
Leaves will keep well when refrigerated.

GAME

Refer to particular species' names.

GARBANZOS (CHICK-PEAS)

See Beans.

GARLIC

Garlic is available dehydrated, fresh, and processed chopped.

DEHYDRATED GARLIC
Dehydrated ground garlic is available both plain and mixed with salt.

Pack:
By weight.

Kitchen Yields
1 tb dehydrated is equivalent to 1 tb minced fresh garlic; ¼ cup (0.06 l) dehydrated is equivalent to 4 tb minced fresh garlic.

FRESH GARLIC
Several varieties of garlic are widely available fresh.

DOMESTIC GARLIC
This is the common white garlic, available domestic and imported. Domestic production starts in July in California. Gilroy is a California community famous for growing garlic.

Season:
Available year-round.

Pack:
By weight.

Kitchen Yields
Peeling waste is about 12 percent.

ELEPHANT GARLIC
Large garlic with milder flavor than ordinary garlic. Can be served raw or cooked as a vegetable.

Season:
May to December.

Pack:
By weight.

Size:
8 to 16 oz (224 to 450 g) each.

Kitchen Yields
There is little waste.

ITALIAN GARLIC
Slightly pink garlic with strong flavor and smaller cloves.

Season:
Fall.

Pack:
By weight.

Kitchen Yield
About 5 percent waste.

TAHITI GARLIC
Large garlic with good yield.

Season:
Fall and winter.

Size:
Bulbs 2 to 3 in (50 to 75 mm) in diameter.

Kitchen Yields
Peeling waste is 5 percent.

PROCESSED CHOPPED GARLIC
Processed garlic is available peeled and chopped.

Pack:
Case of twelve 1-qt (0.9-l) jars. Smaller packs are also available.

Kitchen Yields
1 tb minced is equivalent to 4 to 5 cloves; ¼ cup
(0.06 l) is equivalent to 18 cloves.

GARNISHING PASTE

Solid edible paste made of eggs, starch, and other
ingredients to resemble truffles in appearance, but
not in taste. Available black or white.

Pack:
7¾-oz (220-g) cans.

Kitchen Yields
Depend on application. Paste is solid at room
temperature and can be sliced very thin on a
slicing machine.

GEFILTE FISH

See Fish.

GELATIN

FLAVORED GELATIN
Meat- and fruit-flavored gelatins are available
under different brand names, granulated or in
powder. Follow package directions.

UNFLAVORED GELATIN
Available granulated and in sheets.

Pack:

Granulated:
By weight; normally in 1-lb (450-g) containers;
envelopes of ¼ oz (7 g) each.

Sheets:
Packages of 17½ oz (500 g), often imported.

Kitchen Yields

Weight and volume:
1 cup weighs 5½ oz (154 g), and 1 pint weighs 11
oz (308 g).

Thickening power:
1 oz (28 g) thickens 2 qt (1.8 l) plain liquid.
2 oz (56 g) thickens 1 gal (3.7 l) plain liquid.
1 cup, or 5½ oz (154 g), thickens 2¾ gal (10.3 l)
plain liquid.

The thickening power of gelatin is influenced by
acidity. More gelatin must be used when the liquid
is acidic. In hot weather, the amount of gelatin
should be increased by about 25 percent. It is
always advisable to make a small sample first to
check the firmness of the resulting product.

Calories:
1 oz (28 g) dry gelatin = 100 Calories.

GINGER POWDER

Aromatic spice used in baking.

Pack:
1-lb (450-g) cans.

GINGER ROOT

Brown fibrous root, used in Oriental cooking, as a
flavoring in baking, and in beverages. Available
year-round in fresh, dried, and powdered forms.

Pack:
For fresh ginger, 5-, 10-, 30-lb (2.2-, 4.5-, or
13.5-kg) cartons. Average size varies.

Kitchen Yields
Peeling loss for fresh ginger is about 20 percent.

Calories:
3½ oz (100 g) = 49 Calories.

GNOCCHI

Gnocchi can be made fresh or are available frozen.

FRESH GNOCCHI
Formula
5 lb (2.2 kg) peeled russet potatoes, raw
28 oz (0.7 kg) bread flour
4 whole eggs

1 cup, or 6 oz (170 g), grated Parmesan
cheese.
1 tsp salt
¼ tsp nutmeg

Make sure potatoes are well drained after cooking.
Mash them while they are still hot.

Kitchen Yields
The preceding formula yields about 360 pieces,
weighing ⅓ oz (9 g) each.

Serving size:
Twelve 4-oz (122-g) pieces per portion as appetizer; eight 2½-oz (85-g) pieces per portion as
garnish with main course.

FROZEN GNOCCHI

Pack:
Twenty 1-lb (450-g) packages.

Kitchen Yields
1 lb (450 g) yields about 50 pieces.

Serving sizes:
Twelve 4-oz (122-g) pieces per portion as appetizer; eight 2½-oz (85-g) pieces per portion as
garnish with main course.
1 package yields 4 appetizer servings, or 6½
garnish servings.

GOAT

Available in ethnic markets.

Size:
Carcasses range from 30 to 60 lb (13.5 to 27 kg).

Kitchen Yields
Goat is generally less fatty than lamb. Use lamb
cuts and yields as guidelines. Best size is 30 to 40
lb (13.5 to 18 kg).

GOOSE

Available fresh and frozen, as well as smoked.

Pack:
Four birds each.

Sizes:
8 to 10 lb (3.6 to 4.5 kg); 10 to 12 lb (4.5 to 5.4 kg);
12 to 14 lb (5.4 to 6.3 kg); 14 lb (6.3 kg) and larger.

Kitchen Yields

Best size:
10 lb (4.5 kg), which yields 6 servings.

SMOKED GOOSE
Available whole or as breasts only.

Pack:

Breasts:
2 lb (0.9 kg), on average.

Whole birds:
7 to 9 lb (3.1 to 4 kg).

Kitchen Yields
Purchase breasts only for best yield. Weight of
fatty skin, if removed before service, is 20 percent
of purchased weight.

Serving size:
3 oz (85 g) as appetizer.

GOOSE LIVER
See Foie Gras.

GOOSEBERRIES

Available canned, fresh, and frozen. Fruit is
green or red; berries are sometimes slightly fuzzy
and often tart. Cape gooseberries are listed under
C as a separate entry.

CANNED GOOSEBERRIES
Usually imported. Packed in light syrup or water.

Pack:
Twelve 12½-oz (355-g) cans; six #10 cans.

Kitchen Yields

Drained weights:
One 12½-oz (350-g) can contains 9 oz (255 g)
berries; one #10 can contains 75 oz (2.1 kg)
berries.

FRESH GOOSEBERRIES

Season:
Summer.

Pack:
1-pint (0.47-l) containers. Other packs are available.

Size:
About ½ in (1.2 cm) across.

Kitchen Yields

Serving size:
½ cup (0.232 l); thus, 1 pint (0.47 l) yields 4 servings.

Calories:
4 oz (112 g) = 35 Calories.

FROZEN GOOSEBERRIES

Pack:
30 lb (13.5 kg), IQF.

GOURDS

Ornamental gourds are sold by weight or by the piece.

GRANITE (WATER ICE)

Grainy ice often served as an intermezzo at formal dinners or as a refreshing dessert.

Formula
    6 qt (5.6 l) water
    6 lb (2.7 kg) sugar
    1 cup (0.23 l) lemon juice
    1 qt (0.9 l) fruit brandy

Kitchen Yields
The preceding formula yields 2 gal (7.6 l) granite. NOTE: Water can be flavored with fruit or herbs, or replaced with juice. The sugar quantity should be adjusted as necessary.

GRAPEFRUIT

GRAPEFRUIT JUICE
Grapefruit juice is available canned, freshly squeezed, and as frozen concentrate. Canned juice is available sweetened and unsweetened.

CANNED GRAPEFRUIT JUICE

Pack:
Twelve 46-oz (1.3-l) cans; forty-eight 6-oz (0.17-liter) cans.

Kitchen Yields

Serving size:
6 oz; therefore, one 46-oz (1.3-l) can yields 7½ servings.

Calories:
Unsweetened, 6 oz (0.17 l) = 75 Calories.
Sweetened, 6 oz (0.17 l) = 101 Calories.

FRESH GRAPEFRUIT JUICE

Pack:
Twelve 1-qt (0.94-l) containers.

Kitchen Yields

Serving size:
6 oz; therefore, one 1-qt container yields 5 servings.

Calories:
6 oz (0.17 l) fresh juice = 66 Calories.

FROZEN CONCENTRATED GRAPEFRUIT JUICE

Pack:
Six 46-oz (1.3-l) cans.

Kitchen Yields

Serving size:
6 oz. Dilute 1 part concentrate with 3 parts water. One 46-oz (1.3-l) can yields 30 servings.

GRAPEFRUIT SECTIONS
Grapefruit sections are available canned and fresh in jars.

CANNED GRAPEFRUIT SECTIONS

Pack:
Twelve #3 cylinder cans; twenty-four, thirty-six, or forty-eight #300 cans.

Kitchen Yields

Serving size:
½ cup, or 4½ oz (130 g); thus, one #300 can yields 3 servings, and one #3 cylinder can yields 4 servings with syrup.

FRESH GRAPEFRUIT SECTIONS

Pack:
Four 1-gal (3.7-l) jars.

Kitchen Yields

Serving size:
½ cup, or 4½ oz (130 g); thus, one 1-gal (3.7-l) jar yields 22 servings, with juice.

Calories:
½ cup (130 g) sections in light syrup = 90 Calories.

WHOLE FRESH GRAPEFRUIT

The main varieties are Marsh Seedless White and Ruby, which has pinkish flesh. Duncan grapefruit has the most seeds. Florida and Texas grapefruits are generally juicier than California and Arizona fruits. The Indian River region in Florida and the Rio Grande Valley in Texas are known for producing high-quality grapefruits. Grapefruits are picked when ripe and do not ripen any further once off the tree.

Season:
Available year-round. Winter grapefruit comes from Florida, California, and Texas. Summer fruit is from Arizona and California. Red grapefruit is in season from October to May.

Packs and Counts:

California and Arizona:
38- to 42-lb (17.1- to 18.9-kg) cartons, or $^7/_{10}$ bushel, with 23, 27, 32, 36, 40, 48, 56 or 64 fruits each.

Florida:
40- to 50-lb (18- to 22.5-kg) cartons, or $^4/_5$ bushel, with 23, 27, 32, 36, 40, 48, 56, or 64 fruits each.

Texas:
38- to 42-lb (17.1- to 18.9-kg) cartons, or $^7/_{10}$ bushels, with 18, 23, 27, 32, 36, 40, 48, 56, 76, or 84 fruits each.

Sizes:
#27 = 4$^{11}/_{16}$ in (118 mm) in diameter.
#32 = 4½ in (114 mm) in diameter.
#36 = 4¼ in (107 mm) in diameter.
#40 = 4$^1/_{16}$ in (103 mm) in diameter.
#48 = 3⅞ in (98 mm) in diameter.

Kitchen Yields
One fruit contains 10 to 12 sections. One medium-size raw fruit weighing about 1 lb 1 oz (475 g) yields 8½ oz (238 g) sections or ⅔ cup juice. One and a half medium-size raw fruits yield 1 cup diced fruit.
Common hotel size is #23.

Calories:
For a medium-size (3¾ in in diameter) raw fruit weighing about 1 lb 1 oz (478 g):
One-half fruit, 8½ oz (238 g), pink or red = 50 Calories.
One-half fruit 58½ oz (238 g), white = 45 Calories.

GRAPES

Grapes are available canned, fresh, and whole. Grape juice and grape leaves in brine are also discussed here. Raisins are discussed under a separate entry; *see* Raisins.

CANNED GRAPES
Available packed in light or heavy syrup.

Pack:
Six #10 cans; twenty-four #2½ cans.

Kitchen Yields
One #10 can contains 8 cups (1.8 l) drained fruit. One #2½ can contains 2 cups (0.47 l) drained fruit.

FRESH GRAPES
Domestic table grapes are available year-round, supplemented by imports. However, all varieties have distinct seasons. Grapes are distinguished by

whether they are seedless or seeded and by color (red and green). The shades of color vary widely and can range from light green to purple and dark blue, regardless of whether seedless or seeded. The trade distinguishes between green and colored grapes. Table G-1 lists varieties of domestic table grapes, their characteristics, and their seasons. For foodservice use, seedless grapes are preferred. Both red and green grapes can be seedless. *See also* Champagne Grapes.

Imported seedless grapes are available in winter and spring.

Pack:
23-lb (10.3-kg) lugs; 17-lb (7.6-kg) boxes; 12-lb (5.4-kg) boxes.

Sizes:
Preportioned 2-, 3-, 4-, and 8-oz (56-, 85-, 112-, and 225-g) bunches.

Kitchen Yields
The size of different varieties of grapes varies greatly. Typically, there are 35 to 45 grapes in one cup.

Seedless grapes:
1 lb (450 g) as purchased yields 15 oz (420 g) stemmed grapes. 1 cup weighs 5¾ oz (163 g). One 20-lb (9-kg) lug of grapes yields 50 cups or 12½ qt (11.6 l) stemmed grapes.

Grapes with seeds:
1 lb (450 g) as purchased yields 14½ oz (400 g) stemmed grapes. 1 cup weighs 6 oz (168 g). One 23-lb (10.3-kg) lug yields 55 cups stemmed grapes.

Serving size:
½ cup or 3 oz (84 g); so a 23-lb lug yields 110 3-oz (84-g) servings.

Calories:

Seedless:
1 cup or 5¾ oz (163 g) = 107 Calories.

Seeded:
1 cup or 6 oz (168 g) = 102 Calories.

GRAPE JUICE
Grape juice is available canned or in bottles, or as frozen concentrate.

Table G-1 Varieties and Seasons of Domestic Table Grapes

Variety	Characteristics	Season
Almeria	seeded, green	October through February
Calmeria	seeded, green	October through February
Cardinal	seeded, red	mid-May to mid-August
Concord	seeded, dark blue	September to November
Emperor	seeded, red	September through March
Exotic	seeded, red	June through August
Flame Seedless	seedless, red	mid-June through September
Golden Muscat	green	September to December
Italia	seeded, green	August through September
Perlette	seedless, green	mid-May to mid-July
Queen	seeded, red	August and September
Ribier	seeded, red	August through mid-February
Ruby	seedless, red	mid-August through January
Thompson Seedless	seedless, green	June to November
Tokay	seeded, red	July through November

CANNED GRAPE JUICE

Pack:
Twelve 24-oz (0.7-l) cans, or twelve 32-oz (0.94-l) bottles.

Kitchen Yields

Serving size:
6 oz (0.17 l); thus, one 24-oz (0.7-l) can yields 4 servings, and one 32-oz (0.94-l) bottle yields 5 servings.

Calories:
6 oz (0.17 l), canned or bottled = 124 Calories.

FROZEN CONCENTRATED GRAPE JUICE

Pack:
Six 42-oz (1.2-l) cans.

Kitchen Yields

Serving size:
6 oz (0.17 l). Dilute 1 part concentrate with 3 parts water. One 42-oz (1.2-l) can yields 5¼ qt (4.9 l) juice, which is equivalent to 28 servings.

GRAPE LEAVES

Grape leaves, primarily Dolmas, for stuffing are available imported and from California. The leaves are packed in brine.

Pack:
16-oz (450-g) jars, net weight.

Kitchen Yields
40 leaves per 16-oz (450-g) jar.

GRIDDLE CAKES

Formula
 18 lb (8.1 kg) cake flour
 3 gal (11.4 l) milk
 1 gal (3.8 l), or 80 whole eggs
 4 lb (1.8 kg) sugar
 1 lb (450 g) baking powder
 5 lb (2.25 kg) melted shortening

Kitchen Yield
Total mix: 5 gal (19 l).

Serving size:
Three cakes, 5 in (127 mm) across, which use 5 oz (140 g) batter. The total mix from the preceding formula yields 360 pieces, or 120 servings.

GRITS

See Hominy.

GUAVA

This pear-shaped tropical fruit is available fresh. Ripe fruit gives off a wonderful aroma. It is used mostly in jams and as stewed fruit. *See also* Guyabate, under Mexican Foods.

Season:
Spring and summer. Limited supplies are available year-round.

Pack:
10-lb (4.5-kg) cartons.

Count:
The typical trade count is 30 to 32 pieces per carton.

Kitchen Yields
Fruit is tart and seldom eaten raw.

Size:
4½ in (12 cm) long. Many other sizes can be found in ethnic markets.

Weight:
2⅓ to 2½ oz (65 to 70 g).

Calories:
4 oz (112 g) usable flesh = 70 Calories.

GUINEA HEN

Available fresh and frozen. Normally sold whole. Called *pintades* in French.

Average size:
2¼ to 2½ lb (1 to 1.1 kg).

Kitchen Yields
One bird yields 2 servings.

GYROS

Middle Eastern–style chopped meat cone that is cooked on a revolving vertical spit and served (usually) on pita bread. Available with lamb or beef composition. Shipped fresh or frozen.

Sizes:
10, 20, and 30 lb (4.5, 9, and 13.5 kg).

Pack:
Four 10-lb (4.5-kg) cones; two 20-lb (9-kg) cones; individual 30-lb (13.5-kg) cones.

Kitchen Yields

Serving size:
3½ oz (100 g) cooked meat; therefore, one 10-lb (4.5-kg) cone yields 35 servings.

H

HAMBURGER PATTIES

See Chopped Steaks and Hamburger, under Beef.

HAMS

See Smoked and Cured Pork Products, under Pork.

HARE

Available fresh and frozen. Hare has dark meat, unlike rabbit, which has light meat. Sold skinned or with skin on.

Season:
Fall and winter.

Average size:
4 lb (1.8 kg), skinned and eviscerated.

Kitchen Yields

Serving size:
One leg or one whole loin. One hare thus yields 3 servings—two legs, and one saddle piece.

HARICOTS VERTS

See Beans.

HAZELNUTS

See Filberts.

HEARTS OF PALM

Hearts of palm are available canned.

Pack:
Twenty-four 28-oz (800-g) cans, with drained weight 17¼ oz (490 g); twenty-four 14-oz (400-g) cans, with drained weight 7¼ oz (204 g).

Kitchen Yields
One large can contains 8 to 9 stalks; one small can contains 5 to 6 stalks.

Serving size:
2 stalks, for salad.

HERBS & SPICES

ACHIOTE (ANNATTO)
See Mexican Foods.

ANGELICA
Ancient herb with little modern use. Stems are available candied, dyed green, and used as cake decoration.

Pack:
By weight.

BASIL (SWEET BASIL)
There are a number of varieties of basil on the market.

Season:
Available year-round. Peak is during summer.

Pack:
Bunches of various sizes.

Kitchen Yields
1 cup leaves without stems weighs 2 oz (40 g).
NOTE: Basil wilts quickly.

BAY LEAVES (MONTERY LAUREL)
Available fresh.

Season:
Year-round.

Pack:
Sold on stems, normally by dozen.

Kitchen Yields
Approximately 40 leaves on each stem.

CHILI POWDER

Pack:
By weight.

Kitchen Yields
2 cups weighs 9¼ oz (260 g).

CILANTRO
Also known as *Chinese* or *Mexican parsley,* cilantro constitutes the greens of the coriander plant.

Season:
Available year-round.

Pack:
30-bunch lugs.

Kitchen Yields
Only leaves are used.

CORIANDER
Coriander seed is available ground and whole.

Pack:
By weight.

Kitchen Yields
½ cup weighs 1¼ oz (35 g).

DILL
Fresh dill is available year-round.

Pack:
12 bunches per flat.

Kitchen Yields
Size of bunches varies, depending on season and packer.

FAJITA SEASONING
See Mexican Foods.

GINGER
See Ginger Powder and Ginger Root.

LEMON BALM (MELISSA)
Season:
Summer. The herb is perennial.

Kitchen Yields
Leaves only are used. They are added to fruit salads and drinks and have a slightly lemony taste.

OREGANO
¾ cup dried oregano weighs 1 oz (28 g).

PARSLEY

FRESH PARSLEY
There are two types of parsley: Curly Leaf and Italian. Curly Leaf is mostly used for garnishing, and Italian is used for flavoring.

Season:
Available year-round.

Pack:
Sold in bunches. The size of a bunch varies.

Kitchen Yields
Average weight of a bunch is 2 oz (56 g) but can vary greatly.

SAFFRON
Genuine saffron is imported from Spain. Imitation saffron is available from Mexico.

Pack:
By weight; packs range from 1 oz (28 g) to 1 lb (450 g).

Kitchen Yields
Whole saffron is better than ground saffron. Allow the flower stigmas to steep in liquid, in order to get better flavor extraction.
⅛ oz (3.5 g) saffron flavors 2 gal (7.4 l) stock.

SORREL (SOUR GRASS)
Sorrel is used as a salad green, as a side vegetable, and as a soup ingredient.

Season:
Spring and summer.

Pack:
By weight, usually in 20-lb (9.1-kg) crates.

Kitchen Yields
For vegetable dishes, remove stems, and boil cut leaves in their own juices. It is advisable to cook sorrel separately and add cooked to soups and sauces. In this way, the acidity level of the finished product can be regulated. Sorrel turns gray when cooked due to acidity. It should be added to green sauces at the last moment to limit the color loss of other green ingredients.
1 lb (450 g) as purchased will season 1 qt (0.94 l) soup.

TURMERIC
Turmeric is a root vegetable resembling ginger. The ground root, which is used as a spice, is yellow and is sometimes called erroneously *saffron*.

Turmeric is an important ingredient in curry powder.

Pack:
By weight.

Size:
Roots are 3 to 5 inches (12 to 20 cm) long.

VANILLA
See Vanilla.

HOMINY

Hominy is available canned and as grits, dried and ground.

CANNED HOMINY
Yellow hominy and white hominy are both available fully cooked.

Pack:
Six #10 cans.

Kitchen Yields
One #10 can contains 75 oz (2.1 kg), drained weight.

Serving size:
1 cup, or 8½ oz (238 g), for breakfast. Thus, one #10 can yields 8 servings, and one case of six #10 cans yields 48 servings.

Calories:
1 cup, weighing 8½ oz (238 g) = 125 Calories.

DRY HOMINY GRITS
Uncooked grits are dried hominy that has been ground to the consistency of coarse cornmeal.

Pack:
By weight.

Kitchen Yields
1 lb (450 g) dry measure or 2¾ cups (0.64 l) 4¼ lb (1.9 kg) produces 50 cups cooked.
1 cup dry measure yields 4 cups (0.94 l) cooked mush; 1 lb dry measure yields 11 cups (2.5 l) cooked mush.

Serving size:
1 cup, or 8½ oz.

Calories:
1 cup cooked, weighing 8½ oz (241 g) = 125 Calories.

HONEY

Pack:
Jars in various sizes, or portion pack.

Calories:
1 tb (21 g) = 65 Calories.

HORSERADISH

Horseradish is available whole and fresh, or grated and preserved with vinegar. Most operators use horseradish that has already been grated. Grated horseradish is available plain or mixed with beet juice.

FRESH HORSERADISH
Brown root with white flesh, pungent and hot. It is used raw, grated, and mixed with vinegar as a condiment.

Season:
Available year-round.

Pack:
By weight.

Kitchen Yields
Peeling waste is about 20 percent. To avoid discoloration, keep peeled roots in ice water.

GRATED HORSERADISH
Available plain or flavored with red beet juice.

Pack:
1-qt (0.94-l) jars.

Kitchen Yields
Varies. About 3 oz (85 g) per serving.

HOTCAKES

See Griddle Cakes.

HOT PEPPERS

See Chilies, under Mexican Foods.

HUCKLEBERRY

A variety of blueberry, seldom available commercially. Huckleberries grow wild in many regions of the west coast. The juice of huckleberries is dark purple. The berries are smaller than cultivated blueberries.

Season:
Midsummer to late summer.

Kitchen Yields
See main entry for Blueberries for information on serving size.

Calories:
4 oz (112 g) = 60 Calories.

I AND J

ICE

The production and storage capacity of ice machines is rated in pounds.

Ice cube weights:
1 cubic ft (0.28 cubic m) ice cubes weighs 30 lb (13.5 kg); 1 lb (450 g) cubes will ice 3 to 4 water glasses.

ICE FOR CARVING

Standard size block:

Weight:
300 lb (135 kg).

Size:
40 × 20 × 10 in (1 × 50 × 25 cm).
Other sizes are available.

Melting speed:
1½ in (38 mm) per hour at room temperature. One carved ice piece will melt at the rate of 1½ in per hour of exposed ice surface.

ICE CREAM

Quality in ice cream is measured in terms of butterfat content, weight (overrun), and flavor. *Butterfat content* is measured in percentages, based on weight:

16 to 18 percent: Deluxe quality
14 to 16 percent: High quality
12 percent: Minimum for vanilla ice cream
10 percent: Minimum for ice cream containing added solids, such as chocolate or nuts

Overrun is the amount of expansion in volume that occurs during the freezing process. Some overrun is normal, but it increases if additional air is whipped into the product. Ice cream with high overrun is weak in flavor, light, and has a limited shelf life. The volume will be reduced when this ice cream is processed in the kitchen. The amount of overrun is reflected in percentages in relation to volume: 100 percent overrun means that the product doubled during the freezing process.

100 percent: High
80 percent: Normal
50 percent: High-quality product

Pack:
2½-gal (9.5-l) tubs; 3-gal (11.4-l) tubs. The 3-gal size is standard in many locations.
Weight is an important quality indicator. Ice cream should be weighed occasionally when received to ensure that it meets the quality standards it is supposed to satisfy. The following weights can be used as general guidelines:

1 gal (3.8 l) = 4½ lb (2 kg) minimum weight
1 gal (3.8 l) = 6 lb (2.7 kg) best-quality ice cream with 50 percent overrun
2½-gal (9.5-l) tub = 11¼ lb (5 kg) minimum weight
2½-gal (9.5-l) tub = 15 lb (6.75 kg) high-quality ice cream
3 gal (11.4 l) tub = 13½ lb (6 kg) minimum weight
3-gal (11.4-l) tub = 18 lb (8.1 kg) high-quality ice cream

Kitchen Yields
Scoops are classified by the number of scoops per 1 qt (0.94 l). For instance, there are twelve #12 scoops in 1 qt ice cream. Measurements are approximate, since they depend on how well the portions are dipped, and on the overrun of the product. High-overrun ice cream shrinks during storage. Portion weight depends on the overrun. One #8 scoop of high-quality ice cream weighs around 3 oz (84 g). Other scoop sizes are listed under a separate entry; *see* Scoop Sizes.
   Ice cream rings are often used for banquets. The serving size is 4 fl oz (0.11 l), so 5 cups (1.1 l) provides ice cream for 10 covers.

Calories:
3½ oz (100 g), with 11 percent butterfat = 200 Calories.
3½ oz (100 g), with 16 percent butterfat = 236 Calories.

ICES

See Granite (Water Ice).

ICING

See Royal Icing.

IQF

IQF is the abbreviation for *individually quick-frozen.* IQF products are frozen loose, and therefore are easier to use than products frozen into solid blocks. To prevent freezer burn, processors spray the products with water during the freezing process; this is called *glazing* in the trade.

Kitchen Yields

About 10 to 15 percent lower yield per unit weight, on account of glazing, compared to block-frozen products. The weight loss varies greatly depending on the product.

J

JALAPENOS

See Chilies, under Mexican Foods.

JAPANESE FOODS

ASAKUSA NORI
Asakusa nori, also called *lavar,* is a seaweed, available fresh and as thin, dried sheets. Lack of uniformity in color is an indication of good quality.

Season:
For fresh nori, late summer and fall

Pack:
Varies.

Size:
6×10 in (150×250 mm).

DAIKON
Long white radish, used in condiments and as a vegetable. It may be eaten raw, pickled, or cooked.

Season:
Available year-round.

Pack:
Purchase by weight. Average weight is about 2 lb (0.9 kg). Sold often with leaves on—3 radishes to a bunch, 12 bunches to a case.

Calories:
$\frac{1}{4}$ cup or $1\frac{1}{2}$ oz (42 g) shredded = 25 Calories.

Kitchen Yields

Size:
1 to $1\frac{1}{2}$ lb (0.45 to 0.67 kg).

EDA MAME
Fresh soybeans, most often sold still in their pods.

Season:
Late spring through summer.

Pack:
Sold by weight or in bunches.

Calories:
$1\frac{1}{4}$ cups cooked and shelled = 200 Calories.

GOBO
Called *burdock* in English, this root vegetable is common in most parts of Europe and Asia. The tender roots are peeled and cooked. They resemble salsify.

Season:
August to December.

Size:
10 to 16 oz (228 to 450 g).

JAPANESE EGGPLANT
This small, purple eggplant is available in spring.

Pack:
By weight and by piece.

Size:
4 to 5 oz (113 to 140 g) each.

JAPANESE MUSHROOMS
See Mushrooms.

KANTEN
See Agar-agar.

KATSUO BUSHI
Flakes of dried bonito—the main ingredient for making dashi, the basic stock.

Pack:
2.8- and 5.2-oz (100- and 150-g) bags.

Kitchen Yields
½ cup flakes yields 1½ qt (0.7 l) stock.

Calories:
¼ cup dry flakes = 25 Calories.

KOMBU
Kelp, normally sold dry. Used in making stocks and added to other dishes.

MIRIN
Sweet rice wine.

Pack:
2 qt 2½ oz (1 l).

MISO
Bean paste, available fresh in three basic flavors:

> *Aka:* red, pungent
> *Chu:* gold-colored, mild
> *Shiro:* white, almost sweet

Pack:
Purchase by weight.

OCHA
Green tea. *See* Chinese Foods.

OKOME
Short-grain rice, grown for Japanese cooking. The variety is called California Rose, Blue Rose, or Calrose rice. Grown mostly in California and available under various brand names, this rice is used for sushi and as side dish.

Pack:
1-, 5-, 10-, 25-, and 50-lb (0.45-, 2.2-, 4.5-, 11.2-, and 22.5-kg) bags.

Kitchen Yields

Serving size:
½ cup cooked, equivalent to 1.6 oz (45 g) raw; 10 lb (4.5 kg) yields 100 portions.

Calories:
½ cup cooked = 90 Calories.

SAKE
Alcoholic beverage made from fermented rice; usually served warm.

Calories:
1 cup (0.235 l) = 200 Calories.

TOFU
See Bean Curd.

WAKAME
Seaweed, available fresh or pickled in salt.

WASABI
Powdered green horseradish. Mix with cold water for a mustardlike consistency.

JELLY OKRA

See Roselle, under Flowers.

JERUSALEM ARTICHOKE

See Sunchoke.

JICAMA (MEXICAN POTATO)

Crisp, slightly sweet white tuber resembling a
large turnip. Can be used raw in salads, or can be
steamed, fried, or boiled. The tuber peels easily,
and there is little waste.

Season:
September to June.

Pack:
Sold by weight.

Average weight:
6 to 8 oz (170 to 224 g).

Kitchen Yields
About 25 percent peeling loss.

JUJUBE

Yellowish, olive-shaped fruit with a single stone.
Available fresh.

Season:
Late summer until spring.

Kitchen Yields

Size:
1 to 2 in (2.5 to 5 cm) long.

Weight:
1½ to 3 oz (70 to 85 g).

K

KALE

Kale is available canned, fresh, and frozen.

CANNED KALE

Canned kale is sold chopped.

Pack:
Six #10 cans.

Drained weight:
62 oz (1.7 kg).

Kitchen Yields

Serving size:
¾ cup, or 4 oz (112 g); thus, one #10 can yields 15 servings, and one case yields 90 servings.

Calories:
¾ cup, or 4 oz (112 g) = 40 Calories.

FRESH KALE

Scotch Kale and Blue Kale are important varieties that have curly leaves. Smooth-leaf varieties are also available, especially in the spring. Kale can be purchased whole in bunches or stripped. It is often shipped iced.

Season:
December to April.

Pack:
18- to 25-lb (8.1- to 11.2-kg) bushels.

Kitchen Yields

Yields are difficult to estimate, because of the amount of stripping. Waste is about 30 percent by weight.

Calories:
¾ cup cooked and drained, weighing 4 oz (112 g) = 45 Calories.

FROZEN KALE

Frozen kale is available chopped.

Pack:
Twelve 2-lb (0.9-kg) boxes.

Kitchen Yields

Serving size:
¾ cup, or 4 oz (112 g); one 2-lb (0.9-kg) box yields 7 servings, and one case yields 84 servings.

NOTE: There is weight loss when product is defrosted.

Calories:
¾ cup, or 4 oz (112 g) = 40 Calories.

KASHA

Cracked buckwheat; used as cereal in Jewish and Russian cooking.

Pack:
Twenty-four 1-lb (450-g) packages. Larger packs are available.

Kitchen Yields

1 lb (450 g) kasha is equivalent to 2¼ cups dry.

Serving size:
⅔ (0.15 l) cup; 1 lb (450 g) yields 10 servings.

Kasha Recipe

    1 lb (450 g) kasha
    2 whole eggs, mixed dry into kasha
    ½ cup shortening
    4 cups water or stock

Kitchen Yield

6½ cups (1.5 l).

KELP

See Seaweed.

KIRBY CUCUMBERS

See Cucumbers.

KIWI FRUIT

Also called *Chinese gooseberry*, a green fruit with thin, fuzzy skin. The fruit is ripe when it gives slightly under light pressure. To make a kiwi fruit ripen quickly, store it at room temperature in a plastic bag together with apples or bananas. The fruit stores well for several weeks at 33°F.

Season:

California kiwi:
October until May.

Imported kiwi:
Available year-round.

Pack:
7-lb (3.1-kg) flats; 20-lb (9.0-kg) cartons.

Sizes:
Counts of 25, 28, 30, 33, 36, 39, 42, and 45 in 7-lb flats.

Weight range:
1 to 4 oz (25 to 100 g).

Kitchen Yields

Average weight:
2½ to 3 oz (70 to 84 g) per fruit. One 2½-oz (70-g) fruit yields 5 to 6 slices. Two and one-half fruits, diced large, yield 1 cup, or 6 oz (168 g). One #39 flat yields 16 cups, or 96 oz (2.7 kg), diced fruit.

Calories:
4 oz (100 g) = 39 Calories.

KOHLRABI

Also called *cabbage turnip*, this vegetable has a swollen stem that grows above ground. It is available with green or purple skin. Kohlrabi should not be larger than 2 in (50 mm) across, because larger kohlrabi are often woody and cannot be used.

Season:
May to November, with peak in July and August.

Pack:
By weight or by bunches. When purchasing by weight, ascertain whether the leaves are trimmed off.

Kitchen Yields
Waste is at least 40 percent after trimming off leaves.

KUMQUATS

Kumquats are small citrus fruits resembling oranges; they are available fresh or preserved in syrup.

FRESH KUMQUATS

Season:
Fall and winter.

Pack:
10-lb (4.5-kg) cartons.

Kitchen Yields
Use as is; there is no waste.
NOTE: Kumquats are sometimes shipped in small clusters with leaves still attached.

PRESERVED KUMQUATS
Kumquats are preserved in light or heavy syrup.

Pack:
Four 1-gal (3.8-l) jars.

Kitchen Yields
There is no waste; use as is.

L

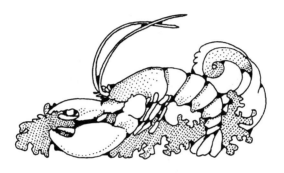

LADLE SIZES

Table L-1 lists common ladle sizes and their equivalents in cups, quarts, and liters.

LAMB AND MUTTON

Lamb generally comes from animals less than 1 year old. Mutton comes from animals over 1 year old but should not be older than 2 years. The term *yearling* is used for animals 1 year old. The term *spring lamb* indicates that the animal was born in spring of the same year. It is generally from a 3-month-old animal, but can be marketed from animals slaughtered as late as October of their year of birth.

LARGER CUTS OF DOMESTIC LAMB AND MUTTON

The American Lamb Council is recommending changes in some of the specifications listed under this heading, in order to make the cuts easier to use. The new specifications are listed under a separate heading in this same general entry.

To make product identification easier, *Meat Buyers Guide* (MBG) numbers are listed when practical.

BABY LAMB
Often sold whole, with the pelt on.

Weight range:
20 to 40 lb (9 to 18 kg).

Table L-1 Ladle Sizes and Equivalents

Size	Fraction of 1 cup	Number per 1 qt	Number per 1 l
1 oz	⅛	32	34
2 oz	¼	16	17
2⅔ oz	⅓	12	13
4 oz	½	8	8.6
6 oz	¾	5⅓	5.7
8 oz	1	4	4.3

Best size:
26 to 30 lb (11.7 to 13.5 kg) with pelt.

Kitchen Yields
The carcass is divided into legs, boneless shoulders, racks, and backs. The parts are very small, and normally slices from various parts are combined to produce a single serving. Meat should be cooked until lightly pink.

Serving size:
5 oz (140 g). One 28-lb (12.6-kg) lamb, pelt on, yields 22 servings.

BACK, MBG #236
Whole back, with rack and loin still attached.

Weights:

Lamb:
8 to 15 lb (3.6 to 6.7 kg).

Mutton:
11 to 26 lb (4.9 to 11.7 kg).

Kitchen Yields
Good buffet piece when roasted whole.

Best size:
15 lb (6.7 kg) for lamb; 20 lb (9 kg) for mutton.

Servings:
One 15-lb (6.7-kg) lamb back yields 25 servings on buffet; one 20-lb (9-kg) mutton back yields 30 servings on buffet.

BREAST, MBG #209A
Cut includes plate and brisket. Best to cut this piece on meat saw for stew or use as barbecue ribs.

Weights:

Lamb:
3 to 8 lb (1.3 to 3.6 kg).

Mutton:
4 to 10 lb (1.8 to 4.5 kg).

Kitchen Yields
Meat is very fatty.

Serving size:
14 oz (400 g), raw weight.

CHUCK, MBG #206
Whole chuck, with bone in.

Weight ranges:

Lamb:
11 to 14 lb (4.9 to 6.3 kg).
14 to 19 lb (6.3 to 8.5 kg).
19 to 23 lb (8.5 to 10.3 kg).

Mutton:
19 to 26 lb (8.5 to 11.7 kg).
26 to 33 lb (11.7 to 14.8 kg).
33 to 40 lb (14.8 to 18 kg).

Kitchen Yields
Chuck can be fatty. Use for stew or make into
boneless roast. Boneless roast is fatty and will not
slice well.

LAMB:

Best weight:
18 lb (8.1 kg). Boned and trimmed, this yields
10 lb (4.5 kg).

Serving size:
For stew, 8 oz (228 g) raw meat, which yields 5 oz
(140 g) cooked stew; thus, 10 lb (4.5 kg) meat
yields 20 servings. For roast, 7 oz (200 g) raw meat,
which yields 5 oz (140 g) cooked roast. Chuck,
boned and tied, yields one 7-lb (3.1-kg) roast, or
3 lb (1.3 kg) stew meat. One 7-lb (3.1-kg) tied roast
yields 16 servings.

Shrinkage loss:
For stew cooked medium well, 35 percent; for
roast, 25 percent.

MUTTON:

Best weight:
24 lb (10.8 kg). Boned and trimmed, this yields
14 lb (6.3 kg).

Serving size:
For stew, 8 oz (228 g) raw meat, which yields 5 oz
(142 g) cooked meat; thus, 14 lb (6.3 kg) stew meat
yields 28 servings. For roast, 7¼ oz raw meat,
which yields 5 oz (140 g) cooked meat; thus 11 lb
(4.9 kg) tied meat yields 22 servings.

Shrinkage loss:
For stew, 35 percent; for roast, 28 percent.
NOTE: Not all chuck meat is suitable for roasting.
About 3 lb (1.3 kg) meat should be used as stew
meat.

Calories:
5 oz (142 g) cooked roast = 575 Calories.

HOTEL-SIZE EIGHT-RIB RACK, MBG #204

Weight ranges:

Lamb:
3 to 5 lb (1.3 to 2.2 kg).
5 to 6 lb (2.2 to 2.7 kg).
6 to 8 lb (2.7 to 3.6 kg).

Mutton:
6 to 8 lb (2.7 to 3.6 kg).
8 to 10 (3.6 to 4.5 kg).
10 to 14 lb (4.5 to 6.3 kg).

Best size:
6 to 8 lb (2.7 to 3.6 kg).

Kitchen Yields

LAMB:

Best size:
Whole. 7 lb (3.1 kg).

Trimmed size:
Two racks, frenched, 2 lb (0.9 kg) each.

Serving size:
For roast rack, two 8½-oz (300-g) pieces, cooked,
with bone. Half a rack yields 3 servings; one
whole rack yields 6 servings; and ten racks yield
60 servings. For rib chops, serving size is one 9-oz
(250-g) piece or two 4½-oz (125-g) pieces. Half a
rack yields 3 servings; one whole rack yields 6
servings; and ten racks yield 60 servings.

Calories:
Lean and fat boneless meat, 3½ oz (100 g) = 370
Calories.

MUTTON:

Best size:
Whole. 10 lb (4.5 kg).

Trimmed size:
Two racks, frenched, 3 lb 5 oz (1.5 kg) each.

Serving size:
For roast rack, two 4½-oz (126-g) pieces cooked, each with bone. Half a rack yields 4 servings; one whole rack yields 8 servings; and ten racks yield 80 servings.
For rib chops, serving size is one 12-oz (336-g) piece with two bones. Half a rack yields 4 chops; one rack yields 8 chops; ten racks yield 80 chops.

LEGS, MBG #233
The weights listed are for pairs, with bone in.

Sizes:

Lamb:
11 to 14 lb (4.9 to 6.3 kg).
14 to 19 lb (6.3 to 8.5 kg).
19 to 23 lb (8.5 to 10.3 kg).
23 to 27 lb (10.3 to 12.1 kg).

Mutton:
19 to 26 lb (8.5 to 11.7 kg).
26 to 33 lb (11.7 to 14.6 kg).
33 to 40 lb (14.6 to 18 kg).
40 to 46 lb (18 to 20.7 kg).

Kitchen Yields

LAMB:

Best size:

Pair:
18 lb (8.1 kg).

Single leg:
9 lb (4 kg).

Serving size:
For roast, 6 oz (170 g). One 7½-lb (3.3-kg) oven-ready single leg, with aitch bone a part of shank removed, trimmed, and leg bone in, yields 8 to 10 servings sliced, with bone in. One 6¼-lb (2.8-kg) boneless and tied roast yields 12 machine-sliced servings.

Shrinkage loss:
20 percent

MUTTON:

Best size:

Pair:
22 lb (9.9 kg).

Single leg:
11 lb (4.9 kg).

Serving size:
For roast, 6 oz (170 g). One 9-lb (4-kg) oven-ready single leg, with aitch bone a part of shank removed, trimmed, and leg bone in, yields 12 to 14 medium rare servings, sliced, with bone in. One 8-lb (3.6-kg) roast, boneless and tied, yields 16 machine-sliced servings.

Shrinkage loss:
25 percent for medium-rare roast.

Calories:
6 oz (170 g) roast, cooked = 480 Calories.

LOIN, MBG #231
Full loin, with kidneys, kidney fat, and flanks attached.

Sizes:

Lamb:
5 to 6 lb (2.2 to 2.7 kg).
6 to 8 lb (2.7 to 3.6 kg).
8 to 10 lb (3.6 to 4.5 kg).
10 to 12 lb (4.5 to 5.4 kg).

Mutton:
8 to 11 lb (3.6 to 4.8 kg).
11 to 14 lb (4.8 to 6.3 kg).
14 to 17 lb (6.3 to 7.6 kg).
17 to 20 lb (7.6 to 9 kg).

Best size:
8 to 10 lb (3.6 to 4.5 kg) for lamb; 8 to 11 lb (3.5 to 4.9 kg) for mutton.

Kitchen Yields

LAMB:

Best size:
10 lb (4.5 kg).

Serving size:

For roast boneless loin, 5 oz (142 g), cooked. Two boned, trimmed, and rolled halves weigh 2½ lb (1.1 kg), so one half weighs 20 oz (568 g). One half yields 3 servings, and one full loin yields 6 servings. For boneless chops, serving size is two 3¼-oz (92-g) pieces. Two halves, boned, trimmed, and rolled, weigh 2½ lb (1.1 kg); and one loin (two halves) yields 12 pieces or 6 servings. For bone-in loin chops serving size is one 7-oz (200-g) piece; one loin (two halves) yields 8 chops.

Shrinkage loss:

20 percent.

MUTTON:

Best size:

12 lb (5.4 kg).

Serving size:

For roast boneless loin, 5½ oz (156 g), cooked. One loin (two halves), boned and trimmed, weighs 3 lb (1.3 kg) and yields 8 servings.

Shrinkage loss:

20 percent.

SHANKS, MBG #210
For braising, whole.

Weights:

1 to 2.5 lb (0.4 to 1.1 kg).

Kitchen Yields

Best size:

1 lb (450 g).

Serving size:

One shank.

NEW SPECIFICATIONS FOR DOMESTIC LAMB AND MUTTON

The American Lamb Council is recommending a change to new specifications that it regards as producing more manageable and "user-friendly" cuts. These new specifications are described individually under this heading. The new cuts are leaner and, in some cases, boneless. They are not always available from all purveyors.

BONELESS SADDLE

Sizes:

1½ to 2 lb (675 to 900 g).

Kitchen Yields

Serving size:

5 oz (140 g) cooked roast, medium rare; one loin yields 4 servings.

BONELESS SARATOGA ROLL
Chuck roll; can be fatty.

Sizes:

1½ to 2 lb (675 to 900 g).

Kitchen Yields

Serving size:

For roast cooked medium well, 5 oz (140 g); one piece yields 4 servings.

BONELESS SIRLOIN

Sizes:

2 to 3 lb (0.9 to 1.3 kg).

Kitchen Yields
Roast whole or cut into medallions.

Serving size:

5 oz (140 g) for cooked roast medium rare, or 6 oz raw weight for medallions (two pieces per serving). One 3-lb (1.3-kg) boneless sirloin yields 7 servings of roast or 7 servings of medallions.

BONELESS SHOULDER ROLL

Sizes:

4 to 6 lb (1.8 to 2.7 kg).

Kitchen Yields

Serving size:

6 oz (170 g) for roast cooked medium well. One 5-lb (2.2-kg) piece yields 9 servings of roast.

DENVER RIB
Whole ribs, trimmed.

Sizes:

12 oz (340 g).

Kitchen Yields

Serving size:

One rib.

DOUBLE BONELESS LOIN

Weight:
3½ to 4½ lb (1.5 to 2 kg).

Pack:
Two loins per box, totaling 7 to 9 lb (3.1 to 4 kg).

Kitchen Yields

Serving size:
For roast, cooked medium rare, 5 oz (140 g). One 4-lb (1.8-kg) piece yields 11 servings of roast. For loin cut into chops, serving size is 6 oz (170 g) raw weight, and one 4-lb (1.8-kg) piece yields 10 chops.

DOUBLE BONELESS LOIN CHOP
Loin with tenderloin removed.

Size:
6 oz (170 g) raw weight.

Kitchen Yields

Serving size:
6 oz (170 g), or one chop per serving.

FRENCH RACK

Sizes:
1¾ to 2¼ lb (0.8 to 1 kg) each, split.

Pack:
Six racks per box, totaling 10½ to 13½ lb (4.7 to 6 kg).

Kitchen Yields
One rack yields 3 servings.

STEAMSHIP LEG
Sirloin removed, aitch bone removed, and shank left attached.

Sizes:
6 to 8 lb (2.7 to 3.6 kg).

Kitchen Yields

Serving size:
6 oz (170 g), cooked medium rare. One 7-lb (3.1-kg) leg yields 7 or 8 servings.

TENDERLOIN
All fat removed, but silver skin left on.

Sizes:
4 to 5 oz (112 to 140 g).

Pack:
5 lb (2.2 kg) per box.

Kitchen Yields

Serving size:
1 piece; one box contains 16 to 18 pieces.

POPULAR LAMB DISHES

BONE-IN LOIN CHOP
Thick single chop, well trimmed, flank removed, back bone in.

Kitchen Yields

Serving size:
One 8-oz (224-g) piece.
One Loin, MBG #231 10 lb (4.5 kg), yields 8 chops. Purchase thirteen 10-lb (4.5-kg) loins for 100 servings.

BONELESS LOIN CHOPS
Also called *medallions*. Same chops as above, but completely boneless and well trimmed to the silver skin.

Kitchen Yields

Serving size:
Two 3-oz (84-g) pieces.
The effective kitchen yield is the same for both MBG #231 (10 lb/4.5 kg), and MBG #232 (7 lb/3.1 kg) which is #231 with the flanks removed. One half loin, trimmed to the silver skin, weighs 18 to 20 oz (504 to 560 g). One half loin yields 3 servings, or 6 pieces; one full loin yields 6 servings; purchase seventeen loins for 100 servings.

BONELESS ROAST LOIN

Serving size:
5 oz (142 g), cooked. One loin yields 6 servings; therefore, to obtain 50 servings, purchase nine 10-lb (4.5-kg) Loins, MBG #231.

GYROS
See Gyros.

LAMB STEW
For dishes such as Irish Stew or Navarin.

Serving size:
8 oz (228 g) raw meat or 5 oz (140 g) cooked stew. To obtain 50 servings, purchase two and one-half 18-lb (8.1-kg) pieces of Chuck, MBG #206, or 25 lb stew meat.

MOUSSAKA

Serving size:
4 oz (113 g) ground lamb. To obtain 50 servings, purchase two 18-lb (8.1-kg) pieces of Chuck, MBG #206.

RIB CHOPS

Serving sizes:
One 9-oz (250-g) piece or two 4½-oz (125-g) pieces. To obtain 50 servings, purchase ten 7-lb (3.1-kg) Hotel-size, Eight-rib Racks, MBG #204. For small chops for receptions, serving size is one 3½-oz (100-g) chop. To obtain 100 chops, purchase seven 5-lb (2.2-kg) Hotel-size, Eight-rib Racks, MBG #204.

ROAST LEG OF LAMB

Serving size:
5 oz (140 g) cooked meat. To obtain 50 servings, purchase two 18-lb (8.1-kg) pairs of Legs, MBG #233, machine-sliced, or five 9-lb (4-kg) single legs, sliced on bone, or three 7- to 8-lb (3.1- to 3.6-kg) boneless Legs, MBG #234A.

SHISH KEBAB

Serving size:
6 oz, raw. To obtain 50 servings, purchase two 18-lb (8.1-kg) pairs of legs, MBG #233, or fifty 6.2-oz (176-g) pieces of New Zealand boneless short loin.

PORTION-CONTROLLED LAMB

LOIN CHOPS
Cut across the loin. All bones are left attached; only the skin is removed.

Sizes:
4 to 10 oz (113 to 280 g), in increments of 1 oz (28 g).

Kitchen Yields
The flank attached is normally 3 in (75 mm) long. Since the bones are left attached, the edible meat portion is smaller than in boneless chops cut in the kitchen.

Serving size:
Varies. Two 6-oz (170-g) chops are an average dinner portion.

RIB CHOPS
Available regular and frenched, with the end of the rib bone exposed. The chops are cut across the rack. Bones are still attached, but the blade bone and surrounding muscle are removed.

Sizes:

Regular Chops:
3 to 10 oz (85 to 280 g), in increments of 1 oz (28 g).

Frenched Chops:
3 to 8 oz (85 to 227 g), in increments of 1 oz (28 g).

Kitchen Yields
Since the feather bone and the aitch bone are still attached, the chops are rather difficult to eat.

Serving size:
Varies. Two 6-oz (170-g) chops is an average dinner portion.

SHOULDER CHOPS
Cut across the blade and arm.

Sizes:
4 to 8 oz (113 to 227 g), in increments of 1 oz (28 g).

Kitchen Yields
These chops are bony and fatty. Suitable for braising with vegetables.

Serving size:
Varies. Two 6-oz (170-g) chops is an average dinner portion.

STEW MEAT

Pack:
By weight.

Kitchen Yields
Stew meat is cut from different muscles, and its degree of tenderness varies. Shrinkage is about 35 to 40 percent.

Serving size:
9 oz (255 g) raw meat or 5½ oz (156 g) cooked meat; 10 lb (4.5 kg) yields 18 servings.

SPECIFICATIONS FOR NEW ZEALAND LAMB
New Zealand lamb is generally about half the size of domestic lamb. It is best purchased fully trimmed and ready for use.

BONE-IN RACKS

Weight:
6 to 7 oz (170 to 200 g).

Pack:
Two pieces per vacuum pack; five vacuum packs per box; four boxes per carton.

Kitchen Yields

Serving size:
One piece per person.

BONELESS SHORT LOIN

Weight:
6.2 oz (176 g).

Pack:
Four pieces per vacuum pack; five vacuum packs per box; four boxes per carton. Thus, there are eighty pieces per carton.

Kitchen Yields

Serving size:
One piece per person, roasted whole or used as shish kebab.

BONELESS STEW MEAT

Pack:
Carton of four 10-lb (4.5-kg) boxes.

Kitchen Yields

Serving size:
8 oz (224 g). One 10-lb (4.5-kg) box yields 20 servings. NOTE: N.Z. is leaner than domestic lamb.

LOIN CHOPS
Bone-in loin chops.

Weight:
3 to 3¼ oz (76 to 91 g).

Pack:
48 to 52 pieces per 10-lb (4.5-kg) box.

Kitchen Yields

Serving size:
Three pieces as main course.

SHANKS

Weight:
9.2 oz (260 g).

Pack:
Twenty pieces per box; four boxes per master carton.

Kitchen Yields

Serving size:
Two shanks; therefore, one box yields 10 servings.

LATKES (POTATO PANCAKES)

Latkes are available frozen or can be made fresh.

FRESH LATKES

Formula
10 lb (4.5 kg) peeled russet potatoes, raw
3 lb (0.9 kg) peeled onion
10 eggs
1 cup (0.23 l) matzo meal
1 cup (0.23 l) flour
1 tb salt

NOTE: Make sure potatoes and onions are well drained after grinding. Squeeze out excess liquid, then add remaining ingredients.

Kitchen Yields

Serving sizes:
3 oz (84 g) per piece: 2 pieces for reception, or 3 pieces as garnish with meat.
The total mixture from the preceding formula yields 60 pieces.

FROZEN LATKES

Pack:
Varies.

LEEKS

Leeks are vegetables with large flat leaves and white stems. They resemble huge scallions. The white part is the part primarily used in cooking, and it should extend at least 3 to 4 in (7.6 to 10 cm) from the roots. Baby leeks are also available; *see* Baby Vegetables.

Pack:
24- to 30-lb (10.8- to 13.5-kg) crates.

Size:
The white stem should be at least ¾ in (1.9 cm) in diameter, but not larger than 1¼ in (3 cm)—the centers of large leeks are often woody.

Count:
12 bunches to a crate.

Kitchen Yields

There are usually between 12 and 25 leeks to a bunch, but sizes vary greatly. For this reason, leeks should be purchased by weight. If only the white part is used, trimming loss is about 50 percent. Leeks are woody in late winter and early spring, and at that time the core cannot be used. This can reduce the normal usable yield of the white parts by an additional 50 percent.

LEMON BALM (MELISSA)

See Herbs & Spices.

LEMONS

FRESH LEMONS

Season:
Available year-round; peak is in May, June, and July.

Pack:
37- to 40-lb (16.6- to 18.0-kg) cartons.

Sizes:
Counts of 63, 75, 95, 115, 140, 165, 200, and 235. The most common sizes are counts of 115 to 165.

Kitchen Yields

When buying for juice, the lowest price per pound is the best buy, because the yield per pound is approximately the same regardless of price. Eight medium lemons yield 1 cup juice; and four #165 lemons weigh 1 lb (450 g). Ten lemons yield 1¾ oz (50 g) grated lemon rind.

One case #165 lemons yields 300 halves, 660 quarter wedges, or 990 sixth wedges.

One lemon yields 7 to 10 slices when sliced on a machine. A lemon crown is half a lemon with six points. Lemon tulips are made by cutting crowns into thirds.

Calories:
1 cup = 60 Calories.

LEMON JUICE

Lemon juice is available in bottles.

Pack:
Twenty-four 10-oz (0.29-l) bottles; twelve 1-qt (0.94-l) bottles.

Kitchen Yields

1 qt (0.47 l) is equivalent to the juice of 32 fresh lemons.

LETTUCE

Lettuce can be distinguished as head lettuce and loose-leaf lettuce. Many varieties are on the market, and new varieties are being developed. Baby lettuce, with one head used as one serving, is becoming popular. Some lettuce is grown hydroponically and is shipped with the roots still attached. This increases its keeping quality.

Season:
Lettuce is available year-round, because growing seasons overlap; but price, quality, and variety can vary greatly, depending on the weather.

BIBB

This small lettuce, related to Boston lettuce, has soft leaves and a firm head. Available with green or slightly red leaves. Kentucky Bibb Limestone lettuce has firm, crisp heads and is considered a delicacy.

Pack:
Baskets containing 18 to 22 heads.

Kitchen Yields
When heads are firm, serving size is one-half head.

BOSTON (BUTTERHEAD)
Varieties range from lettuce with firm heads and crisp yet tender leaves to rather loose-headed lettuce.

Pack:
Cartons containing 24 heads.

Kitchen Yields
Heads are larger than Bibb lettuce, but less firm.

Serving size:
Half a head.

Calories:
One half 4-oz (112-g) head, cleaned = 13 Calories.

CHICORY (ENDIVE)
Also referred to as *endive*, this slightly bitter lettuce has a loose head with curly, edge-indented leaves that can be dark green at the edges and almost white at the center.

Season:
Summer.

Pack:
35- to 40-lb (15.7- to 18-kg) cartons with 24 heads each; 18-lb (8.1-kg) cartons with 12 to 18 heads each.

Kitchen Yields

Waste:
About 30 percent.

Calories:
1 cup, or 2 oz (56 g), cut = 10 Calories.

CORN SALAD
See Mache, under this same heading.

COS
See Romaine, under this same heading.

ENDIVE
See Chicory, under this same heading, for the domestic variety; *see* Belgian Endive for the imported form.

ESCAROLE
Variety of lettuce closely related to curly endive or chicory. It has a looser head and broader, less ruffled leaves. The lettuce should be crisp.

Season:
Year-round, with peak in December.

Pack:
35- to 40-lb (15.7- to 18-kg) cartons with 24 heads each; 18-lb (8.1-kg) cartons with 12 to 18 heads each.

Kitchen Yields

Waste:
About 45 percent.

Calories:
1 cup, or 2 oz (56 g), cut = 10 Calories.

FRISEE
Curly chicory. *See* Chicory, under this same heading. Some frisee is imported from Italy in 11-lb (5-kg) crates.

GREEN OAK LEAF
Baby lettuce with lobed green leaves. Sharper flavored than Red Oak Leaf lettuce.

Season:
Summer.

Pack:
Individual pack.

Kitchen Yields

Serving size:
One head.

LEAF LETTUCE
Also called *garden lettuce,* this is a leafy variety that does not form a head.

Season:
Available year-round, with peak in summer.

Pack:
6-lb (2.7-kg) baskets.

Kitchen Yields

Waste:
40 percent.

Calories:
One cup, or 2 oz (56 g), cut = 10 Calories.

LAMB'S LETTUCE
Also called *corn salad. See* Mache.

LOLLO BIONDO
Ruffled, crinkly baby leaf lettuce with white tips.
It is most commonly grown hydroponically.

Pack:
Individual packs.

Kitchen Yields
There is no waste.

LOLLO ROSA
Ruffled, crinkly baby leaf lettuce with rose tips. It
is most commonly grown hydroponically.

Pack:
Individual packs.

Kitchen Yields
There is no waste.

MACHE
Also known as *corn lettuce* or *lamb's lettuce,*
Mache is a delicate, teaspoon-shaped salad.

Pack:
11-lb (5-kg) cases.
Hydroponically grown Mache is shipped in 8-oz
(225-g) plastic trays.

Kitchen Yields
Mache is very light. It wilts quickly once dressing
is applied.

Serving size:
1½ oz (42 g); 8 oz (225 g) hydroponically grown
Mache, with roots, yields 4½ oz (125 g) salad.

ICEBERG
Firm head lettuce that keeps well under
refrigeration.

Season:
Available year-round, but weather can influence
supply and quality.
Types of trim available include chopped; shredded;
whole, cored and trimmed; and whole, uncut.

CHOPPED OR SHREDDED

Pack:
20-lb (9.0-kg) cartons, consisting of either four
5-lb (2.25-kg) poly bags or two 10-lb (4.5-kg) poly
bags.

Kitchen Yields
One 20-lb (9.0-kg) carton can be used to produce
160 small tossed salads of 1 cup or 2 oz (56 g), or
80 large tossed salads of 2 cups or 4 oz (112 g).

Calories:
1 cup, or 2 oz (56 g), chopped = 8 Calories.
One wedge weighing 5 oz (140 g) = 20 Calories.

WHOLE, CORED AND TRIMMED

Pack:
30 lb (13.5 kg), with 24 or 30 heads packed in poly
bags of 6 heads each.

Kitchen Yields
One 24-head carton yields 120 5-oz (140-g) wedges
or 120 to 144 large leaves, or 280 small tossed salads
of 1 cup or 2 oz (56 g), 140 large tossed salads of
2 cups or 4 oz (112 g), 15 gal (57 l) torn or
shredded lettuce, or 10 gal (38 l) lettuce chunks.

WHOLE, UNCUT

Pack:
50-lb (22.5-kg) cartons.

Sizes:
24 heads per carton; cartons with 30 or 18 heads
are also available.

Weight:
Average head, with outer leaves trimmed, weighs
1¾ lb (790 g).

Kitchen Yields
Same as from whole, cored and trimmed.

PERELLA
Red and green baby lettuce.

Pack:
Grown hydroponically.

Kitchen Yields
Basically no waste, because lettuce is grit-free.

RADICCHIO
Red leaf lettuce of the chicory family. Resembling a small head of red cabbage, this salad/vegetable is often used as garnish on cold platters or as flavor component in salads. It can also be used as a steamed or broiled vegetable.

Season:
Summer, fall, and winter. Low supply in spring.

Pack:
4½-lb (2-kg) box.

Count:
12 heads.

Kitchen Yields

Serving size:
One half head as vegetable.
One head contains 8 leaves. One case yields 4 lb (1.8 kg) cleaned pieces, or 96 leaves.
Size of heads can vary greatly toward the end of the season.

RED OAK LEAF
Baby lettuce with deeply cut, finely divided leaves that have burgundy-colored centers. About 8 leaves per head.

RED ROMAINE
Also called *Rouge d'Hiver,* this is a red-tipped baby Romaine lettuce.

Pack:
Grown hydroponically.

Kitchen Yields
There is basically no waste, because the product is delivered clean and grit-free.

ROMAINE (COS)
Loaf-shaped head lettuce with broad, white-stemmed leaves.

Season:
Available year-round.

Pack:
40-lb (18-kg) cartons with 24 heads; 18-lb (8.1-kg) cartons with 12 to 18 heads.

Kitchen Yields

Waste:
45 percent cleaning loss.

Calories:
1 cup, or 2 oz (56 g) chopped = 10 Calories.

TREVISE
Red lettuce that is hothouse-grown.

Pack:
11-lb (5-kg) case.

LILY ROOT

See Lotus Root, under Chinese Foods.

LIMES

Limes are available fresh and as juice.

FRESH LIMES
There are two varieties; acid limes and sweet limes. Almost all limes sold commercially are classed as acid limes. The Florida Key West lime is the only sweet lime variety of some commercial importance.

ACID LIMES
Persian lime, produced in Florida and the Caribbean Islands, is the most important variety.

Season:
Available year-round. Peak is in spring.

Pack:
Flats with 63 or 72 fruits each. The most common hotel size is 63 count.

Kitchen Yields
Normally, limes are cut in quarters for garnish; thus, one 63-count flat yields 250 pieces.
1 lb (450 g) fruit yields ¾ cup (0.17 l) juice.

Calories:
1 cup (0.23 l) juice = 65 Calories.

KEY WEST LIMES
Yellow, thin-skinned limes that have a pleasant
taste. They are no longer grown commercially in
Key West, but some supply comes from the
Caribbean Islands and Mexico. Some bottled
Key West lime juice is available.

Formula for Key West Lime Pie
>   One 14-oz (0.4-l) can sweetened condensed
>   milk
>   4 egg yolks
>   ½ cup (0.11 l) Key West lime juice
>   4 egg whites
>   4 oz sugar
>   One 9-in prebaked pie crust

Blend egg yolks and milk well, and stir in only
lime juice. Make meringue, and bake until brown.

Kitchen Yields
One 9-in (228-mm) pie yields 8 portions.

LIME JUICE
Lime juice is available unsweetened and sweet.

Pack:
Twelve 12-oz (0.35-l) bottles; twelve 25-oz (0.72 l)
bottles.

Kitchen Yields
Use unsweetened juice just as if it were fresh
juice.

Calories:
1 cup (0.23 l) unsweetened juice = 65 Calories.

LINGONBERRIES

Lingonberries are a variety of cranberry found in
Europe. They are smaller than the American
cranberry, and are tart and acidic. Whortleberry
is a related species found wild in North America.

Pack:
Twelve 14-oz (400-g) cans; six #10 cans solid pack.
Other packs are available.

Kitchen Yields

Serving size:
1½ oz (42 g) as condiment.
One #10 can yields 60 servings.

LIQUID SMOKE

A number of liquid-smoke products are on the
market.

Formula
>   For marinating meat, use 1 part liquid smoke to
>   2 parts cold water.

Marinating time:
20 minutes for chops, ribs, or chicken.
2 hours for brisket.

LITCHIS

See Lychees.

LITER

Metric volume measure.
The liter (l) contains 10 deciliters, *OR* 100 centiliters
(cl), *OR* 1000 milliliters (ml). 1 l equals 33.8 fl oz;
750 ml equal 24 fl oz.

LO BOK (CHINESE RADISH)

See Chinese Foods.

LOBSTER

Lobster is available canned, fresh (live), and
frozen.

CANNED ATLANTIC LOBSTER MEAT
Available packed in brine; often shipped frozen.

Pack:
12-oz (340-g) cans

Kitchen Yields
Typical pack contains 2 small tails, some claws, plus shredded meat.

Drained weight:
9 oz (255 g).

FRESH LOBSTER

ATLANTIC LOBSTER
Also called *Maine lobster,* this crustacean is trapped from the waters off New England and the eastern coast of Canada. Large numbers of freshly caught lobster are shipped live—some by air—throughout the world. Raw lobster, whole or split, are available frozen. Lobster farming has been successful in some places.

Tomalley is the green liver of the lobster, a delicacy that becomes pasty when cooked. *Coral* is the undeveloped egg mass, which turns solid and red when cooked. It, too, is considered a delicacy.

Season:
Available year-round. Peak in summer.

Pack:
Purchased by piece and weight.

Sizes:

Culls:
1 lb (450 g) and under; animals are live but damaged, normally with one claw missing.

Chicken:
1 lb (450 g).

Regular:
1½ lb (0.675 kg).
1¾ to 2 lb (0.78 to 0.9 kg).
2 to 2½ lb (0.9 to 1.1 kg).
2½ to 3¼ lb (1.1 to 1.6 kg).
Over 3½ lb (1.6 kg).
Fresh shelled lobster meat is available by weight. It is normally sold in 1-gal (3.8-l) cans, weighing 8 lb (3.6 kg).

Kitchen Yields
The yield depends to a large extent on freshness, because live lobsters, when stored, sustain themselves on their own body juices.

One 1-lb (450-g) lobster weighs approximately 14 oz (400 g) when cooked. The shelled meat weighs 3½ to 4 oz (100 to 112 g).
Four 1-lb (450-g) lobsters provide approximately 1 lb (450 g) shelled meat. The yield depends on the freshness of the lobster, and on the care taken when the meat is removed.

Serving sizes:

Shelled meat:
3½ oz (100 g) as appetizer.
6 oz (170 g) as main course with sauce.
5 oz (140 g) for buffet service, hot.
4½ oz (130 g) for salad.

Half lobster:
1½-lb (0.67-kg) size, split, as cold appetizer.
2-lb (0.9-kg) size, split, as cold main course.

Whole lobster:
2½ lb (1.1 kg).

Calories:
3½ oz (100 g) = 100 Calories.

SPINY LOBSTER (ROCK LOBSTER)
A clawless lobster harvested in both tropical and temperate to cold waters, spiny lobster is available in Florida live. It is seldom shipped whole out of state.

Season:
December to May.

Sizes:
2 to 5 lb (0.9 to 2.2 kg).

Kitchen Yields
Known under the name *langouste* in Europe, the spiny lobster makes an attractive buffet centerpiece. It is sold as lobster in Caribbean resorts and in South America.

FROZEN LOBSTER TAILS
These come from the tails of spiny lobsters. Most are imported. They are available as cold-water lobster tails and as warm-water lobster tails; cold-water tails are better than warm-water tails.

Pack:
Five 10-lb (4.5-kg) boxes.

Sizes:
5 to 6 oz (140 to 170 g) equal 30 tails; 8 to 10 oz (226 to 284 g) equal 18 tails. Other sizes are available.

Kitchen Yields
Lobster tails are frozen ready to use. Best use is broiled to order. When lobster meat is boiled, it tends to be dry.

Serving sizes:
Two 5- to 6-oz (140- to 170-g) tails as main course; one 8-oz (226-g) tail with Surf and Turf.

Calories:
4½ oz (127 g) meat from 8-oz tail = 130 Calories.

LOGANBERRIES

Loganberries resemble blackberries in shape and raspberries in color, but are not directly related to either plant. They are very tart unless picked ripe.

Season:
Summer.

Pack:
Flats of twelve ½-pint (0.235-l) containers.

Kitchen Yields
Used primarily for jams and jellies.

Calories:
4 oz (112 g) = 29 Calories.

LONGANS

Fruit resembling lychees. Available pitted and dried, or canned.

LOQUAT

Also known as *Japanese plum*. Small fruit with a yellow to orange skin and white to pink flesh.

Season:
Spring.

Pack:
10-lb (4.5-kg) carton.

Size:
About 3 in (76 mm) long.

LYCHEES

Lychees are available dried and fresh.

CANNED LYCHEES

Pack:
Twenty-four #2 cans.
Other packs are available.

Drained weight:
12½ oz (350 g); approximately 35 to 40 pieces.

Kitchen Yields

Serving size:
½ cup (0.11 l), with syrup. One #2 can yields 5 servings.

DRIED LYCHEES (LYCHEE NUTS)
So-called *lychee nuts*, used in Oriental cooking, are actually dried lychee fruits. The whole fruit is dried; and as it shrivels around the seed, it acquires a different flavor. The seed itself is not edible.

Pack:
By weight.

Kitchen Yields

Count:
One 1-lb (450-g) bag contains about 70 to 80 pieces; 1 oz (28 g) equals 45 pieces.

FRESH LYCHEES
Lychee fruits grown in Florida are usually of a red variety. Imports may be green, yellow, or pink.

The flesh is white and perfumed. Shelf life is limited, but the fruits can and freeze very well.

Season:
June until late July.

Pack:
By weight. Normally, the whole fruit cluster—including the tip of the branch—is shipped.

Size:
About 1 in (25 mm) in diameter and 1½ in (38 mm) in length. The pit is not edible, but it slips off easily; it is about ¾ in (19 mm) long.

Kitchen Yields
Ten fruits yield 4 oz (113 g) fresh pulp.

Calories:
Ten fruits = 66 Calories.

M

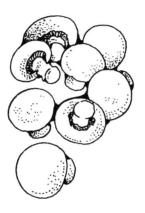

MACADAMIA NUTS

This soft, round nut is available shelled and in the shell.

Pack:
5-lb (2.3-kg) carton, shelled. Other packs are available. Macadamia nuts are most commonly packed in jars.

Kitchen Yields
Nuts are normally purchased shelled.

MACAROONS

Formula for Almond Macaroons
>   10 lb (4.5 kg) almond paste
>   8 lb (3.6 kg) sugar
>   3 lb (1.3 kg) 6X sugar
>   2 qt (1.88 l) egg whites

Dress on kraft paper to bake. Moisten paper to remove macaroons.

Kitchen Yields

Serving size:
1 oz. The total mix from the preceding formula yields 380 pieces.

MACHE

See Lettuce.

MANDARIN ORANGES

Mandarin oranges are available peeled and canned (in sections) and whole.

CANNED MANDARIN ORANGE SECTIONS
Available packed in light or heavy syrup.

Pack:
Six #10 cans.

Drained weight:
74 oz (2 kg).

Kitchen Yields
Count varies. Sections are seldom used alone, but are popular as garnish.

FRESH MANDARIN ORANGES
The term *mandarin orange* is a generic name and is used for many variety of kid-glove oranges, such as the Clementines, Dancy, Kings, Satsumas, Tangerines, and Temple oranges.

Season:

California and Arizona:
November to January.

Florida season:
November to January.

Texas season:
November to March.

Pack:
Varies according to growing area. Available in 37- to 45-lb (16.6- to 20.2-kg) cartons.

Count:
Ranges from 80 to 130. The counts for mandarin-type oranges are not as defined as for oranges in general.

Kitchen Yields
The average weight of the fruit is 4 to 6 oz (112 to 168 g). The largest sizes available are bought for foodservice use.

MANGOES

Mangoes are available canned, dehydrated, and fresh.

CANNED MANGO
Normally packed in heavy syrup. Product is imported.

Pack:
Twenty-four #2 cans.
Twenty-four #2½ cans.

Drained weight:
One #2 can equals 10 oz (280 g).
One #2½ can equals 17 oz (476 g).

Kitchen Yields

Serving size:
½ cup (0.11 l), with syrup.
One #2 can yields 5 servings.
One #2½ can yields 7 servings.

DRIED MANGO

Called *amchooor* in India, this is raw mango that has been dried and ground. The powder is acidic and is used as a spice. Candied dried Mango strips are also available.

Pack:
By weight.

Kitchen Yields
1 lb (450 g) dried mango strips yield 2½ cups (0.58 l) cooked.

FRESH MANGO

Kidney-shaped fruit with large pit and fibrous flesh. Mangoes vary greatly in size. Much production is used in the manufacture of chutney. The fruit is green when unripe, but yellow and soft when ripe.

Season:
May to September. Peak is in August, with imports available year-round.

Pack:
10- to 12-lb (4.5- to 5.4-kg) cartons.

Counts:
8, 9, 10, 12, 14, 15, 16, 18, 20, 24, 28, or 30.

Weight:
For 15 or 16 size, 10 to 12 oz (280 to 340 g) each.

Kitchen Yields
It is very difficult to get a good yield. Pits are hard to remove, and sometimes the fruit's flesh is woody and stringy.
One 12-oz (340-g) fruit yields ¾ cup, or 4½ oz (130-g) flesh.

MANZANITA BANANAS

See Bananas.

MARASCHINO CHERRIES

See Cherries.

MARGARINE

Margarine is available salted, sweet, whipped, and mixed with butter. Specialty margarine for baking is also available.

Pack:

Prints:
Thirty 1-lb (450-g) boxes.

Bulk:
50-lb (22.5-kg) boxes.

Whipped:
Six 40-lb (18-kg) tubs.

Pats:
Same counts as for butter.

Kitchen Yields
Basically the same as for butter. For whipped margarine, 1 lb (450 g) is equivalent to 6 sticks and yields 12 oz, or 1½ cups, melted clear fat.

Calories:
Regular margarine, 1 stick, or ½ cup (112 g) = 815 Calories.
Regular margarine, 1 tb, or ⅛ stick (14 g) = 100 Calories.
Regular margarine, 1 pat, 90 count (5 g) = 35 Calories.
Soft spread, 8-oz (224-g) container = 1,635 Calories.
Whipped margarine, ½ cup (76 g) = 545 Calories.
Whipped margarine, 1 tb, or ⅛ stick (9 g) = 70 Calories.

MARRONS GLACÉS

See Chestnuts.

MARZIPAN

See Almonds.

MAYONNAISE

Mayonnaise is available commercially as regular and as light (or low-calorie) mayonnaise, or it can be made fresh.

COMMERCIAL MAYONNAISE

Pack:
Four 1-gal (3.7-l) jars. Other packs are available.

Kitchen Yields
Proportions of main ingredients and mayonnaise in salads:

    10 lb (4.5 kg) cooked meat, chicken, or
        seafood
    3 lb (1.3 kg) diced celery
    2 qt (1.8 l) mayonnaise

Calories:
Regular mayonnaise, 1 oz (28 g), or 2 tb = 200 Calories.
Light mayonnaise, 1 oz (28 g), or 2 tb = 100 Calories.

HOME-MADE MAYONNAISE

Formula
    120 egg yolks or 5 pints (2.35 l) egg yolks
    1¼ cup salt (280 g)
    1 cup dry mustard (200 g)
    5 gal (19 l) oil
    1 qt (0.94 l) warm water
    3 cups (0.87 l) vinegar

Kitchen Yield
The preceding formula produces 6 gal (22.2 l).

MEATBALLS

Formula
    10 lb (4.5 kg) ground meat (beef or other),
        about 25 percent fat content
    1 lb (450 g) stale rolls, soaked
    1 lb (450 g) onions, peeled
    2 tb chopped garlic
    6 eggs
    1 bunch parsley
    Spices

Kitchen Yields
The preceding formula produces 75 meatballs of 2½ oz (70 g) each, using a #12 scoop, and these yield 25 servings of spaghetti and meatballs. Alternatively, the formula produces 200 meatballs of 1 oz (28 g) each, using a #30 scoop, for hors d'oeuvres.

MEAT LOAF

A cheaper grade of beef could be used for meat loaf.

Formula
    10 lb (4.5 kg) ground meat (usually beef),
        about 25 percent fat content
    1 lb (450 g) stale rolls, soaked
    1 lb (450 g) onions
    2 tb chopped garlic
    6 eggs
    1 bunch parsley
    Spices

Kitchen Yield

Serving sizes:
4 oz (113 g) cooked, in 2 slices. One loaf yields 20 slices, or 10 servings. Therefore, four 3-lb (1.3-kg) loaves yield 40 servings.

MELONS

CANARY MELON
Yellow melon with light green to yellow flesh. Also called *Juan canary melon.*

Season:
Summer.

Pack:
26- to 27-lb (11.7- to 12.1-kg) cases, containing 6, 7, 8, or 10 melons; 29- to 30-lb (13- to 13.5-kg) cartons, containing 4, 5, or 6 melons.

Weight range:
2¼ to 4½ lb (1 to 2 kg).

CANTALOUPE
Cantaloupe melons, with their netted skins and characteristic orange flesh, are members of the broad group of muskmelons. They are widely available fruits. Much of the market supply is domestically grown, and there are imports in

off-season. Some small muskmelons are imported from Europe as specialty items.

Season:
Available year-round. Peak is in June to August.

Pack:
75- to 85-lb (33.7- to 38.2-kg) standard crates.

Counts:
18, 23, 27, 36, or 45 melons.

Pack:
53- to 55-lb (23.8- to 24.7-kg) ⅔ crates.

Counts:
12, 13, 18, 24, or 30 melons.

Pack:
38- to 41-lb (17.1- to 18.4-kg) half-crates.

Counts:
12, 15, and 18 melons.

Sizes:
The most common sizes are 45 or 36 counts in an 85-lb (38.2-kg) standard crate, or 15 or 18 counts in a 41-lb (18.4-kg) half-crate.

Kitchen Yields
One 45-size melon yields twenty-five ⅞-in (22-mm) melon balls, or four wedges. 100 melon balls weigh 2¼ lb (1 kg).

Serving sizes:

Breakfast:
Half a 45-size melon.

Main course:
Half a 36-size melon.

CASABA MELON
Late-variety melon with soft, white, and juicy flesh. Because the melon is normally vine ripened, it is very sweet.

Season:
Fall and early winter.

Pack:
26- to 27-lb (11.7- to 12.1-kg) cases.

Count:
6, 7, or 8 melons.

Pack:
29- to 30-lb (13- to 13.5-kg) cartons.

Count:
4, 5, or 6 melons.

Weight range:
4 to 6 lb (1.8 to 2.7 kg).

Kitchen Yields
4 servings from small melons; 6 servings from large melons.

CHRISTMAS MELON
See Santa Claus Melon, under this same heading.

CRANSHAW MELON
Also spelled *crenshaw.* These store well, and have a rich, sweet flavor. The flesh is a bright salmon color.

Season:
Summer, fall, and winter.

Pack:
26- to 27-lb (11.7- to 12.1-kg) cases.

Count:
6, 7, or 8 melons.

Pack:
29- to 30-lb (13- to 13.5-kg) cartons.

Count:
4, 5, or 6 melons.

Weight range:
4 to 6 lb (1.8 to 2.7 kg).

Kitchen Yields
4 servings from small melons; 6 servings from large melons.

HAND MELON
Sweet, juicy, and expensive melon cultivated at the Hand Farm in Greenwich, New York. The season is very short, and the melons are shipped only at the peak of ripeness. The melon is a musk melon, and is identified by a red hand decal.

Season:
August.

Pack:
40-lb (22.5-kg) cartons.

Count:
16 melons.

Average weight:
3 lb (1.3 kg) or less.

Kitchen Yields

Serving size:
⅓ melon for appetizer or dessert.

HONEYDEW MELON
Honeydew is a large, round melon with flesh that is light green, sweet, and delicate.

Season:
July to October for domestic products; winter to spring for imports.

Pack:
26- to 27-lb (11.7- to 12.1-kg) cases, containing 6, 7, or 8 melons; 29- to 30-lb (13- to 13.5-kg) cartons, containing 4, 5, or 6 melons.

Weight range:
4 to 6 lb (1.8 to 2.7 kg).

Kitchen Yields

Serving size:
Quarter of a 6- or 8-size melon; sixth of a 5-size melon. One 5-size melon yields 35 ⅞ in (22-mm) melon balls; 100 melon balls weigh 2¼ lb (1 kg).

Calories:
8 oz (224 g) = 55 Calories.

PERSIAN MELON

Season:
Summer and fall.

Pack:
6 melons per half-crate.

Size:
Average 7 lb (3.1 kg).

Kitchen Yields
36 servings per case.

Serving size:
⅙ melon.

SANTA CLAUS MELON
Also called *Christmas melon,* this fruit resembles watermelon, with a light green, mottled rind and green flesh.

Season:
Late summer. Peak is in winter.

Pack:
26- to 27-lb (11.7- to 12.1-kg) cases, containing 6, 7, or 8 melons; 29- to 30-lb (13- to 13.5-kg) cartons, containing 4, 5, or 6 melons.

Weight range:
4 to 6 lb (1.8 to 2.7 kg).

Kitchen Yields
4 servings from small melons; 6 servings from large melons.

SPANISH MELON
This melon is hard-skinned with a green to deep yellow exterior and sweet, orange-colored flesh.

Season:
Winter.

Pack:
26- to 27-lb (11.7- to 12.1-kg) cases, containing 6, 7, or 8 melons; 29- to 30-lb (13- to 13.5-kg) cartons, containing 4, 5, or 6.

Weight range:
4 to 6 lb (1.8 to 2.7 kg).

Kitchen Yields
4 servings from small melons; 6 servings from large melons.

WATERMELON
This is a very large melon with pink to deep red flesh with dark seeds. A smaller, seedless variety is also available. Watermelon with yellow flesh is also available in selected markets.

Season:
Mid-April to mid-December. Peak is in late summer. Imports in winter and in spring.

Pack:
70- to 85-lb (31.5- to 38.2-kg) cartons, containing 2, 3, 4, or 5 melons.

Weight ranges:

15 to 40 lb (6.7 to 18.0 kg). Larger sizes are available.

Kitchen Yields

For buffet display, purchase 30-lb (13.5-kg) melons. One 22-lb (9.9-kg) melon yields 22 cups bite-size pieces. One 32-lb (14.4-kg) melon yields 16 large wedges, 2 lbs (0.9 kg).
NOTE: There is little waste because melon is normally served with rind.

Calories:

2-lb (0.9-kg) slice = 110 Calories.

MERINGUE

Formula

     1 lb (450 g) egg whites
     2 lb (900 g) sugar

Kitchen Yields

The preceding formula produces 25 individual shells for dessert.

MEXICAN FOODS

The components for assembling Mexican dishes are available canned, dried, fresh, or frozen. Complete prepared Mexican dishes are also available frozen.

ACHIOTE (ANNATTO)

These very hard, reddish/yellowish seeds from the tropical annatto tree are used as a dyeing and flavoring agent. Available also in paste form.

Pack:
By weight.

Kitchen Yields
Use according to taste.

CHILIES

Chilies are available canned, dried, and fresh. As a general rule, fresh chilies impart more flavor than do dried chilies. Normally, the seeds are hotter than the flesh.

CANNED CHILIES

CALIFORNIA CHILIES

Also known as *Anaheim chilies*; normally moss-green, but also available red. Available whole, diced, or in strips.

Kitchen Yields

Sweet to slightly hot. California chilies are canned already peeled. Remove seeds before use.

CASCABEL CHILIES

Small, rather peppery chilies.

CHIPOTLE CHILIES

Jalapeño chili that has been ripened, dried, and smoked. This reddish brown chili is canned in either vinegar or adobo sauce.

GREEN CHILIES

Green chilies are available diced, in strips, and whole in cans.

Pack:

Diced:
Twelve or twenty-four #2½ cans weighing 29 oz (820 g), containing about 3½ cups (0.82 l).
Six #10 cans, containing 13 cups (3 l); individual 5-gal (19-l) cans.

Strips:
Twelve or twenty-four #2½ cans, weighing 29 oz (820 g), containing about 3½ cups (0.8 l).

Whole:
Twelve or twenty-four #2½ cans, weighing 29 oz (820 g), containing about 3½ cups (0.8 l).

JALAPEÑOS

Like green chilies, jalapeños are available diced, in slices, and whole in cans. They may be slightly hot to very hot.

Pack:

Diced:
Twelve #2½ cans, weighing 29 oz (820 g), containing about 3½ cups (0.8 l); six #10 cans, containing 13 cups (3 l).

Sliced:
Six #10 cans, containing 13 cups (3 l).

Whole:
Twelve #2½ cans, weighing 29 oz (820 g), containing about 3½ cups (0.82 l); six #10 cans, containing 13 cups (3 l).

PIMIENTOS
Mild red chilies that are peeled before canning. Pimientos are available whole and diced.

Pack:
Twenty-four #2½ cans, weighing 29 oz (0.820 l); twelve 14-oz (400-g) cans.

DRIED CHILIES

ANCHO
Ancho means wide or broad. Dried mature poblano chilies with dark, reddish brown color are called *anchos.* Widely used in Mexican cooking.

Kitchen Yields
Relatively mild. Soak in water or vinegar, and use shredded or ground in sauces.

PASILLA
Long, thin chili that is dark brown to black. It is usually toasted and ground.

Kitchen Yields
Medium hot.

FRESH CHILIES

ANCHO
Resembles a bell pepper and turns red when mature. Often called *poblano* on the market. Anchos are wider than the genuine poblanos, but the names are often used interchangably.

Size:
About 4 to 5 in (100 to 127 mm) long.

Kitchen Yields
Mildly peppery.

CALIFORNIA CHILIES
Also called *Anaheim Chilies*, they are about 5 to 8 in (127 to 203 mm) long, and dark green.

Season:
Available year-round. Peak is in summer and fall.

FRESNO CHILIES
Bright green to reddish orange when ripe. Often referred to as "hot peppers."

Size:
About 2 in (50 mm) long.

Kitchen Yields
Slightly hot to very hot.

JALAPEÑOS
Dark green chilies, about 2½ in (63 mm) long.

Kitchen Yields
Very hot.

POBLANOS
Large green pepper that resembles a deflated bell pepper and is used for stuffing.

Kitchen Yields
Most varieties are relatively mild. The chili's skin and seeds are removed before it is stuffed.

SERRANOS
Small green chilies about 3 in (76 mm) long.

Kitchen Yields
Flesh is very hot, and seeds are dynamite. Base ingredient for Salsa Cruda.

CHEESE SAUCE FOR NACHOS

Pack:
Six #10 cans, each weighing 106 oz (3 kg).

Kitchen Yields

Serving size:
4 oz (112 g), for topping. Therefore, one #10 can yields 25 servings.

Calories:
4 oz (112 g) = 190 Calories.

CHORIZOS
Fatty pork sausages, available mild or hot.

Pack:
By weight.

Kitchen Yields
30 to 40 percent shrinkage, depending on brand.

CILANTRO
See Herbs & Spices.

CORN HUSKS
Available dry, corn husks are used for making tamales.

Pack:
By weight.

Kitchen Yields
1 lb (450 g) contains 40 leaves for medium-size tamales.

ENCHILADA SAUCE
Red sauce made of mild chili pulp, tomatoes, onions, and other ingredients. Available canned.

Pack:
Six 106-oz (3-kg) #10 cans.

Kitchen Yields

Serving size:
½ cup (0.235 l), with main course. One #10 can yields 25 servings.

FAJITA SEASONING
Seasoning mix consisting of chili, cumin, garlic, salt, and peppers.

Pack:
By weight.

GUYABATE
Firm, sweet guava paste, usually served with cheese as a dessert.

Pack:
3¼-lb (1.5-kg) block. Other sizes are available.

Kitchen Yields

Serving size:
2 oz (56 g). One 3¼-lb (1.5-kg) block yields 25 servings.

JICAMA
See Jicama (Mexican Potato).

MASA HARINA
Trade name for specially treated corn flour. It is also known as *tamale flour* and as *corn tortilla flour.*

MOLE
Seasoning that contains chocolate and chile; available as a paste or as a powder.

NOPALES (CACTUS LEAVES)
Nopales, or cactus leaves, are broad green pads with thorns. The flavor is mild. They can be eaten raw in salads or cooked as vegetables.

Season:
February to November.

Pack:
Tray with twelve 8-oz (226-g) leaves. Smaller sizes are available.

Sizes:
Each leaf weighs about 3 to 8 oz (85 to 226 g).

Kitchen Yields
About 15 percent cleaning loss.

REFRIED BEANS
Commercially produced refried beans are available in cans; the product can also be home-made.

CANNED REFRIED BEANS
Called *frijoles refritos* in Spanish they are most often made from pinto beans.

Pack:
Six #10 cans, each containing 13 cups (3.0 l) refried beans.

Kitchen Yields

Serving size:
¾ cup; therefore, one #10 can yields 17 servings.

HOME-MADE REFRIED BEANS

Formula
> 1 lb (450 g) pinto beans or red kidney beans
> 5 cup (1.17 l) water
> 1 cup, or 6 oz (170 g), diced onions
> ½ cup, or 4 oz, bacon drippings

Kitchen Yields
The preceding formula produces 5½ cups (1.3 l) refried beans.

Serving size:
¾ cup; therefore, the preceding formula yields 7 servings.

SALSA

Hot sauce made of jalapeños, onions, and tomatoes. Available red or green, in mild, medium, and hot spiciness levels.

Pack:
Twenty-four #2½ cans, weighing 29 oz (810 g), containing about 3½ cups (0.8 l).

Kitchen Yields
Serving size varies according to individual tastes.

TACO SAUCE

Made with tomatoes, vegetables, and chilies. Available hot and mild.

Pack:
Six #10 cans, containing 13 cups (3.0 l) sauce each; five hundred ⅓-oz (9-g) individual packets.

Kitchen Yields
Serving size varies according to tastes.

TACO SHELLS

Ready-to-fill shells that resemble crispy corn tortillas.

Pack:
200 shells per case.

Weight:
½ oz (14 g) each.

Kitchen Yields

Serving sizes:
One shell per person as snack; two shells per person as main course.

TAMALES

Corn husks stuffed with corn masa dough. They can be sweet or meat-filled.
Tamales are available canned and frozen. Pack varies according to manufacturer.

Tamale Dough Formula
2 lb (0.9 kg) lard
4½ lb (2 kg) masa harina
6 tb salt
2 qt (1.9 l) warm water or chicken broth

Kitchen Yields
The preceding formula produces 4 qt (3.7 l) tamale dough, which—when shaped, filled, and cooked—yields 85 tamales.

Serving size:
1½ oz (42 g) masa dough; 1½ oz (42 g) meat or sweet filling.

TOMATILLO

Also called *tomate verde.* Sour green tomato with a parchmentlike covering outside the skin. Available fresh and canned.

Pack:
36-lb (16.2-kg) flats.

TORTILLAS

Available fresh and frozen as corn tortillas and as flour tortilla, in various sizes.

Corn Tortilla Formula
6 cups, or 2¼ lb (1 kg), masa harina
4½ cups (1 l) warm water

Kitchen Yields
The preceding formula yields thirty-six 2-oz (56-g) tortillas.

TUNAS (CACTUS FRUIT)

Prickly pears are the fruits from a cactus of the same name. The Mexican word for them is *tunas.* The spines on prickly pears are sharp, but most have been removed by the time the fruit reaches the market.

Season:
September to December, and March to May.

Pack:
By weight.

Size:
2½ to 4 in (7 to 10 cm) long.

Kitchen Yields
Two large fruits yield 1 cup (0.23 l) purée.

Calories:
4 oz (113 g) edible flesh = 65 Calories.

MILK & MILK PRODUCTS

CREAM

Cream is discussed in greater detail under its own alphabetical entry; *see* Cream. Cream must contain at least 18% percent butterfat content to be labeled *cream.* The prescribed percentages of butterfat for different types of cream are as follows:

Coffee cream (light cream): 18 to 30 percent butterfat content.
Half and half: 11.5 percent butterfat content.
Sour cream: 18 percent or more butterfat content.
Whipping cream (light): 30 to 35 percent butterfat content.
Whipping cream (heavy): 36 percent butterfat content.

MILK

Milk is available condensed or evaporated, dehydrated, and fresh.

CONDENSED OR EVAPORATED MILK

Types include concentrated milk, condensed milk, and evaporated milk.

CONCENTRATED MILK

Canned milk product made by evaporation, without sugar added.
It can be made with whole milk and with skim milk.

Pack:
6-oz (0.17-l) cans; six #10 (3-l) cans. Other packs are available.

Kitchen Yields
One #10 can + 13 cups water yields 6½ qt (6 l) whole milk.

CONDENSED MILK

Evaporated, sweetened milk that has a higher milk-solids and fat content than evaporated milk. Sugar content before condensation is equivalent to 19 to 20 lb (8.5 to 9 kg) per 100 lb (45 kg) fresh milk. Proportions of the finished product include 8.5 percent butterfat, 28 percent milk solids, and 45 percent sugar.

Pack:
6 oz (0.17 l) cans; six #10 (3-l) cans. Other packs are available.

Calories:
6 oz (0.17 l) condensed milk = 780 Calories.

EVAPORATED MILK

Canned evaporated milk is whole milk with about 50 percent water removed. Available sweetened and unsweetened. Evaporated milk contains not less than 7.9 percent butterfat and 25 percent milk solids.

Pack:
Six #10 cans. Other sizes are available.

Kitchen Yields
One #10 can contains 13 cups.
1 cup evaporated milk + 1 cup water is equivalent to 2 cups (0.47 l) whole milk; thus, one #10 can mixed with 13 cups (3 l) water yields 6½ qt (6 l) whole milk.

Calories:
1 cup (0.23 l), unsweetened, diluted = 170 Calories.
1 cup (0.23 l), unsweetened, not diluted = 340 Calories.
1 cup (0.23 l), sweetened, not diluted = 980 Calories.

DEHYDRATED MILK

Dehydrated milk is available as dry crystal milk, dry malted milk, dry nonfat milk, and dry whole milk.

DRY CRYSTAL MILK

Pack:
By weight.

Kitchen Yields
1 lb (450 g) is equivalent to 6½ cups dry milk; 1½ cups weigh 3¾ oz (106 g). 1½ cups (0.34 l) + 3¾ cups (0.88 l) water yield 1 qt (0.94 l) milk.

DRY MALTED MILK

Dry malted milk is whole dried milk, with 55 to 60 percent malt extract added before drying. Extra-strength malted milk has double the normal amount of malt extract.

DRY NONFAT MILK
Dry nonfat milk has 1.25 percent butterfat content.

Pack:
By weight.

Kitchen Yields
1 lb (450 g) is equivalent to 3¼ cups dry milk; ¾ cup weighs 3¾ oz (106 g).
¾ cup + 3¾ cup (0.88 l) water yields 1 qt (0.94 l) milk.

DRY WHOLE MILK
Dry whole milk has 26 percent butterfat content.

Pack:
By weight.

Kitchen Yields
1 lb (450 g) is equivalent to 3½ cups; 1 cup weighs 4½ oz (128 g). 1 cup + 3½ cups (0.82 l) water yields 1 qt (0.94 l) milk.

FRESH MILK AND MILK PRODUCTS

BUTTERMILK
This cultured milk product contains at least 8.25 percent nonfat milk solids.

Pack:
½ pint; 1 qt.

Calories:
1 cup (0.235 l) = 100 Calories.

CHOCOLATE MILK
Chocolate milk is available with whole milk or low-fat milk as the base.

Pack:
½ pint, 1 cup, or 8 fl oz (0.23 l); 1 qt (0.94 l).

Calories:
1 cup (0.23 l), regular = 210 Calories.
1 cup (0.23 l), low-fat, 2 percent = 180 Calories.
1 cup (0.23 l), low-fat, 1 percent = 160 Calories.

HALF AND HALF

Pack:
1-qt (0.94-l) containers. Other packs are available.

Calories:
Half and half, 12 percent fat: 1 cup (0.23 l) = 315 Calories.
1 tb (0.015 l) = 20 Calories.

LOW-FAT MILK
Low-fat milk contains approximately 2 percent (or in some cases, 1 percent) butterfat and 10 percent milk solids.

Pack:
½ pint, 1 cup, or 8 fl oz (0.23 l). Other packs are available.

Calories:
1 cup (0.23 l), 2 percent fat = 120 Calories.
1 cup (0.23 l), 1 percent fat = 100 Calories.

SKIM MILK
Skim milk is nonfat (it has less than 0.1 percent butterfat content).

Pack:
½ pint, 1 cup, or 8 oz (0.23 l); numerous larger packs.

Calories:
1 cup (0.23 l) = 85 Calories.

WHOLE MILK
Fresh whole milk has a minimum fat content of 3.5 percent and contains 8.25 percent milk solids.

Pack:
½ pint, 1 cup, or 8 fl oz (0.23 l); numerous larger packs.

Calories:
1 cup (0.23 l) = 155 Calories.

MIREPOIX

Mirepoix consists of mixed vegetables and is used for flavoring stewed meats, sauces, and gravies.

Formula
    50 percent onions, coarse-cut
    25 percent carrots, coarse-cut
    25 percent celery, coarse-cut
    Crushed peppercorns and bay leaves (optional)
    Herbs (optional)

MIRLITON SQUASH (CHAYOTE)

See Squash.

MOUSSE

Mousse can be classified as either hot or cold.
Both can be sweet, or based on meat, fish, or
vegetables. Frozen mousse is a rich dessert, also
known as *parfait.*

BASIC COLD MOUSSE
Made with either meat, fish, or vegetables.

Formula
    5 lb (2.2 kg) cooked meat, fish, shellfish, or
        vegetables
    1 qt (0.94 l) cold cream sauce or mayonnaise
    6 cups aspic jelly of the same flavor as the
        main ingredient
    6 cups heavy cream, whipped

Kitchen Yields

Serving size:
For appetizer, 3 oz (85 g). The mixture produced
from the preceding formula yields 60 servings.

BASIC COLD SWEET MOUSSE

Formula
    2 gal (7.6 l) milk
    48 egg yolks
    12 oz (340 g) gelatin
    1½ lb (675 g) cornstarch
    3 lb (1.3 kg) sugar
    1 qt (0.94 l) concentrated fruit
    48 egg whites
    1½ lb (675 g) sugar
    2 gal (7.6 l) heavy cream

Make pastry cream with first six ingredients. Beat
separately and fold in egg whites and heavy
cream.

Kitchen Yields

Serving size:
¾ cup (0.17 l). The preceding formula produces 8
gal (30 l) mousse, which yields 170 servings.

CHOCOLATE MOUSSE
See Chocolate.

HOT FISH MOUSSE
See Frozen or Prepared Fish Products, under Fish.

FROZEN SWEET MOUSSE

Formula
    32 egg yolks
    1 qt (0.94 l) sugar syrup
    1 qt (0.94 l) heavy cream
    8 oz (0.23 l) licorice or other flavor

To make the sugar syrup, boil 4 lb (1.8 kg) white
sugar with 5 cups (1.1 l) water for 10 minutes.

Kitchen Yields
The preceding formula produces 1 gal (3.8 l)
mousse.

Serving size:
½ cup (0.1 l). Total mix yields 30 servings.

MUFFINS

Muffins can be prepared from scratch, from mix,
or from ready batter.

DRY MUFFIN MIX

Pack:
Six 5-lb (2.2-kg) bags.

Kitchen Yields

Sizes:
For 3.2-oz (90-g) portion of batter, use #10 scoop;
the yield is 240 muffins per case.
For 1½-oz (45-g) portion of batter, use #24 scoop;
the yield is 480 muffins per case. Yields vary
slightly according to type of muffin.

MIXED AND FROZEN MUFFIN BATTER

Pack:
Four 5-lb (2.2-kg) buckets.

Kitchen Yields

Sizes:
For 3.2-oz (90-g) portion of batter, use #10 scoop;
the yield is 100 muffins per case.

For 1½-oz (45-g) portion of batter, use #24 scoop; the yield is 212 muffins per case. Yields vary slightly according to type of muffin.

MUSHROOMS

CULTIVATED MUSHROOMS
Cultivated mushrooms are available canned, dehydrated, fresh, and in some instances frozen. Many types of cultivated mushrooms are available fresh.

CANNED CULTIVATED MUSHROOMS

CHAMPIGNONS OR COMMON MUSHROOMS
Available as whole buttons, in slices, and as stems and pieces. Some products are imported.

Pack:
Twenty-four #303 cans; twenty-four #2 cans; twenty-four 16-oz (450-g) cans; six #10 cans. Many other packs are available.

Sizes:

#1 tiny: ½- to ⅝-in (12- to 15-mm) diameter.
#2 small: ⅝- to ⅞-in (15- to 22-mm) diameter.
#3 medium: ⅞- to 1⅛-in (22- to 28-mm) diameter.
#4 large: 1⅛- to 1⅜-in (28- to 34-mm) diameter.
#5 extra larger: 1⅜-in (34-mm) diameter and larger.

Kitchen Yields

Drained weights:
#303 can: 10 oz (280 g).
#2 can: 12 oz (340 g).
16-oz can: 12 oz (340 g).
#10 can: 68 oz (1.9 kg).

Counts:
For buttons, one 16-oz (450-g) can contains 10 to 15, 15 to 20, 20 to 25, 25 to 35, or 35 to 45 mushrooms.

DEHYDRATED MUSHROOMS
Dried mushrooms are very light. About 10 lb (4.5 kg) fresh mushrooms produce 1 lb (450 g) dried mushrooms. In some varieties, the flavor is much intensified, in comparison to fresh mushrooms of the same variety.

BLACK CHANTERELLES (TRUMPETS OF DEATH)
Dried black chanterelles are somewhat more attractive as an alternative to fresh than are dried regular chanterelles. They are nontoxic, and are *not* related to the poisonous death cap and anger of death mushrooms.

Kitchen Yields
5 oz (140 g) dried mushrooms are equivalent to 2 lb (900 g) fresh mushrooms.

CHAMPIGNONS OR COMMON MUSHROOMS

Pack:
By weight.

Kitchen Yields
Rather flavorless, dried champignons are seldom used, because fresh and canned mushrooms are readily available.
4 oz (112 g) dried mushrooms are equivalent to 2½ lb (1.1 kg) basket-fresh mushrooms.

CHANTERELLES
Chanterelles are available dried, but they tend to be a little tough.

Pack:
By weight.

Kitchen Yields
5 oz (140 g) dried mushrooms are equivalent to 2 lb (900 g) fresh mushrooms.

MORELS
Morels are available imported and domestic. Little product comes from Europe; most of it is imported from India and Kashmir. The smoky smell of Indian morels is caused by the mushrooms' being dried over cow dung. Domestic morels are normally a mix of white and black varieties, but only professionals notice the difference. Some are picked after forest fires, and these have weak walls and a muddy flavor. Better-quality morels are picked in clear-cut areas.

Pack:
Sold by weight; 3-lb (1.3-kg) bags are common.

Kitchen Yields
Dried morels have more intense flavor than fresh morels, so the high price is justified. The price of

dried morels should be around 7 to 8 times more than the price of fresh.

PORCINI

One of the best dried mushrooms, with strong flavor. The best-quality porcinis are imported from Italy. Many different quality levels are on the market. Smaller mushrooms have stronger flavor than larger ones.

Pack:
By weight.

Size:
Some packers market very large mushrooms, which can be tough.

Kitchen Yields
Since flavor levels vary greatly, it is best to make a sample with small amount. Dried porcini can be soaked, and then simmered for about ½ hour to extract flavor. In many cases, the mushroom is discarded after the flavor is imparted to the liquid.

SHIITAKE
Dried shiitake mushrooms are seldom used in Western cooking.

WOOD EARS
Oriental mushrooms, popular in Chinese cooking.

Pack:
By weight.

FRESH CULTIVATED MUSHROOMS

CHAMPIGNONS OR COMMON MUSHROOMS
Champignons are marketed as white, off-white, and brown mushrooms; the most common variety is white. The mushrooms are sized by number per 1 lb (450 g). Mushrooms are perishable; they store best refrigerated and in darkness.

Season:
Available year-round; low season is the middle of the summer.

Pack:
3-, 5-, and 10-lb (1.3-, 2.2- and 4.5-kg) cartons; individual baskets weighing 2 to 2½ lb (0.9 to 1.1 kg). The basket is being phased out in many markets.

Sizes:
Table M-1 identifies diameters and numbers per pound for champignons of different sizes. Medium-size mushrooms are often marketed as "Silver Dollar" size. Nonselect mushrooms are also on the market, usable for chopping or slicing.

Kitchen Yields
1 lb (450 g) yields 1 qt whole, raw; 5 cups sliced, raw; or 6 cups chopped, raw. The same quantity yields 2 cups sliced cooked, or 2 cups diced cooked.

Waste:
About 5 percent.

Calories:
1 lb (450 g) raw = 120 Calories.
1 cup raw, chopped 2½ oz (70 g) = 20 Calories.

CORALS
Corals look like hens-of-the-woods. They are golden tinged with white at the base of the florets. However, these mushrooms do not taste as good as the hen-of-the-woods; some, especially the cultivated ones, can be bitter. These are best just for show.

Table M-1 Champignon Diameters and Numbers per Pound

	Small	*Medium*	*Large*	*Extra Large*
Diameter	¾ to 1¼ in (1.9 to 3.1 cm)	1¼ to 1¾ in (3.1 to 4.5 cm)	1¾ to 3 in (4.5 to 7.6 cm)	3 in and up (7.6 cm and up)
Numbers per 1 lb (450 g)	30 to 40	18 to 20	12 to 14	7 to 10

Season:
Summer.

Pack:
Sold by weight.

CRAB MUSHROOMS
Crab mushrooms look like a lady's powder puff. They look much better than they taste, however. They have an unpleasantly bitter taste, although they are safe to eat, and are not recommended as a food item.

CREMINI
Cremini mushrooms are the progenitors of today's common cultivated mushroom. They are more like the ones our grandparents would have known in America. The shelf life for creminis is about 1 week.

Season:
Available year-round.

Pack:
Sold by weight, often in 5- to 6-lb (2.3- to 2.7-kg) boxes.

ENOKI
Enoki mushrooms look like enlarged pins. They have a long, skinny stem, about 3 to 4 in (76 to 100 mm) in length, and a tiny round head or cap. They have almost no taste, but they look great and are common decorations in Japanese cuisine.

Season:
Available year-round.

Pack:
10-, 16-, 32-oz (228-, 450-, or 900-g) packages.

Kitchen Yields
There is some trimming loss. Enokis are usually purchased in small quantities.

HEN-OF-THE-WOODS (CAULIFLOWER)
Hens-of-the-woods are uncommon but delicious mushrooms. They resemble the head of a cauliflower, with a brownish gray tinge.

Season:
Late summer.

Pack:
3-lb (1.3-kg) flats, or individual by weight.

Kitchen Yields
Although hens-of-the-woods are expensive to purchase, there is no trimming loss. They should be served cut into florets, but showing one whole makes quite an impression.

PLEUROTES (OYSTER MUSHROOMS)
Pleurotes are grown in straw or sawdust. Look for nonleggy mushrooms with short stalks. Four key varieties are in commercial cultivation—some grown domestically, and others imported.

• *American Golden Pleurotes*

Also known as *golden trumpets,* because of their shape and color, these mushrooms are from an Italian strain. The American varieties come trimmed, with or without the stalk. The American pleurotes are usually not as large as the Italian ones. As they become larger, they exude more spores, making them difficult for pickers because of allergic reactions.

Pack:
3- or 5-lb (1.4- to 2.3-kg) boxes.

• *American White Pleurotes*

Pack:
1-lb (450-g) boxes.

• *Italian Golden Pleurotes*

Imported yellowish to white mushrooms.

Pack:
3-, 4-, or 5-kg (105-oz, 128-oz, or 11-lb) wooden flats.

• *Italian White Pleurotes*

Also known as *white trumpets,* these imported mushrooms are very difficult to grow, are usually quite small, and have a short shelf life. They are nicely curved and look attractive. The mushrooms are shipped untrimmed.

Pack:
1-lb (450-g) boxes.

PORTOBELLO (ROMAN MUSHROOMS)
These are actually the same mushroom species as creminis, but they have been left to mature longer

in the field. As they mature, they become flatter and their flavor intensifies. When cooking with them, use an acidic ingredient such as lemon juice to avoid having these mushrooms turn very dark.

Season:
Available year-round.

Pack:
Sold by weight, often in 5-lb (2.3-kg) boxes.

Kitchen Yields
About 6 large mushrooms weigh 1 lb (450 g).

SHIITAKE
Shiitake mushrooms are the most commonly cultivated mushrooms in the world. American production is expected to surpass the production of cremini mushrooms in the next 20 years, because of the influences of Oriental cuisines, and also because shiitake mushrooms taste delicious. Commercially cultivated shiitake mushrooms taste better than those found in the wild. Shiitake mushrooms are marketed in two basic varieties: indoor-grown and outdoor-grown. Outdoor-grown mushrooms are usually denser, woodier, and heavier than indoor-grown ones. Fresh shiitakes have a long shelf life.

Grades:

A:
Uniform in size, with clear, neatly structured gills.

B:
Larger and nonconforming in shape and size.

Pack:
3-, 5-, 7-, and 10-lb (1.3-, 2.2-, 3.1-, and 4.5-kg) flats.

Kitchen Yields
Use grade A for presenting the cap whole. The stems can be cut julienne style.
Use grade B for cutting up, or select the large caps for grilling.

WOOD EARS
Wood ears are most often sold dried, but some are sold fresh. When reconstituted or fresh, they have a slick, slippery feel and an al dente texture.

WILD MUSHROOMS
Available canned, fresh, and in some instances frozen.

BLACK CHANTERELLES (TRUMPETS OF DEATH)
This edible mushroom is available fresh in small quantities.

Season:
Spring and fall.

CANNED WILD MUSHROOMS

CHANTERELLES
Most canned wild chanterelles are imported, but the mushrooms often originate in the United States and are canned in Europe. Their flavor is briny.

Pack:
Twenty-four 29-oz (830-g) cans, with a drained weight of 14.1 oz (400 g) each; thirty-six 14.6-oz (415-g) cans, with a drained weight of 6.7 oz (190 g) each. Other packs are available.

Kitchen Yields
Mushrooms are fully cooked, and there is no additional shrinkage.

MORELS
Canned morels are available but have little commercial importance because dried and fresh morels are readily available.

PORCINI

Pack:
Twelve 22-oz (616-g) cans.

Drained weight:
16 oz (450 g).

STRAW MUSHROOMS
Straw mushrooms are popular in Oriental cooking. They are packed in water.

Pack:
Thirty-six 1-lb (450-g) cans.

Drained weight:
8 oz (224 g).

TRUFFLES
Preserved truffles are available in tins and in jars. Truffles in jars are considered to be of better

quality than ones in tins. Canned truffles are available in the following forms:

Whole brushed truffle
Peeled truffle
Truffle peelings
Truffle pieces
Truffle juice
Truffle paste
Truffle powder

Pack:
1- to 8-oz (28- to 226-g) tins or jars.

Kitchen Yields
Truffles are very expensive. They dry quickly when not covered with liquid. For economical truffle sauce, one 8-oz (226-g) can truffle peelings produces ½ gal (1.8 l) sauce, which yields 50 servings.

FRESH WILD MUSHROOMS

Many wild mushrooms picked in the United States are exported. Some of these mushrooms are processed abroad and then reimported canned or dried. The location where the mushrooms are grown is the most important quality factor. The Midwest and eastern states grow the best-tasting mushrooms. Nova Scotia also produces excellent wild mushrooms. The Pacific Northwest, however, is the most prolific producer.

Professional mushroom pickers are very fastidious, and some put every mushroom in a separate bag to avoid infestation by worms, especially when picking porcini. Wild mushrooms are inspected a number of times before being shipped and are very safe; there has never been a reported case of mushroom poisoning attributed to commercially picked wild mushrooms.

CHANTERELLES
These mushrooms are available domestic and imported. American chanterelles are related to the French girolles but are not exactly the same species. Fresh chanterelles *should be dry* when picked, because they are susceptible to worm infestation. They should smell like apricots.

Season:
From May until almost February. The season begins in May in Morocco and North Africa;

in July and August in Pennsylvania, Nantucket (Massachusetts), and Nova Scotia; and in late August in California, Oregon, Washington, and western Canada.

Pack:
By weight.

Size:
There is no count. Early chanterelles are small and weigh between ¼ and ½ oz (7 and 14 g) each. Small chanterelles have a better flavor than later-picked mushrooms. Late mushrooms can weigh as much as 1 lb (450 g).

Kitchen Yields
To preserve chanterelles, sauté quickly and freeze. There is little shrinkage.

CORALS
Available in spring and fall in small quantities.

GOAT'S BEARD
This rare mushroom looks like a goat's beard.

Season:
Fall.

HEDGEHOG MUSHROOMS
The caps are beige to orange, and the underside is white.

Season:
Winter and very early spring.

HEN-OF-THE-WOODS (CAULIFLOWER)
This excellent mushroom is very rare and expensive. They are delicious raw. Only domestic wild hens-of-the-woods are available.

Season:
Spring and fall.

Pack:
By weight.

HON SHIMEJI MUSHROOMS

Season:
Summer.

Pack:
By weight.

LOBSTER MUSHROOMS
Orange to red in color.

Season:
July and August.

Pack:
By weight.

MORELS
Nearly all fresh morels available in U.S. markets
are domestic. The United States exports large
quantities to Europe. These are sometimes
reimported to America dried or canned. Cultivation of morels is not yet possible.

Morels, like all mushrooms, are underground
plants; the visible hat is the fruit. Morels picked
in the United States are normally not as sandy
as their imported counterparts. Over twenty-
two varieties of morels are found in the United
States, but only black and white morels are of
commercial importance. White morels are of
superior quality, because they are lighter and
more delicate than black morels. The best come
from Michigan and Wisconsin. White morels are
rarer than black morels, but they are not necessarily more expensive.

Season:
End of March until end of June in the northern
hemisphere. Little supply comes from the southern hemisphere as yet.

Pack:
By weight. When morels are shipped they can
generate heat of up to 100°F. Heated morels
develop an ammonia smell and should not be
accepted. Morels are not graded by size. A packer
might pick large morels upon request for a
premium price.

False morels, called *snow morels*, reach the
market occasionally. They are less expensive than
real morels but should never be used. Although
not toxic, they can cause stomach cramps and
indigestion if eaten in large quantities.

Kitchen Yields
Morels do not shrink much. Large morels are
often stuffed.

PIEDS DE MOUTON
Called *lamb's feet mushrooms,* they look like
chanterelles but have more gills, which come off
in cooking and make the product look muddy.

Season:
November and December.

Size:
Small, about 1¼ in (32 mm) across.

Pack:
By weight.

PORCINI
Porcinis are considered the best-flavored wild
species of mushrooms other than truffles. The
German name is *Steinpilze*; the French name is
cèpes. There are many species, but only two of
these—Boletus edulis and Boletus miraculus—
should be used.

Season:
Imports from Europe during summer and early
fall. There are two domestic seasons: a short
season in spring and a longer season in fall.

Pack:
By weight.

Size:
Size is no indication of quality. Large mushrooms
are as tasty as small mushrooms. Large caps can
be up to 15 in (380 mm) across and are used for
grilling; whole mushrooms can weigh as much as 3
lb (1.3 kg), while small ones are as tight as a baby's
fist.

Kitchen Yields
Place of origin does not influence quality. The
whole mushroom can be used. Porcinis are very
perishable and subject to infestation. To preserve,
sauté and freeze. There is some shrinkage, especially when the mushrooms are sautéed. Very
large caps have dark brown gills, which are often
mushy and should be removed. Infestation by
snails can be a problem, and the trim loss
sometimes exceeds 20 percent.

PUFFBALLS
Not commonly available, although not rare in the
wild.

Season:
Late spring to fall.

Size:
About ½ lb (225 g) each, up to 3 lb (1.3 kg).

STRAW MUSHROOMS
Seldom available fresh. They are slimy and very perishable.

TRUFFLES
Fresh truffles are available domestic and imported. By far the majority (and those of the best quality) are imported. Two varieties of domestic truffles come to the market. They differ in size and smell from the imported varieties. Like imported truffles, they are available either black or white—the white ones being more plentiful and slightly cheaper than the black ones. Most come from the Pacific coast, especially from Oregon. Some domestic truffles may have a camphor smell, which is not acceptable.

Imported truffles come mostly from France and Italy. They are available either black or white—the black variety being slightly more abundant than the white. The flavor is carried in the volatile oils of the truffle and is easily imparted to other foods. Truffles can be flash-frozen successfully.

Season:

Black Truffles:
November to December.

White Truffles:
October to December.

Summer Truffles:
Black truffles with less flavor than winter truffles are imported from France from July until November.

Pack:
Sold by weight.

Size:
Varies from 1 to 4 oz (28 to 113 g).

Kitchen Yields
Truffles are very expensive, and maximum use must be made of the product to realize a return. Since truffles impart their flavor easily to other foods, they can be stored for a short time, such as one week, in oil or sherry wine. Truffles should be sliced thin and to order. White truffles are excellent grated raw, to order, over pasta dishes.

WINE CAPS
Lavender-colored caps with gills.

Season:
Spring and fall.

YELLOW FOOT CHANTERELLES
They are very different from other chanterelles. Because they are very light and tiny, they look like miniature yellow carnations.

Season:
Spring and fall.

Size:
1 oz (28 g) comprises 20 to 30 mushrooms.

FROZEN WILD MUSHROOMS

CHANTERELLES
Available in Europe but seldom imported.

Pack:
1-kg (35-oz) bags.

PORCINI
Commercially flash-frozen whole and sliced mushrooms are available, most often imported from Europe. The quality is good.

Pack:
1-kg (35-oz) bags.

MUSSELS

Mussels are available canned, fresh, and frozen. Fresh mussels are sold cultivated and wild. Cultivated mussels are free of grit and are very large.

CANNED MUSSELS
Canned mussels are available smoked and plain.

Pack:
Varies.

FRESH MUSSELS

Season:
Available year-round.

Pack:
Normally sold by weight.

Counts:

Small:
11 to 14 pieces per 1 lb (450 g).

Medium:
8 to 11 pieces per 1 lb (450 g).

Large:
5 to 8 pieces per 1 lb (450 g).

Extra Large:
3 to 5 pieces per 1 lb (450 g).

Kitchen Yields

Serving size:
1 lb (450 g), any size, for steamed mussels. The best size for receptions is medium.

FROZEN MUSSELS
Frozen mussels are available as shucked meat only IQF and on the half-shell.

Pack:
Varies.

MUSTARD GREENS

Mustard greens are available canned, fresh, and frozen. They are used as a cooked green leafy vegetable.

CANNED MUSTARD GREENS
These are chopped mustard greens.

Pack:
Six #10 cans, with a drained weight of 60 oz (1.7 kg) each.

Kitchen Yields

Serving size:
$2/3$ cup, or $3\frac{1}{4}$ oz (90 g). One #10 can yields 18 servings, so one case yields 108 servings.

Calories:
$2/3$ cup, or $3\frac{1}{4}$ oz (90 g) = 20 Calories.

FRESH MUSTARD GREENS
Mustard greens are grown extensively in the South, but supplies also come from other states.

Season:
Winter.

Pack:
By weight.

Kitchen Yields

Serving size:
$2/3$ cup, or $3\frac{1}{4}$ oz (90 g) cooked; 1 lb (450 g) raw yields 3 servings.

Calories:
$2/3$ cup, or $3\frac{1}{4}$ oz (90 g) cooked = 20 Calories.

FROZEN MUSTARD GREENS

Pack:
Twelve $2\frac{1}{2}$-lb (1.1-kg) packages. Other packs are available.

Kitchen Yields

Serving size:
$2/3$ cup, or $3\frac{1}{4}$ oz (90 g). One package yields 10 servings; one case yields 120 servings.

Calories:
$2/3$ cup, or $3\frac{1}{4}$ oz (90 g) = 20 Calories.

MUTTON

See Lamb.

N AND O

NECTARINES

Juicy fruit closely related to peaches. Each fruit has a single large pit. Freestone varieties should be purchased for foodservice. There is large domestic production, and imports are available in the off-season.

Season:
May to September, with peak in July and August.

Pack:
19- to 23-lb (8.5- to 10.3-kg) two-layer lugs, with counts of 48, 56, 64, 72, 80, or 84; 25- and 35-lb (11.2- and 15.7-kg) loose-fill cartons.

Kitchen Yields
One medium (64-size) nectarine weighs 5 oz (140 g). Three medium fruits weigh 1 lb (450 g) and are equivalent to 2 cups (0.47 l) sliced, 1¾ cups (0.4 l) diced, or 1½ cups (0.34 l) puréed. One 22-lb case (9.9-kg) yields 2¾ gal (10.4 l) sliced nectarines.

Calories:
1 cup sliced fruit = 75 Calories.

NOODLE DOUGH

Besides being used for making noodles of various shapes and sizes, this dough can be used for making baskets and other ornamental pieces. Other pasta products are discussed separately; *see* Pasta.

Formula
   5 lb (2.2 kg) bread flour
   16 eggs
   ½ cup water
   1 oz (28 g) oil

Kitchen Yields
The preceding formula produces 7 lb (3.1 kg) raw noodles.

Serving sizes:

Main course:
3½ oz (98 g) raw; 1 cup (0.23 l) cooked.

Garnish:
1½ oz (42 g) raw; ⅓ cup cooked.
Mixture yields thirty-two 1-cup (0.23-l) main course servings and seventy-four 1½-oz (42-g) garnish servings.

Calories:
½ cup (0.16 l) = 100 Calories.

NOPALES (CACTUS LEAVES)

See Mexican Foods.

O

OCTOPUS

Octopus is available fresh and frozen.

Season:
Available year-round.

Average sizes:
From 3 lb (1.3 kg) and up.

Kitchen Yields
Most octopus is shipped frozen in 5-lb (2.2-kg) boxes. There is no waste because only the legs are shipped.

OKRA

Okra is available canned, fresh, and frozen. It is also called *gumbo*.

CANNED OKRA
Okra in cans is available cut or whole.

Pack:
Six #10 cans, with a drained weight of 60 oz (1.7 kg); twenty-four #2½ cans, with a drained weight of 18 oz (500 g); twenty-four #2 cans with a drained weight of 12 oz (340 g).

Kitchen Yields

Calories:
Ten pods, or 3¾ oz (106 g) cooked = 30 Calories.

FRESH OKRA
Long and short varieties are on the market in both green and yellow. Green okra is the more common variety.

Season:
Available year-round. Peak is from July to October.

Pack:
By weight, in hampers, bushels, or baskets.

Kitchen Yields
Best size are pods 2 to 3½ in (50 to 89 mm) long. About 35 pods weigh 1 lb (450 g).

Calories:
Eight pods, or 3¾ oz (106 g) cooked = 30 Calories.

FROZEN OKRA
Frozen okra is available whole, cut, and breaded.

Pack:

Cut okra:
Twelve 3-lb (1.3-kg) boxes, 20-lb (9-kg) boxes, cut okra.

Whole okra:
Twelve 2½-lb (1.1-kg) boxes, 20-lb (9-kg) boxes.

Breaded okra:
20-lb (9-kg) boxes, IQF.

OLIVES

Olives are available as canned black, canned or pickled green, and cured ripe olives. Because olives are an ancient food, many different styles are available in ethnic markets. Domestic and imported types are available.

CANNED BLACK OLIVES
The process of canning was developed in the United States. Large black olives in cans are made with unripe green olives and often lack flavor. Canned black olives are available whole pitted, whole unpitted, sliced, chopped, and in wedges.

Pack:
Six #10 cans.
Other packs are available.

SLICED, WEDGED, AND CHOPPED BLACK OLIVE PIECES

Kitchen Yields
One #10 can of sliced olives weighing 55 oz (1.5 kg) drained yields 12 cups (2.7 l).
One #10 can of wedged olives weighing 55 oz (1.5 kg) drained yields 11¼ cups (2.6 l).
One #10 can of chopped olives weighing 90 oz (2.3 kg) drained yields 13 cups (3 l).

Calories:
Three small or two large olives = 15 Calories.
1 cup sliced, weighing 4½ oz (126 g) = 174 Calories.
1 cup wedged, weighing 4¾ oz (135 g) = 193 Calories.
1 cup chopped, weighing 6⅞ oz (190 g) = 250 Calories.

WHOLE PITTED OLIVES
Table O-1 lists data for canned pitted black olives.

WHOLE UNPITTED OLIVES
Table O-2 lists data for canned unpitted black olives.

Imported tiny olives are also available canned and unpitted whole. They are sold in packs of three 10-lb (4.5-kg) cans; the drained weight of each can is 5 lb 12 oz (2.7 kg), and each can contains 2,000 olives.

CANNED OR PICKLED GREEN OLIVES
The most important varieties of green (or queen or Spanish) olives are Sevillano, Manzanillo, Ascolana, and Mission. Olives are available unpitted, pitted, and stuffed with various foods.

Table O-1 Yields for Canned Pitted Black Olives

Size	Drained Weight	Number per #10 Can	Number per 1 lb (450 g)
Small	51 oz (1.4 kg)	578	177 to 193
Medium	51 oz (1.4 kg)	486	150 to 165
Large	51 oz (1.4 kg)	430	123 to 128
Extra Large	51 oz (1.4 kg)	350	105 to 120
Jumbo	49 oz (1.39 kg)	245	69 to 90
Colossal	49 oz (1.39 kg)	199	54 to 70
Super Colossal	49 oz (1.39 kg)	163	44 to 56

Table O-2 Yields for Canned Unpitted Black Olives

Size	Drained Weight	Number per #10 Can	Number per 1 lb (450 g)
Small	66 oz (1.9 kg)	557	128 to 140
Medium	66 oz (1.9 kg)	466	106 to 121
Large	66 oz (1.9 kg)	404	91 to 105
Extra Large	66 oz (1.9 kg)	288	65 to 88
Jumbo	64 oz (1.8 kg)	228	51 to 60
Colossal	64 oz (1.8 kg)	192	41 to 50
Super Colossal	64 oz (1.8 kg)	128	26 to 40

Table O-3 Yields for Canned Unpitted Green Olives

Size	Name	Count per 1 lb (450 g)	Count per 1 kg (2.2 lb)
00	Peewee	181 to 220	
0	Midget	141 to 180	
1	Small	128 to 140	280 to 300
2	Medium	106 to 127	220 to 240
3	Large	91 to 105	200 to 220
4	Extra Large	76 to 90	170 to 190
5	Mammoth	65 to 75	150 to 160
6	Giant	53 to 64	120 to 130
7	Jumbo	42 to 52	100 to 110
8	Colossal	33 to 41	80 to 90
9	Super Colossal	32 or fewer	70 to 80

Pack:
Many sizes are available. The label normally indicates drained weight.

Common drained weight:
½ pint (0.23 l) = 5 oz (140 g).
1 pint (0.47 l) = 10 oz (280 g).
1 qt (0.94 l) = 21 oz (588 g).
1 gal (3.8 l) = 88 oz (2.4 kg).

WHOLE UNPITTED GREEN OLIVES
Table O-3 lists data for canned unpitted green olives.

Calories:
Four medium, three extra large, or two giant = 15 Calories.

CURED RIPE OLIVES
Cured ripe olives may range from brown to purple to black, and may be cured in brine, in oil, or by some other process.

IMPORTED OLIVES
Available canned, cured, and salted.

IMPORTED CANNED OLIVES

Pack:
3 10-lb (4.5-kg) cans; drained weight 5 lb 12 oz (2.7 kg).

Count:
2000 per can.

IMPORTED PICKLED AND CURED OLIVES
A large variety of loose black olives is available in ethnic stores. There are basically two varieties: olives shipped in brine, and dry cured olives. Dry cured olives can be very salty. All olives are processed with pits.

Pack:
Varies. Most olives are sold by weight.

Size:
Varies.

Kitchen Yields

Brine cured olives:
1 cup (23 l) weighs 8 oz (224 g).

Salted olives:
1 cup (23 l) weighs 7 oz (196 g).

Count:
1 cup (23 l) equals about 40 to 50 medium olives.

ONIONS

Onions are available canned, dried, fresh, fresh processed, and frozen. *See also* Shallots.

CANNED ONIONS

PEARL ONIONS

Pack:
Six #10 cans.

Counts:
100 to 125, 200 to 250, 375 to 400, and 400 to 500.

Kitchen Yields
Use as is; there is no waste.

DEHYDRATED ONIONS

Pack:
Six #10 cans.

Net weight:
28 oz (784 g).

Kitchen Yields
1 lb (450 g) dry = 6¾ cups (1.4 l) dry, or 13 cups (3 l) reconstituted onions.

FRESH ONIONS

BOILING ONIONS
See Pearl Onions, under this same heading.

CREAMER ONIONS
See Pearl Onions, under this same heading.

GREEN ONIONS (SCALLIONS)

Season:
Available year-round. Peak in spring.

Pack:
15- to 25-lb (6.8- to 11.3-kg) cartons containing 48 bunches; 24- and 12-bunch cartons are also available.

Kitchen Yields
Waste depends on whether the green part, the white part, or both are used. If the whole vegetable is used, cleaning waste is about 10 percent by weight.

Calories:
6 stalks, weighing 1½ oz (42 g) = 20 Calories.

MATURE ONIONS
Onions are classified as storage onions and fresh onions. Storage onions can be recognized by their thicker, darker-colored outer skin. Storage onions are known for their firmness. Fresh onions can be recognized by their lighter color and thinner skin. They have a higher water and sugar content than do storage onions, and they are susceptible to bruising and decay. Both varieties are available most of the time in three colors: red, white, and yellow.

Sweet onions are sweeter than normal onions and do not irritate the eyes during processing. They come from various growing regions. Sweet Spanish onions are large red storage onions from Idaho and eastern Oregon.

Fresh Onion Season:

Arizona:
May to June

Imperial Valley Sweets, CA:
April to June

San Joaquin Valley, CA:
May to August

Colorado:
July to September

Vidalia Sweets, GA:
April to June

Maui Sweets, HA:
Year-round

Las Cruces, NM:
June to August

High Plains, TX:
July to August

Rio Grande, TX:
March to June

Trans-Pecos, TX:
June to July

Winter Gardens, TX:
April to June

Walla Walla Sweets, WA:
June to August

Storage Onion Season:
July until April of the following year.

Pack:
5-, 10-, 25-, and 50-lb (2.2-, 4.5-, 11.2-, and 22.5-kg) bags; 40- and 50-lb (18.0- and 22.5-kg) cartons. Table O-4 lists colors, diameters, and weights for different sizes of mature onions.

Counts:
Table O-5 identifies counts of different sizes of mature onions, by pack.

Kitchen Yields
1 cup chopped weighs 6 oz (170 g); 1 cup sliced weighs 4 oz (112 g). One 50-lb (22.5-kg) bag yields 110 cups chopped, or 170 cups sliced.

Table O-5 Counts for Different Containers of Mature Onions

Container	Colossal	Jumbo	Large Medium	Prepack
50 lb (22.5 kg)	45 to 50	80 to 100	180	350
25 lb (11.2 kg)	22	45	90	170
10 lb (4.5 kg)	12	23	45	85
5 lb (2.2 kg)	6	11	22	44

Table O-4 Trade Names and Average Sizes for Mature Onions

Trade Name	Color	Diameter	Weight
Colossal	yellow only	4 in & up (100 mm & up)	14 to 18 oz (400 to 500 g)
Jumbo	yellow & red	3¼ to 4¼ in (82 to 114 mm)	8 to 10 oz (226 to 280 g)
Large Medium	yellow, white & red	2¼ to 3¼ in (57 to 82 mm)	3 to 5 oz (85 to 140 g)
Prepack	yellow & white	1¾ to 2¼ in (45 to 57 mm)	1½ to 3 oz (45 to 85 g)
Boiler	yellow & white	½ to ⅞ in (12 to 22 mm)	1 to 1½ oz (0.28 to 45 g)
Creamer	yellow & white	½ in (12 mm)	1 oz or smaller (0.28 g or less)

Waste:

Peeling loss is about 15 percent by weight.

Calories:

1 cup, or 6 oz (170 g), raw, chopped = 65 Calories.
1 cup, or 4 oz (112 g), raw, sliced = 45 Calories.

PEARL ONIONS

Also called *creamer* or *boiler onions,* these are small white onions used in stews and in vegetable preparations. They are also available canned, fresh, and frozen.

Season:

Available year-round.

Pack:

28-lb (12.6-kg) lugs. Other packs are available.

Count:

Varies.

Kitchen Yields

Waste:

15 percent peeling loss.

Serving size:

3 oz (84 g) as garnish with stew; 1 lug yields 130 servings.

Calories:

3 oz (84 g) = 35 Calories.

SCALLIONS

See Green Onions, under this same heading.

SHALLOTS

See Shallots.

FRESH PROCESSED ONIONS

Available peeled, sliced, or diced.

Pack:

20-lb (9.1-kg) box containing four 5-lb (2.2-kg) bags; 20-lb (9.1-kg) box containing two 10-lb (4.5-kg) bags.

FROZEN ONIONS

Available diced or sliced, IQF, or as whole pearl onions. Many ready-to-use products are also on the market.

DICED OR SLICED MATURE ONIONS

Pack:

12-, 16-, 20-, or 45-lb (5.4-, 7.2-, 9.0-, or 20.2-kg) boxes, loose or in 2-lb (0.9-kg) boxes.

PEARL ONIONS

Pack:

Twelve 2½-lb (1.1-kg) cartons. Larger packs of IQF onions are available.

Kitchen Yields

Use as is; there is no waste.

ONION SOUP

See Soups.

ORANGES

See also Mandarin Oranges, Shamouti, Tangerines.

ORANGE JUICE

Orange juice is available canned, dehydrated, freshly squeezed (in some markets), fresh, and as frozen concentrate.

CANNED ORANGE JUICE

Available sweetened and unsweetened.

Pack:

Twelve 46-oz (1.3-l) cans.

Kitchen Yields

Serving size:

6 oz (0.17 l).

Calories:

6 oz (0.17 l), unsweetened = 90 Calories.

DEHYDRATED ORANGE JUICE

Pack:

1-lb (450-g) jars. Other packs are available.

Kitchen Yields

Serving size:

6 oz (0.17 l); 1 lb (450 g) mixed with 1 gal (3.8 l) water yields 21 servings.

Calories:

6 oz (0.17 l) = 75 Calories.

FRESH ORANGE JUICE

Pack:

1-qt (0.94-l) cartons or bottles; ½-gal (1.8-l) cartons or bottles. Other packs are available.

Kitchen Yields

Serving size:

6 oz (0.17 l). Thus, 1 qt (0.94 l) yields 5 servings, and ½ gal (1.8 l) yields 10 servings.

Calories:

6 oz (0.17 l) unsweetened = 90 Calories.

FROZEN ORANGE JUICE CONCENTRATE

Pack:

Various packs are available. Common pack is a 12-oz (0.35-l) can.

Kitchen Yields

Dilute 1 part concentrate with 3 parts water; thus, one 12-oz (0.354-l) can mixed with 36 oz, or 4½ cups (1 l), water yields 48 oz (1.4 l) juice.

Serving size:

6 oz (0.17 l); thus, one 12-oz (0.354-l) can diluted yields 8 servings.

Calories:

6 oz (0.17 l) = 90 Calories.

ORANGE SECTIONS

Orange sections are available canned and fresh.

CANNED ORANGE SECTIONS

Pack:

Twenty-four #3 cylindrical cans; twenty-four or thirty-six #2 cans; twenty-four or thirty-six #303 cans.

Kitchen Yields

Serving size:

½ cup (0.11 l); 3½ oz (98 g).

Drained weights:

#3 cylindrical can weighs 30 oz (850 g) and yields 8½ servings.

#2 can weighs 12 oz (340 g) and yields 3½ servings.
#303 can weighs 10 oz (280 g) and yields 3 servings.

FRESH ORANGE SECTIONS

Pack:

Four 1-gal (3.8-l) jars.

Kitchen Yields

Serving size:

½ cup (0.11 l); 3½ oz (98 g).

Drained weight:

6 lb (2.7 kg); yields 25 to 26 servings.

WHOLE ORANGES

Whole oranges are available fresh. Their marketing season is year-round, with a general peak from December through May. Valencia oranges from California and Arizona peak in August through September. Oranges are produced in Florida, California, Texas, and Arizona. Varieties include Valencia (good eating and juice orange), Navel (large, seedless, peels and sections easily), Hamlin (seedless, thin peel), Pineapple (juicy, has seeds), and Temple (few seeds, peels easily). Valencia is a summer orange; Navel is a winter orange. Blood oranges are in season during the summer.

Seasons:

California/Arizona:
Navel: November to June.
Valencia: March to January.
Temple: November to February.

Florida:
Hamlin: October to January.
Navel: November to January.
Pineapple: December to February.
Temple: January to March.
Valencia: March to July.

Texas:
Valencia: February to June.
Temple: February to June.

Pack:
Varies, depending on growing area.

California/Arizona:
37- to 45-lb (16.6- to 20.2-kg) cartons with counts of 48, 56, 72, 88, 113, 138, or 168 oranges.

Florida:
37- to 45-lb (16.6- to 20.2-kg) cartons containing ⁴/₅ bushel with counts of 64, 80, 100, or 125 oranges. Counts for navels are 32, 36, 40, 48, or 56.

Texas:
38- to 44-lb (17.1- to 19.8-kg) cartons with counts of 56, 64, 80, 100, 125, 144 oranges; 82- to 87-lb (36.9- to 39.1-kg) cartons with counts of 100, 125, 163, 200, 252, or 288 oranges.

Sizes:
Florida sizes are based on the number of oranges in a 40-lb (18-kg) carton. Sizes and diameters are as follows:

125 size: 2½ in (63 mm) diameter.
100 size: 2¹¹/₁₆ in (68 mm) diameter.
80 size: 2¹⁵/₁₆ in (75 mm) diameter.
64 size: 3¹/₁₆ in (81 mm) diameter.

Common hotel size for fruit baskets is sizes 56, 64, or 72.

Weights:
48 size: very large, 12 to 14 oz (360 to 400 g).
88 size: medium, 7½ oz (200 g).
163 size: small, 4 oz (113 g).

Kitchen Yields
For fruit baskets buy Navel or Valencia oranges.
One large navel orange, weighing 13 oz (364 g), yields 8 oz (224 g) peeled fruit, 6 to 7 large slices, or 1 cup sections totaling 5 oz (140 g).
Three to four medium oranges yield 1 cup, or 8 oz (0.235 l), juice.
Two medium oranges yield 1 cup, or 6 oz (168 g) bite-size pieces.
One medium orange yields 4 tsp grated peel.

Calories:
One orange, 80 size = 70 Calories.

JUICE ORANGES
Florida oranges have a higher juice content than do California oranges. The three best juice oranges are Valencia, Hamlin, and Pineapple.

Season:

Florida:
Valencia: March to July.
Hamlin: October to January.
Pineapple: December to February.

California:
Valencia: March to January.
Storage orange are available from July until October, but their juice yield is less.

Pack:

Florida:
size 125.

California:
size 113 or 138.

Kitchen Yields
Yield is influenced by season, climate, count, and type of machine used. Higher-count oranges give slightly better yields.
One case of size 125 oranges yields 2¼ to 2½ gal (8.5 to 9.5 l) juice.

Calories:
6 fl oz (0.17 l) = 82 Calories.

OREGANO

See Herbs & Spices.

OTTAHITIA APPLES

Also spelled *otaheite apple,* this is a pear-shaped tropical fruit (not a true apple) with a thin, edible skin.

Season:
Spring and fall.

Pack:
By weight.

Size:
About 2 oz (56 g).

Kitchen Yields
Serve raw or poached. Center pit is easily removed
About two fruits (four halves) per serving. Do not
peel.

OYSTERS

CANNED SMOKED OYSTERS

Pack:
Forty-eight 3.66-oz (103-g) cans.

Count:
Varies; approximately 14 to 16 pieces.

FRESH OYSTERS
Many varieties of oysters are available, from both
the Atlantic and Pacific oceans. Atlantic oysters
represent about 85 percent of all domestic
production. Oysters are successfully cultivated.
Imports from Canada, Asia, and Europe are also
available.

Oysters are sold whole, live in the shell, and
shucked fresh. Fresh oysters should be stored in a
cool, dark place, covered with wet rags. Fresh
water and ice kill oysters, which are saltwater
creatures.

ATLANTIC OYSTERS
Many communities produce oysters, and they are
marketed under the site name. Following is a
listing of the major market varieties and their
season. Generally, cultivated oysters are available
year-round. Wild oysters are normally not shipped
during the summer. A large amount of oysters is
produced in Louisiana. They are not shipped
during the summer.

BELON OYSTER
European oyster, now also grown in Maine.

Season:
Winter for domestic Belons; September to
February for imported ones.

Pack:
144 per case for domestic Belons; 200 per case
for imported ones.

BLUEPOINT OYSTER
Primarily found off Long Island, this variety is
marketed whole and live in the shell and fresh
shucked with juice.

Season:
Cultivated oysters are shipped year-round.

Pack:
Bushels or cartons for whole live oysters in the
shell; many food buyers purchase them by the
piece.

Count:
220 to 230 medium oysters in shell per bushel; 220
to 240 select-size shucked oysters per 1-gal (3.8 l)
container.

Sizes:
Some packers classify Bluepoints as medium or
large; others use select as the standard.

Kitchen Yields

Serving size:
6 medium-size oysters in shell.

Calories:
One portion, or 6 medium-size oysters in shell = 65
Calories.
1 cup (0.235 l), or 13 to 19 select shucked
oysters = 160 Calories.

CAPE BRETON OYSTER

Season:
September to January.

Count:
425 oysters per bushel.

CAPE COD OYSTER

Season:
Available year-round.

Count:
150 oysters per bushel.

CHINCOTEAGUE OYSTER
Also called *Virginia oyster.*

Season:
Winter.

Count:
240 to 250 oysters per bushel.

DELAWARE BAY OYSTER

Season:
Winter.

Count:
300 oysters per bushel.

GARDINERS BAY OYSTER

Season:
Available year-round.

Count:
250 oysters per bushel.

GREAT SOUTH BAY OYSTER

Season:
Winter.

Count:
250 oysters per bushel.

LYNHAVEN OYSTER

Season:
Available year-round.

Count:
125 oysters per bushel.

MALPEQUE OYSTER
Wild Canadian oyster.

Season:
September to January, and late spring.

Count:
225 oysters per bushel.

POCOMOKE SOUND
Maryland oyster.

Season:
Winter.

Count:
300 oysters per bushel.

PRINCE EDWARD ISLAND OYSTER

Season:
September to January.

Count:
225 oysters per bushel.

WELLFLEET OYSTER

Season:
Winter.

Count:
150 oysters per bushel.

WHITESTABLE OYSTER
Imported oyster from the Thames River estuary in England.

Season:
September to February.

Count:
250 oysters per bushel.

PACIFIC OYSTERS

KUOMOMOTO OYSTER

Season:
Fall and winter.

Count:
180 oysters per bushel.

OLYMPIA OYSTER
Also called *western oyster,* this variety is very tiny. Available whole live in shell and shucked.

Season:
Available year-round.

Count:
400 oysters in shell per bushel; 500 to 600 shucked oysters per 1-gal (3.8-l) container.

PACIFIC GOLDEN OYSTER

Season:
Available year-round.

Count:
240 oysters per bushel.

FROZEN PROCESSED OYSTERS

BREADED OYSTERS
Commercially breaded oysters are available frozen from a number of manufacturers.

Pack:
3-lb (1.4-kg) boxes.

Kitchen Yields
Sizes range from 1 to $1\frac{1}{3}$ oz (28 to 36 g).

OYSTER CRABS

See Crabs.

OYSTER PLANT

See Salsify.

P

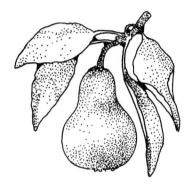

PANCAKES

See Griddle Cakes.

PAPADOM

Indian flat bread made with udad-dal flour in a number of flavors, some of them very hot.

Pack:
8¾-oz (250-g) packages.

Count:
16 or 17 pieces, each 7 in (177 mm) across.

Kitchen Yields
Papadoms must be fried quickly in very hot oil to puff up. For garnish with curry dishes, allocate ½ piece per person.

PAPAYA

Also called *tree melon,* this oval to pear-shaped fruit can vary greatly in size. The flesh is hard when the fruit is unripe (indicated by green skin), but soft and very perishable when ripe (indicated by yellow skin). Papayas can reach 10 lb (4.5 kg) in some tropical countries, but Hawaiian papayas shipped to the mainland are uniform in size.

Pack:
10-lb (4.5-kg) containers.

Count:
8 to 12 fruits per container.

Kitchen Yields
Half of a fruit, peeled and with seeds removed weighs 5⅓ to 5¾ oz (150 to 160 g).

Calories:
1 cup cubed fruit, weighing 5⅓ oz (150 g) = 80 Calories.

PARSLEY

See Herbs & Spices.

PARSLEY ROOT

Also called *Hamburg parsley,* this vegetable looks like a yellow carrot and is used as a garnish in soups and stews.

Season:
Available year-round.

Pack:
By weight.

Size and Count:
Vary.

Kitchen Yields
Peeling loss is about 15 percent.

PARSNIPS

Root vegetable that tastes best when left in the ground until after the ground freezes.

Season:
October to January. A small amount is available until spring.

Pack:
25- and 50-lb (11.2- and 22.5-kg) bags; twelve 20-oz (560-g) bags.

Size:
Count varies. About four parsnips weigh 1 lb (450 g).

Kitchen Yields
Large parsnips can have a woody core, which reduces yields. 1 lb (450 g) fresh yields 2 cups cooked and diced.

Calories:
1 cup, or 6 oz (168 g), cooked and diced = 108 Calories.

PARTRIDGE

Chukar and Bartavelle partridge are available.

Average size:
14 to 16 oz (400 to 450 g).

Kitchen Yields

Serving size:
One bird.

PASSION FRUIT

Also called *grenadilla,* this is a purple-skinned fruit with yellow flesh and many edible seeds.

Season:
November to July.

Pack:
By weight.

Size:
3 oz (85 g), on average.

Kitchen Yields
Use the whole fruit.

Calories:
3¾ oz (100 g) = 75 Calories.

PASTA

Pasta is available canned, fresh, and dry. Canned pasta is of minor importance to foodservice and is not listed. *See also* Noodle Dough.

DRY PASTA
The quality of pasta depends on the quality of the flour used in making it. Since the base price of pasta is low, foodservice operators should only use high-quality products. There are hundreds of different pasta shapes on the market.

Pack:
1-, 10- and 20-lb (450-g, and 4.5- and 9-kg) boxes.

Kitchen Yields
The relation of weight to volume of cooked pasta varies according to shape. Macaroni has the greatest weight per unit of dry volume.
1 lb (450 g) lasagna consists of 24 sheets, 2¼ in × 9½ in (57 mm × 240 mm).
1 lb (450 g) dry medium-sized macaroni equals 4½ cups (1.3 l) and produces 9 cups (2 l) cooked pasta.
1 lb (450 g) dry noodles measures 8 cups (1.8 l) and produces 8 cups (1.9 l) cooked pasta.
1 lb (450 g) dry spaghetti produces 8 cups (1.8 l) cooked pasta.

Serving sizes:

For any pasta, except lasagna:
½ cup (0.235 l) side order.
1½ cup (0.35 l) main course.

Yields for various pastas:

Macaroni:
1 lb (450 g) produces 18 side-order servings or 6 main-course servings.
10 lb (4.5 kg) produce 180 side-order servings or 60 main-course servings.

Spaghetti or noodles:
1 lb (450 g) produce 16 side-order servings or 5 main-course servings.
10 lb (4.5 kg) produce 180 side-order servings or 50 main-course servings.

Lasagna:
26 oz (730 g) fill one hotel pan 20 in × 12 in (508 × 304 mm) with four layers.

Calories:
½ cup (0.232 l) cooked pasta without sauce = 200 Calories.

FRESH PASTA
Fresh pasta can be purchased in many shapes and flavors.

Kitchen Yields

Serving size:
Main course 3½ oz (98 g). Serving size varies according to pasta variety.
1 lb (450 g) fresh pasta yields approximately 5 to 6 cups (1.1 to 1.2 l) cooked pasta.

TORTELLINI
Tortellini are available fresh or frozen with both meat and cheese fillings, and can be made with dough of different flavors. There is no noticeable difference in yield between fresh and frozen merchandise.

Pack:
1 lb (450 g) packages.

Kitchen Yields
1 lb (450 g) medium size contains about 140 pieces; 1 cup weighs 5 oz (140 g) and contains about 40 pieces.

Serving sizes:
Twenty 2¼-oz (63-g) appetizer pieces.
Thirty-five 4-oz (112-g) main-course pieces.
1 lb (450 g) yields 7 appetizer servings or 4 main-course servings.

PASTILLAGE

Formula
1½ oz (42 g) plain gelatin
6 lb (2.7 kg) confectioners sugar
4 oz (112 g) cornstarch
1 pint (0.47 l) warm water

Kitchen Yields
The preceding formula produces about 7 lb (3.1 kg) pastillage—enough to make four simple cookie stands.

PASTRY

See Danish Pastry.

PASTRY CREAM

Formula 1
7½ qt (7 l) milk
3½ lb (7 cups, or 1.5 kg) sugar
36 whole eggs (1 qt + 3 cups, or 1.65 l)
1 lb (450 g) cornstarch

Kitchen Yield
The preceding formula produces 9½ qt (8.8 l), or 38 cups pastry cream.

Formula 2
10 qt (9.3 l) milk
5 lb (2.2 kg) sugar
50 (2½ qt or 2.3 l) whole eggs
22 oz (616 g) cornstarch

Kitchen Yield
The preceding formula produces 13 qt (12.2 l) or 52 cups pastry cream.

PÂTE À CHOU

Also called *cream puff paste.*

Formula
1 qt (0.94 l) milk
1 lb (450 g) butter
1¼ lb (560 g) bread flour
¼ oz (7 g) salt
1 qt (32 oz or 0.94 l) or 20 whole eggs

Kitchen Yields
The preceding formula produces 3 qt (2.8 l) pâté à chou.

PÂTE DOUGH

Formula
3 lb 5 oz (1.5 kg) cake flour
1½ lb (675 g) shortening
1 pint (0.47 l) warm water
1 oz (28 g) salt

Kitchen Yields
The preceding formula produces 5 lb 12 oz (2.4 kg) pâté dough. Mixture will line four standard pâté molds.

PEACHES

Peaches are available canned, dehydrated, fresh, and frozen.

CANNED PEACHES
Canned peaches are available packed in extra-heavy, heavy, or light syrup, or in water. They are packed whole, in halves, in quarters, in slices, and diced. Some varieties are marketed natural or spiced.

Pack:
Twenty-four #2½ cans; six #10 cans. Many other packs are available.

Sizes:
Table P-1 identifies canned peach weights and volumes.

Table P-1 Weights and Volumes of Canned Peaches

Can Size	Net Weight	Total Contents	Drained Weight	Volume of Drained Fruit
#2½	29 oz (820 g)	3½ cups (0.8 l)	18 oz (500 g)	2 cups (0.47 l)
#10	6 lb 12 oz (3 kg)	12 cups (2.8 l)	66 oz (1.87 kg)	8⅓ cups (1.96 l)

Counts:

For peach halves in #10 cans, counts are 25 to 30, 30 to 35, 35 to 40, and 40 to 50.

Kitchen Yields

Averages:

Halves:
#10 can: 35 to 40 pieces.
#2½ can: 10 to 12 pieces.

Slices:
#10 can: 6 lb 14 oz (4 kg) drained.
#2½ can: 1 lb 14 oz (840 g) drained.

Serving sizes:

Halves:
2 fruit pieces.
One #10 can yields 17 to 20 servings.
One #2½ can yields 5 to 6 servings.

Slices:
½ cup (0.11 l).
One #10 can yields 25 servings.
One #2½ can yields 7 servings.

Calories:

½ cup (0.11 l) or two halves syrup pack = 100 Calories.
½ cup (0.11 l) or two halves water pack = 38 Calories.

DEHYDRATED PEACHES

Dehydrated peaches are available as halves, pieces, dices, and slices, and as canned low-moisture slices.

Pack:

Regular dried:
10-lb (4.5-kg) lugs.
Other packs are available.

Low-moisture slices:
Six #10 cans with a net weight of 3 lb (1.35 kg) each.

Count:
Varies.

Kitchen Yields

1 lb (450 g) dried peaches yields 5¼ cups (1.2 l) cooked fruit.
1 lb (450 g) low-moisture slices yield 8 cups (1.8 l) cooked fruit.

Serving size:

½ cup (0.11 l).
1 lb (450 g) dried peaches yields 10 servings; 5 lb (2.2 kg) dried peaches yield 50 servings.
1 lb (450 g) low-moisture peaches yields 8 servings; 8 lb (3.6 kg) low-moisture peaches yield 50 servings.

Calories:

½ cup (0.11 l) cooked, unsweetened fruit = 100 Calories.
NOTE: Calorie count for constituted dried and low-moisture peaches is about the same.

FRESH PEACHES

Two types of peaches are important: Clingstone and Freestone. Early-season fruits are often Clingstone peaches.

Season:

Domestic fresh peaches are available from late May until September, peaking in July and August. Imports are available during the winter. Many varieties are on the market.

Pack:

19- to 23-lb (8.5- to 10.3-kg) two-layer lugs with counts of 50, 56, 60, 64, 72, or 80; 17- to 18-lb (7.6- to 8.1-kg) boxes with counts of 40, 45, 50, 55, 60, or 65; 38-lb (17-kg) boxes of loose fruit in sizes 2, 2¼, and 2½ in (51, 57, and 63 mm) diameter; 45- to 48-lb (20.2- to 21.6-kg) bushel baskets.

Common hotel size:
60-count lug.

Kitchen Yields
1 lb (450 g) is equivalent to 3 to 4 medium fruits, which yield 2 cups (0.47 l) sliced peaches or 1½ cups (0.350 l) pulp.

Calories:
One medium peach, weighing about 4 oz (112 g) with pit = 38 Calories.
½ cup (0.117 l) sliced peaches = 43 Calories.

FROZEN PEACHES
Frozen peaches are packed with approximately 25 percent sugar by weight. They are available as halves and as slices.

Pack:
1 gal (3.8 l) cans; 10-, 25-, and 30-lb (4.5-, 11.2-, and 13.5-kg) cans.

Serving size:
½ cup sliced peaches. One 30-lb (13.5-kg) can yields 100 servings.

Calories:
½ cup, or 4½ oz (126 g), sliced and sweetened = 110 Calories.

PEARS

Pears are available canned and fresh.

CANNED PEARS
Canned pears are available packed in extra-heavy syrup, heavy syrup, light syrup, slightly sweetened water, slightly sweetened fruit juice, or fruit juice.

Pack:
Six #10 cans.
Other packs are available.

Counts:

Halves:
20 to 25, with a drained net weight of 66 oz (1.85 kg); 25 to 30, 30 to 35, 35 to 40, 40 to 45, 45 to 50, 50 to 60, or 60 to 70, each with a drained net weight of 67.5 oz (1.9 kg).

Slices or pieces:
Drained net weight 70 oz (2 kg).

Diced:
Drained net weight 74.5 oz (2.11 kg).

Kitchen Yields

Serving sizes:
Use one #25 pear for stuffed pears; two #30 pears supply 1 portion for stewed fruit; three #35 pears supply 1 portion for pear salad.

Calories:
3½ oz (100 g) in fruit juice = 56 Calories.
3½ oz (100 g) in water = 35 Calories.
3½ oz (100 g) in light syrup = 75 Calories.
3½ oz (100 g) in heavy syrup = 92 Calories.

FRESH PEARS

ASIAN PEAR
Round fruit that tastes like a pear but looks like an apple. Available fresh.

Season:
Late summer through winter.

Pack:
9- to 10-lb (4- to 4.5-kg) crates.

Counts:
20 to 22 pieces per crate.

Kitchen Yields
Use in fruit baskets. Fruit is expensive. One Asian pear weighs 8 oz.

DOMESTIC PEARS
Domestic pears are harvested green and ripened under controlled temperature conditions. Numerous varieties are the market. Table P-2 lists these, together with the seasons when they are most plentiful and their primary uses. Many pear varieties are available year-round.

Pack:
44- to 46-lb (19.8- to 21.1-kg) layer-packed boxes; 36-lb (16.1-kg) cartons, tight-filled.

Counts:
70, 80, 90, 100, 110, 120, 135, 150, and 165 in layer-packed boxes. Carton counts, which roughly

Table P-2 Pear Varieties, Availability, and Uses

Name of Variety	Peak Season	Uses
Anjou	October through May	Fresh and salads
Bartlett	August through December	Fresh and cooking
Bosc	September through May	Fresh and cooking
Comice	October through March	Fresh
Forelle	October through February	Fresh
Nelis	October through April	Fresh and cooking
Red Bartlett	August through December	Fresh and cooking
Seckel	August through January	Fresh

correspond to box counts, are 56, 64, 72, 80, 90, 96, 108, 120, and 125.

Sizes:
Large pear: 90 to 100 size.
Medium pear: 135 size.
Small pear: 165 size.
Not all varieties are available in all sizes.

Weights:
90 size: 8 oz (226 g).
135 size: 5½ oz (155 g).
165 size: 4½ oz (126 g).

Kitchen Yields
1 cup (0.23 l) sliced pear weighs 5½ oz (155 g).
Three medium pears yield 2 cups sliced pears and a 1-layer box of #135 pears yields 5½ gal (21 l) sliced, peeled, and cored pears.

Calories:
One whole medium pear, weighing 5½ oz (155 g) = 65 Calories.
1 cup sliced pear, weighing 5½ oz (155 g) = 90 Calories.

PEAS

Peas are available canned, dried, fresh, and frozen.

CANNED PEAS

BLACK-EYED PEAS
Black-eyed peas, closely identified with Southern cooking, are also called *cowpeas* and *black-eyed beans*. A number of varieties and combinations with other vegetables are on the market, canned.

Pack:
Six #10 cans, containing 13 cups (3 l) each.

Kitchen Yields
1 #10 can contains 85 oz (2.4 kg) drained weight.

Serving size:
⅔ cup, or 4 oz (112 g); thus, one can yields 20 servings, and one case yields 120 servings.

Calories:
⅔ cup, or 4 oz (112 g) = 126 Calories.

GREEN PEAS
Canned peas are graded by size, as indicated by a sieve number. Sieve #1 is the smallest size, and sieve #6 is the largest size. Many packers no longer indicate sieve size. The designation of Early or Fancy does not indicate size. Puréed peas are available from at least one packer in #303 cans.

Pack:
Six #10 cans.

Kitchen Yields
One #10 can contains 70 oz (2 kg) drained weight, so one #10 can yields 20 servings.
Six #10 cans yield 120 servings.

Serving size:
½ cup, or 3½ oz (100 g).

Calories:
½ cup, or 3½ oz (100 g) = 88 Calories.

DRIED PEAS

BLACK-EYED PEAS

Pack:
Twenty-four 1-lb (450-g) boxes; individual 25-lb (11.2-kg) bags.

Kitchen Yields

Serving size:
½ cup (0.11 l) cooked.
1 cup dry measure weighs 7 oz (200 g).
1 lb (450 g) dried product yields 4½ cups (1.3 l), cooked.
1 lb (450 g) dried product yields 9 servings.

Calories:
½ cup (0.11 l) = 95 Calories.

WHOLE AND SPLIT DRIED PEAS
Dried peas are classified as green or mature yellow peas. In most cases, the outer skin is removed during the drying process, and the pea splits into two natural halves.

Pack:
Twenty-four 1-lb (450-g) boxes; individual 25-lb (11.2-kg) bags.

Kitchen Yields
1 lb (450 g) dried product is equivalent to 2¼ cups (0.5 l).

Serving size:
½ cup (0.11 l), cooked.
1 lb (450 g) produces 5 cups (1.1 l), cooked; therefore, 10 lb (4.5 kg) produce 100 servings.

Calories:
½ cup (0.11 l), cooked = 110 Calories.

FRESH PEAS

BLACK-EYED PEAS
Available shelled.

Season:
Mid- to late summer.

Pack:
By weight.

Kitchen Yields

Serving size:
½ cup (0.11 l) cooked.

Calories:
½ cup (0.11 l) = 90 Calories.

GREEN PEAS
Green peas have large pods that must be shelled and discarded. The actual size of the peas can be seen through the pod, because they bulge out. The sizes of the kernels in a pack vary greatly; and for this reason, unshelled peas are seldom used in the food industry. Peas must be very fresh when used.

Season:
Available year-round, with peak in early summer.

Pack:
10- and 30-lb (4.5- and 13.5-kg) lugs.

Kitchen Yields

Serving size:
½ cup (0.11 l), or 2¼ oz (63 g).
1 lb (450 g) is equivalent to 1 cup, or 5½ oz (155 g) shelled peas.
One 30-lb (13.5-kg) carton yields 30 cups (7 l), which amounts to 10 lb (4.5 kg) shelled peas. Therefore, one 30-lb (13.5-kg) carton yields 60 servings.

Calories:
½ cup, or (0.11 l) cooked and drained = 55 Calories.

SNOW PEAS
Snow peas are a cross between green peas and sugar snap peas.

Season:
Available year-round. Peaks are from January to February and from July to August.

Pack:
10- and 30-lb (4.5- and 13.6-kg) cartons.

Kitchen Yields

Waste:
Cleaning loss by weight is 15 percent.

Serving size:
1¼ oz (35 g); therefore, 1 lb (450 g) yields 11 servings.

SUGAR SNAP PEAS
Sugar snap peas can be eaten whole; only the ends must be snapped off, and the string along the back removed.

Season:
February to September.

Pack:
10- and 30-lb (4.5- and 13.5-kg) cartons.

Kitchen Yields

Waste:
Trimming loss is 5 percent by weight.

Serving size:
½ cup (0.11 l), or 2 oz (58 g), untrimmed.
1 lb (450 g) contains approximately 100 pieces, which yield 8 portions.

FROZEN PEAS

BLACK-EYED PEAS
Frozen while still tender and green.

Pack:
Twelve 3-lb (1.3-kg) packages; individual 20-lb (9-kg) bulk packs.

Kitchen Yields

Serving size:
½ cup cooked. One 3-lb (1.3-kg) package yields 12 servings.
One case of twelve packages yields 144 servings; one case of 20-lb (9-kg) bulk pack yields 80 servings.

Calories:
½ cup (0.11 l) = 80 Calories.

GREEN PEAS
Peas are graded by size and tenderness. They are marketed as Petit Peas, Small Peas, and under a number of other names. Size is an important quality factor. They are also on the market mixed with either pearl onions or cubed carrots.

Pack:
Twelve 2½-lb (1.1-kg) boxes; individual 20-lb (9-kg) cartons.

Kitchen Yields

Serving size:
½ cup cooked.
One 2½-lb (1.1-kg) package yields 10 to 12 servings; one case of twelve packages yields 120 to 144 servings.
20 lb (9 kg) yields 80 to 90 servings.

Calories:
½ cup, or 3 oz (85 g) = 60 Calories.

SNOW PEAS
Frozen snow peas have come onto the market. They overcook easily and lose crispness unless served right away.

Pack:
Twelve 2-lb (940-g) packages.

Kitchen Yields

Serving size:
3½ oz (100 g), as purchased; thus, one 2-lb (940-g) package yields 10 servings.
Twelve packages yield 120 servings.

Calories:
3½ oz (100 g) = 55 Calories.

SUGAR SNAP PEAS

Pack:
Twelve 32-oz (900-g) bags, IQF.

Kitchen Yields

Serving size:
3½ oz (100 g), as purchased. Thus, one 32-oz (900-g) bag yields 8 or 9 servings.

Calories:
3½ oz (100 g) = 50 Calories.

PECANS

Available shelled and in the shell. Pecan halves are graded by size; pieces are not graded by size.

Table P-3 Pecan Grades and Numbers

Name	Numbers per 1 lb (450 g)
Mammoth	200 to 250
Junior Mammoth	251 to 300
Jumbo	301 to 350
Extra Large	351 to 450
Large	451 to 550
Medium	551 to 600

Pack:
By weight.

Sizes:
Table P-3 lists pecan names and number per 1 lb (450 g).

Calories:
1 cup (0.23 l) chopped = 425 Calories.
1 cup (0.23 l) halves = 465 Calories.

Kitchen Yields
1 cup (0.23 l) pecan halves weighs 4 oz (113 g).

PEPPERS

HOT PEPPERS
See Chilies, under Mexican Foods.

SWEET PEPPERS (BELL PEPPERS)
Sweet peppers are available canned (often under the name pimiento), fresh, and frozen.

CANNED SWEET PEPPERS
These are diced or whole red peppers.

Pack:
Six #10 cans. Other packs are available.

Kitchen Yields
One #10 can contains 70 oz (1.9 kg) drained, or 8 cups (1.8 l).

FRESH SWEET PEPPERS
Most sweet peppers (also known as *bell peppers*) are sold in the immature stage, while they are green. All peppers turn red or yellow when they mature. Numerous varieties have been developed, including red, yellow, purple, brown, and white. Some are imports from Holland or from Mexico. The market differentiates between Choice and Fancy grades. The prices of colored peppers vary greatly according to season and where grown. Red sweet peppers are cheap and plentiful in season, but they can command a premium price when out of season.

Season:
Available year-round. Peak season from July to October. Domestic red peppers are most plentiful in fall. Mexican peppers are available in winter in both green and red. Hothouse-grown peppers are European imports and are available year-round.

Pack:
26- to 30-lb (11.7- to 13.5-kg) bushels; 10-lb (4.5-kg) cartons. Specialty colored peppers should be purchased by weight.

Count:
Varies greatly. About 5 pieces per 1 lb (450 g).

Kitchen Yields
For chopping, purchase Choice; for other applications, purchase Fancy.

Waste:
Cleaning loss is 20 percent by weight.
Ten medium peppers yield 5 cups (1.17 l) diced; 20 lb (9 kg) yields 40 cups diced and cooked.

Calories:
1 cup, or 4 oz (112 g), raw and diced = 28 Calories.

FROZEN SWEET PEPPERS
Sweet green peppers are available diced and in strips.

Pack:
Twelve 2½-lb (1.1-kg) packages.

Kitchen Yields
2½-lb (1.1-kg) packages yield 9 cups (2.1 l).

PERSIMMONS

Two varieties of persimmons are marketed. The Fuyu persimmon has orange-colored skin and flesh. It should be eaten while still firm. The whole fruit is edible. The Hachiya variety is more pointed than the Fuyu variety and should be eaten when soft. Both varieties are used in salads and as a fruit garnish.

Season:
Fall and early winter.

Pack:
Flats with 24 or 30 fruits.

Kitchen Yields
One fruit yields 4 oz (112 g) edible flesh.

Calories:
4 oz (117 g) edible flesh = 90 Calories.

PESTO

Prepared pesto sauce is available under a number of brand names. It can be made fresh, as well.

Formula
    10 cups (2.3 l) basil leaves
    1 cup (0.23 l) chopped garlic
    2 cups (0.47 l) pine nuts
    3 cups (0.7 l) grated Parmesan cheese
    3 cups (0.7 l) olive oil

Kitchen Yields
The preceding formula yields 12 cups pesto.

Serving size:
3 tb pesto with 1 cup cooked pasta. Therefore, the preceding formula yields pesto for 64 servings.

PHEASANT

FRESH OR FROZEN PHEASANT
Pheasant is available eviscerated, either fresh or frozen. Male birds in feathers for display are also available.

Season:
Available year-round, because birds are farm-raised.

Average sizes:
15 to 18 oz (420 to 504 g); 20 oz (560 g); 1¾ to 2 lb (0.8 to 0.9 kg); 2 to 2½ lb (0.9 to 1.1 kg); 2½ to 3 lb (1.1 to 1.3 kg).

Kitchen Yields

Serving sizes:
15- to 18-oz (420- to 504-g) whole birds.
2-lb (0.9-kg) whole birds, when serving half birds.
3-lb (1.3-kg) whole birds, when serving breast only.

SMOKED PHEASANT
Smoked pheasant is available as whole bird or as breasts in some markets.

Sizes:
For whole birds, 2¼ to 2¾ lb (1 to 1.2 kg).

PIE

CANNED PIE FILLING
Available are most fruit fillings, ready for baking.

Pack:
Six #10 cans.

Kitchen Yields
Varies, depending on fruit variety. One #10 can yields, on average, five 9-in-diameter (288-mm-diameter) pies.

PIE DOUGH
Formula
    3 lb (1.3 kg) pastry flour
    2 lb (900 g) shortening
    1 pint, or 2 cups (0.47 l), cold water
    1 oz, or 2 tb (28 g), salt

Kitchen Yields
Ten 9-in-diameter (228-mm-diameter) pie shells.

PINEAPPLE

Available canned, fresh, and fresh processed.

CANNED PINEAPPLE
Available sliced, in chunks, in tidbits, coarse-crushed, fine-crushed, and in broken slices. Most items are packed in heavy syrup, light syrup, or juice.

Table P-4 Counts and Weights for Canned Pineapple

Product Name	Can Weight	Drained Weight	Count
Sliced	108 oz (3.06 kg)		52
Sliced	108 oz (3.06 kg)		66
Sliced	108 oz (3.06 kg)		100 to 110
Chunks	109 oz (3.09 kg)	66 oz (1.87 kg)	
Small tidbits	108 oz (3.06 kg)	70 oz (2 kg)	
Coarse crushed	107 oz (3.03 kg)	90 oz (2.5 kg)	
Fine crushed	107 oz (3.03 kg)	90 oz (2.5 kg)	
Broken slices	107 oz (3.03 kg)	63 oz (1.8 kg)	

Pack:
Six #10 cans. Table P-4 lists weights and counts for #10 cans of pineapple in different styles.

Kitchen Yields

Serving sizes:

Chunks:
4½ oz (126 g); therefore, one #10 can yields 20 servings.

Large slices:
1 slice; therefore, one #10 can yields 52 or 66 servings.

Small slices:
2 slices; therefore, one #10 can yields 50 to 55 servings.

Calories:
½ cup, or 4½ oz (126 g), chunks in heavy syrup = 95 Calories.
One large 3⅝-oz (105-g) slice, with 2¼ tb syrup = 80 Calories.

FRESH PINEAPPLE
Fruit should be picked almost ripe, but ripeness of fruit is difficult to judge. For this reason, brand is important. Domestic fruits and imports come to the market at various times. Baby pineapples, about 2½ to 3 in (63 to 76 mm) tall, are available from Hawaii. They are used primarily for decorative purposes.

Season:
Available year-round. Peak is in April and May.

Pack:
20-lb (9-kg) half cartons; 40-lb (18-kg) full cartons.

Counts:

Half cartons:
4, 5, 6, or 7.

Full cartons:
8, 9, 10, 12, 14, 15, 16, or 18.

Kitchen Yields

Common hotel sizes:
#5 for salads; #14 for appetizer baskets.
One medium pineapple weighs 4 lb (1.8 kg) and yields 5½ cups diced pineapple.
One #5 pineapple yields 1⅓ lb (0.58 kg) clean meat, which amounts to 17 slices when sliced with machine at #34 or to 68 sliced quarters.

Calories:
1 cup, or 5½ oz (156 g), raw and diced = 80 Calories.

FRESH PROCESSED PINEAPPLE
Available are chilled fresh pineapple chunks.

Pack:
5-lb (2.25-kg) pouches.

Counts:

Wedges:
23 to 32.

Spears:
10 to 12.

Tidbits:
139 to 153.

Kitchen Yields
Use in fruit salads. There is little juice in packages.

Calories:
4 oz (112 g) = 90 Calories.

PINEAPPLE JUICE
Pineapple juice is available canned and fresh, sweetened and unsweetened.

Pack:
Forty-eight 6-oz (0.176-l) cans; twelve 46-oz (1.3-l) cans.

Kitchen Yields
6 oz (0.17 l) per serving; therefore, one 46-oz can (1.3-l) yields 7½ servings.
For fresh juice, one medium #5 pineapple yields 2½ cups (0.58 l) juice.

Calories:
6 oz (0.17 l) unsweetened = 110 Calories.

PINE NUTS

Also called *pignoli nuts.* Available shelled.

Pack:
By weight.

Kitchen Yield
1 cup dry measure weighs 5 oz (140 g).

PISTACHIOS

Pistachios are available in the shell (often dyed red) and shelled. The shelled nuts can be purchased raw or roasted, salted or unsalted. They are usually still covered with a thin skin, which can be removed from raw nuts by blanching them in boiling water.

Pack:

Shelled nuts:
#10 cans with a net weight of 3½ to 4 lb (1.5 to 1.8 kg) each. 25-lb (11.25-kg) cartons.

Unshelled nuts:
By weight. Many sizes are available.

Kitchen Yields
1 cup shelled nuts weigh 4½ oz (126 g).

PITA BREAD

Flat round bread of Middle Eastern origin that forms a pocket inside.

Pack:
Bags of 10 or 12 pieces.

Size:
2 oz (56 g) each, with a diameter of about 7 in (177 mm).

Kitchen Yields
One piece per person for sandwich. Product freezes well.

PIZZA

HOME-MADE PIZZA INGREDIENTS
PIZZA DOUGH

Formula
50 lb (22.5 kg) high-gluten flour
2 gal + 3 pints (8.8 l) water
1 cup, or 8 oz (226 g), oil
1 cup, or 8 oz (226 g), salt
½ cup, or 4 oz (110 g), sugar
8 oz (226 g) fresh yeast

Kitchen Yields
The preceding formula produces 70 large 16-in (40-cm) pies scaled at 1 lb (450 g), or 110 medium 9-in (23-cm) pies, scaled at 10 oz (284 g), or 640 hors d'oeuvre pies, scaled at 1¾ oz (78 g).

PIZZA SAUCE

Formula
5 #10 cans tomato sauce
3 #10 cans crushed tomatoes
1 #10 can tomato catsup
½ cup (0.11 l) oregano

Kitchen Yields
12 oz (0.7 l) sauce for one 16-in (400-mm) pie.
Recipe yields sauce for 75 pies.

PROCESSED PIZZA INGREDIENTS
BAKED PIZZA CRUST

Sizes and packs:
Twenty-four 16-in (400-mm) pie crusts; twenty-four 15-in (375-mm) pie crusts; twenty-four or thirty 12-in (300-mm) pie crusts; thirty 10-in (250-mm) pie crusts; twenty-four or thirty 9-in (225-mm) pie crusts; sixty 6½-in (184-mm) pie crusts; one hundred twenty 5½-in (156-mm) pie crusts; twenty-four 8 × 12 in (200 × 300 mm) pie crusts; twenty or twenty-four 9 × 10 in (225 × 250 mm) pie crusts; twenty 12 × 16 in (300 × 400 mm) pie crusts.

PIZZA CHEESE
Mozzarella cheese is normally used.

Pack:
5- to 6-lb (2.2- to 2.7-kg) loaves; 20-lb (9-kg) loaves; 40-lb (18-kg) block; six 4-lb (1.8-kg) bags, shredded cheese.

Kitchen Yields
1 lb (450 g) cheese provides topping for one 16-in (40-cm) pie.
10 oz (280 g) cheese provides topping for one 10-in (25-cm) pie.

PIZZA DOUGH BALLS

Sizes and packs:
Twenty-four 22-oz (624-g) dough balls; twenty-four 20-oz (568-g) dough balls; twenty-four 16-oz (450-g) dough balls; forty 10-oz (280-g) dough balls.

PIZZA SAUCE

Pack:
Six #10 cans.

Kitchen Yields

Serving size:
18 oz (0.5 l) sauce for one 16-in (400-mm) pie.
1 #10 can yields sauce for 5½ pies.

READY-TO-BAKE PIZZA
Ready-to-bake pizzas are available in many sizes.

Sizes and packs:
Forty-eight 4 × 6 in (100 × 150 mm) pies; forty-eight 4 × 6 in (100 × 150 mm) pies with extra cheese; forty-eight 4 × 5 in (100 × 125 mm) pies. Other packs and sizes are available:

PLANTAINS

Called *platanos* in Spanish, these are cooking bananas. The color ranges from green to dark yellowish brown (which indicates maturity).

Season:
Imports are available year-round.

Pack:
48-lb (21.6-kg) cartons.

Size:
Average 8 to 10 oz (226 to 284 g) each.
Larger sizes, up to 1 lb (450 g), come to the market occasionally.

Kitchen Yields

Waste:
Peeling loss is about 20 percent.

Serving size:
4 oz (112 g).

Calories:
4 oz (112 g) = 175 Calories.

PLUMS

Plums are available canned and fresh.

CANNED PLUMS
Available canned varieties include Purple, Green Gage, Yellow Egg, and others, whole and in halves. Whole plums are usually not pitted. Canned plums may be packed in heavy syrup, light syrup, or water.

Pack:
Six #10 cans; twenty-four #2½ cans; twenty-four #2 cans.

Kitchen Yields

Drained weights:

Whole plums:
#10 can weighs 60 oz (1.7 kg).
#2½ can weighs 15½ oz (440 g).
#2 can weighs 10½ oz (300 g).

Plum halves:
#10 can weighs 63 oz (1.8 kg).
#2½ can weighs 16¼ oz (460 g).
#2 can weighs 12 oz (340 g).

Serving size:
½ cup. One #10 can yields 16 servings, and one #2½ can yields 6 servings.

DRIED PLUMS
See Prunes.

FRESH PLUMS
There are two major varieties: Freestone and Clingstone. The Clingstone variety is marketed as plum for eating fresh, while the Freestone variety is marketed as fresh prune.

Varieties (by color):

Purple: Italian or French, Damson.
Red: Clayman, Climax, Hungarian, Santa Rosa, Beauty.
Yellow or green: Yellow Egg, Wickson, Kelsey, Greengage.

Season:
Domestic supplies peak during the summer and early fall. Various domestic and imported varieties are available year-round. Italian plums are available from late August to October.

Pack:
28-lb (12.6-kg) cartons or lugs.

Count:
Differs, depending on variety. Yellow Egg plums can be as large as 2 in (50 mm) across, while Damson plums can be as small as cherries.

Kitchen Yields

Quantities:

Large plums:
4 to 5 per 1 lb (450 g).

Small plums:
8 to 10 per 1 lb (450 g).

Calories:
4 oz (117 g) edible flesh = 50 Calories.
One 3-oz (84-g) plum, 2 in in diameter = 30 Calories.

POLENTA

Polenta is yellow cornmeal mush, sometimes flavored with grated Parmesan cheese.

Formula
6 cups (1.4 l) coarse cornmeal
10 cups (2.3 l) chicken stock
8 oz (224 g) butter
1 cup (0.11 l) heavy cream
2 cups grated cheese
nutmeg, salt to taste

Kitchen Yields

Serving size:
½ cup (0.11 l). The preceding formula produces 1 gal (3.7 l), and will fill one 18- by 26-in sheet pan, and yield 32 servings.

POMEGRANATES

Red-skinned fruit, used mostly in the manufacture of grenadine syrup.

Season:
August to December.

Pack:
22-lb (9.9-kg) lug.

Size and count:
3 to 4 in (80 to 120 mm) across.

Kitchen Yields
Primary use is for flavoring sauces and syrups, because numerous seeds are imbedded in the flesh.

Calories:
4 oz (117 g) edible flesh = 90 Calories.

POPCORN

Many different brands are available. Smaller kernels make better tasting popcorn than larger kernels. Natural blue popcorn and black popcorn have come on the market.

Pack:
By weight.

Kitchen Yields
Yield varies, as high-quality popcorn gives a better yield than cheaper popcorn.
¼ cup (0.05 l) dry measure weighs 2 oz (56 g) and makes 9 to 10 cups (2 to 2.3 l) popped corn.
1 cup (0.232 l) dry measure weighs 8 oz (224 g) and makes 2¼ to 2½ gal (8.3 to 9.2 l) popped corn.

Calories:
2 oz (56 g), without fat, 9 to 10 cups popped = 220 Calories.
2 oz (56 g), with ⅔ oz (19 g) oil, 9 to 10 cups popped = 386 Calories.

POPOVERS

Formula
    24 whole eggs
    3 lb (1.3 kg), bread flour
    2½ qt (2.3 l) milk
    1 oz (56 g), or 2 tb salt
    Nutmeg to taste
    Fat to fill muffin tins about one-quarter full

NOTE: Fat must be very hot when batter is poured in. Bake at 450°F.

Kitchen Yields
The preceding formula produces 96 medium-sized popovers.

PORK

LARGER CUTS OF PORK
Pork products generally come from animals under 1 year of age, and for this reason all cuts are relatively tender. Pork parts are not graded, although the carcass is. Selection #1 is normally used for foodservice. For clarity, the *Meat Buyers Guide* (MBG) identification numbers established by the National Association of Meat Purveyors are used with some items.

BACK RIBS, MBG #422
Rib bones, with some loin meat still attached.

Weight ranges:
Under 1½ lb (0.6 kg).
1½ to 3 lb (0.6 to 1.3 kg).
3 lb (1.3 kg) and up.
Ribs weighing more than 3 lb (1.3 kg) can be tough.

Kitchen Yields

Serving size:
1 lb (450 g).

BUTT, MBG #406
Called the *Boston butt,* this piece is from the shoulder, with the blade bone in.

Sizes:
4 to 8 lb (1.8 to 3.6 kg).
8 to 12 lb (3.6 to 5.4 kg).

Kitchen Yields
Meat for roasts, stews, or as ground pork.

Best size:
7 lb (3.1 kg).

Boned and trimmed:
6 lb (2.7 kg).

CAUL FAT
Thin, netlike covering of the lower part of the intestines; available fresh or salted. Keep caul fat in water in refrigerator.

Pack:
Sold by weight.

HAM, BONED AND NETTED, MBG #202B
Boneless ham, with all skin removed.

Sizes:
6 to 8 lb (2.7 to 3.6 kg).
8 to 10 lb (3.6 to 4.5 kg).
10 to 12 lb (4.5 to 5.4 kg).

Kitchen Yields

Smaller hams are generally leaner and easier to slice than larger ones.

Best size:
7 lb (3.1 kg).

Serving sizes:
6 oz roast ham for main course, or 5 oz for sandwich meat. One 7-lb (3.1-kg) roast will yield 12 to 14 main-course servings; 15 to 16 sandwich servings.

HAM, REGULAR, SHORT SHANK, MBG #401A
Basic ham, with shank cut short and aitch bone left in.

Weight ranges:
10 to 14 lb (4.5 to 6.3 kg).
14 to 17 lb (6.3 to 7.6 kg).
17 to 20 lb (7.6 to 9.0 kg).

Kitchen Yields

Best size:
14 lb (6.3 kg).
Bones, fat, skin, and cooking shrinkage is about 50 percent.

Serving size:
6 oz (170 g) roast ham; thus, one 14-lb (6.3-kg) ham yields 16 to 20 servings.

HAM, SKINNED, SHORT SHANK, MBG #402A
Same items as regular ham, but with skin and underlying fat partly removed.

Kitchen Yields

The removed skin and fat accounts for about 8 to 10 percent of weight.

Best size:
12 lb (5.4 kg).

KNUCKLES

Average size:
12 oz (340 g).

Kitchen Yields

Serving size:
One knuckle.

LIVER

Weights:
3 to 4 lb (1.3 to 1.8 kg).

LOIN, MBG #410
Full split loin, including tenderloin and blade.

Weight ranges:
10 to 14 lb (4.5 to 6.3 kg).
14 to 17 lb (6.3 to 7.6 kg).
17 to 20 lb (7.6 to 9 kg).

Kitchen Yields

Serving size:
5 oz (140 g) cooked.

Best size:
12 lb (5.4 kg).
1 lb (450 g) as purchased yields 8 oz (227 g) boneless cooked meat. One 12-lb (5.4-kg) loin roasted whole yields 8 lb (3.60 kg) raw boneless meat, or 20 boneless servings.

LOIN, BONELESS, MBG #413
Full loin, including end pieces, but fully boned.

Weight ranges:
6 to 8 lb (2.7 to 3.6 kg).
8 to 10 lb (3.6 to 4.5 kg).
10 to 12 lb (4.5 to 5.4 kg).

Kitchen Yields
Use boneless loin for roasting whole.

Serving size:
5 oz (140 g) cooked.

Best size:
8 lb (3.6 kg). One 8-lb (3.6-kg) loin, yields 19 servings.

LOIN, CENTER-CUT, MBG #412

Weight ranges:
4 to 6 lb (1.8 to 2.7 kg).
6 to 8 lb (2.7 to 3.6 kg).
8 to 10 lb (3.6 to 4.5 kg).

Kitchen Yields
Purchase this cut when there is no use for trimmings.

Best size:
8 lb (3.6 kg).
One 8-lb (3.6-kg) loin yields 6 lb (2.7 kg) raw boned meat.

RIBS, COUNTRY-STYLE MBG #423
Basically a loin chop from the shoulder end, with shin bone removed, cut horizontally into two pieces—one piece containing the feather bones, and the other piece containing the ribs.

Weight ranges:
1 to 2 lb (0.45 to 0.9 kg).
2 to 4 lb (0.9 to 1.8 kg).
4 lb (1.8 kg) and up.

Kitchen Yields

Serving size:
1 lb (450 g) and up.

SHOULDER HOCKS, MBG #417
Weights range from ½ lb (226 g).

SHOULDER, SKINNED, MBG #404
This is a bone-in shoulder, with most of the fat removed.

Weight ranges:
8 to 12 lb (3.6 to 5.4 kg).
12 to 16 lb (5.4 to 7.2 kg).
16 to 20 lb (7.2 to 9.0 kg).

Kitchen Yields
Use for stew meat and ground meat. For roasting, purchase Boston butt instead of whole shoulder.

Best size:
12 lb (5.4 kg).
12 lb (5.4 kg) skinned shoulder yield 7 lb (3.1 kg) boned meat, with skin, shank, and most fat removed.

Serving size:
For roast, 5 oz (142 g) roasted; thus, one shoulder, boned and tied, yields 15 servings. For stew, 8 oz (227 g) raw, or 5½ oz (156 g) cooked; thus, one 12-lb (5.4-kg) shoulder, as purchased, yields 14 servings.

SPARERIBS, MBG #416
Ribs from belly and breast.

Weight ranges:
1½ to 3 lb (0.6 to 1.3 kg).
3 to 5 lb (1.3 to 2.2 kg).
5 lb and (2.2 kg) and up.

Kitchen Yields
Available as spareribs, breast off, MBG #416A, the weights are about 10 to 16 oz (280 to 450 g) less.

Serving size:
1 lb (450 g) and up.

SUCKLING PIG
Weights vary from 8 to 40 lb (3.6 to 18 kg).

Kitchen Yields

Best sizes:

Roasted whole pig for buffet:
25 to 30 lb (11.2 to 13.5 kg).
NOTE: A pig of 25 to 30 lb (11.2 to 13.5 kg) will still fit in a convection oven.

Servings:
15 to 20 main-course servings, or 40 to 50 appetizer servings on buffet, from a 25- to 30-lb (11.2- to 13.5-kg) pig; purchase one 10-lb (4.5-kg) suckling pig for making galantine.

TENDERLOINS, MBG #415
Most commonly available frozen.

Weight ranges:
4 to 8 oz (112 to 224 g).
8 to 12 oz (224 to 340 g).
12 to 16 oz (340 to 450 g).

Kitchen Yields
Very little trim is needed. Roast or braise whole, or cut into small medallions.

Serving size:
Varies. For braising whole, use 8 to 10 oz (227 to 340 g) raw weight per person.

TRIMMINGS
Trimmings are available 90 and 80 percent lean. Good buy for making sausages.

POPULAR PORK DISHES

BARBECUED SPARE RIBS
Purchase Spareribs, MBG #416 (ribs from belly and breast), or Back Ribs, MBG #422 (rib bones with some loin meat still attached).

Best weight:
1½ to 3 lb (0.6 to 1.3 kg) for Spareribs, MBG #416; 1½ lb (1.3 kg) for Back Ribs, MBG #422.

Kitchen Yields

Serving size:
1½ lb (675 g) raw weight, which yields 1 lb (450 g) cooked weight.
10-lb (4.5-kg) ribs yield 7 servings.

BROILED CHOPS
Purchase Loin, Center-cut, MBG #412.

Best weight:
8 lb (3.6 kg).

Kitchen Yields

Serving size:
Two chops, 4 oz (112 g) each, with only rib bones still attached and all other bones removed, well trimmed.
One 8-lb (3.6-kg) loin yields 12 servings.

ROAST FRESH HAM
Purchase Ham, Boned and Netted, MBG #202B (boneless ham, with all skin removed).

Best size:
7 lb (3.1 kg).

Kitchen Yields
Smaller hams are generally leaner and easier to slice than larger pieces.

Serving sizes:
6 oz (170 g) roast ham for main course, or 5 oz (142 g) for sandwich meat.
One 7-lb (3.1-kg) ham yields 12 main-course servings or 16 sandwich-meat servings.

Calories:
6 oz (170 g) = 620 Calories.

ROAST FRESH SHOULDER
Purchase Butt, MBG #406. Also called *Boston butt* (piece from the shoulder, with the blade bone in).

Best weight:
7 lb (3.1 kg).

ROAST LOIN
Purchase Loin, Boneless, MBG #413 (full loin, including end pieces, but fully boned).

Best size:
8 lb (3.6 kg).

Kitchen Yields

Serving size:
6 oz (170 g) cooked meat.
One 8-lb (3.6-kg) loin yields 16 servings.

Kitchen Yields

Serving size:
6 oz (170 g).
One 7-lb (3.1-kg) butt yields 10 to 12 servings.

Calories:
6 oz (170 g) = 640 Calories.

PORTION CUTS OF PORK

BUTT STEAKS
Available bone-in and boneless. This is rather fatty meat.

Weight ranges:
4, 5, 6, and 8 oz (113, 142, 170, and 226 g).

Kitchen Yields
Braise with vegetables or with sauerkraut.

Serving size:
6 oz (170 g) raw weight.

CHOPS
Available in many sizes and configurations.

BONE-IN CHOPS
Cut across the loin, with all bones still attached, starting at the shoulder end. These are least expensive chops.

Weights:
3, 4, 5, and 6 oz (85, 113, 142, and 170 g).

Serving size:
Two 4-oz (113-g) chops.

BONELESS CHOPS
Cut from the boned full loin, from end to end.

Weights:
3, 4, 5, 6, and 8 oz (85, 112, 140, 170, and 224 g).

Serving size:
Varies.

CENTER-CUT CHOPS
Available with or without the shin bone removed; and also available completely boneless. The completely boneless chops are the most expensive cuts.

Weights:
3, 4, 5, 6, and 8 oz (85, 112, 140, 170, and 224 g).

Serving size:
Varies.

CHOPS WITH POCKET
Available as rib chops or cut from the full loin. Rib chops have the incision made at the rib bone; the other chops have the incision from the outside.

Weights:
5, 6, and 8 oz (140, 170, and 224 g).

Serving size:
One chop 6 or 8 oz (170 or 227 g), stuffed.

SMOKED AND CURED PORK PRODUCTS

BACON

CANADIAN BACON
Cured and smoked boneless loin. Genuine Canadian bacon is a product in its natural shape. There is also a pressed and rolled domestic product of the same name on the market.

Weights:

Imported:
5 to 7 lb (2.2 to 3.1 kg).

Roll:
7 to 9 lb (3.1 to 4 kg).
Canadian bacon is also available sliced in packages of various sizes.

Kitchen Yields
The imported product is packaged on top of a thin wooden board. Waste and trim loss amount to about 5 percent. The rolled product has very little waste.

Serving size:
Two 2-oz (56-g) slices, or 4 oz (112 g) total.
6 lb (2.7 kg) imported product yields 24 servings.
8 lb (3.6 kg) rolled product yields 30 servings.

PANCETTA
Italian rolled bacon; used for cooking or eaten uncooked.

Weight:
4½ lb (2 kg).

SLICED BACON

Pack:
10-, 12-, and 15-lb (4.5-, 5.4-, and 6.7-kg) boxes. Other sizes are available.

Counts:

Regular bacon:
1 lb (450 g) consisting of 16 to 18 slices.
1 lb (450 g) consisting of 18 to 22 slices.

Special lean:
1 lb (450 g) consisting of 30 slices.

Precooked:
1 lb (450 g) consisting of 50 slices.

Kitchen Yields
Serving sizes:
Three slices for breakfast; three slices, chopped fine, as salad garnish; four slices, chopped fine, as garnish for pasta carbonara.
Thus, for breakfast, 1 lb (450 g) regular bacon of 16 to 18 size yields 5½ servings; 9 lb (4 kg) yields 50 servings, 18 lb (8.1 kg) yields 100 servings.
Also, 1 lb (450 g) regular bacon of 18 to 22 size yields 6½ breakfast portions; 8 lb (3.6 kg) yields 50 portions, and 15½ lb (7 kg) yields 100 portions. For garnishes, 1 lb (450 g) raw bacon produces 5 oz (142 g) cooked bacon, and 1 cup crisp bacon bits, chopped fine, weighs 4 oz (170 g). 13 oz (370 g) raw bacon yields 1 cup (0.235 l) cooked chopped bits, and 5 lb (2.3 kg) raw bacon yields 6 cups cooked bacon bits.

Hence, 3¾ lb (1.7 kg) uncooked bacon yield 25 servings for salad garnish, while 5 lb (2.2 kg) uncooked bacon yields 25 servings for pasta carbonara garnish.

Calories:

16 to 18 size:
Three crisp 1-oz (28-g) slices = 175 Calories.

18 to 22 size:
Three crisp ¾-oz (21-g) slices = 130 Calories.

WHOLE OR SLAB BACON
Normally sold with skin on.

Purchase:
By weight.

Kitchen Yields

Waste:
Trimming waste is about 8 percent.
Use for garnishes, or slice thick for special applications.

BOLOGNA (MORTADELLA)
See Sausages, under this same heading.

BRATWURST
White sausage with smooth filling. Bratwurst with coarse filling is normally sold as Italian sausage.

Pack:
10-lb (4.5-kg) cartons.

Count:
Forty 4-oz (112-g) pieces per pound and up.

Kitchen Yields

Serving size:
Two sausages, 4 oz (112 g) each.

BUTTS
Smoked boneless butts.

Weight range:
1½ to 2½ lb (0.6 to 1.1 kg).

Kitchen Yields
Shrinkage after boiling is 20 percent. Excellent braised with root vegetables, cabbage, or sauerkraut.

FATBACK
Available fresh (called *green*) or salted. The product is also called *larding pork*.

Weight range:
12 to 14 lb (5.4 to 6.3 kg).

Kitchen Yields
Weight of skin is about 8 to 10 percent of total weight. When product is used for pâté, make sure to specify unsalted fatback.

HAM

CANNED HAM
Available in natural shape, square shape, and rectangular shape (called *pullman ham*) in many quality levels, ranging from very lean to fatty. Pullman ham is available in 4 × 4 in (100 × 100 mm) blocks—the standard size of sandwich bread.

Sizes:
Vary greatly according to manufacturers.

Kitchen Yields
Basically there is very little waste.

Serving size:
3 to 4 oz (85 to 113 g) for sandwiches.

Calories:
4 oz (113 g), very lean = 260 Calories.

COOKED HAM
Boneless ham, fully cooked, and lightly smoked. This ham is often used as breakfast ham. A number of manufacturers produce hams under trade names.

Sizes:
7 to 10 lb (3.1 to 4.5 kg).

Kitchen Yields

Trimming waste:
5 percent on most brands.

Serving sizes:
3 to 4 oz (85 to 113 g) for breakfast ham; 6 to 7 oz (170 to 200 g) for ham steak.
One 8-lb (3.6-kg) ham yields forty 3-oz (85-g) breakfast servings.

Calories:
4 oz (113 g), lean and fat = 325 Calories.

HAM STEAKS
Produced by many manufacturers. Fully trimmed and ready to eat, with center bone in.

Weights:
12 to 16 oz (340 to 450 g).

Packs:
15- or 30-lb (6.7- to 13.5-kg) boxes.

PICNIC HAM
Shoulder ham; often fatty.

Sizes:
From 2 to 6 lb (0.9 to 2.7 kg).

PROSCIUTTO HAM
Available bone-in, boneless in natural shape, and boneless shaped round.

Sizes:

Bone-in:
11 to 14 lb (4.9 to 6.3 kg).

Boneless:
6 to 10 lb (2.7 to 4.5 kg).

Kitchen Yields
The waste factor of bone-in ham is high, because skin, shank, and bones (which have only limited kitchen use) must be removed. Boneless hams in natural shape have a high waste factor, too, because shank and skin must be removed. Fat cover can also be high in both ham varieties.

Serving size:
1½ oz (42 g)—about two large or three medium lean slices.
For a 12-lb (5.4-kg) bone-in prosciutto, the following weights and servings will be obtained.

> *Bones and trim:* 5 lb 6 oz (2.4 kg).
> *Usable meat:* 6 lb 10 oz (2.9 kg).
> *Servings:* 70 if slices of different sizes and shapes are used.

NOTE: Some trimmings can be used.
For a 9-lb (4-kg) boneless prosciutto in natural shape, the following weights and servings will be obtained.

> *Shank and trim:* 3 lb 3 oz (1.4 kg).
> *Usable meat:* 5 lb 13 oz (2.6 kg).
> *Servings:* 60, if slices of different shapes are used.

For a 7-lb (3.1-kg) round boneless prosciutto, the following yields will be obtained:

> *Usable meat:* 6¼ lb (2.8 kg).
> *Servings:* 65 if slices of different shape are used.

SMITHFIELD HAM
Another name for Virginia ham.

VIRGINIA HAM
Genuine Virginia ham is from razorback hogs; it is air-dried and lightly smoked, and then coated with pepper. Available raw or fully cooked, bone in or boneless.

Weights:

Whole, uncooked:
12 to 16 lb (5.4 to 7.2 kg).

Ready-to-eat, bone in:
10 to 12 lb (4.5 to 5.4 kg).

Ready-to-eat, boneless:
8 to 10 lb (3.6 to 4.5 kg).

Kitchen Yields
Soak overnight. Change water during boiling, if necessary to remove salt.

Waste:

Uncooked Ham, bone in:
Waste is about 50 percent.

Cooked Ham, bone in:
Boning and trimming waste is about 40 percent.

WESTPHALIAN HAM
Smoked, dried ham that is served uncooked and sliced very thin. Available from specialty butchers.

Weights:
3 to 5 lb (1.3 to 2.2 kg) boneless. Other sizes are available.

Kitchen Yields
Better-quality hams have skin and fat layer still attached, and each piece has an irregular shape.

Trimming waste:
20 percent.

Serving size:
3 oz (100 g), for cold plate or sandwich.

WHOLE SMOKED HAM
Available both fully cooked (referred to as *ready-to-eat*) and uncooked. Most smoked ham on the market is fully cooked.

Pack and weights:

Ready-to-eat cooked Ham:
10 to 12 lb (4.5 to 5.4 kg).
14 to 17 lb (4.5 to 7.6 kg).

Uncooked Ham:
12 lb (5.4 kg) and up.

Kitchen Yields

Serving sizes:
6 oz (168 oz) as main course; 4 oz (112 g) as sandwich.
One 14-lb (6.3-kg) ready-to-eat ham has the following yields:

> *Bone and trim:* 4 lb 5 oz (1.9 kg)
> *Usable meat:* 9 lb 9 oz (4.2 kg)
> *Servings:* 20 main-course servings.
>   25 sandwich servings.
> *Usable trimmings:* 1 lb 15 oz (0.9 kg)

One 15-lb (10.1-kg) uncooked ham undergoes a cooking loss of 2 lb 8 oz (680 g).
After cooking, the yield is same as for ready-to-eat ham.

Calories:
4 oz (112 g) = 330 Calories.

KASSLER
Another name for smoked pork loin.

LOIN
Smoked pork loin is also known as Kassler. Product is normally sold as full loin, with all bones attached.

Weights:
9 to 11 lb (4 to 4.9 kg).

Kitchen Yields

Serving size:
8 oz (224 g), consisting of two slices, boneless (except rib bones), cooked. One 10-lb (4.5-kg) loin yields 10 servings.

LUNCHEON MEAT
Available canned in various sizes.

Kitchen Yields
There is no waste; use as is.

Calories:
4 oz (112 g) = 350 Calories.

MORTADELLA
See Sausages, under this same heading.

PANCETTA
See Bacon, under this same heading.

PROSCIUTTO
See Ham, under this same heading.

SALAMI
See Sausages, under this same heading.

SALT BELLY
Cured in salt only. Normally sold with skin on.

Weight:
12 to 14 lb (5.4 to 6.3 kg).

CORNED SALT BELLY
Cured with salt and saltpeter. Meat portion is slightly red. Normally sold with skin on.

Weight:
12 to 14 lb (5.4 to 6.3 kg).

SMOKED SALT BELLY
See Whole or Slab Bacon, under this same heading.

SAUSAGES

BREAKFAST SAUSAGES
Available in different sizes. Sausages made with other meats—without pork—are also available.

Pack:
5-lb (2.2-kg) packages.

Sizes:
Eight pieces per 1 lb (450 g), or twelve pieces per 1 lb (450 g).

Kitchen Yields
The fat content of sausages varies greatly. Average shrinkage by weight is 35 percent. Precooked products with little shrinkage are on the market.

Serving size:
Three pieces, for breakfast. Thus, one 5-lb (2.2-kg) box, size 8, yields 13 servings; and one 5-lb (2.2-kg) box, size 12, yields 20 servings.

Calories:
6 oz, raw = 360 Calories.

ITALIAN SAUSAGES
Available mild (also called *sweet*) and sharp.

Pack:
By weight; normally 5-lb (2.2-kg) boxes.

Kitchen Yields
Sausages are available in different lengths or are portioned eight pieces per 1 lb (450 g) or larger.

Serving size:
Varies.

MORTADELLA
Large pork sausage; often sold as *Bologna sausage*.

Weights:
5 to 50 lb (2.2 to 22.5 kg).

SALAMI
Pork salami is often referred to as *Genoa salami*.

Weights:
4 to 7 lb (1.8 to 3.1 kg). Smaller sizes are also available.

SAUSAGE MEAT
Breakfast sausage mix that is sold in rolls to be sliced or used in stuffing.

Pack:
By weight; usually in 3-lb (1.3-kg) rolls.

Kitchen Yields

Serving size:
Two 2-oz (56-g) pieces, raw weight; cooked weight is 2½ oz (70 g).

POTATO CHIPS

Available in many shapes and many flavors.

Pack:
By weight.

Kitchen Yields

Serving size:
1 oz (28 g) or less, as garnish with sandwich.

POTATO GNOCCHI

See Gnocchi.

POTATO LATKES

See Latkes (Potato Pancakes).

POTATOES

Available canned, dehydrated, fresh, and processed frozen.

CANNED POTATOES
Canned potatoes are available whole, sliced, and diced.

Pack:
Six #10 cans.

Counts:
For whole canned potatoes, 80 to 100, 100 to 120, 130 to 150, and 200 and up.

Drained weight:
For diced and sliced potatoes, one #10 can weighs 108 oz (3 kg). Drained weight is 75 oz (2.1 kg).
NOTE: Counts and weights vary according to manufacturer.

Kitchen Yields

Serving size:
3 oz (85 g) each. One 1 #10 can yields 25 servings.

DEHYDRATED POTATOES
Dehydrated potatoes are available as flakes, granules, slices, dices, hash browns, and french fry mix.

FLAKES

Pack:

For Idaho Instant Flakes:
Six 2-lb (0.9-kg) bags; six 2-lb (0.9-kg) #10 cans; six 2½- or 5-lb (1.1- or 2.2-kg) bags; twelve 1-lb or

Table P-5 Ingredients and Yields for Idaho Instant Flakes

Ingredients	25/20	50/40	100/80
Water	1¾ qt (1.6 l)	3½ qt (3.2 l)	1¾ gal (6.4 l)
Margarine or butter	⅓ cup (74 g)	¾ cup (168 g)	1½ cups (336 g)
Milk	3 cups (0.69 l)	1½ qt (1.4 l)	3 qt (2.7 l)
Salt	1½ tsp	1 tbsp	2 tbsp
Potato flakes	1 lb (450 g)	2 lb (0.9 kg)	4 lb (1.8 kg)

2-lb (450- or 900-g) cartons. Larger packs are also available.

Kitchen Yields
Instant flakes produce mashed potatoes. Table P-5 lists serving yields for Idaho Instant Flakes.

Serving sizes:
#10 scoop equals ⅜ cup (0.08 l); #8 scoop equals ½ cup (0.11 l).

GRANULES

Pack:

For Idaho Granules:
Granules are available plain, seasoned, with milk and with vitamin C added. They are used to produce mashed potatoes. Table P-6 lists available forms of Idaho Instant Mashed Potatoes.
NOTE: Flakes and granules cannot always be used interchangeably in recipes, because in dehydrated form they are not equal by volume measure. However, substitutions can be made based on weight measure. Follow directions on package.

SLICES
Slices are available plain or seasoned.

Pack:

Plain:
Six #10 cans; individual 5-lb (2.25-kg) bags; individual 1-gal (3.8-l) pour packs. Larger packs are available.

Table P-6 Available Forms of Idaho Instant Mashed Potatoes

Granule Type	Packing Size	Yield per Can
Plain	Six 1-lb (2.7-kg) #10 cans	5 gal (19.5 l)
With vitamin C	Six 1-lb (2.7-kg) #10 cans	5 gal (19.5 l)
Complete	Six 87-oz (2.4-kg) #10 cans	4½ gal (17.1 l)
Complete, with vitamin C	Six #10 cans	4½ gal (17.1 l)
Seasoned, complete	Six 5-lb 8-oz (2.4-kg) *or* 3½-lb (1.5-kg) #10 cans	4 gal (15.2 l)

Seasoned:
Individual 2½-lb (1.1-kg) bags; six 2¼-lb (1-kg) cartons.

Kitchen Yields
Table P-7 lists rehydration and yields for slices, dices, and hash browns.

Serving size:
¼ cup (0.11 l).

DICES

Pack:
Six 2½-lb (1.1-kg) #10 cans; individual 2½-lb (1.1-kg) bags; individual 5-lb (2.25-kg) and larger bags.

Kitchen Yields
Table P-7 lists rehydration and yields for slices, dices, and hash browns.

Serving size:
¼ cup (0.116 l).

Table P-7 Rehydration and Yields for Slices, Dices, and Hash Browns

Ingredient	25 servings	50 servings	100 servings
Potato product	22 oz (616 g)	42 oz (1.1 kg)	5 lb 5 oz (2.3 kg)
Water, at 140 to 150°F	3 qt (2.7 l)	6 qt (5.5 l)	3 gal (11.4 l)

HASH BROWNS

Pack:
Six 2-lb (0.9-kg) pour packs; individual 5-lb (2.25-kg) bags.

Kitchen Yields

Serving size:
4 oz (113 g). One 5-lb (2.25-kg) bag, as purchased, yields 90 servings.
See also Table P-8.

FRENCH FRY MIX

Pack:
Two 2-lb (0.9-kg) packages; fifteen 2-lb (0.9-kg) bags.

Kitchen Yields

Serving size:
For mashed potatoes, ½ cup (0.11 l), or one #8 scoop, weighing 4 oz (113 g). One #10 can produces 5 qt (4.7 l) mashed potatoes, which yields 40 servings.

FRESH POTATOES

Potatoes are classified into four broad groups:

> *Long Whites:* Boiling and salads
> *Round Reds:* Boiling and salads
> *Round Whites (Irish potatoes):* Boiling, salads, and frying
> *Russets:* Baking and frying

Each group includes a number of varieties. Potatoes are available year-round, although fall is the harvesting season in most states. Potatoes are grown in many states—in particular, Idaho, Washington, Colorado, and Maine. Washington

Table P-8 Yields for Unpeeled Potatoes, 80 to 120 size

Form of potato	25 servings	50 servings	100 servings
¼-in fries, unpeeled	10¼ lb (4.6 kg)	21 lb (9.4 kg)	41½ lb (18.6 kg)
Jacket fries, skin on	9½ lb (4.2 kg)	18½ lb (8.3 kg)	37 lb (16.6 kg)
Shoestring fries, unpeeled	9½ lb (4.2 kg)	19 lb (8.5 kg)	37½ lb (16.8 kg)
¼-in fries, peeled	20 lb (9.0 kg)	40 lb (18.0 kg)	80 lb (36.0 kg)
Round fries	15¼ lb (6.8 kg)	30½ lb (13.7 kg)	61 lb (27.4 kg)
Shoestring fries, peeled	14¼ lb (6.4 kg)	28½ lb (12.8 kg)	57 lb (25.6 kg)

potatoes have a slightly higher nutrient content than the average American potato. Table P-8 lists purchasing requirements for unpeeled fresh potatoes.

Kitchen Yields

Serving size:
4 oz (112 g) cooked.
2 lb (0.9 kg) potatoes yield 3 servings.

Calories:
One 4-oz (112-g) portion = 293 Calories.

LONG WHITE POTATOES
Good variety for salads, hash browns, and home-fried potatoes.

Season:
Available year-round.

Pack:
50-lb (22.5-kg) bags.

Kitchen Yields
1 lb (450 g) raw, boiled in jacket, yields 14 oz (400 g) peeled, which produces 3 portions hash browns or home fries.

Calories:
One 6-oz (170-g) potato, cooked, and peeled after boiling = 126 Calories.
5 oz (140 g) hash browns = 310 Calories.
NOTE: Calorie count varies according to amount of fat used in preparation.

ROUND RED (RED BLISS) POTATOES
These potatoes are available small and large; in many markets, grade A indicates a larger potato than grade B. The small variety is often served whole as boiled potato, with only part of the peel removed before cooking.

Season:
Available year-round.

Pack:
50-lb (22.5-kg) bags.

Kitchen Yields
1 lb (450 g) is equivalent to 7 to 9 small potatoes or 5 to 6 medium-sized potatoes.

Serving sizes:
Two to three small potatoes or one medium-size potato, with peel partly removed; thus, 1 lb (450 g) yields 3 to 4 servings in restaurant, and one 50-lb (22.5-kg) bag yields 190 servings in restaurant. For banquet servings, use two small potatoes; thus, 50 lb (22.5 kg) yields 200 servings, and 25 lb (11.2 kg) yields 100 servings.

Calories:
Two small or one medium-sized potato, 5 oz (140 g), boiled = 105 Calories.

ROUND WHITE POTATOES (IRISH POTATOES)
Also called chef's potatoes.

Season:
Available year-round.

Pack:
50-lb (22.5-kg) bags.

Kitchen Yields
1 lb (450 g) is equivalent to four or five potatoes, which yield 3 portions boiled potatoes or 3 portions potato salad; therefore, 50 lb (22.5 kg) yield 150 portions potato salad.

Calories:
Two potatoes, 4¾ oz (130 g), boiled and peeled = 90 Calories.

RUSSET POTATOES
Most russet potatoes are grown in Idaho, Washington, and Colorado.

Season:
Fresh harvest in October; available year-round.

Pack:
50-lb (22.5-kg) cartons, net weight.

Count:
Ranges from 35 to 140 per carton, as detailed in Table P-9.
Most common restaurant sizes are from 80 to 100.

Shrinkage:
About 25 percent, by weight after baking.

Kitchen Yields

• *Baked:*

35, 50, or 60 size: Good for complete entrée.
80 size: Common hotel size.

Table P-9 Counts and Weights of Russet Potatoes

Count	Average Weight per Potato
35	22 oz (638 g)
50	14 to 17 oz (400 to 475 g)
60	12 to 13 oz (335 to 365 g)
70	11 to 13 oz (300 to 320 g)
80	9 to 12 oz (250 to 335 g)
90	8 to 11 oz (225 to 300 g)
100	7 to 9 oz (200 to 250 g)
110	6 to 8 oz (170 to 225 g)
120	5 to 7 oz (140 to 200 g)
140	3 to 4 oz (85 to 110 g)

90 size: Good for scooped out skins.

100 or 110 size: Good for commercial operations.

120 size: Perfect for elementary schools as side dish.

140 size: Weighs 3 oz (85 g) cooked; meets ⅔ cup vegetable requirement for school foodservice.

• *French-fried:*

4 oz (112 g) cooked as side order.

Table P-10 gives weight yields for 4 lb of french-fried Idaho potatoes.

• *Mashed:*

Table P-11 lists formulas for different yields of mashed potatoes.

Quantities:

1 lb whole, unpeeled potatoes (450 g) yields 2 cups (0.23 l) mashed potatoes; and 8 lb whole, unpeeled potatoes (3.6 kg) yield 1 gal (3.7 l) mashed potatoes.

1 gal mashed potatoes yields 30 servings.

Table P-10 Weight Yields for 4 lb (1.8 kg) Fresh Idaho Potatoes

Form of Potato	Cooked Weight	Number of Servings
¼-in fries, unpeeled	44 oz (1.2 kg)	11
Jacket fries, skin on	42 oz (1.1 kg)	10
Shoestring fries, unpeeled	48 oz (1.3 kg)	12
¼-in fries, peeled	20 oz (560 g)	5
Round fries	26 oz (728 g)	6
Shoestring fries, peeled	28 oz (784 g)	7

Calories:

½ cup (110 g) mashed, with milk and butter = 100 Calories.

One #8 scoop, 4 oz (112 g), mashed, with milk and butter = 125 Calories.

One baked potato, #100, 6 oz (168 g) = 150 Calories.

FROZEN PROCESSED POTATOES

Many products are available in processed frozen form, such as french fries, ranch or country fries, hash browns, ranch-style potatoes, and potato rounds.

Packs:

French fries:

Six 5-lb (2.25-kg) bags. Some varieties are also packed in 4-lb and 4½-lb (1.8- and 2-kg) bags.

Shredded hash browns:

Eight 2½-lb (1.1-kg) layers; ninety-six 3-oz (85-g) portions.

Table P-11 Ingredients Needed for Different Quantities of ½-cup (#8-scoop) Servings Mashed Potatoes

Ingredient	25 Servings	50 Servings	100 Servings
Whole, unpeeled russet potatoes	6 lb (2.7 kg)	12 lb (5.4 kg)	24 lb (10.8 kg)
or			
Whole, peeled russet potatoes	5 lb (2.25 kg)	10 lb (4.5 kg)	20 lb (9 kg)
Milk, hot	3 to 4 cups (0.7 to 0.9 l)	1½ to 2 qt (1.4 to 1.9 l)	3 to 4 qt (2.8 to 3.8 l)
Butter	¼ lb (112 g)	½ lb (225 g)	1 lb (450 g)
Salt to taste			

Long shredded hash browns:
Three 5-lb (2.2-kg) layers; eight 4-lb (1.8-kg) layers; six 3-lb (1.3-kg) bags, IQF.

Skin-on hash browns:
Six 5-lb (2.25-kg) bags.

Shells:
Six 5-lb (2.25-kg) bags, with 200 shells per case.

Wedges:
Six 5-lb (2.25-kg) bags.

Cubes:
Six 4-lb (1.8-kg) bags.

Kitchen Yields
Use as is. There is no waste.

Calories:
3 oz (85 g) french fries = 229 Calories.
¾ cup, or 4 oz (113 g) hash browns = 250 Calories.

POUSSIN

See Baby Chicken, under Chicken.

PRAWNS

See Shrimp.

PRICKLY PEARS (CACTUS FRUIT)

See Tunas, under Mexican Foods.

PRUNES

DRIED PRUNES
Dried prunes are available in bulk packs, fully cooked, and canned. Prunes are dried plums, but not all varieties of plums can be dried. The most commonly used drying variety is the California French Prune. Prunes are available pitted and with pit in.

BULK-PACK DRIED PRUNES
Pitted prunes are classified into three types, which indicate size and quality. For restaurant foodservice,

Table P-12 Sizes and Counts for 25-lb (11.2-kg) Cartons of Pitted Dried Prunes

Count per 1 lb (450 g)	Average Number per Case	Servings per 1 lb (450 g)	Servings per Case
Jumbo, 39 and larger	950	8 (5 prunes)	200
Extra Large, 40 to 49	1125	7½ (6 prunes)	150
Large, 50 to 61	1375	9 (6 prunes)	229
Medium 62 to 79	1750	10 (7 prunes)	250
Small 80 and smaller	2000	10 (8 prunes)	250

Table P-13 Sizes and Counts for 25- and 30-lb (11.2- and 13.5-kg) Cartons of Unpitted Dried Prunes

Carton Weight	Count per 1 lb (450 g)	Average Number per Case	Servings per 1 lb (450 g)	Servings per Case
25 lb (11.2 kg)	20 to 30	625	6½ (4 prunes)	160
	25 to 35	800	8 (4 prunes)	200
	30 to 40	900	9 (4 prunes)	225
	40 to 50	1,125	9 (5 prunes)	225
30 lb (13.5 kg)	25 to 35	850	7 (4 prunes)	212
	30 to 40	1,080	9 (4 prunes)	270
	40 to 50	1,350	9 (5 prunes)	270

types I and II are used. The sizes of types I and II are identical.

Pack:
Table P-12 identifies sizes, counts, and servings in a 25-lb (11.2-kg) carton of dried pitted prunes. NOTE: Use Jumbo or Extra Large sizes for stuffing. Table P-13 lists sizes, counts, and servings in 25- and 30-lb (11.2- and 13.5-kg) cartons of dried unpitted prunes.

Table P-14 Sizes and Counts for Canned Prunes without Pits

Can size and Drained Weight	Type of Pack	Approximate Equivalent Size with Pit	Prunes per Can	Number of Portions
#10: 70 oz (1.9 kg)	Regular	20 to 30	140 to 160	30 (5 prunes)
#10: 92 oz (2.6 kg)	Nectarized	20 to 30	190 to 210	40 (4 prunes)
#10: 112 oz (3.1 kg)	High-moisture	40 to 50	330 to 370	70 (5 prunes)

Kitchen Yields

Average weight of one Extra Large prune is $\frac{1}{3}$ oz (9 g).

Serving size:

Pitted Prunes:

Five large prunes; thus, 1 lb (450 g) Extra Large prunes yields 9 portions.

Whole Prunes:

Four to five large prunes; thus, 1 lb (450 g) 25 to 35 size yields 7 to 8 portions.

Calories:

Four Extra Large prunes, with pits, uncooked = 110 Calories.
Five Large prunes, with pits, uncooked = 110 Calories.

CANNED DRIED PRUNES

Canned prunes are available pitted and with pits in. There are three standard packs of canned prunes:

> *Regular:* Packed in syrup.
> *Nectarized:* Packed in water, with higher fruit count.
> *High-moisture:* No liquid added.

Pack:

Many can sizes are available. For institutional use, #10 cans are normally purchased. Table P-14 lists sizes, packs, and counts for pitted canned prunes. Table P-15 lists sizes, packs, and counts for unpitted canned prunes.

Table P-15 Sizes and Counts for Canned Prunes with Pits

Can Size and Drained Weight	Type of Pack	Prunes per can	Number of Portions (and Portion Size)
#10: 70 oz (1.9 kg)	Regular	70 to 85	26 (3 prunes)
#10: 70 oz (1.9 kg)	Regular	115 to 135	32 (4 prunes)
#10: 70 oz (1.9 kg)	Regular	140 to 160	30 (5 prunes)
#10: 96 oz (2.7 kg)	Nectarized	155 to 175	40 (4 prunes)
#10: 7 lb (3.1 kg)	Moist pack	238 to 273	52 (5 prunes)

Calories:

7 or 8 extra-large prunes, $3\frac{1}{2}$ oz (100 g), packed in syrup, drained = 110 Calories.

PRUNE JUICE

Canned or bottled prune juice is prepared from a water extract of dried prunes.

Pack:

Glass:

4 oz (0.11 l); 8 oz (0.23 l); 32 oz = 1 qt (0.94 l); 40 oz = 5 cups (1.1 l); 48 oz = 6 cups (1.4 l).

Cans:
5½ oz (0.16 l); 6 oz (0.17 l); 46 oz (1.3 l).

Kitchen Yields

Serving size:
5½ oz (0.16 l); therefore, 1 qt (0.94 l) yields 5½ servings, and one 46-oz can yields 8 servings.

Calories:
5½ oz (0.16 l) = 120 Calories.

PRUNE PASTE
Called *lekvar* on the East Coast, prune paste is used for baking—particularly in Danish pastries. *See* Danish Pastries.

Pack:
25- to 40-lb packs (11.2- to 18-kg); six #10 cans of 7 lb (3.1 kg) each.

Kitchen Yields

Serving size:
1 oz (28 g) filling for one piece Danish; therefore, one #10 can yields 110 fillings.

Calories:
1 oz (28 g) = 70 Calories.

PULLED SUGAR

See Sugar.

PUMPKINS

Pumpkin is available as canned purée and fresh.

CANNED PUMPKIN
Canned pumpkin is primarily used in pies, but it is also used in soups.

Pack:
Six #10 cans.

Kitchen Yields

Serving size:
½ cup. One #10 can yields 13 cups (3 l) pumpkin purée, which yields 25 servings.
NOTE: Some brands of pumpkin purée are very liquidy.

Calories:
½ cup, or 4⅓ oz (122 g) = 40 Calories.

FRESH PUMPKIN

Weights:
Vary greatly.

Kitchen Yields

Waste:
Trimming loss is about 30 percent by weight.

Serving size:
½ cup (0.11 l), mashed.
50 lb (22.5 kg), as purchased, yield 4 gal (15.2 l), mashed, or 110 servings.

Calories:
½ cup, or 4⅓ oz (112 g), plain, baked, and mashed = 40 Calories.

Q AND R

QUAIL

Farm-bred quails are available fresh or frozen in the following forms: whole, with bone in; whole, boned; and split.

• *Whole Quails*

Pack:
12, 24, 40, or 56 birds to a case; 4 or 6 birds per tray, with 72 per master.

Size:
4 to 5 oz (112 to 140 g) each, whole.
5 to 6 oz (140 to 170 g) each, whole.
4 oz (112 g) each, split.

• *Boned Quails*

Pack:
Eight 3½-oz (100-g) birds, with 40 per case.

Kitchen Yields

Serving size:
Two birds.
The meat stuffing needed to stuff one bird is 1½ oz (42 g).
The meat stuffing needed to stuff 50 birds is 3½ lb (1.5 kg), or 7 cups (1.6 l).

QUAIL EGGS

Quail eggs are available fresh in flats and hard-boiled in jars and cans.

CANNED QUAIL EGGS
Canned quail eggs are packed in plain or flavored brine.

Pack:
Twelve 15-oz (425-g) cans, with a drained weight of 8 oz (225 g) each.

Count:
30 eggs. Other packs are available.

Kitchen Yields
One egg weighs ¼ oz (7.0 g).

FRESH QUAIL EGGS

Pack:
30 eggs per flat, and 18 flats per case, or 540 eggs per case; 30 eggs per flat, and 6 flats per case, or 180 eggs per case.

QUICHE

QUICHE CUSTARD

Formula
For custard:

> 6 qt (5.6 l) light cream
> 36 whole eggs
> 3 tb salt
> 1 tb white pepper
> 1 tsp nutmeg

Garnish quantity for basic quiche lorraine:

> ½ cup chopped chives
> 8 cups (0.6 kg) diced Swiss cheese
> 6 lb (1.8 kg) raw bacon, then cooked and diced

Kitchen Yields
Twelve 9-in (228-mm) quiches.

QUICHE DOUGH

Formula
> 4 lb (1.4 kg) pastry flour
> 2 lb (0.9 kg) shortening
> 14 fl oz, or 1¾ cup (0.4 l) cold water
> 2 oz (56 g) sugar
> 1 oz (28 g) salt

Do not overmix. Prebake at 375°F for 15 minutes.

Kitchen Yields
Twelve 9-in (228-mm) crusts.

QUINCE

Quinces are fruits that have a high pectin content and resemble yellow apples. They are used in making jams. Quinces are available fresh.

Season:
September to December.

Pack:
20-lb (9-kg) lug. Fruit is often sold in units of 1 dozen.

Average weight:
10 to 12 oz (280 to 340 g).

Kitchen Yields

Waste:
Peeling and coring loss is about 25 percent. One lug yields 15 lb (6.7 kg) peeled fruit.

Quince jam proportions:
Mix 1 lb (450 g) peeled and cored fruit with 12 oz (340 g) sugar.

QUINOA

High-protein grain that originated in the Peruvian Andes. Quinoa is used as a starch garnish, in place of rice or pasta.

Pack:
12 oz (340 g); 1 lb (450 g); 25 lb (11.2 kg).

Kitchen Yields

Serving size:
½ cup (0.11 l).
1 cup, or 6 oz (170 g), produces 3 cups cooked, which yields 6 portions.
1 cup quinoa + 2 cups water = 3 cups cooked quinoa.
NOTE: Rinse grain before cooking.

R

RABBIT

Rabbit is available fresh or frozen, whole or in pieces. Rabbit meat is white. *See also* Hare.

Pack:
For whole, skinless rabbit, with head and feet off, eviscerated, 26-, 28-, or 44-lb (11.7-, 12.6-, or 19.8-kg) cases, in sizes 4 to 6 lb (1.8 to 2.7 kg), 1½ to 3½ lb (0.6 to 1.5 kg), or 1¾ to 2½ lb (0.7 to 1 kg). For irregular pieces, 15-lb (6.7-kg) cases. For boneless loins, pack is by weight and piece, in sizes 6 to 9 oz (170 to 255 g).

Average size:

Pieces of one 2-lb (1-kg) rabbit:
Two 8-oz (224-g) hind legs;
one 8-oz (224-g) back piece;
two 5-oz (140-g) shoulders, plus 2 oz (56 g) of trim.

Kitchen Yields
One 2½-lb (1-kg) rabbit yields 3 servings.
NOTE: Shoulders and trimmings have very limited use.

Calories:
5 oz (142 g) cooked meat = 291 Calories.

RADICCHIO

See Lettuce.

RADISHES

Many varieties and types of radishes are marketed.

BLACK RADISHES
Black roots with white flesh; sharp and pungent when eaten raw. They are popular in Germany with beer. Black radishes can also be cooked as a vegetable. Baby black radishes are also available; *see* Baby Vegetables.

Pack:
Sold by weight.

DAIKON (JAPANESE RADISH)
See Japanese Foods.

HORSERADISH
See Horseradish.

LO BOK (CHINESE RADISH)
See Chinese Foods.

RED RADISHES
Available whole with the green leaves still attached, whole trimmed, and sliced.

Season:
Available year-round.

Pack:
12- to 14-oz (340- to 400-g) fresh bunches, including leaves; twelve cello packs, trimmed, in a 30-lb (13.5-kg) carton; sliced radishes in individual 5-lb (2.3-kg) bags.

Count:
Varies greatly.

Kitchen Yields
One bunch fresh contains 12 to 13 pieces in vastly different sizes. One bunch fresh, without leaves, weighs 8 oz (225 g); 1 cup sliced weighs 4½ oz (120 g).

Calories:
1 cup sliced, or 4½ oz (120 g) = 33 Calories.

RAISINS

Raisins are dried grapes. They are available seedless, from either seedless grapes or seeded grapes whose pits are removed during processing. Unseeded raisins, which contain their pits, are also on the market, but are less important to foodservice. The color of raisins can range from golden yellow to dark brown. Very light raisins are often bleached during processing. The important varieties are Thompson Seedless and Muscat. Currants are small, dark raisins produced mainly in Greece. Sultanas are large, light-colored raisins.

Pack:
20-lb (9-kg) cartons, or 1-lb (450-g) boxes. Other packs are available.

Sizes:
Seedless raisins are sized as midget, small, or select. Unseeded raisins are sized from one to four crowns, four being the largest. The sizes vary according to variety; for example, a select Thompson seedless is similar in size to a Muscat midget.

Kitchen Yields
1 cup (0.23 l) seedless raisins equals 5½ oz (154 g); 1 lb (450 g) seedless raisins equals 3 cups (0.7 l).

Calories:
1 cup (0.232 l) = 430 Calories.

RAMPS

Wild leeks with strong, garlic smell, indigenous from Maine to Georgia. Bulbs and leaves are used. Harvesting plant with bulbs destroys plant.

Season:
From late March to June.

Pack:
By weight.

Size:
Varies.

Kitchen Yield
1 lb (450 g) with leaves yields 45 to 50 pieces. Waste about 50 percent by weight if leaves are discarded.

RAPINI

Bitter broccoli. *See* Broccoli Rabe.

RASPBERRIES (BUSHBERRIES)

Raspberries are available canned, fresh, and frozen.

CANNED RASPBERRIES

Pack:
Six #10 cans; twenty-four #303 cans.

Kitchen Yields

Serving size:
½ cup fruit and juice. One #10 can contains 8 cups drained fruit and yields 26 servings with juice. One #303 can yields 4 servings fruit and juice.

FRESH RASPBERRIES

Season:
June until November for domestically grown raspberries. Imports are available during the rest of the year.

Pack:
Flats of twelve ½-pint (0.23 l) baskets.

Kitchen Yields
There is virtually no waste when merchandise is fresh.

Serving sizes:
For breakfast or dessert service, ½ pint yields 1⅓ servings, so 1 flat yields 16 portions. For garnish with desserts and ice cream, ½ pint yields 3 portions, so 1 flat yields 32 portions. There are about 60 to 75 berries in ½ pint.

Calories:
¾ cup, or 3 oz (84 g) = 53 Calories.

FROZEN RASPBERRIES
Available straight and with sugar added at a ratio of 4 parts fruit to 1 part sugar.

Pack:
Six #10 cans, weighing 6½ lb (3 kg) each; 30-lb pack with sugar added, 4 to 1; 28-lb straight pack.

Kitchen Yields

Serving size:
½ cup fruit and juice. One #10 can yields 24 servings.

Calories:
½ cup, or 4 oz (112 g), with juice and sugar = 112 Calories.

RHUBARB
Rhubarb is available fresh and frozen.

FRESH RHUBARB

Season:
Spring to early summer and late fall. Hot-house rhubarb is often available from January to April.

Pack:

Hot-house:
5-lb (2.2-kg) cartons.

Regular:
15- and 20-lb (6.7- and 9.1-kg) cartons.

Kitchen Yields

Waste:
Cleaning waste is 10 percent by weight. Hot-house rhubarb might have a slightly smaller waste.

Serving size:
½ cup (0.11 l).
5 lb (2.2 kg) as purchased yield 17 servings.
30 lb (13.5 kg) as purchased yield 100 servings.

Sugar ratio:
1 lb (450 g) cleaned rhubarb to 8 oz (224 g) sugar. NOTE: Cooked weight is same as raw weight due to added sugar.

Calories:
½ cup (0.11 l), with sugar = 190 Calories.

FROZEN RHUBARB

Pack:
25-lb (11.2-kg) can; twelve 2½-lb (1.1-kg) packages.

Kitchen Yields

Serving size:
½ cup (0.23 l). One 25-lb (11.2-kg) can yields 90 servings, and one 2½-lb (1.1-kg) package yields 9 servings.

Calories:
½ cup (0.11 l), with sugar = 192 Calories.

RICE

The leading varieties are Long Grain, Medium Grain, and Short Grain. Long Grain rice is commonly used in foodservice, except for some ethnic dishes. The following types of rice are available:

White rice: Polished Long Grain Rice; the most popular kind.
Converted rice: Rice steam-treated to retain vitamins.
Brown rice: Whole, unpolished grains.
Precooked rice: Fully cooked and then dehydrated rice; also called *instant rice.*

The following specialty varieties are available:

Wild rice; *see* Wild Rice.
Blends of Long Grain and wild rice.
Flavored rice mixes.
Arborio rice, used for risotto.
Basmati rice, used for Indian and Asian dishes.
Okome rice; *see* Japanese Foods.

Pack:
Two 10-lb (4.5-kg), or individual 25-, 50-, or 100-lb (11.2-, 22.5-, and 45.0-kg) bags. Special packs are available for flavored rice mixes.

Kitchen Yields

Serving size:
Between ⅓ and ½ cup.

- *White Rice*

1 cup (0.23 l) dry measure equals 7 oz (200 g).
1 lb (450 g) dry measure equals 2¼ cups (0.5 l).
1 cup (0.23 l) raw rice produces 3 cups (0.7 l) cooked rice; and 1 lb (450 g) raw rice produces 7½ cups cooked rice. Therefore, 10 lb (4.5 kg) produce 4½ gal (16.6 l) cooked rice.
To make 1 gal cooked rice, use 3 lb (1.3 kg) uncooked rice. Table R-1 lists the proper formulas for different yields of white rice.

- *Converted Rice*

1 cup (0.232 l) dry measure: 8 oz (224 g).
1 lb (450 g) dry measure: 2 cups (0.47 l).

1 lb (450 g) produces 7½ cups cooked rice; thus, 10 lb (4.5 kg) produce 75 cups, which is equivalent to 4⅝ gal (17.3 l) cooked rice.
To make 1 gal cooked rice, use 2¾ lb (1.2 kg) uncooked rice.

- *Brown Rice*

1 cup (0.23 l) dry measure equals 8 oz (224 g).
1 lb (450 g) dry measure equals 2 cups (0.47 l).
1 cup (0.23 l) raw rice produces 3 to 4 cups cooked rice. Use more liquid and longer cooking time for brown rice than for white rice.
1 lb (450 g) raw rice produces 8 cups (1.9 l) cooked rice; thus, 10 lb (4.5 kg) produce 80 cups cooked rice, which is equivalent to 5 gal (19 l).

- *Instant Rice*

1 cup (0.23 l) dry measure equals 4 oz (112 g).
1 lb (450 g) dry measure equals 1 qt (0.94 l).
1 lb (450 g) raw rice produces 8 cups cooked rice.

- *Wild Rice and Long Grain Blend*

1 lb (450 g) raw rice produces 12 cups (2.3 l) cooked rice.

2½ gal (9.5 l) cooked rice (any type) provides stuffing for 100 chicken breasts.

Calories:
1 cup raw Long Grain, weighing 6⅝ oz (185 g) = 670 Calories.
1 cup boiled Long Grain, weighing 7⅓ oz (205 g) = 225 Calories.
1 cup cooked instant rice, weighing 5¾ oz (165 g) = 180 Calories.

Table R-1 Formulas for White Rice

Rice	Water	Fat	Salt	Yield	Portions
1 lb	5 cups	2 oz	1 tb	6 cups	10
5 lb	6½ qt	10 oz	½ cup	30 cups	50
10 lb	13 qt	20 oz	1 cup	3¾ gal	100

RISOTTO

Also spelled *rizotto,* this is an Italian rice dish flavored with meats or seafood, and often with saffron or grated Parmesan cheese. The dish should be soupy, yet the kernels should still be hard. Arborio Rice is best. The formula below is for basic risotto.

Formula

    1 pint (0.4 l) Arborio rice
    1 cup (0.23 l) chopped onion
    1 cup (0.23 l) melted butter
    1½ qt chicken stock or other stock
    1 cup (0.23 l) Parmesan cheese
    4 oz (113 g) fresh butter

Kitchen Yields

Serving size:
1 cup (0.23 l), as appetizer. The preceding formula produces 6 servings.
NOTE: Add garnish, such as meat or seafood, according to taste.

ROUX

Roux consists of 3 parts bread flour to 2½ parts fat by volume, such as oil or clarified butter. White roux is heated long enough to cook the flour without causing it to change color. Brown roux is cooked slowly for a long time to produce its brown color.

Kitchen Yields

Quantities:

White Roux:
3 oz (80 g) yield thickening for 1 qt 32 oz (0.94 l) stock for soup.
4 oz (100 g) yield thickening for 1 qt 32 oz (0.94 l) milk for medium-thick cream sauce.

Brown Roux:
Roux loses thickening power through roasting. Brown roux has approximately 25 percent less thickening power than white roux.

ROYAL ICING

Formula

    4 lb (1.8 kg) confectioners sugar
    ¾ lb (340 g) egg whites
    ½ tsp cream of tartar

NOTE: Royal icing gets hard and brittle when dry. Use for decorative cakes only.

Kitchen Yields
The preceding formula produces enough for one 20-in (50.8-cm) dummy cake.

RUTABAGAS

These large yellow root vegetables are available fresh.

Season:
Fall and winter.

Pack:
50-lb (22.5-kg) bags or cartons.

Sizes and weights:
Vary.

Kitchen Yields

Waste:
20 percent, by weight.

Serving size:
½ cup (0.23 l) cubed and cooked. One 50-lb (22.5-kg) bag yields 5 gal (19 l) cubed and cooked rutabagas. One 4½-in (114-mm) diameter bulb yields 4 cups cooked (0.92 l) and diced rutabaga.

Calories:
½ cup, or 4 oz (112 g) = 40 Calories.

S

SAFFRON

See Herbs & Spices.

SALAD DRESSING

See Dressing Formulas.

SALAD GREENS

See also Cabbage, Lettuce, and Sprouts.

ALFALFA SPROUTS
See Sprouts.

ARUGULA
Salad plant with peppery mustard flavor. As a salad ingredient, arugula is always mixed with other greens, because it would be too sharp if served alone.

Season:
Available year-round.

Pack:
6- to 7-lb (2.7- to 3.1-kg) flats, 24-count bunches.

Kitchen Yields
Use one part arugula with three parts milder salad greens.

BEAN SPROUTS
See Sprouts.

BELGIAN ENDIVE
See Belgian Endive.

DANDELION GREENS
See Dandelion Greens.

SORREL
See Sorrel.

SPINACH
See Spinach.

WATERCRESS

Season:
Available year-round. Peak is from May to July.

Pack:
By the bunch.

Size:
Varies, but usually 4 oz (112 g) per bunch.

Kitchen Yields

Waste:
Trimming waste is about 10 percent by weight, if stems are cut 2 in (50 mm) from bottom.
1 lb (450 g) yields 8 cups (1.8 l) chopped.

SALSIFY

Salsify is available canned and fresh. Also called *oyster plant,* this vegetable is most often used canned. It resembles white asparagus in shape and parsnip in flavor, when cooked.

CANNED SALSIFY

Pack:
Six #10 cans, weighing 6½ lb (3 kg) each; twenty-four 15-oz (426-g) cans.

Kitchen Yields

Serving size:
4 oz (113 g). One #10 can has a drained weight of 5 lb 10 oz (2.5 kg) and yields 20 servings. One 15-oz (426-g) can has a drained weight of 12 oz (340 g) and yields 3 servings.

FRESH SALSIFY
Available with black or white skin. The inner flesh is always white.

Season:
Imported from March through summer.

Pack:
By weight.

Size:
Varies. 1 lb (450 g) yields 4 to 5 roots without leaves.

Kitchen Yields
Peeling waste about 25 percent by weight. Cooking loss is very low.

SALT DOUGH

Formula 1
    2 cups (300 g) flour
    1 cup (224 g) salt
    1 cup (23 l) water

Dough can be dried or can be baked at low temperature.

Formula 2
    1 pint (0.47 l) water
    12 oz (336 g) cornstarch
    ½ oz (14 g) gelatin
    3 tb, or 1½ oz (42 g) water
    2 lb (0.9 kg) extra-fine salt

Boil the starch with 1 pint water; dissolve the gelatin in 3 tb water, and add it and the salt to the starch solution. Dough will dry well.

SANDWICH FILLINGS

BUTTER OR MARGARINE
1 lb (450 g) softened product supplies spread for 70 slices of #2 bread.

CHEESE FILLINGS

Serving size:
2 to 3 oz (56 or 85 g) cheese per sandwich.

MEAT FILLINGS

Serving size:
2 to 4 oz (56 to 112 g).
Meat should be sliced very thin. Weight of meat varies according to moisture content.

Average yields:
1 lb (450 g) canned ham yields filling for 5 to 6 sandwiches.
1 lb (450 g) cold roast beef yields filling for 5 sandwiches.

SALAD FILLINGS

Serving sizes:
For 2 oz (56 g), use #16 scoop; for 2½ (70 g), use #12 scoop; for 3½ oz (100 g), use #10 scoop; for 4 oz (113 g), use #8 scoop.

For 30 tuna salad sandwiches use the following sample recipe:

    1 can tuna weighing 55 oz (1.5 kg) drained
    1 pint (0.47 l) mayonnaise
    1 pint (0.47 l) diced celery

Use #12 scoop to measure out filling.

SAPODILLA

Also known as *dilly fruit* or *maseberry* in Florida, this round to oval tropical fruit has a thin brown or orange skin. Some varieties are seedless, but most have two or more inedible seeds. Fruit is sweet when ripe.

Season:
Available year-round.

Pack:
10-lb (4.5-kg) flats.

Sizes:
Large, medium, and small.

SAPOTA

See Mamey Sapote, Sapodilla, and White Sapota.

SATSUMA

See Mandarin Orange.

SAUCES

BASIC SAUCE INGREDIENTS
BONNE FEMME SAUCE FOR FISH

Formula
    One 3-lb (1.3-kg) basket sliced mushrooms
    1 cup (0.23 l) chopped shallots
    ½ lb (224 g) butter
    1 pint (0.47 l) dry white wine
    1 cup (0.23 l) cut chives

1 gal (3.8 l) heavy fish velouté (*see* Fish
  Velouté, under this same heading)
1 qt (0.94 l) Hollandaise sauce
1 qt (0.94 l) heavy cream, whipped

Kitchen Yields
The preceding formula produces 1½ gal (5.7 l)
sauce—enough for 100 portions of fish.

BROWN MUSHROOM SAUCE

Formula
One 3-lb (1.3-kg) basket sliced mushrooms
1 cup, or 8 oz (0.23 l) chopped shallots
½ gal (1.9 l) white wine
1 gal (3.8 l) brown sauce
Herbs and spices to taste

Kitchen Yields
The preceding formula produces 1¼ gallon (4.7 l)
sauce.

CHICKEN VELOUTÉ

Formula
4 gal (15.2 l) strong chicken stock
1 gal (3.8 l) light cream
3 lb (1.4 kg) mushroom trimmings
3 qt (2.8 l) white roux
1 lb (450 g) fresh butter

Kitchen Yields
The preceding formula produces 5 gal (19 l) sauce.

CUMBERLAND SAUCE

Formula
Three #10 cans red currant jelly
3 qt (2.8 l) sweet port wine
3 cups (0.7 l) orange juice concentrate
1½ cups (0.3 l) lemon juice
1 cup (0.23 l) chopped shallots
3 tb dry mustard
¼ cup (0.06 l) chopped ginger
1 pint (0.47 l) water

For garnish:

3 cups (0.7 l) orange zest
2 cups (0.47 l) lemon zest

Kitchen Yields
The preceding formula products 5 gal (19 l) sauce.

FISH VELOUTÉ

Formula
3 gal (11.4 l) fresh fish stock
1 gal (3.8 l) chicken stock
1 bottle (0.75 l) dry white wine
3 lb (1.4 kg) mushroom trimmings
3 qt (2.8 l) white roux
1 gal (3.7 l) light cream
1 lb (450 g) fresh butter

Kitchen Yields
The preceding formula produces 5 gal (19 l)
sauce.

HOLLANDAISE SAUCE

Formula
9 lb (4 kg) butter, when melted will yield
  3½ qt (3.2 l) clear butter fat
24 egg yolks
2 cups (0.47 l) water
¼ cup (0.06 l) vinegar
¼ cup (0.06 l) lemon juice
Salt and cayenne pepper to taste

Kitchen Yield
The preceding formula produces 1¼ gal (4.75 l)
sauce.

Serving size:

For vegetables:
1 oz (0.29 l). Mixture will yield 125 servings.

LEMON SAUCE FOR DUCKLING

Formula
3 cups (0.7 l) vinegar
3 cups (0.7 l) sugar
3 cups (0.7 l) frozen lemonade concentrate
2 cups (0.46 l) red currant jelly
8 lemons, cut into quarters
2 qt (0.9 l) brown duckling stock
¾ cup (0.17 l) corn starch
1 cup (0.23 l) dry sherry wine

For garnish:

2 cups (0.47 l) lemon peel, cut julienne style

Kitchen Yield
The preceding formula produces 1 gal (3.8 l)
sauce.

MINT SAUCE

Formula

1 gal (3.8 l) white vinegar
1½ qt (1.4 l) sugar
1½ qt (1.4 l) water
2 qt (1.8 l) chopped mint leaves
1 pint (0.47 l) mint jelly

Kitchen Yield

The preceding formula produces 1½ gal (5.7 l) sauce.

NEWBURG SAUCE

Formula

1 pint (0.47 l) chopped onions
1¼ cup (0.3 l) Spanish paprika
2 lb (0.9 kg) butter
½ gal (1.9 l) dry sherry
1 gal (3.7 l) light cream
3½ gal (13 l) heavy cream sauce

Kitchen Yields

The preceding formula produces 5 gal (19 l) sauce.

ORANGE SAUCE FOR DUCKLING

Formula

3 cups (0.7 l) vinegar
3 cups (0.7 l) sugar
3 cups (0.7 l) orange juice concentrate
2 cups (0.47 l) red currant jelly
4 large oranges, cut into quarters
4 lemons, cut into quarters
2 qt (0.9 l) brown duckling stock
¾ cup (0.17 l) cornstarch
1 cup (0.235 l) dry sherry wine

For garnish:

2 cups (0.47 l) orange peel, cut julienne style

Method

Caramelize sugar. Add remaining ingredients except cornstarch and sherry. Reduce to 1 gal. Thicken with cornstarch and sherry. Strain.

Kitchen Yield

The preceding formula produces 1 gal (3.8 l) sauce.

SAUCE VERTE (GREEN SAUCE)

Formula

Purée in food processor:

1 bunch watercress, stems discarded
4 bunches chives
½ bunch parsley, stems discarded
1 bunch chervil
1 cup, or 6½ oz (180 g), cooked spinach
3 pieces anchovy fillets
1 tb chopped garlic
1 qt (0.94 l) mayonnaise

Kitchen Yields

The preceding formula produces 3 pints (1.4 l) sauce.

TARTAR SAUCE GARNISH

Formula

1 gal (3.8 l) coarse-cut onions
1½ gal (5.7 l) dill pickle, drained
½ bunch parsley
1 bunch watercress
1 pint (0.47 l) capers, drained
1½ tb chopped garlic

Grind all ingredients through medium plate of food chopper.

Kitchen Yields

Recipe will yield 2½ gal (8.7 l) garnish. Blend 1 pint garnish (0.47 l) and 3 qt (2.8 l) mayonnaise.

TONNATO SAUCE

Formula

Two 42-oz (1.15-kg) cans tuna in oil
1 cup, or 8 oz (0.23 l) capers, drained
24 pieces anchovy fillets
2 tb grated lemon peel
2 cups (0.47 l) olive oil
2 pints (0.94 l) mayonnaise

Kitchen Yields

The preceding formula produces 1 gal (3.8 l) sauce.

SAUCE QUANTITIES

RESTAURANT USE

BROWN SAUCES

Serving size:
1½ oz (0.05 l).

BANQUET USE

BROWN SAUCES
5 qt (4.7 l) serves 100 covers.
2 gal (7.6 l) serves 200 covers.

CREAM SAUCES
1½ gal (5.7 l) serves 100 covers.
3 gal (11.4 l) serves 200 covers.

JUS (FOR ROAST BEEF)
3 qt (2.8 l) serves 100 covers.
1½ gal (5.7 l) serves 200 covers.

SAUERKRAUT

Sauerkraut is most commonly available canned, although fresh sauerkraut might be available locally. Varieties include shredded kraut, chopped kraut, sweet sauerkraut, and kraut with either celery seeds or caraway seeds.

Pack:
Six #10 cans, with a drained weight of 80 oz (2.3 kg) each. Smaller packs are available.

Kitchen Yields

Serving sizes:
With hot dog, 1½ oz (42 g); therefore, one #10 can yields 50 servings. As a vegetable, ½ cup cooked; therefore, one #10 can yields 18 servings cooked kraut.

Calories:
½ cup, or 4 oz (112 g) plain, raw sauerkraut = 20 Calories.

SAVOY CABBAGE

See Cabbage.

SCALLOPS

Scallops are available fresh, frozen, and processed. Scallops are classified as bay scallops, which have an edible muscle of about ½ in (12.7 mm) across, and sea scallops, which can develop a muscle of up to 2 in (50.8 mm) across. Imported scallops are often shipped with the pink edible roe still attached. Domestic scallops are almost always fully cleaned and white.

Sea scallops are harvested mostly in the North Atlantic. An important source of sea scallops is the waters around Alaska and along the Pacific coast as far south as Oregon. Bay scallops are harvested in the estuaries along the Atlantic coast as far south as Florida. The southern variety is slightly larger than the northern bay scallop, and is called a *calico bay scallop*.

FRESH BAY SCALLOPS
Bay scallops are sold shucked.

Season:
Available year-round, with peak season in the summer.

Pack:
Sold in 1-gal (3.7-l) cans. Net weight per can is about 8 lb (3.6 kg).

Kitchen Yields
There is no waste.

Count:
450 to 480 per gal (3.7 l).

Serving size:
For main course, 7 oz (200 g); 1 gal (3.8 l) yields 16 portions.
7 oz (200 g) raw scallops is equivalent to 4½ oz (127 g) cooked.

FRESH SEA SCALLOPS
Sea scallops are almost always sold shucked.

Pack:
Sold in 1-gal (3.7-l) containers. Net weight is about 7 lb 12 oz (3.5 kg).

Kitchen Yields
There is no waste.

Count:
Varies; about 160 to 240 per 1-gal container.

Serving size:
For main course, 7 oz (200 g).

FROZEN SEA SCALLOPS
Frozen scallops are available loose (IQF) or in
a block.

Pack:

Block Scallops:
One case of ten 5-lb (2.25-kg) boxes.
One 50-lb (22.5-kg) individual case.

IQF Scallops:
One case of six 3-lb (1.4-kg) boxes.
One 30-lb (13.5-kg) individual case.

Kitchen Yields

Counts:
Up to 20, 20 to 30, 30 to 40, and 40 to 50 per 1 lb
(450 g).

PROCESSED SCALLOPS
Frozen breaded scallops are available in two sizes:
bay scallop size and sea scallop size. The breading
is about 45 percent, by weight.

Pack:
Four 3-lb (1.4-kg) trays.

Kitchen Yields

Serving size:
6 oz uncooked; one 3-lb (1.4-kg) tray yields 8
servings.

Calories:
Eight fried scallops, weighing about 4¼ oz
(120 g) = 240 Calories.

SCOOP SIZES

Scoops are classified according to the approximate number of scoops contained in 1 qt (0.47 l).
Table S-1 lists scoop volumes and weights. NOTE:
Weight is approximate and depends on density of
product.

Table S-1 Scoop Volumes and Weights

Scoop #	Measure	Approximate Weight
30	2 tb	1 oz (28.4 g)
24	2¾ tb	1½ oz (42.6 g)
20	3 tb	1¾ oz (49.7 g)
16	4 tb	2 oz (56.8 g)
12	5 tb	2½ oz (71.0 g)
10	6 tb	3 oz (85.2 g)
8	8 tb	4 oz (112 g)
6	10 tb	5 oz (142 g)

SEAWEED

ASAKUSA NORI
See Japanese Foods.

DULSE
Purplish red seaweed, available fresh and
dehydrated.

Season:
April, May, and June.

Pack:
By weight.

KELP
Seaweed available fresh, dried, and pickled.
Powdered kelp can be used as a salt substitute.

Season:
April, May, and June.

Pack:
By weight.

KOMBU (DRIED KELP)
See Japanese Foods.

SEA BEANS

Season:
Available fresh year-round.

Pack:
By weight.

Kitchen Yield

Waste:
Large stems are tough and must be discarded.
Cleaning loss by weight is 20 percent.

SEA LETTUCE
Seaweed that has the texture of romaine and a
spicy taste. It is available fresh.

Season:
April to August.

Pack:
By weight.

SEA PALM
Seaweed found on the coast of the Pacific
Northwest. It is available fresh.

Season:
April to August.

Pack:
By weight.

WAKAME
See Japanese Foods.

SHALLOTS

Available fresh and processed, shallots are small
bulbs that resemble onions but have a milder
flavor. Used for flavoring sauces and as vegetable.

FRESH SHALLOTS

Season:
Available year-round.

Pack:
1-pint (0.47-l) cartons; 5-lb (2.3-kg) bags.

Sizes and counts:

Large:
40 to 50 pieces per 1 lb (450 g).

Jumbo:
20 to 25 pieces per 1 lb (450 g).

Kitchen Yields
1 cup chopped weighs 4 oz (112 g); 1 lb as
purchased produces 2¼ cups chopped.

PROCESSED SHALLOTS
Chopped shallots have become available dehydrated, frozen, or packed in oil.

Pack:
Varies, depending on packer.

Kitchen Yields
Use as is. There is no waste.

SHAMOUTI

Also known as *Jaffa orange,* this fruit is now
grown in limited quantities in the United States.

Season:
Domestic production in fall; imports in winter.

SHARON FRUIT

This fruit, which resembles a persimmon, is
imported from Israel. It is seedless and can be
eaten raw.

Season:
Winter.

SHELLFISH
See individual types, such as Crabs, Lobsters, and
Shrimp.

SHISH KEBAB
See Lamb.

SHRIMP

Shrimp are caught in most seas and come in many
sizes and quality levels. There are three principal
kinds of shrimp: white, pink, and brown. Large
shrimp are often called prawns. Price depends on
size and color. Pink shrimp are considered most
desirable in foodservice. Shrimp are always shipped
frozen, except in local markets.

COOKED SHRIMP

CANNED COOKED SHRIMP

Pack:
Six #10 cans. Other packs are available.

Kitchen Yields
Product is fully cooked and ready to serve.
Drained weight varies, depending on the
manufacturer.

Calories:
3 oz (85 g) = 100 Calories.

FROZEN COOKED COCKTAIL SHRIMP
These are fully cooked and peeled shrimp; most
brands have the tails still attached, for eye appeal.
IQF shrimp only should be purchased, because the
ice glazing protects the product from freezerburn.

Counts:
Generally, 1 lb (450 g) raw green headless shrimp
produces ½ lb (226 g) peeled cooked shrimp. For
this reason, peeled cooked shrimp are often
packed in 2½-lb (1.1-kg) boxes, so that the
number of cooked shrimp per box corresponds
roughly with the count of green headless shrimp.
However, other packs are also available.

Pack:
Four 2½-lb (1.1-kg) boxes. Table S-2 identifies
standard industry terms for shrimp sizes and
compares counts of cooked cocktail and green
headless shrimp.
Terminology varies from one packer to another.

Kitchen Yields

Serving size:
For shrimp cocktail, 5 pieces of size 31 to 40. One
2½-lb (1.1-kg) box yields 18 servings.

Calories:
5 oz (142 g) = 166 Calories.
4 oz (113 g), or 7 to 8 Super Jumbo pieces = 125
Calories.

FROZEN COOKED TINY SHRIMP
Alaska is the largest producer of these shrimp.

Pack:
Six 5-lb (2.3-kg) blocks or bags containing IQF
shrimp. Other packs are available.

Counts:

Regular:
350 to 500 per 1 lb (450 g).

Table S-2 Size Comparisons between Cooked Cocktail and Green Headless Shrimp

Name	Tail Style	Cooked Count per 1 lb (450 g)	Raw Count (Green Headless) per 1 lb (450 g)	Cooked Count per 2½-lb (1.1-kg) Box
Super Colossal	tail on or off	18 to 25	10 to 12	52 pieces
Colossal	tail on or off	21 to 30	10 to 15	65 pieces
Super Jumbo	tail on or off	31 to 40	16 to 20	90 pieces
Jumbo	tail on or off	41 to 50	21 to 25	115 pieces
Extra Large	tail on or off	51 to 60	26 to 30	140 pieces
Large	tail on or off	61 to 70	31 to 35	165 pieces
Salad	tail off only	70 to 90, 110 to 130, 130 to 200, 200 to 300, or 300 to 500	36 to 42, 50 to 60	200 pieces or more

Medium:
250 to 350 per 1 lb (450 g).

Defrosted weight:
4 lb 13½ oz (2.2 kg).

Kitchen Yields
One regular block contains 2,250 shrimp; one medium block contains 1,500 shrimp.

Serving size:
6 oz (170 g) for shrimp cocktail; one 5-lb (2.3-kg) block yields 13 servings.

Calories:
6 oz (170 g) = 200 Calories.

PROCESSED SHRIMP
Processed breaded shrimp are classified as hand-breaded or machine-breaded. Generally, the tails are left unbreaded on hand-breaded shrimp. On most machine-breaded shrimp, the tails are also breaded, although some brands of machine-breaded shrimp are available with unbreaded tails. Many different types of breading are available.

Pack:
Eight 3-lb (1.3-kg) boxes; four 3-lb (1.3-kg) boxes; twelve 8-oz (224-g) bags; twelve 6-oz (170-g) bags.

Kitchen Yields
Counts for breaded shrimp are basically the same as those for green headless shrimp. The count on the box is the actual count. By government regulation, weight of breading cannot exceed 50 percent. If breading does exceed 50 percent, the product must be labeled *Imitation Shrimp.* Miniature shrimp (very tiny shrimp) are available in 40 to 50 counts. They are often referred to as popcorn shrimp. Portion sizes vary according to count.

Calories:
Six medium shrimp, fried, weighing 6 oz (170 g) = 270 Calories.

RAW SHRIMP

GREEN HEADLESS SHRIMP
Green headless shrimp are uncooked shrimp in the shell, with the head removed. They are sold on the basis of count per 1 lb (450 g).

Pack:
5-lb (2.3-kg) boxes, frozen in a solid block. Table S-3 lists counts per 1 lb and total number per box for green headless shrimp.

Kitchen Yields

Waste:

Peeling and deveining loss:
About 25 percent by weight.

Cooking loss:
25 percent by weight.

Total loss:
50 percent by weight.

Serving sizes:
For broiled stuffed shrimp served as main course, 4 shrimp of size Under 8; therefore, one 5-lb (2.2-kg) box yields 9 servings. For shrimp cocktail, 4 shrimp of size 16 to 20; therefore, one 5-lb (2.2-kg) box yields 22 to 24 portions. For shrimp

Table S-3 Green Headless Shrimp per 1 lb (450 g) and per Box

Count per 1 lb (450 g)	Number per 5-lb (2.2-kg) Box
Under 8	36 to 38
Under 10	42 to 48
10 to 15	60 to 75
16 to 20	90 to 95
21 to 25	110 to 120
26 to 30	135 to 145
31 to 35	160 to 170
36 to 42	185 to 195
40 to 50	215 to 260
50 to 60	270 to 280

Table S-4 Size Comparisons between Green Headless and P & D Shrimp

Green Headless Count per 1 lb (450 g)	P & D Count per 1 lb (450 g)	P & D Count per 3-lb (1.4-kg) Box
10 to 15	18	54
16 to 20	23	69
21 to 25	28	84
26 to 30	32	96
31 to 35	38	114
36 to 42	44	132
40 to 50	53	159
50 to 60	63	190

salad course, 9 or 10 shrimp of size 21 to 25; therefore, one 5-lb (2.2-kg) box yields 13 servings.

Calories:
5 oz (142 g) = 166 Calories.

P & D SHRIMP
P & D shrimp are peeled and deveined. They are normally shipped as individually quick-frozen (IQF) shrimp. P & D shrimp are available by count per 1 lb (450 g), and by weight as broken pieces. Broken pieces are usable in salads and in shrimp dishes with sauce.

Pack:
Six 3-lb (1.4-kg) boxes; 12½-lb (5.6-kg) bulk pack. Other packs are available. Table S-4 compares counts of green headless and P & D shrimp.

Kitchen Yields
There is no peeling loss. Cooking loss is about 30 percent, because the IQF process involves glazing each piece with ice, which increases the water content of the product.

Calories:
5 oz (142 g) = 166 Calories.

SNAIL EGGS

Imported and domestic snail eggs have come onto the market. Some are flavored with saffron, ginger, or other flavorings.

Pack:
1-oz (28.4-g) jars, pasteurized.

SNAILS

See Escargots.

SNOW PEAS

See Peas.

SORREL (SOUR GRASS)

See Herbs & Spices.

SOUFFLÉ

Basic Mix Formula
    2 lb (900 g) flour
    1¾ lb (784 g) butter
    8 oz (224 g) sugar

Method:
Blend ingredients and store, scaled, in refrigerator.

Two-serving Soufflé Formula
    3½ oz (100 g) basic mix
    ½ pint (0.232 l) boiling milk
    4 egg yolks
    3 egg whites
    2 oz (56 g) sugar
    ½ oz (0.01 l) cordial or flavor

Kitchen Yields
The preceding formula yields 2 servings.

Forty-serving Soufflé Formula
    Full basic mix formula
    6 qt (5.6 l) milk
    70 egg yolks

54 egg whites
2½ lb (1.1 kg) sugar
10 oz (0.30 l) cordial or flavor

Kitchen Yields
The preceding formula yields 40 servings.

SOUPS

BASIC SOUP INGREDIENTS
Only basic ingredients are listed in the formulas presented under this entry.

BEAN SOUP WITH TOMATO
20 lb (9 kg) navy beans
12 gal (45.6 l) chicken stock
One #10 can chopped tomatoes
1½ gal (5.7 l) light cream

Kitchen Yields
The preceding formula produces 10 gal (37 l) soup.

BEEF CONSOMMÉ
10 lb (4.5 kg) clarification meat
30 egg whites, or 1 qt (0.9 l)
One #10 can peeled tomatoes
1 gal mirepoix (diced soup vegetables)
12 gal (45.6 l) beef stock

Kitchen Yields
The preceding formula produces 10 gal (37 l) soup.

BLACK BEAN SOUP
15 lb (6.7 kg) black turtle beans
12 gal (46.6 l) chicken stock
5 lb (2.2 kg) navy beans
1½ gal (5.7 l) light cream

Kitchen Yields
The preceding formula produces 10 gal (37 l) soup.

CHILLED CHERRY SOUP
6 gal (22.8 l) frozen pitted sour cherries
4 gal (15.2 l) water
2 lb (0.9 kg) cornstarch
2 lb (0.9 kg) sugar

4 cinnamon sticks
Peel from 8 lemons
1 tb cayenne pepper

Kitchen Yields
The preceding formula produces 10 gal (37 l) soup.

CRAYFISH BISQUE
10 dozen crayfish
1 gal (3.8 l) mirepoix (including garlic)
2 cups (0.47 l) oil
¾ gal (2.8 l) white roux
12 gal (45.6 l) strong chicken stock
1 gal (3.8 l) light cream
½ gal (1.9 l) white wine
1 qt (0.9 l) cream sherry
1 qt (0.9 l) brandy

Kitchen Yields
The preceding formula produces 10 gal (37 l) soup.

CREAM OF ASPARAGUS
10 lb (4.5 kg), or 4 boxes frozen asparagus
¾ gal (2.8 l) white roux
12 gal (45.6 l) strong chicken stock
1 gal (3.8 l) light cream

Kitchen Yields
The preceding formula produces 10 gal (37 l) soup.

CREAM OF BROCCOLI
10 lb (4.5 kg), or 4 boxes frozen broccoli
¾ gal (2.8 l) white roux
12 gal (45.6 l) strong chicken stock
1 gal (3.8 l) light cream

Kitchen Yields
The preceding formula produces 10 gal (37 l) soup.

CREAM OF CAULIFLOWER
10 lb (4.5 kg), or 4 boxes frozen cauliflower
¾ gal (2.8 l) white roux
12 gal (45.6 l) strong chicken stock
1 gal (3.8 l) light cream

Kitchen Yields
The preceding formula produces 10 gal (37 l) soup.

CREAM OF CHICKEN
>   ¾ gal (2.8 l) white roux
>   12 gal (45.6 l) strong chicken stock
>   1 gal (3.8 l) light cream
>   1 gal (3.8 l) diced chicken meat (as garnish)

Kitchen Yields
The preceding formula produces 10 gal (37 l) soup.

CREAM OF CORN
>   Two #10 cans creamed corn
>   One #10 can kernel corn (for garnish)
>   ½ gal (1.9 l) white roux
>   10 gal (38. l) strong chicken stock
>   1 gal (3.8 l) light cream

Kitchen Yields
The preceding formula produces 10 gal (37 l) soup.

CREAM OF CURRY
>   ½ lb (225 g) curry powder
>   ¾ gal (2.8 l) white roux
>   12 gal (45.6 l) strong chicken stock
>   1 gal (3.8 l) light cream

Kitchen Yields
The preceding formula produces 10 gal (37 l) soup.
NOTE: Soup can be garnished with diced chicken, banana, and unsweetened coconut.

CREAM OF MUSHROOM
>   9 lb (4 kg) fresh mushrooms
>   ¾ gal (2.8 l) white roux
>   12 gal (45.6 l) strong chicken stock
>   1 gal (3.8 l) light cream

Kitchen Yields
The preceding formula produces 10 gal (37 l) soup.

CREAM OF TOMATO
>   Three #10 cans tomato purée
>   ¾ gal (2.8 l) white roux
>   12 gal (45.6 l) strong chicken stock
>   1 gal (3.8 l) light cream
>   One #10 can chopped tomatoes (as garnish)

Kitchen Yields
The preceding formula produces 10 gal (37 l) soup.

CUCUMBER SOUP
>   25 lb (11.2 kg) potatoes
>   20 lb (9 kg) peeled, seeded cucumbers
>   12 gal (45.6 l) chicken stock

>   2.5 gal (9.5 l) dry white wine
>   2.5 gal (9.5 l) heavy cream

Kitchen Yields
The preceding formula produces 10 gal (37 l) soup.
NOTE: Save 6 lb diced, cooked cucumbers as garnish.

FENNEL (OR ANISE) SOUP
>   2 gal (4.6 l) chopped fennel or anise, no greens
>   ½ gal (1.9 l) chopped fennel or anise, with greens
>   ½ cup, or 2 oz (56 g) fennel or anise seed
>   ¾ gal (2.8 l) white roux
>   12 gal (45.6 l) strong chicken stock
>   1 gal (3.8 l) light cream

For garnish:

>   ½ gal (1.9 l) diced fennel
>   1 qt (0.47 l) chopped fennel green

Kitchen Yields
The preceding formula produces 10 gal (37 l) soup.

GAME CONSOMMÉ
>   15 lb (6.7 kg) browned venison or other game bones
>   5 lb (2.2 kg) clarification meat (venison and beef trimmings)
>   15 egg whites, or 1 pint (0.47 l)
>   One #10 can peeled tomatoes
>   1 gal (3.8 l) mirepoix (diced soup vegetables)
>   ¼ cup, or 2 oz (56 g) crushed juniper berries
>   12 gal (45.6 l) beef stock
>   1 qt (0.9 l) dry sherry
>   1 qt (0.9 l) cream sherry

Kitchen Yields
The preceding formula produces 10 gal (37 l) soup.

GAZPACHO
>   10 lb (4.5 kg) onions
>   10 lb (4.5 kg) seeded green peppers
>   15 lb (6.7 kg) peeled, seeded cucumbers
>   One #10 can peeled whole tomatoes
>   5 lb (2.2 kg) celery stalks
>   One #10 can tomato purée
>   2 46-oz cans (2.6 l) tomato juice
>   2 qt (0.94 l) vinegar
>   1 qt (0.47 l) olive oil

½ cup crushed garlic
24 whole eggs
½ cup salt
¼ cup ground pepper
½ cup sugar
1 oz (28 g) dried tarragon

Kitchen Yields
The preceding formula produces 10 gal (37 l) soup.

GIBLET AND BARLEY SOUP
2.5 gal (9.5 l) ground raw giblets
½ gal (1.9 l) oil
5 lb (2.2 kg) pearl barley
½ gal (1.9 l) diced onions
½ gal (1.9 l) diced celery
½ gal (1.9 l) diced carrots
½ gal (1.9 l) diced turnips
1 qt (0.9 l) brown roux
12 gal (45.6 l) beef stock

Kitchen Yields
The preceding formula produces 10 gal (37 l) soup.

GUMBO
½ gal (1.9 l) diced green peppers
½ gal (1.9 l) diced onions
½ gal (1.9 l) diced celery
½ gal (1.9 l) diced cabbage
One #10 can chopped tomatoes
10 lb (4.5 kg) frozen diced okra
    or
Two #10 cans diced okra
1 gal (3.8 l) cooked rice
5 lb (2.2 kg) diced ham
½ gal (1.9 kg) cooked chicken
1 lb (450 g) filé powder
4 gal (15.2 l) chicken stock
4 gal (15.2 l) beef stock

Kitchen Yields
The preceding formula produces 10 gal (37 l) soup.

JELLIED MADRILENE CONSOMMÉ
Four 46-oz cans (5.3 l) tomato juice
Two #10 cans peeled tomatoes
1 lb (450 g) plain gelatin
½ gal (1.9 l) chopped celery
10 lb (4.5 kg) clarification meat
30 egg whites, or 1 qt (0.47 l)
One #10 can peeled tomatoes
8 gal (30.4 l) beef stock

Kitchen Yields
The preceding formula produces 10 gal (37 l) soup.

LOBSTER SOUP
35 cooked lobster heads and carcasses from
    1¼ lb (560 g) lobsters, or 25 lb (11.2 kg) raw
    culls
1 pt (0.47 l) oil
One #10 can tomato purée
1 gal (3.8 l) mirepoix (including garlic)
¾ gal (2.8 l) white roux
12 gal (45.6 l) strong chicken stock
⅛ cup (28 g) dried tarragon
1 gal (3.8 l) light cream
½ gal (1.9 l) white wine
1 qt (0.9 l) cream sherry
1 qt (0.9 l) brandy

Kitchen Yields
The preceding formula produces 10 gal (37 l) soup.
NOTE: If available, use lobster stock instead of
chicken stock.

MINESTRONE
1 cup (8 oz) chopped fresh garlic
½ gal (1.9 l) olive oil
5 lb (2.2 kg) ham hocks
3 lb (1.3 kg) navy beans
½ gal (1.9 l) diced green peppers
½ gal (1.9 l) diced onions
½ gal (1.9 l) diced celery
½ gal (1.9 l) diced carrots
½ gal (1.9 l) diced cabbage
One #10 can chopped tomatoes
One #10 can tomato purée
3 lb (1.3 kg) broken spaghetti
7 gal (26.6 l) beef stock

Kitchen Yields
The preceding formula produces 10 gal (37 l) soup.

ONION SOUP
4 gal (15.2 l) sliced onions
½ gal (1.9 l) oil
12 gal (45.6 l) strong beef stock
¼ cup dried thyme
1 qt (0.9 l) applejack

Kitchen Yields
The preceding formula produces 10 gal (37 l) soup.

PEA SOUP

20 lb (9 kg) green split or yellow peas
12 gal (45.6 l) chicken stock
1½ gal (5.7 l) light cream

Kitchen Yields

The preceding formula produces 10 gal (37 l) soup.
NOTE: Ham bones can be added for flavor if desired, and ½ gal (1.9 l) diced ham added for garnish.

PHILADELPHIA PEPPER POT

1 gal (3.8 l) diced green peppers
1 gal (3.8 l) diced onions
1 gal (3.8 l) diced potatoes
1 gal (3.8 l) diced celery
1 gal (3.8 l) cooked spaetzle
1 gal (3.8 l) cooked, diced tripe
8 gal (30.4 l) beef stock

Kitchen Yields

10 gal (38 l)
NOTE: Spaetzle are tiny dough dumplings. They are available dried or can be made on premise. *See* Spaetzle for recipe.

PUMPKIN SOUP

½ gal (1.9 l) white roux
Three #10 cans pumpkin purée
12 gal (45.6 l) strong chicken stock
¼ cup, or 2 oz (56 g), nutmeg
½ cup, or 4 oz (113 g), lemon juice
1 gal (3.8 l) light cream

Kitchen Yields

The preceding formula produces 10 gal (37 l) soup.
NOTE: Canned pumpkin can be replaced by 25 lb (11.2 kg) cleaned, diced, fresh pumpkin.

VEGETABLE SOUP

½ gal (1.9 l) diced green peppers
½ gal (1.9 l) diced onions
½ gal (1.9 l) diced potatoes
½ gal (1.9 l) diced celery
½ gal (1.9 l) diced carrots
½ gal (1.9 l) diced cabbage
One #10 can chopped tomatoes
7 gal (26.6 l) beef stock

Kitchen Yields

10 gal (37 l)

VICHYSSOISE (POTATO SOUP)

25 lb (11.2 kg) potatoes
8 lb (3.6 kg) onions
8 lb (3.6 kg) white part of leeks
12 gal (45.6 l) strong chicken stock
2 gal (7.6 l) light cream

NOTE: Soup should be sprinkled with chives before service.

SOUP QUANTITIES

Kitchen Yields

Serving size:
6 oz (0.17 l).
1 gal (3.7 l) yields 20 servings.
5 gal (19 l) yield 100 servings.
10 gal (37 l) yield 200 servings.
25 gal (95 l) yield 500 servings.
38 gal (145 l) yield 750 servings.
NOTE: Always make about 10 percent more soup than needed, to allow for spillage.

SOUR CREAM

See Cream.

SOUVLAKI

This is a Greek preparation of pork on skewers. It is available frozen, fully seasoned.

Pack:
15-lb (6.7-kg) case.

Count:
Fifty-four 4-oz (113-g) skewers.

Kitchen Yields

Serving size:
Two pieces, as main course.

SOYBEANS

See Eda Mame, under Japanese Foods; *see also* Bean Curd.

SPAETZLE

Small dumplings from southwestern Germany and neighboring Switzerland.

Formula

    3 lb (1.3 kg) bread flour
    12 eggs
    1 qt (0.94 l) milk
    ½ cup (0.11 l) oil
    1 tb salt
    1 tb baking powder

This formula yields forty ½-cup (0.11-l) servings. NOTE: To shape spaetzle, use a food mill with very large holes. Some chefs shape spaetzle on a wet, wooden board, then scrape them directly into the boiling water.

SPAGHETTI

See Pasta.

SPANISH LIME

This fruit resembles lychee nuts. It has a brown, tough skin. The fruit is eaten by sucking the milky flesh from the seeds.

SPICES

See Herbs & Spices.

SPINACH

Spinach is available canned, fresh, and frozen.

CANNED SPINACH
Available chopped and whole-leaf.

Pack:
Six #10 cans.

Kitchen Yields

Serving size:
½ cup, or 4 oz (100 g). One #10 can has a drained weight of 58 to 60 oz (1.6 to 1.7 kg) and yields 15 servings; one case yields 90 to 100 servings.

Calories:
½ cup: 4 oz (100 g) plain = 29 Calories.

FRESH SPINACH
There are two basic varieties: curly-leaf Savoy spinach and flat-leaf spinach, also called *broadleaf spinach*. Curly-leaf Savoy spinach ships better than flat-leaf spinach. Semi-Savoy spinach is occasionally available. Loose spinach is shipped both clipped (with some stems removed) and in bunches.

Season:
Available year-round, with peaks in spring.

Pack:
20- to 22-lb (9- to 9.9-kg) bushels; cases with eight 10-oz (280-g) cello packs.

Kitchen Yields

Waste:
From bushel spinach, as purchased, ready-to-cook or serve as salad, the waste is 30 percent by weight. One 20-lb (9-kg) bushel as purchased produces 13 to 14 lb (5.8 to 6.3 kg) cleaned spinach.
From trimmed cello pack spinach, ready-to-cook or serve as salad, the waste is 15 percent by weight. One carton of eight cello packs as purchased produces 68 oz (1.9 kg) cleaned spinach.

Salad serving sizes:

For main course salad:
2 cups, or 4 oz (112 g).

For side order salad:
1 cup, or 2 oz (56 g).
One cello pack yields 2 main-course salad servings and 4 side-order salad servings.
One case yields 16 to 17 main-course salad servings or 32 to 34 side-order salad servings.
One bushel spinach yields 54 main-course salads or 100 side-order salads.

Serving size:

Cooked spinach:
½ cup (0.23 liter).
One case cello pack spinach produces 7½ cups (1.7 l) cooked spinach, or 15 servings.

One bushel, as purchased, produces 10 lb (4.5 kg) cooked spinach.
10 lb (4.5 kg) cooked spinach equals 20 cups (4.6 l), or 40 servings.

Cooking loss:
10 lb (4.5 kg) trimmed spinach produces 7½ lb (3.3 kg) cooked spinach.
7½ lb (3.3 kg) cooked spinach equals 15 cups (3.5 l).

Calories:
1 cup, or 2 oz (56 g) raw, chopped = 15 Calories.
½ cup, or 4 oz (116 g) cooked, drained = 28 Calories.

FROZEN SPINACH
Available whole-leaf, chopped, and IQF.

Pack:
Twelve 3-lb (1.3-kg) boxes, chopped or whole; twelve 2-lb (0.9-kg) bags, IQF.

Kitchen Yields
There is some draining loss, especially from chopped spinach.

Serving size:
½ cup (0.23 l). One 3-lb (1.3-kg) box yields 10 servings; therefore, one case yields 120 servings.

Calories:
½ cup, or 4 oz (100 g), cooked, chopped, and drained = 28 Calories.
1 cup, or 6¾ oz (190 g), cooked leaf = 47 Calories.

SPONGE CAKE

Formula
  1 qt (0.47 l) egg yolks
  3 qt (1.4 l) whole eggs
  4 lb (1.8 kg) sugar
  3 lb (1.3 kg) cake flour
  1 lb (450 g) patent flour
  8 oz (222 g) cornstarch
  1 lb (450 g) melted butter
  Salt, vanilla, or lemon peel to taste

Kitchen Yields
The preceding formula produces twenty 8-in (200-mm) layer cakes.

SPROUTS

Sprouts include alfalfa sprouts and bean sprouts. Brussels sprouts are listed separately; *see* Brussels Sprouts. Sprout varieties are available canned, cut, fresh, and live in planter boxes.

ALFALFA SPROUTS

Pack:
Twelve 4- or 6-oz (112- or 170-g) containers; 4-lb (1.8-kg) flats.

Kitchen Yields
There is no waste.

Serving size:
For salad garnish, 1 oz (28 g); one flat of 4-oz (113-g) containers yields 48 garnish servings. One 4-lb (1.8-kg) flat yields 64 garnish servings.

Calories:
1 oz (28 g) = 5 Calories.

BEAN SPROUTS
Bean sprouts are grown from mung beans.

CANNED BEAN SPROUTS

Pack:
Six #10 cans. Other packs are available.

Drained weight:
58 oz (1.6 kg).

Kitchen Yields
1 cup weighs 4 oz (113 g).

Calories:
1 cup, or 4 oz (112 g) = 35 Calories.

FRESH BEAN SPROUTS

Pack:
5- and 10-lb (2.25- and 5.5-kg) bags.

Kitchen Yields
There is no waste; use as is.
1 cup weighs 3½ oz (100 g).

Calories:
1 cup, or 3½ oz (100 g) = 33 Calories.

SPUN SUGAR

See Sugar.

SQUAB

Squab is a young pigeon; it should not be confused with the squab chicken, which is a baby chicken. Squab is available fresh and frozen and is shipped whole, bone-in and boneless. Fresh whole bone-in birds are often shipped with head on.

Season:
Available year-round, with a larger supply in spring.

Pack:
Twelve birds to a carton.

Sizes:

Whole:
12 oz (340 g), 14 oz (400 g), 16 oz (450 g), and 20 oz (560 g).

Boneless:
13 oz (370 g).
NOTE: Sizes quoted by purveyor can be for squabs with or without heads.

Kitchen Yields

Best size:
14 oz (400 g), with head.

Serving sizes:
One bird.

Breast only:
5 to 6 oz (140 to 170 g).
One 20-oz bird will yield 2 breasts.

SQUASH

Squash are available canned, fresh, and frozen. They are classified as soft-shell (also called *summer squash*) or hard-shell (also called *winter squash*).

FRESH SQUASH

Season:
Despite their classification into summer and winter types, many varieties are available year-round.

Pack:
25-lb (11.2-kg) cartons. Other packs are available.

Sizes:
Vary greatly. When sizes are indicated, they are the ones most suitable for foodservice operators.

Kitchen Yields
Yields vary greatly, depending on season and size of vegetable. For summer squash, the smallest pieces are the best, because they give the most highest percentage yield, are firm, and shrink little.

SUMMER SQUASH VARIETIES

BITTER MELON
Also called *Balsam Asiatic pear*, this squash has a sour/bitter taste. Seeds should be removed before cooking. Soaking in salted water removes some of the sourness. The vegetable looks like a crinkled cucumber.

Season:
Available year-round.

Pack:
By weight.

Size:
6 to 12 oz (170 to 340 g).

Kitchen Yields
Use with peel. Little waste.

BUTTERNUT

Season:
Summer for squash with soft edible skin and seeds. Winter for squash with harder shell.

CHAYOTE
Also called *Mirliton squash*, this is a member of the melon family used for cooking. The squash is round to pear-shaped and varies in color from light to dark green.

Season:
Available year-round.

Pack:
10- and 15-lb (4.5- and 6.8-kg) boxes.

Count:
Varies according to pack.

Size:
1 lb (450 g) average.

Kitchen Yield

Cleaning waste:
30 percent.

CUSTARD SQUASH
Also called *pattypan squash*.

Season:
Summer and fall.

SCALLOP SQUASH

Season:
Fall.

YELLOW CROOKNECK

Season:
Summer and fall.

Average sizes:

Small:
4 oz (113 g).

Medium:
5 oz (142 g).

YELLOW STRAIGHTNECK

Season:
Summer and fall.

ZUCCHINI

Season:
Available year-round.

Kitchen Yields

Trimming waste:
10 percent.

Serving sizes:
For restaurant service, 3 oz (85 g) raw, cleaned weight sautéed or breaded; one 25-lb (11.2-kg) carton yields 120 servings sautéed or breaded. For banquet service, one 25-lb (11.2-kg) carton yields 140 servings, and 18 lb yield 100 2½-oz (70-g) servings.

Calories:
½ cup, or 2¾ oz (77 g) cooked, drained, and diced = 11 Calories.

WINTER SQUASH VARIETIES

ACORN SQUASH
Available green and gold.

Season:
Peak is from October to December.

Pack:
38-lb (17.1-kg) box.

Kitchen Yields
About 25 percent waste.

BANANA SQUASH
Straightneck squash with a hard rind.

Season:
October to December.

Pack:
40-lb (18-kg) cartons.

BUTTERNUT

Season:
September to December.

Pack:
38-lb (17.1-kg) bushel.

CALABASA
Also called *Cuban squash*, the vegetable has a better yield than pumpkin. Buff color indicates maturity.

Season:
Winter.

Kitchen Yields
1 lb as purchased yields 11 oz (312 g) squash, ready to cook.

COCOZEALLA
Straightneck squash with a hard rind.

Season:
September to December.

Pack:
40-lb (18-kg) cartons.

HUBBARD

Season:
September to November.

Average size:
4 lb (1.8 kg).

ORNAMENTAL SQUASH

Season:
October to December.

Pack:
By weight.

PUMPKIN
See Pumpkin.

SPAGHETTI SQUASH

Season:
September to December.

Pack:
35-lb (15.7-kg) carton.

Average sizes:
3 to 4 lb (1.3 to 1.8 kg).

WINTER MELON
Large vegetable, round or football-shaped, with green skin and white inner meat that contains many seeds. Must be cooked.

Season:
Year-round; peak is in winter.

Pack:
Sold by weight and piece.

Kitchen Yields

Size:
Up to 20 in (500 mm) across.

PROCESSED SQUASH

CANNED PUMPKIN
See Pumpkin.

FROZEN SQUASH
Available are a number of varieties, including sliced zucchini and sliced yellow squash. Cooked squash purée is also available. Many different packs are available.

Pack:
Twelve 4-lb (1.8-kg) boxes squash purée; twelve 2-lb (0.9-kg) boxes IQF zucchini or yellow squash; individual 20-lb (9-kg) packages IQF zucchini or yellow squash; twelve 2½-lb (1.1-kg) zucchini or yellow squash; twelve 3-lb (1.3-kg) yellow southern squash.

Kitchen Yields

Serving size:
½ cup, or 4 oz (0.112 l).
One 4-lb (1.8-kg) box squash purée yields 17 servings, so one case squash purée yields 200 servings.
One 2-lb (0.9-kg) box IQF squash yields 8 servings, so one case IQF squash yields 100 servings.
One 2½-lb squash box yields 10 servings, so one case yields 120 servings.

Calories:
½ cup, or 4 oz (112 g) summer squash = 15 Calories.
½ cup, or 4 oz (112 g) winter squash = 60 Calories.

SQUID

Available fresh or frozen.

WHOLE SQUID

Squid, also called *calamare*, is normally sold fully cleaned, except for the center cartilage, which is easily pulled out.

Pack:
By weight.

Season:
Available year-round.

Kitchen Yields
Waste is about 5 percent by weight. Cleaned squid does not contain the squid ink, which is prized for pasta and sauce flavoring.

PROCESSED SQUID

Frozen breaded squid sections are available from specialty purveyors.

Pack:
Twelve 2½-lb (1.1-kg boxes).

Kitchen Yields
Use as is. There is no waste.

Serving size:
3 oz (84 g) as appetizer. One package yields 13 servings.

STARFRUIT

There are two varieties on the market: Green Star Fruit (also called *Cucumber Tree Fruit*) and a yellow variety called Star Apple. Both have the shape of a five-pointed star when cut across. The Green Star Fruit is sour and cannot be eaten raw. The Star Apple is slightly sweet.

Season:
Available year-round, with peak in fall and winter.

Pack:
By weight and by piece.

Size:
Green Star Fruit:
3 in (8 cm) long.

Star Apple:
4 in (12 cm) long.

STEAM TABLE PAN SIZES

Table S-5 lists sizes and capacities of different steam table pans.
NOTE: The capacities shown are to the rim of the pan. The effective capacity is considerably smaller when pans are filled and transported.

STRAWBERRIES

Strawberries are available canned, fresh, and frozen.

CANNED STRAWBERRIES
Available sliced or whole.

Pack:
Six #10 cans; twelve or twenty-four or thirty-six #303 cans.

Kitchen Yields
One #10 can, drained weight, is 74 oz (2.0 kg).
One #303 can, drained weight, is 11 oz (0.3 kg).

Serving size:
½ cup (0.11 l) fruit and juice. One #10 can yields 25 servings, while one #303 can yields 4 servings.

FRESH STRAWBERRIES
Common cultivated strawberries are available year-round. Marshall strawberries are extra-large berries with the stem still attached. *Fraises des bois* is the French name for imported or domestic wild strawberries.

COMMON CULTIVATED STRAWBERRIES

Season:
Available year-round. Peak is from March through June. Worst quality is in December. Imported strawberries come onto the market in the winter.

Pack:
Twelve 1-pint (0.47-l) baskets, with a total tray volume of 6 qt (5.6 l); 1-qt (0.94-l) baskets are also on the market.

Weights:
1 pint weighs 14 oz (400 g).
1 tray weighs 10 lb (4.5 kg).
1 qt weighs 1¾ lb (780 g).

Counts:
1 pint (0.47 l) contains 12 to 14 large berries or 20 to 25 smaller berries. Large berries are packed on top. One 12-pint tray contains 150 large berries or 240 to 300 smaller berries.

Kitchen Yields

Waste:
Cleaning loss is 10 percent by weight; percentage varies by season and depending on size of berries.
1 pint contains 2 cups (0.47 l) whole berries, cleaned, or 1¾ cups (0.4 l) sliced berries.
1 cup whole berries, cleaned, weighs 5 oz, and one tray contains 24 cups.

Serving sizes:

Restaurants:
For breakfast or dessert (without ice cream), 1 pint yields 2 portions, and one flat yields 24

Table S-5 Steam Table Pan Sizes and Capacities

Size	Approximate Exterior Dimensions	Depth	Capacities	4 fl oz (0.11 l) Portions
Full	12¾ × 20¾ in (323 × 527 mm)	1 in (25 mm)	3½ qt (3.3 l)	28
		2 in (50 mm)	7 qt (6.5 l)	56
		2½ in (63 mm)	9 qt (8.4 l)	72
		3 in (76 mm)	11 qt (10.3 l)	88
		4 in (101 mm)	15 qt (14.1 l)	120
		6 in (152 mm)	22 qt (20.6 l)	176
		8 in (203 mm)	31½ qt (29.6 l)	252
Two-thirds	13¾ × 12¾ in (349 × 323 mm)	1 in (25 mm)	2¼ qt (2.1 l)	18
		2 in (50 mm)	4½ qt (4.2 l)	36
		2½ in (63 mm)	6 qt (5.6 l)	48
		3 in (76 mm)	7¼ qt (6.8 l)	58
		4 in (101 mm)	10 qt (9.4 l)	80
		6 in (152 mm)	14¼ qt (13.3 l)	114
		8 in (203 mm)	21⅜ qt (20.0 l)	171
One-half	10⅜ × 12¾ in (263 × 323 mm)	1 in (25 mm)	1½ qt (1.4 l)	12
		2 in (50 mm)	3½ qt (3.3 l)	28
		2½ in (63 mm)	4 qt (3.7 l)	32
		3 in (76 mm)	5 qt (4.7 l)	40
		4 in (101 mm)	7 qt (6.6 l)	56
		6 in (152 mm)	10 qt (9.4 l)	80
		8 in (203 mm)	15 qt (14.1 l)	120
One-third	6⅞ × 12¾ in (175 × 323 mm)	1 in (25 mm)	1 qt (0.9 l)	8
		2 in (50 mm)	2 qt (1.9 l)	16
		2½ in (63 mm)	2⅝ qt (2.5 l)	21
		3 in (76 mm)	3¼ qt (3.0 l)	26
		4 in (101 mm)	4½ qt (4.2 l)	36
		6 in (152 mm)	6½ qt (6.2 l)	52
One-quarter	10⁵⁄₁₆ × 6⁵⁄₁₆ (261 × 160 mm)	1 in (25 mm)	⅝ qt (0.6 l)	5
		2 in (50 mm)	1¼ qt (1.2 l)	10
		2½ in (63 mm)	1⅝ qt (1.5 l)	13
		3 in (76 mm)	2 qt (1.9 l)	16
		4 in (101 mm)	3 qt (2.8 l)	24
		6 in (152 mm)	4¾ qt (4.5 l)	38
One-sixth	6⅞ × 6⁵⁄₁₆ in (174 × 160 mm)	1 in (25 mm)	½ qt (0.47 l)	4
		2 in (50 mm)	1 qt (0.94 l)	8
		3 in (76 mm)	1½ qt (1.4 l)	12
		4 in (101 mm)	2 qt (1.9 l)	16
One-ninth	6¾ × 4¼ in (171 × 108 mm)	1 in (25 mm)	⅜ qt (0.35 l)	3
		2 in (50 mm)	⅗ qt (0.70 l)	6

portions. For garnish with ice cream, mousse, or cake, 1 pint yields 3½ portions, and one flat yields 40 portions.

Banquets:
With ice cream, one flat yields 60 to 70 servings.

Calories:
1 cup, or 5½ oz (150 g) = 55 Calories.

EXTRA-LARGE STRAWBERRIES WITH STEMS
These are also called *Marshall strawberries.*

Season:
Available by special order. They are difficult to get in late fall and early winter.

Pack:
Tray or box with twelve 1-pint (0.47-l) baskets.

Count:
1 pint contains about 8 large berries.

Kitchen Yields

Serving size:
For garnish, 1 fruit; for dessert portion, 2 to 3 fruits. Therefore, 1 pint (0.47 l) yields 3 portions.

WILD STRAWBERRIES
Called *fraises de bois* in French, wild strawberries are available domestic and imported.

Season:
Spring and early summer.

Pack:
Twelve ½-pint (0.23-l) baskets.

Kitchen Yields
Berries are very small. Cleaning waste is about 20 percent by volume.

FROZEN STRAWBERRIES
Frozen strawberries are available sliced and mixed with sugar, or IQF whole.

Pack:

Sliced, sweetened berries:
6½-lb (3-kg) can; 10-lb (4.5-kg) can; 30-lb (13.6-kg) tin.

Whole berries IQF:
30-lb (13.6-kg) carton.

Kitchen Yields

Serving size:
½ cup (0.11 l) sliced fruit and juice for dessert; ¼ cup (0.05 l) as garnish with ice cream.
One 6½-lb (3-kg) can yields 24 ½-cup servings or 48 ¼-cup servings.
One 10-lb (4.5-kg) can yields 38 ½-cup servings or 75 ¼-cup servings.
One 30-lb (13.6-kg) can yields 115 ½-cup servings or 230 ¼-cup servings.
Serving sizes for whole berries IQF are about the same as for sliced berries, because berries get very soft when defrosted.

Calories:
½ cup (0.11 l) sweetened, sliced = 118 Calories.

STRUDEL DOUGH

See Filo Dough, under Filo.

SUGAR

1 cup granulated sugar weighs 7 oz (200 g).
1 cup confectioners sugar weighs 4 oz (113 g).

PULLED SUGAR

Formula
> 5 lb (2.25 kg) granulated sugar
> 1 pint (0.47 l) water
> ¼ oz (6.75 g), or 2 tsp cream of tartar
> Boil the mixture to 318°F.

Kitchen Yields
The preceding formula yields one medium-size basket.

SPUN SUGAR

Formula
> 5 lb (2.3 kg) sugar
> 1 lb (0.450 g) glucose
> 1 pint (0.47 l) water
> Boil ingredients to 320°F.

Kitchen Yields
The preceding formula produces garnish for 50 desserts.

SUNCHOKES (JERUSALEM ARTICHOKES)

Pack:
12-lb (5.4-kg) carton.

Kitchen Yields

Waste:
20 percent by weight.

Calories:
3½ oz (100 g) = 75 Calories.

SURIMI

See Crab Meat Substitutes.

SWEET POTATOES AND YAMS

Various sweet potatoes and yams are available canned, fresh, and frozen. The names *yam* and *sweet potato* are often used interchangeably, although there is a difference between the two.

BONIATO
Sweet potato with red skin and white flesh.

Season:
Available year-round.

Kitchen Yields
Use as you would a sweet potato.

CANNED YAMS
Whole, cut, and mashed yams are available canned. Whole and cut sweet potatoes are available in syrup pack, vacuum pack, and dry pack.

Pack:
Six #10 cans; twelve #3 vacuum cans.

Kitchen Yields
Whole potato counts and weights in #10 can are as follows:

40 to 50: 2½ oz (70 g) each.
30 to 40: 3¼ oz (90 g) each.
20 to 30: 4½ oz (125 g) each.

Serving size:
½ cup (0.11 l). One #10 can syrup pack yields 20 servings; one #3 can vacuum pack yields 5 servings; one #10 can dry pack yields 25 servings.

Calories:
½ cup, or 5 oz (140 g), syrup pack = 177 Calories.

FRESH SWEET POTATOES OR YAMS
Little distinction is made on the market between sweet potatoes and yams. Yams are considered to be more moist than sweet potatoes.

Season:
Available year-round, with peak in the winter months.

Pack:
Cartons with varying counts and weights.

Kitchen Yields
Shape is important for good yield. Look for clearly identifiable pieces.

Average weight:
5 to 6½ oz (140 to 185 g) for raw, unpeeled potato.

Serving size:

Mashed:
½ cup (0.11 l).
1 lb (450 g) yields 12 oz (340 g); 1 lb (450 g) yields 2¾ servings.

Sliced:
½ cup (0.11 l).
1 lb (450 g) yields 12 oz (340 g); 1 lb (450 g) yields 3 servings.

Calories:
4 oz (112 g), baked in skin = 160 Calories.
5 oz (140 g), boiled in skin = 160 Calories.
4 oz (112 g), candied = 175 Calories.

FROZEN YAMS
Frozen yams are available whole, sliced, and in patties.

Pack:
Twelve 2½-lb (1.1-kg) packages, whole or sliced; six 5-lb (2.2-kg) boxes, sliced; 24-lb case of 2-oz (56-g) patties.

Kitchen Yields

Serving size:
½ cup (0.11 l). One 2½-lb (1.1-kg) package yields 10 servings; one 5-lb (2.2-kg) box yields 20 servings.

Calories:
½ cup, or 4 oz (112 g), candied = 175 Calories.

SWISS CHARD

This vegetable in the beet family, grown for its leaves and stems, is available fresh.

Season:
Fall and winter, with some supplies available in early summer.

Pack:
20- to 25-lb (9- to 11.2-kg) bushel basket; 30- to 35-lb (13.5- to 15.7-kg) cartons, in bunches.

Kitchen Yields
Trimming loss is about 30 percent. Yield depends to large extent on how the vegetable is used. Some chefs braise the stems and cream the chopped leaves; others use the stems only.

T

Table T-1 Common Banquet Table Sizes

Shape	Size	Seating Capacity	Buffet Capacity
Round	2 ft (0.6 m)	2	0
	2½ ft (0.76 m)	3	0
	3 ft (0.91 m)	4	0
	4½ ft (1.36 m)	6	0
	5 ft (1.52 m)	8	0
	5½ ft (1.67 m)	10	0
	6 ft (1.82 m)	12	0
Rectangular	1½ × 6 ft (0.45 × 1.82 m)	4 schoolroom or theater style	10
	2½ × 4 ft (0.76 × 1.21 m)	6	20
	2½ × 6 ft (0.76 × 1.82 m)	10	25
	3 × 6 ft (0.9 m × 1.82 m)	8	12
	3 × 8 ft (0.9 × 2.4 m)	12	30
Crescent	6 × 3 ft (1.82 × 091 m)	4	30

TABLE AND TABLECLOTH SIZES

Table T-1 list the most common banquet table sizes.

The following is a list of table sizes and corresponding tablecloth sizes for standard banquet tables.

Round banquet tables:

Table Size	Tablecloth Size
2 ft (0.6 m)	72 × 72 in (1.82 m²)
2½ ft (0.76 m)	72 × 72 in (1.82 m²)
3 ft (0.91 m)	72 × 72 in (1.82 m²)
4½ ft (1.36 m)	90 × 90 in (2.29 m²)
5 ft (1.52 m)	90 × 90 in (2.29 m²)
5½ ft (1.67 m)	108 × 108 in (2.73 m²)
6 ft (1.82 m)	108 × 108 in (2.73 m²)

Rectangular banquet tables:

Table Size	Tablecloth Size
18 × 6 ft (0.45 × 1.82 m)	two 62 × 62-in (1.57-m²) tablecloths
2½ × 4 ft (0.76 × 1.21 m)	72 × 72 in (1.82 m²)
2½ × 6 ft (0.76 × 1.82 m)	two 72 × 72 in (1.82 m²) tablecloths

Table T-2 Table Skirting Sizes

Skirt Length	Round Tables	Head Tables	Buffet Tables
12 ft (3.64 m)		2½ × 6 ft (0.76 × 1.82 m) *or* 3 × 6 ft (0.91 × 1.82 m)	
13 ft (3.9 m)	4 ft diameter (1.2 m)	2½ × 8 ft (0.76 × 2.4 m)	
16 ft (4.8 m)	5 ft diameter (1.5 m)		
17½ ft (5.25 m)	5½ ft diameter (1.65 m)	two 2½ × 6 ft (0.76 × 1.8 m), side-by-side	2½ × 6 ft (0.76 × 1.8 m), freestanding
19 ft (5.7 m)	6 ft diameter (1.8 m)		3 × 6 ft (0.9 × 1.8 m), freestanding
21½ ft (6.3 m)		two 2½ × 8 ft (0.76 × 2.4 m), side-by-side	2½ × 8 ft (0.76 × 2.4 m)

Crescent-shaped tables:

Table Size	Tablecloth Size
6 × 3 ft (1.82 × 0.91 m)	two 90 × 90 in (1.82 m²) tablecloths

To calculate the skirting length required for round tables, use the following equation:

$$\frac{\text{Diameter (in inches)} \times 1.14}{12} = \text{Length (in feet)}$$

Then round off to the next 6-in increment. Table T-2 lists skirting sizes for different tables.

TALLOW

Two varieties of tallow are used for decorating. One is pliable at room temperature; the other is hard enough to be carved.

Formula for Pliable Tallow
5 lb (2.3 kg) shortening
5 lb (2.3 kg) rendered beef fat
4 lb (1.8 kg) paraffin

Formula for Carving Tallow
5 lb (2.3 kg) beeswax
5 lb (2.3 kg) rendered beef fat
5 lb (2.3 kg) paraffin

TAMARIND

The fruit, which resembles large, brown bean pods, is used for making syrups.

Season:
Available year-round.

Pack:
10-lb (4.5-kg) carton.

TANGELOS

A tangerine/grapefruit hybrid with thin skin, easily separated sections, and many seeds.

Season:
From October to May.

Pack:

Florida:
45-lb (20.2-kg), or ⅘-bushel cartons, with counts of 40, 48, 56, 64, 80, 100, or 125.

California:
27- to 32-lb (12.1- to 14.4-kg) cartons, with counts of 42, 54, 72, 84, 90, 100, 105, 135, or 165.

TANGERINES

See also Mandarin Oranges. Tangerines are related to the satsumas. The fruits have few seeds. Tangerines peel and section easily.

Season:
October to mid-May.

Pack:

Florida:
45-lb (20.2-kg), or ⅘-bushel cartons, with counts of 80, 100, 120, 150, 176, 180, or 210.

California:
27- to 32-lb (12.1- to 14.4-kg) cartons, with counts of 72, 84, 90, 100, 135, or 165.

Kitchen Yields
Four #176 fruits weigh 1 lb (450 g).

Calories:
One 4-oz (12-g) tangerine = 40 Calories.

TARO ROOT

Potatolike root used in Oriental, Hawaiian, and South American cooking.

Season:
Year-round.

Pack:
By weight. Also available in 10-lb (4.5-kg) cartons.

Kitchen Yields
About 20 percent peeling loss.

TEA

The best tea is grown on shrubs at high elevations. The smallest leaves are considered best; however, broken leaves are inferior. Fermented tea leaves are referred to as *black tea.* This tea has the typical tea flavor. Unfermented tea is called *green tea* and is the standard tea in Asia. Both black and green teas come from the same shrub. Almost all brands are blends, and the quality of the tea depends on the place where it is grown, the type of fermentation used, the size of the tea leaves, and the care exercised during packing, shipping, and storing.

Pack:
By weight. Many package sizes of loose or packed tea are available.

Kitchen Yields
For fermented (black) tea, 1 tsp yields 2 cups steeped tea; 1 oz (28.4 g) dry tea is equivalent to 12 tsp and yields 24 cups steeped tea.
For iced tea, double amount of tea.
For green tea, 1¾ oz (50 g) dry tea yields 30 cups steeped tea.

TERRAPIN

Small North American turtle that inhabits both brackish and fresh water. The diamondback is the best type. Only females should be used. Terrapins are sold live.

Season:
Summer and fall.

Sizes:
2- to 4-lb (0.9- to 1.8-kg).

Kitchen Yields

Serving size:
Average terrapin yields 4 appetizer servings.

TOFU

See Bean Curd.

TOMATILLOS

See Mexican Foods.

TOMATOES

Tomatoes are available canned and processed, fresh, and sun-dried.

CANNED AND PROCESSED TOMATOES
A wide variety of canned and processed tomato products are on the market.

CHILI SAUCE
Tomato-based sauce flavored with chili peppers. Some brands contain seeds.

Pack:
Six #10 cans. Other packs are available.

Kitchen Yields
Sauce is often mixed with cocktail sauce. One #10 can contains 13 cups (3 l).

TOMATO CATSUP

Packs:
Six #10 cans. Many other packs are available.

Calories:
¼ cup, or 2½ oz (70 g) = 72 Calories.

TOMATO JUICE

Pack:
Forty-eight 6-oz (0.17 l) containers; twelve 46-oz (1.33-l) cans.

Kitchen Yields

Serving size:
6 oz (0.17 l); therefore, one 46-oz can yields 7½ servings.

Calories:
6 fl oz (0.17 l) = 35 Calories.

TOMATO PASTE

Pack:
Six #10 cans. Other packs are available.

Kitchen Yields
Tomato paste is used in cooking, but can also be reconstituted as tomato juice.

Serving size:
6 oz (0.17 l) reconstituted tomato juice. One #10 can + three refilled cans water produces 100 servings.

TOMATO PURÉE

Pack:

Six #10 cans. Other packs are available.

Kitchen Yields

Tomato purée has many uses in cooking, but it can also be reconstituted as tomato juice.

Serving size:

6 oz (0.17 l) reconstituted tomato juice. One #10 can + one refilled can water produces 34 servings.

WHOLE OR CRUSHED TOMATOES

Available as solid pack (no added liquid), with juice added, and with purée added. Canned tomatoes may be whole or crushed.

Pack:

Six #10 cans. Other packs are available.

Kitchen Yields

Drained weight for grade A should be 66 percent of total can content.

Calories:

1 cup (0.23 l) solids and liquid = 50 Calories.

FRESH TOMATOES

Fresh tomatoes are available year-round. They are harvested green or turning and are then ripened though exposure to carefully regulated temperatures and ethylene gas. Tomatoes should not be stored in the refrigerator. Imports are available from a number of countries. Yellow tomatoes have come onto the market as a specialty item.

Tomatoes are best when vine-ripened, but because tomatoes are very perishable when fully ripe, only locally grown fruits are marketed ripe. The flavor of vine-ripened tomatoes is much superior to that of warehouse-ripened tomatoes. Many varieties are on the market, including regular tomatoes, cherry tomatoes, and plum-shaped tomatoes (often referred to as *Italian tomatoes*). Baby pear tomatoes are also available; *see* Baby Vegetables.

CHERRY TOMATOES

Season:

Available year-round.

Pack:

Flats of twelve 1-pint (0.47-l) containers.

Count:

1 pint (0.47 l) contains 23 to 26, or 35 to 45 tomatoes; one flat of twelve 1-pint (0.47-l) or six 1-qt (5.6-l) containers, or 312 pieces.

REGULAR TOMATOES

Regular tomatoes are shipped according to type. Mature, but still-green tomatoes are shipped in cartons with volume-fill pack and are locally repacked when red. Pink and vine-ripened tomatoes are shipped in one- or two-flats, lugs, loose-pack cartons, and basket-packed cartons.

Packs:

18- to 20- lb (8.1- to 9-kg) flats; 28- to 30-lb (12.6- to 13.5-kg) lugs; 25-lb (11.2-kg) cartons; 10-lb (4.5-kg) baskets.

Weights of individual tomatoes:

Maximum large:
8 to 10 oz (224 to 280 g).

Extra large:
5 to 7 oz (140 to 200 g).

Large:
3 to 5 oz (84 to 140 g).

Small:
Under 3 oz (84 g).

Counts:

Flats containing 40 (maximum large) to 60 (extra large) tomatoes; lugs with three layers contain 108 large, 236 medium, and 147 small tomatoes; cartons and baskets have varying counts.

Size classifications refer to the number of tomatoes packed in a carton or lug in rows. Thus, a straight-pack 6 × 6 lug contains 108 tomatoes. However, additional rows of the next size are permitted in lower layers, increasing the number of tomatoes per layer in a carton. A lug of 5 × 5 tomatoes can contain 85 tomatoes. Table T-3 lists size classifications and corresponding diameters for tomatoes.

Table T-3 Tomato Size Classifications and Diameters

Size Classifications	Minimum Diameter	Maximum Diameter
7 × 7	2⁵⁄₃₂ in (54 mm)	2⁵⁄₁₆ in (58 mm)
6 × 7	2¼ in (56 mm)	2⁹⁄₁₆ in (64 mm)
6 × 6	2½ in (62 mm)	2¹³⁄₁₆ in (71 mm)
5 × 6	2¾ in (69 mm)	3³⁄₁₆ in (80 mm)
5 × 5	2⅞ in (72 mm)	3⅜ in (84 mm)
4 × 5	3 in (76 mm)	3⅝ in (91 mm)

Kitchen Yields

1 lb (450 g) is equivalent to 3 to 4 medium tomatoes, or 1½ cups peeled, diced, and seeded tomatoes.

Serving size:
½ cup (0.11 l) raw diced or sliced tomato; therefore, 1 lb (450 g) yields 4½ servings.

Calories:
One raw, large tomato, 5 oz (140 g) = 27 Calories.
3½ oz (100 g) raw tomatoes = 22 Calories.

SUN-DRIED TOMATOES

Available dry or packed in oil.

Pack:

Dry product:
By weight.

Wet product:
In jars.

Kitchen Yields

Yield depends on use. Good-quality sun-dried tomatoes have very concentrated flavor.

TORTELLINI

See Pasta.

TORTILLA

See Mexican Foods.

TRUFFLE PASTE

See Garnishing Paste.

TRUFFLES

See Mushrooms.

TURMERIC

See Herbs & Spices.

TURKEY

FRESH OR FROZEN WHOLE TURKEY

Whole turkeys are available fresh and frozen, although most production is frozen.

Pack:

Fryers and roasters:
4 per carton.

Toms and hens:
2 per carton.
Weight varies according to sizes of birds.

Sizes:

Fryer/roaster:
5 to 9 lb (2.2 to 4.0 kg).

Hen:
8 to 16 lb (3.6 to 7.2 kg).

Tom:
16 lb (7.2 kg) and up.

Kitchen Yields

Whole turkeys have the following percentages of edible meat, before cooking:

Fryer: 75 percent of weight.
Hen: 78 percent of weight.
Tom: 81 percent of weight.

Whole turkey parts have the following percentages of edible meat, before cooking:

Breast: 41 percent of weight.
Drumstick: 14 percent of weight.
Thigh: 17 percent of weight.
Wing: 11 percent of weight.
Necks and giblets: 8 percent of weight.

The larger the bird, the higher the percentage of edible meat. The approximate edible yield after cooking is 55 percent. The usable yield after cooking is 40 percent of purchased weight. Cooking loss by weight is 27 percent.

Serving size:
6 oz (170 g) cooked meat. One 22-lb (10.4-kg) tom turkey, roasted, produces 12 lb (5.4 kg) meat, including all scraps, which yields 22 à la carte portions if hand-sliced directly from the frame or 24 portions if boned after cooking and sliced on machine.
For buffets, 12 lb (5.4 kg) meat yields about 40 portions when served with other meats and salads. For turkey galantine, one 25-lb (11.2-kg) turkey, produces four 4-lb (1.8-kg) rolls.

Calories:
6 oz (170 g) roasted white meat only, without skin = 300 Calories.
5 oz (140 g) roasted dark meat only, without skin = 360 Calories.
6 oz (170 g) roasted diced, mixed meat, 1 cup = 320 Calories.

RAW TURKEY PARTS

BREAST

Weights:
8 to 22 lb (3.6 to 9.9 kg).

Pack:
Two to eight pieces per case.

Kitchen Yield

Serving size:
3½ oz (100 g) cooked. Bone-in breast yields 2 to 3 servings per 1 lb (450 g). Boneless breast yields 3 to 3½ servings per 1 lb (450 g).

Calories:
3½ oz (100 g) cooked meat = 136 Calories.

DRUMSTICKS

Weights:
½ to 1½ lb (227 to 675 g).

Pack:
Bulk.

Kitchen Yields

Serving size:
10 oz (100 g).
Purchase 10-oz (100-g) portions.

Calories:
10 oz raw, 3½ oz (100 g) cooked meat with skin = 200 Calories.

THIGHS

Thighs are normally available with bone in and skin on.

Weight:
½ to 1½ lb (227 to 675 g).

Pack:
Bulk.

Kitchen Yields

Serving size:
3½ oz (100 g) cooked. Bone-in thighs yield 2 to 3 servings per 1 lb (450 g).

Calories:
3½ oz (100 g) cooked meat without skin = 170 Calories.

WINGS

Weights:
¾ to 1¼ lb (337 to 560 g).

Pack:
Bulk.

Kitchen Yields

Serving size:
12 oz (100 g).
Purchase 12-oz portions.

Calories:
12 oz raw, or 3½ oz (100 g) cooked meat with skin = 200 Calories.

TURKEY PRODUCTS
BREADED TURKEY PRODUCTS

BREADED TURKEY CUTLETS
Cut from whole-muscle breast meat, breaded or batter dipped. Precooked or fried.

Weight:
3.2 oz (90 g).

Count:
Five pieces per 1 lb (450 g).

Pack:
10-lb cartons, containing 50 pieces.

Kitchen Yields
Ready-to-use product.

Serving size:
Two pieces.

BREADED TURKEY NUGGETS
Available batter-fried or breaded, fully cooked.

Weights:
½ to ¾ oz (14 to 20 g).

Pack:
8 to 12 lb (3.6 to 5.4 kg).

Count:
215 to 390.

Kitchen Yields
Ready-to-use product for buffets.

Calories:
4 oz (113 g) = 328 Calories.

BREADED TURKEY PATTIES
Ground product, shaped into patties and pre-cooked or browned.

Weights:
Five to seven pieces per 1 lb (450 g).

Pack:
48 to 72 lb (21.6 to 32.4 kg).

Kitchen Yields

Serving size:
One or two patties.

COOKED TURKEY PRODUCTS

BREAST AND THIGH
Boneless combination of natural proportions white and dark meat.

Weight:
7 to 10 lb (3.1 to 4.5 kg).

Pack:
Two to four pieces per case.

Kitchen Yields
Product is available flavored and browned. Economical, easy-to-slice white and dark meat. Shape of product varies and affects yield.

Calories:
4 oz (112 g) = 140 Calories.

FORMED BREAST
All-breast meat, made with large sections and held together with a number of extenders, including ground meat and water.

Weights:
4 to 10 lb (1.8 to 4.5 kg).

Pack:
Two to four pieces per case.

Kitchen Yields
Product is available flavored and browned. Economical, easy-to-slice all-breast meat. Shape of product varies and affects yield.

Calories:
4 oz (112 g), skinless = 125 Calories.
4 oz (112 g), skin on = 145 Calories.

PULLED OR DICED BONELESS MEAT
Frozen IQF.

Pack:
Normally, four 5-lb (2.2-kg) bags.

Kitchen Yields
Product can be used for any kind of hot turkey dish.

Serving size:
5 oz, frozen. Therefore, 5 lb (2.2 kg) yields 16 servings.

THIGH
Boneless, all-dark meat.

Weights:
4 to 10 lb (1.8 to 4.5 kg).

Pack:
Two to four pieces per case.

Kitchen Yields
Use for sandwiches.

Calories:
4 oz (112 g) = 144 Calories.

TURKEY ROLLS
Ground turkey, available as all-white meat or in combination of white and dark meat. Can include extenders, binders, and extra water.

Weights:
7 to 10 lb (3.1 to 4.5 kg).

Pack:
Two to four rolls per case.

Kitchen Yields
Least expensive turkey for sandwiches.

Calories:
4 oz (112 g) = 168 Calories.

WHOLE-MUSCLE BREAST
Boneless, fully cooked and hand-packed. Available with skin on or skinless. Up to 98 percent fat-free.

Weight:
2 to 10 lb (0.9 to 4.5 kg).

Pack:
Two to eight pieces per carton.

Kitchen Yields
Many brands are available from different packers. Product is available colored with caramel, browned, and with low salt content. Includes up to three breast muscles. This is the best-quality, but also the most expensive cooked breast.

Serving size:
2 to 4 oz (56 to 112 g) for sandwiches.

Waste:
There is about 3 percent cutting waste.

Calories:
4 oz (112 g), skinless = 125 Calories.

RAW PROCESSED TURKEY PRODUCTS

ALL-WHITE NETTED, BONELESS BREAST ROAST

Weights:
8 to 12 lb (3.6 to 5.4 kg).

Pack:
Four to six pieces per case. Weight of case varies from 48 lb (21.6 kg) down.

Kitchen Yields

Serving size:
For sandwich, 3½ oz (100 g) cooked. Boneless breast roast yields 3 to 3½ servings per 1 lb (450 g).

Calories:
3½ oz (100 g) cooked = 190 Calories.

BONELESS BREAST AND THIGH ROAST

Weights:
4 to 14 lb (1.8 to 6.3 kg).

Pack:
Two to four pieces per case.

Kitchen Yields

Serving size:
For sandwich, 3½ oz (100 g) cooked. Boneless breast and thigh roast yields 3 to 3½ servings per 1 lb (450 g). Therefore, one 8-lb (3.6-kg) roast yields 26 servings.

Calories:
3½ oz (100 g) cooked = 203 Calories.

GROUND TURKEY
Mostly dark meat.

Weight:
10 lb (4.5 kg).

Pack:
Two to four rolls.

Kitchen Yields
Ground turkey is at least 85 percent lean, but the product can contain skin. Use it for patties, meat sauce, and pizza.

Calories:
4 oz (112 g) cooked = 202 Calories.

TURKEY BREAST SLICES/CUTLETS
All boneless and skinless meat, sliced across the grain. Available frozen.

Weights:
Approximately 2 oz (56 g) each, ⅛ to ⅓ in (3 to 8 mm) thick.

Pack:
30- to 40-lb (13.5- to 18.0-kg) cases.

Kitchen Yields
Product is packed with paper or plastic film between slices. It can be breaded or flattened for roulades or turkey scallopini. There is no trimming loss.

Serving size:
Two pieces, breaded, for main course; one piece for buffet; two pieces, flattened, for scallopini. One 30-lb (13.5-kg) case yields 120 servings.

Calories:
4 oz (113 g) cooked = 176 Calories.

TURKEY TENDERLOINS
Whole muscle from inside the center of the breast.

Weights:
6 to 12 oz (170 to 340 g).

Pack:
20- to 40-lb (9- to 18-kg) cases.

Kitchen Yields
Frozen, with plastic film between layers. Cut pieces across the grain into medallions, kebabs, or stir-fry dishes. There is some cutting waste, depending on portion size.

Serving size:
4 oz (112 g).

Calories:
4 oz (112 g) cooked = 176 Calories.

TURKEY THIGH STEAKS
Boneless and skinless raw dark meat.

Weights:
3 to 4 oz (85 to 112 g).

Pack:
40 to 54 individual steaks.

Kitchen Yields
Thigh steaks can be braised, broiled, or baked.

Serving size:
One piece.

Calories:
4 oz (112 g) cooked = 232 Calories.

TURKEY DELICATESSEN ITEMS

SMOKED BREAST
Available boneless and on the frame.

Weights:
On frame:
6 to 12 lb (2.7 to 5.4 kg).

Boneless:
2 to 4 lb (0.9 to 1.8 kg).

Pack:
Two to ten pieces per case.

Kitchen Yields
Purchase bone-in breast for buffet display, boneless for slicing.

SMOKED WHOLE TURKEY
Weights:
8 to 10 lb (3.6 to 4.5 kg).
10 to 12 lb (4.5 to 5.4 kg).
12 to 14 lb (5.4 to 6.3 kg).
14 to 16 lb (6.3 to 7.2 kg).

Pack:
Four per case.

Kitchen Yields
Product is available fresh or frozen. It is best used as a display piece on buffets. If sliced meat is needed, purchase boneless breasts. Check quality carefully; some products are flavored with artificial smoke flavor and are boiled in the bag.

Serving size:
For buffet, 10 lb (4.5 kg) yields 20 servings.

TURKEY HAM
Available whole-muscle, chopped, as roll, pastrami-shaped, and as salami.

Weights:
5 lb (2.2 kg) and up.

Kitchen Yields
Ready-to-eat product, often less expensive than similar pork products. Items should be identified on menu as turkey products.

Calories:
4 oz (112 g) whole-muscle ham = 150 Calories.
4 oz (112 g) salami = 224 Calories.

WILD TURKEY

Available fresh or frozen.

Sizes:
10 to 20 lb (4.5 to 9 kg).

Kitchen Yields
1 lb (450 g) as purchased produces 35 percent usable cooked meat.

TURNIP GREENS

Turnip greens are available canned, fresh, and frozen.

CANNED TURNIP GREENS

Pack:
Six #10 cans, with a drained weight of 60 oz (1.6 kg) each.

Kitchen Yields

Serving size:
½ cup; thus, one #10 can yields 14 servings.

Calories:
½ cup (112 g) = 30 Calories.

FRESH TURNIP GREENS
Available with and without roots attached. Sometimes broccoli greens are shipped as turnip greens. Roots should be no larger than 1½ in (38 mm) across.

Pack:
By weight.

Kitchen Yields

Waste:
Trimming loss is about 25 percent by weight if some thin stews are used.

Serving size:
½ cup; thus, 1 lb (450 g) as purchased yields 2 servings.

Calories:
½ cup, or 4 oz (112 g), chopped with stems = 34 Calories.

FROZEN TURNIP GREENS
Available chopped, with or without diced turnips.

Pack:
Twelve 3-lb (1.3-kg) boxes.

Kitchen Yields

Serving size:
½ cup; one package yields 10 servings.

Calories:
½ cup, or 4 oz (112 g) chopped = 32 Calories.

TURNIPS

Season:
Fall, winter, and spring. Smaller supply in summer.

Pack:
25- and 50-lb (11.2- and 22.5-kg) bags; 43- to 47-lb (19.3- to 21.1-kg) cartons containing 24 bunches each, with greens still attached.

Counts:
Vary greatly.

Kitchen Yields
Smaller turnips are better than larger turnips. If the vegetable is not fresh, regardless of its size, it can be spongy. This reduces yield considerably.

Best size:
About 2 in (50 mm) across.

Waste:
Peeling loss is 20 percent by weight for turnips without greens.

Serving size:
½ cup, or 3 oz (84 g).

Calories:
½ cup, or 3 oz (84 g), cooked and diced = 20 Calories.

U AND V

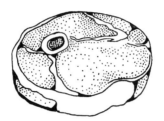

UGLI FRUIT

Ugli fruit is a juicy citrus hybrid with spotted, loose-looking skin.

Season:
Winter.

Pack:
By count.

Kitchen Yields
This fruit is slightly smaller than a grapefruit, with thick skin. Use it as if it were a grapefruit.

UNIFORM SIZES

MEN'S SIZES
Table U-1 identifies uniform measurements for male personnel. This table is a general guideline

Table U-1 Uniform Sizes for Male Personnel

Height	Weight	Chest	Coat Length	Waist	Trouser Inseam
5 ft 4 in (1.6 m)	120 lb (54 kg)	34 in (0.86 m)	27½ in (0.69 m)	36¾ in (0.93 m)	27 in (0.68 m)
	150 lb (67.5 kg)	38 in (0.96 m)	28 in (0.71 m)	37 in (0.93 m)	27 in (0.68 m)
	180 lb (81 kg)	42 in (1.06 m)	28 in (0.71 m)	37½ in (0.95 m)	27 in (0.68 m)
5 ft 6 in (1.67 m)	165 lb (74.2 kg)	40 in (1.01 m)	28½ in (0.72 m)	38 in (0.96 m)	27½ in (0.67 m)
	200 lb (90.0 kg)	44 in (1.11 m)	29 in (0.73 m)	39 in (0.99 m)	27½ in (0.69 m)
5 ft 8 in (1.72 m)	170 lb (76.5 kg)	40 in (1.01 m)	29½ in (0.75 m)	40 in (1.01 m)	29 in (0.73 m)
	185 lb (83.2 kg)	42 in (1.06 m)	30 in (0.76 m)	40½ in (1.02 m)	29 in (0.73 m)
5 ft 10 in (1.77 m)	175 lb (78.7 kg)	40 in (1.01 m)	30½ in (0.76 m)	41 in (1.04 m)	29½ in (0.75 m)
	190 lb (85.5 kg)	42 in (1.06 m)	31 in (0.78 m)	41 in (1.04 m)	29 in (0.73 m)
6 ft (1.82 m)	180 lb (81 kg)	40 in (1.01 mm)	31½ in (0.80 m)	42 in (1.06 m)	30½ in (0.76 m)
	195 lb (87.7 kg)	42 in (1.06 m)	32 in (0.81 m)	42 in (1.07 m)	30 in (0.76 m)
6 ft 2 in (1.87 m)	198 lb (89.1 kg)	42 in (1.06 m)	33 in (0.84 m)	43½ in (1.10 m)	31½ in (0.80 m)

Table U-2 Uniform Sizes for Female Personnel

Dress Size	Height	Weight (Regular)	Bust Girth	Waist Girth	Hip Girth
4	5 ft 2½ in (1.58 m)	85 to 90 lb (38.3 to 40.5 kg)	30 in (0.76 m)	23½ in (0.60 m)	33 to 34 in (0.84 to 0.86 m)
6	5 ft 3 in (1.60 m)	95 to 100 lb (42.7 to 45 kg)	31 in (0.78 m)	25 in (0.63 m)	34 to 36 in (0.86 to 0.91 m)
8	5 ft 3½ in (1.61 m)	105 to 110 lb (47.2 to 49.5 kg)	32 in (0.81 m)	25½ in (0.67 m)	35 to 37 in (0.89 to 0.94 m)
10	5 ft 4 in (1.62 m)	115 to 120 lb (51.7 to 54 kg)	33 in (0.84 m)	26½ in (0.67 m)	36 to 38 in (0.91 to 0.96 m)
12	5 ft 4½ in (1.63 m)	125 to 130 lb (56.2 to 58. 5 kg)	34½ in (0.88 m)	28 in (0.71 m)	38 to 39 in (0.96 to 0.99 m)
14	5 ft 5 in (1.65 m)	135 to 140 lb (60.7 to 63 kg)	36 in (0.91 m)	29 in (0.73 m)	39 to 41 in (0.99 to 1.04 m)
16	5 ft 5½ in (1.66 m)	150 to 155 lb (67.5 to 69.7 kg)	37 ½ in (0.95 m)	31 in (0.78 m)	41 to 42 in (0.99 to 1.06 m)
18	5 ft 6 in (1.67 m)	165 to 170 lb (74.2 to 76.5 kg)	39½ in (1.0 m)	32 to 33 in (0.81 to 0.84 m)	43 to 44 in (1.09 to 1.11 m)

for ordering uniforms. The chest size indicates the jacket size; the waist and inseam size indicates pant size. Most jacket sizes are 38, 40, 42, and 44. Most pant sizes are 37/27, 39/27, 40/29, 41/30, and 42/30.

WOMEN'S SIZES
Table U-2 identifies uniform measurements for female personnel.

VANILLA

Vanilla is available in whole vanilla pods, as pure vanilla extracts, and as vanilla powder. Imitation vanilla concentrates are also marketed.

IMITATION VANILLA CONCENTRATES
A number of imitation vanilla products are available in varying strengths, based on Vanillin, a synthetic product.

Pack:
1-qt (0.94-l) bottles; 1-gal (3.8-l) bottles. Other packs are available.

Kitchen Yields
Common dilution ratio is 1 part extract to 9 parts water.

PURE VANILLA EXTRACTS
Genuine vanilla extract must contain a minimum of 32 percent alcohol.

Pack:
1-qt (0.94-l) bottle; 1-gal (3.8-l) bottle. Other packs are available.

Kitchen Yields
Use 4 oz (0.116 l) for 5 gal (19 l) ice cream mix or for 50 lb (22.5 kg) dough.

VANILLA PODS
The quality depends on the location where they were grown and on the care exercised in curing them. The best vanilla pods come from Mexico. The Bourbon grades are grown in Madagascar and other tropical islands. The best grades are the longest beans.

Pack:
By weight. Common pack is 8 oz (227 g).

Size:
Up to 10 in (254 mm) long for best grade.

Kitchen Yields
Difficult to determine, because pods can be used a number of times until all flavor is extracted.

VANILLA POWDER
Available pure or mixed with Vanillin, with or without ground bean specks.

Pack:
By weight.

Kitchen Yields
Strength varies according to product. With common-strength pure vanilla powder, use 3 oz (85 g) for 5 gal (19 l) ice cream mix or 50 lb (22.5 kg) dough.

VEAL

Animals up to 3 months of age are classified as veal; animals between 3 months and 1 year are classified as calves. For foodservice, veal is more likely to be specified, except in the case of liver, which comes from calves; veal liver is too small for commercial use.

Veal is normally not graded by the USDA. Some veal is raised and marketed with proprietary names, such as Plume de Veau and Provini. The animals are heavy, but have light-colored meat. Nature veal is an industry term for heavy veal with light meat.

LARGER CUTS OF VEALS
When purchasing, make sure to specify veal, because some cuts are available in veal and calf weight ranges. Veal has soft, almost white meat; calf has redder and coarser meat. The *Meat Buyers Guide* (MBG) specification numbers are used to further identify the cuts.

BACK, MBG #341
Whole back with nine ribs, trimmed.

Weight ranges:
10 to 30 lb (4.5 to 13.5 kg).

Kitchen Yields
Use for buffet display.

Recommended weight:
18 lb (8.1 kg).

Serving quantities:
On buffet, one back yields 50 servings.

BONES
Bones from the neck and loin are soft and render flavor; knuckle bones provide gelatin for stocks and sauces.

Pack:
By weight.

Kitchen Yields
50 lb (22.5 kg) veal bones flavors 10 gal (38 l) brown stock.
Judging the strength of stock is subjective. The preceding proportions are for good-quality stock.

BRAINS
Brains should only be purchased fresh, because the skin and membranes are difficult to remove from frozen brains.

Pack:
½ lb (224 g) per piece, in trays; 16 pieces per 10-lb (4.5-kg) box, with four boxes per carton. Also available by weight.

Kitchen Yields
Soak in lukewarm water to remove skin.

Average size:
½ lb (224 g) per piece.

Usable meat:
12 to 13 oz (340 to 370 g) per 1 lb (450 g).

BREAST, MBG #313

Weight ranges:
3 to 6 lb (1.3 to 2.7 kg).
6 to 8 lb (2.7 to 3.6 kg).
8 to 10 lb (3.6 to 4.5 kg).
10 to 12 lb (4.5 to 5.4 kg).

Kitchen Yields

Best use:
Bone and stuff, bone and roll, or braise with bones in.

ROLLED BREAST, BONELESS:

Recommended size:
10 lb (4.5 kg).

Bones:
24 oz (670 g).

Trim, fat:
8 oz (224 g).

Breast, ready to roast:
8 lb (3.6 kg).

Weight after roasting:
5 lb 10 oz (2.5 kg).

Serving size:
Twelve 7-oz (200-g) servings.

STUFFED BREAST

Recommended size:
10 lb (4.5 kg).

Bones:
24 oz (670 g).

Trim, fat:
8 oz (224 g).

Breast, ready to stuff:
8 lb (3.6 kg).

Stuffing:
3 lb (1.3 kg).

Breast, ready to roast:
11 lb (5 kg).

Weight after roasting:
8 lb 5 oz (3.7 kg).

Serving size:
Fifteen to sixteen 8-oz (224-g) servings.

CHUCK, BONELESS, MBG #309B
Economic piece for cutting stew meat.

Weight range:
For whole or double chuck, 12 to 40 lb (5.4 to 18 kg).

Kitchen Yields

Trimming waste:
8 percent.
1 lb (450 g) produces 10 oz (280 g) cooked meat.

Serving size:
6 oz (170 g) cooked meat. Thus, 20 lb (9 kg) yield 30 servings.

CHUCK ROLL, TRIMMED

Size:
3 to 4½ lb (1.3 to 2 kg).

Pack:
By weight. One purveyor offers cases of five 4½-lb (2-kg) pieces.

Kitchen Yields
1 lb (450 g) as purchased produces 12 oz (336 g) cooked meat.

Serving size:
5 oz (140 g) cooked. One 4½-lb (2-kg) chuck roll yields 14 servings.

Calories:
5 oz (140 g) cooked = 380 Calories.

HEART

Average size:
1 to 2 lb (0.45 to 0.9 kg) per piece.

Pack:
By weight and piece. One purveyor offers 50-lb (22.2-kg) boxes, containing twenty-five to thirty 2-lb (0.9-kg) pieces.

Kitchen Yields
Braise to boil. Remove the thin fatty top after cooking.

Serving size:
5 oz (140 g) cooked; one 1-lb heart yields 2½ servings.

Calories:
5 oz (140 g) cooked = 262 Calories.

HIND SHANK

Weight ranges:
1 to 4½ lb (0.45 to 2 kg).

Pack:
One purveyor offers 55-lb (24.7-kg) boxes of fifteen 3½-lb (1.5-kg) trimmed shanks.

Kitchen Yields
When purchasing, specify hock bone cut off. For osso buco, purchase 4½-lb (2-kg) or larger shanks, and cut each shank into four pieces. For roasting whole, purchase 3-lb (1.3-kg) shanks.

Serving size:
For osso buco, two pieces; for whole roasted shanks, one-half shank.

KIDNEYS
Available with fat on or peeled and with fat removed. Most purveyors sell peeled kidneys only.

Size:
½ to ¾ lb (226 to 340 g) peeled.

Pack:
By piece and weight. One purveyor offers boxes of fourteen ¾-lb (340-g) kidneys.

Kitchen Yields

Waste:
Trimming loss from peeled kidney is 5 percent. Purchase 10- to 12-oz (280- to 340-g) kidneys.

Serving size:
6 oz (170 g).

LEG, MBG #334
Legs are normally sold whole, bone in, in pairs. When a number of single legs are purchased, make sure that only every other leg has the tail still attached. Tails weigh about 8 to 10 oz (227 to 280 g).

Weight ranges:

For single legs:
12 to 20 lb (5.4 to 9 kg).
20 to 28 lb (9 to 12.6 kg).
28 to 35 lb (12.6 to 15.7 kg).
35 to 45 lb (15.7 to 20.5 kg).

Kitchen Yields
For boning and cutting into scallopini or cutlets, purchase the largest legs. For roasting whole, purchase smaller legs.

Recommended size:
For boning, 45 lb (20.5 kg).
The following are approximate weights of pieces, bones, and scrap from one 42-lb 12-oz (19.2-kg) leg, best quality:

Clean, ready-to-cut meat, fully trimmed:
6 lb 6 oz (2.8 kg)—15 percent.

Clean meat, good quality:
7 lb (3.1 kg)—16 percent.

Stew meat, second quality:
4 lb 5 oz (1.9 kg)—10 percent.

Scraps, usable for stock:
6 lb 10 oz (3 kg)—16 percent.

Fat:
6 lb 6 oz (2.8 kg)—15 percent.

Bones:
8 lb 9 oz (4 kg)—20 percent.

Shank:
3 lb 8 oz (1.5 kg)—8 percent.
Common uses for veal leg include scallopini, breaded cutlets, roast veal, stew, and veal strips sauté.

- *Scallopini*

  Serving size:
  Three 6-oz (170-g) pieces. The above leg yields 37 servings, providing all clean meat is used.

- *Breaded Cutlets*

  Serving size:
  5 oz (140 g). The above leg yields about 36 servings cutlets, and six scallopini servings.

Calories:
Scallopini, 6 oz (170 g), raw weight = 370 Calories.

LEG, BONELESS, SHANK OFF, MBG #336

Weight range:
7 to 23 lb (3.1 to 10.3 kg).

Kitchen Yields
Good piece for roasting whole.

Recommended size:
12 lb (5.4 kg).

Serving size:
4 oz (117 g) cooked.

Cooking loss:
1 lb (450 g) reduces to 13 oz (370 g) cooked meat.
Therefore, one 12-lb (5.4-kg) boneless leg, yields
20 to 22 main-course servings, 25 banquet servings
(if cut on machine), or 30 buffet servings.

LIVER (CALF'S LIVER)
On the New York market, the term *kosher calf
liver* is used to indicate freshness, although the
liver might not be certified kosher. The livers
should be light in color and fresh. They may come
from heavy veal or from small calves.

Weight ranges:
2½ to 7 lb (1.1 to 3.1 kg).

Pack:
By the piece and by weight. One purveyor offers
55- to 56-lb (24.7- to 25.2-kg) cases of eight 7-lb
(3.1-kg) whole livers.

Kitchen Yields
The liver must be skinned. There is a small flap,
and some trimming waste, which can be used in
pâté or as julienne of liver sauté.

Best size:
3 to 3½ lb (1.3 to 1.6 kg).

Serving size:
5 to 6 oz (142 to 170 g) in two slices; thus, one 3-lb
(1.3-kg) liver yields 7 servings.

Calories:
5 oz (140 g) raw = 210 Calories.

LOIN, WHOLE, MBG #231
Whole loin, with two ribs, kidneys, and tenderloins.
The same piece trimmed to 4-in (102-mm) flank,
with kidneys removed, is called MBG #332. The
same piece is also available boneless and rolled.
The loin is the best part of the animal and is very
expensive.

Weight ranges:
6 to 10 lb (2.7 to 4.5 kg).
10 to 14 lb (4.5 to 6.3 kg).
14 to 18 lb (6.3 to 8.1 kg).
18 to 23 lb (8.1 to 10.3 kg).

Kitchen Yields

Recommended size:
22 lb (9.9 kg). One 22-lb (9.9-kg) consists of 7 lb
(3.1 kg) usable meat.
Common uses of veal loins include loin chops,
medallions, scallopini, and roasted and split loins.

   • *Boneless Loin Chop*

Serving size:
One 6½-oz (180-g) piece per serving; thus,
one 22-lb (9.9-kg) loin yields 16 servings.

   • *Medallion (Completely Skinned)*

Serving size:
One 5-oz (112-g) piece; thus, one 22-lb
(9.9-kg) loin yields 16 servings.

   • *Scallopini*

Serving size:
5½ oz (154 g); thus, one 22-lb (9.9-kg) loin
yields 17 servings.

   • *Roasted and Split Loin*

Serving size:
5 oz cooked meat; thus, one 22-lb (9.9-kg)
loin yields 8 to 9 servings from each side.

Recommended size for roasted whole loin, presented cold on buffet, is 14 to 18 lb (6.3 to 8.1 kg).
This size yields approximately 30 servings.

LOIN, BONELESS
Cap-on, 1-in (25-mm) flank.

Weight range:
3¼ to 4 lb (1.5 to 1.8 kg).

Pack:
One purveyor offers sixteen 3¼-lb (1.5-kg) loins in
a 51-lb (23-kg) master carton.

Kitchen Yields
This is a boneless, well-trimmed piece of meat. It
can be cut into boneless chops without additional
trimming.

LOIN, BONELESS, TRIMMED

Weight range:
6 to 9 lbs (2.7 to 4 kg).

Pack:
One purveyor offers seven 8-lb (3.6-kg) loins in a 56-lb (25.2-kg) master carton.

Kitchen Yields
Refer to yields for whole loins.

LOIN, TRIMMED TO SILVER SKIN

Weight range:
2½ to 3 lb (1.1 to 1.3 kg).

Pack:
One purveyor offers sixteen 2¾-lb (1.2-kg) loins in a 45-lb (20-kg) carton.

Kitchen Yields
Completely trimmed loin with no waste factor.

NECK, BONELESS

Weight range:
9 to 11 lb (4 to 4.9 kg).

Kitchen Yields
Good piece for cutting stew meat.

Trimming waste:
5 percent.

Cooking loss:
1 lb (450 g) stew meat reduces to 11 oz (308 g) cooked meat.

Serving sizes:
8 oz (224 g) raw meat or 5½ oz (154 g) cooked meat, for main course; 5 oz (140 g) raw meat or 3½ oz (100 g) cooked meat, for buffet. Thus, 10 lb (4.5 kg) raw stew meat yield 20 main-course servings or 30 buffet servings.

RACK, MBG #306
Racks with seven ribs are standard.

Weight range:
5 to 20 lb (2.2 to 9.0 kg).

Kitchen Yields
The piece provides very low yield on account of the bone structure it contains. The proportion of usable meat to bone is better in larger pieces. However, chops cut from 16-lb (7.2-kg) and larger racks are very heavy due to the large rib bone.

Recommended size:
16 to 18 lb (7.2 to 8.1 kg).

Breakdown of one 19-lb 4-oz (8.6-kg) rack:

Fat:
1 lb 8 oz (0.6 kg) — 8 percent.

Bones:
4 lb 4 oz (1.9 kg) — 22 percent.

Scraps:
2 lb 8 oz (1.1 kg) — 13 percent.

Stew meat:
3 lb 8 oz (1.5 kg) — 18 percent.

Rack, two pieces, frenched (with rib bones):
7 lb 8 oz (3.3 kg) — 39 percent.

Serving sizes:

Rib chop, bone in:
9 oz (252 g).
The above rack yields ten rib chops and two 6-oz (170-g) servings scallopini.

Roast rack of veal:
7½ oz (210 g) including rib bone. The above rack yields 12 servings.

RIB-EYE
New way of cutting the carcass. This piece is available from at least one packer.

Size:
3 lb (1.3 kg).

Pack:
Ten 3-lb (1.3-kg) pieces in 30-lb (13.5-kg) cartons.

Kitchen Yields
The piece is boneless and well-trimmed. It can be cut into boneless steaks, or it can be roasted whole.

RIBLETS

Pack:
40-lb (18-kg) case.

Count:
Varies; about four pieces to the 1 lb (450 g).

Kitchen Yields
Short-cut riblets, ready to use.

Serving size:
12 to 16 oz (340 to 450 g) raw weight.

SCOTCH TENDER
Fully trimmed piece from the shoulder.

Size:
1-lb (450-g) piece, vacuum-packed.

Pack:
Sixty 1-lb (450-g) pieces in a 60-lb (27-kg) box.

Kitchen Yields
Relatively new and convenient piece. It can be used for roasting or braising whole, or it can be cut for stew. The piece is very practical for banquet or buffet use.

Cooking loss:
1 lb (450 g) roasted whole reduces to 11 oz (312 g) cooked meat.

SHOULDER, BONE-IN
The shoulder is cut from the chuck. The best part is the clod, which can be rolled and tied for a roast.

Weight:
16 to 20 lb (7.2 to 9 kg).

Kitchen Yields
Use for stew meat or for roast clod.

Recommended weight:
18 lb (8.1 kg).

Weight of parts:

Usable meat, including shank, cubed:
9 lb 12 oz (4.3 kg).

Scraps and bones:
8 lb 4 oz (3.6 kg).

Cooking loss:
1 lb (450 g) stew meat reduces to 11 oz (312 g) cooked meat.

Serving sizes:
8 oz (224 g) raw meat or 5½ oz (154 g) cooked meat, for main course; 5 oz (140 g) raw meat or

3½ oz (100 g) cooked meat, for buffet. Therefore, 10 lb (4.5 kg) raw stew meat yield 20 main-course servings or 30 buffet servings.

SHOULDER CLOD, BONELESS, MBG #310

Weight ranges:
4 to 9 lb (1.8 to 4 kg). Fully trimmed pieces weigh 3 to 4 lb (1.3 to 1.8 kg).

Pack:
By piece and weight. One purveyor offers five 4-lb (1.8-kg) pieces in 20-lb (9-kg) boxes.

Kitchen Yields

Serving size:
5 oz (140 g) cooked meat; thus, one 4-lb (1.8-kg) piece yields 8 servings.

STEW MEAT
Purchase by weight.

Kitchen Yields
Refer to Neck or Shoulder under this same heading for yield information.

SWEETBREADS
Make sure to specify veal sweetbreads, because calf's sweetbreads can be very tough. Specify fresh when possible. Veal sweetbreads are lighter in color than calf's sweetbreads.

Pack:
By weight; usually 5-lb (2.2-kg) baskets or 40-lb (18-kg) boxes.

Size:
1 lb (4.5 g) average, per pair.

Kitchen Yields
Sweetbread pairs consist of two uneven parts. They are often sold separated.

Trimming waste:
10 percent by weight.

Cooking loss:
10 percent by weight.

Serving size:
7 oz (226 g) cooked, as main course; thus, 5 lb (2.2 kg) sweetbreads yield 9 servings.

TENDERLOINS
Short, fully trimmed tenderloins.

Size:
½ lb (224 g) each.

Pack:
Sixty-four ½-lb (224-g) pieces in a 37-lb (16.6-kg) master carton.

Kitchen Yields
Very tender pieces. Best use is for scallopini or for breaded cutlets.

TONGUE

Size:
1 to 1½ lb (450 to 675 g).

Pack:
By piece and by weight. One purveyor offers thirty-two pieces in a 40-lb (18-kg) case.

Kitchen Yields

Cooking loss:
1 lb (450 g) as purchased reduces to 10 oz (280 g) cooked, peeled, and trimmed.

TOP ROUND, FULLY TRIMMED

Pack:
Eight 4½-lb (2-kg) pieces in a 37-lb (16.6-kg) master case.

Kitchen Yields
Meat can be cut into cutlets or scallopini. There is little trimming waste. For portion sizes, refer to Leg, MBG #334, under this same heading.

PORTION CUTS OF VEAL

CUBED STEAKS
Boneless slices that have been mechanically tenderized. The meat can be dry.

Sizes:
3, 4, 5, 6, and 8 oz (85, 112, 140, 170, and 224 g).

Kitchen Yields
Best use is breaded.

Serving size:
4 oz (112 g) lunch size, when breaded.

CUTLETS
Boneless slices made from leg meat only. The meat may be cut against or with the grain. Slices must be pounded before use in order for meat to be sufficiently tender.

Sizes:
2, 3, 4, 5, and 6 oz (85, 112, 140, and 170 g).

Pack:
256 pieces of 2 oz (56 g) each in four 8-lb (3.6-kg) boxes; 170 pieces of 3 oz (85 g) each in four 8-lb (3.6-kg) boxes; 128 pieces of 4 oz (112 g) each in four 8-lb (3.6-kg) boxes.

Kitchen Yields
Meat can be tough and dry on account of the loss of juices after thawing. Best use is breaded, but the product can also be used as veal marsala or for scallopini.

Serving sizes:
One 4-oz (112-g) slice, cut in half, for reception; one 5-oz slice for braised roulade.

GROUND PATTIES
Available in different sizes. Low cholesterol substitute for beef hamburger patties. Available plain and breaded.

PLAIN PATTIES

Sizes:
3 oz (85 g); 4 oz (112 g).

Packs:
170 pieces of 3 oz (85 g) each in four 8-lb (3.6-kg) boxes; 128 pieces of 4 oz (112 g) each in four 8-lb (3.6-kg) boxes.

BREADED PATTIES

Size:
4 oz (112 g).

Pack:
128 pieces of 4 oz (112 g) each in four 8-lb (3.6-kg) boxes.

LIVER (CALF'S LIVER)
Calf's liver is available sliced. Not to be confused with baby beef liver.

Weights:
3- and 4-oz (85- and 112-g) slices.

Pack:
170 pieces of 3 oz (85 g) each in four 8-lb (3.6-kg) boxes; 128 pieces of 4 oz (112 g) each in four 8-lb (3.6-kg) boxes.

LOIN CHOPS
Cut from the loin, with bones still attached. Up to 3 in (75 mm) of flank can be left on.

Sizes:
3, 4, 5, 6, 8, and 10 oz (85, 112, 140, 170, 224, and 280 g).

Kitchen Yields
This piece is rather expensive and is best used as a dinner item.

Serving size:
One 8- or 10-oz (224- and 280-g) piece; two 5-oz (140-g) pieces.

OSSO BUCO
Cut veal shank; available precut.

Weights:
6- to 8-oz (170- to 224-g) pieces.

Pack:
Four 10-lb (4.5-g) cartons.

Count:
80 to 90 pieces.

RIB CHOPS
Cut from the rack. All bones are still attached, but the blade is removed.

Sizes:
3, 4, 5, 6, 8, and 10 oz (85, 112, 140, 170, 224, and 280 g).

Pack:
Varies, depending on size and packer.

Kitchen Yields
This item is rather expensive and is best used as a dinner item.

Serving size:
8 or 10 oz (224 and 180 g).

SHOULDER CHOPS
Cut from the chuck, with bones still in.

Sizes:
3, 4, 5, 6, 8, and 10 oz (85, 112, 140, 170, 224, and 280 g).

Kitchen Yields
Best used for braising. Shoulder chops make a good lunch item.

Serving size:
6 oz (170 g).

YIELDS OF POPULAR VEAL DISHES

FRICASSEE
Use high-quality stew meat from the shoulder.

Kitchen Yields

Serving size:
7 oz raw meat for lunch.

LOIN ROAST
Loin roast can be stuffed with any stuffing or with kidneys; the latter type of presentation is called *rognonnade* in French. It can be made with loin halves, flank still attached, or with the whole, small loin.

Kitchen Yields

Best sizes:

Half loin roast:
4 lb (1.8 kg) boneless, oven-ready meat plus stuffing. This size yields 10 servings.

Full loin roast:
7 lb (3.1 kg) boneless, oven-ready meat plus stuffing. This size yields 16 servings.

OSSO BUCO
Purchase large shanks of about 4 lb (1.8 kg) each. Cut the center of the shank into four pieces. There will be about 1½ lb (680 g) bone without meat left over.

Kitchen Yields

Serving size:
Two 8- to 10-oz (224- to 280-g) pieces.

PAILLARD
Very thin, pounded cutlet, grilled or sautéed to order. Use best-quality leg meat.

Kitchen Yields

Serving size:
5 oz (140 g).

PICCATA
Veal scallopini served with lemon juice and sliced lemon.

Kitchen Yields

Serving size:
Three pieces per serving, with a total weight of 6 oz (170 g). One 45-lb (20.2-kg) leg yields 40 servings scallopini.

ROASTED VEAL SHANKS (HAXEN)
Haxen is the German word for whole roasted shanks. Use 3-lb (1.3-kg) shanks, trimmed.

Kitchen Yields

Serving size:
One-half shank.

ROGNONNADE
See Loin Roast, under this same heading.

ROLLATINE
Italian name for stuffed, rolled cutlet. It is often sliced for service. Use thin cutlets.

SALTIMBOCCA ALLA ROMANA
Veal scallopini with prosciutto and sage.

Kitchen Yields

Serving size:
Three 2-oz (56-g) pieces, plus 1 oz (28 g) prosciutto sliced into three pieces.

SCALLOPINI
Scallopini, cut from leg.

Kitchen Yields

Serving size:
Three 2-oz (56-g) pieces.

VEAL BIRDS
Rolled, stuffed, and braised cutlets. Cubed cutlet can be used.

Kitchen Yields

Serving sizes:
For main course, 6 oz (170 g) meat plus 1 oz (28 g) stuffing; for buffet, 3 oz (84 g) meat plus ½ oz (14 g) stuffing.

VEAL MARSALA
Scallopini flavored with marsala wine.

VEAL OSCAR
Veal cutlet topped with asparagus, crab meat, and Hollandaise sauce.

Kitchen Yields

Serving size:
6 oz (170 g) boneless cutlet, plus 1 oz crab meat, plus 3 asparagus tips.

VITELLO TONNATO
Cold veal roast covered with cold tuna-based sauce. Any roast can be used. Tonnato sauce formula is given elsewhere; see Sauces.

Kitchen Yields

Serving size:
For main course, 4 oz (112 g) cooked roast, sliced thin, with 3 oz (0.17 l) sauce.

WIENER SCHNITZEL
German name for boneless breaded cutlet.

Kitchen Yields

Serving sizes:
4 oz (112 g) for lunch; 5 oz (140 g) for dinner.

VENISON

Available fresh, frozen, or smoked, domestic and imported.

FRESH OR FROZEN VENISON

Pack:

Whole animal, hide on:
80 to 180 lb (36 to 81 kg).

Hind leg, shank cut short:
16 to 25 lb (7.2 to 11.2 kg).

Saddles:
10 lb to 14 lb (4.5 to 6.3 kg).

Boneless stew meat:
10-lb (4.5-kg) bags.
Also available are fully trimmed hind leg and shoulder cuts.

Kitchen Yields

• *Leg*

Best size:
16 to 18 lb (7.2 to 8.1 kg); this yields 14 to 16 servings when roasted medium, or 12 to 14 servings when braised.

• *Rack*

Best size:
12 lb (5.4 kg); this yields 20 servings of two 2½-oz (70-g) boneless filet steaks or 16 servings roasted whole, on the bone.

SMOKED VENISON LEG

Available as a specialty item. Serve sliced very thin, like prosciutto ham.

VIANDE DE GRISON

See Buendnerfleisch, under Beef, Smoked and Cured.

VESIGA

Gelatinous sturgeon marrow; available dried and frozen.

Pack:
By weight.

Kitchen Yields

Use in soups and in coulibiac (baked salmon loaf). Soak and boil.
3 oz (85 g) dried vesiga produce 15 oz (420 g) cooked vesiga.
NOTE: Soak dried vesiga for at least 5 hours.

W, Y, AND Z

WAFFLE BATTER

Formula
30 eggs
1½ lb (0.675 g) sugar
8 lb (3.6 kg) cake flour
2½ lb (1.1 kg) melted shortening
5 qt (4.7 l) milk
2 oz (56 g) salt
8 oz (226 g) baking powder
Vanilla flavor to taste

Kitchen Yields

Serving size:
For 7-in (177-mm) waffles, 5 oz (0.29 kg) batter.
The preceding formula produces a total yield of
75 servings.

Calories:
1 waffle = 324 Calories.
Batter will get stiff if stored in refrigerator. It can
be diluted with milk. Additional baking powder
must be added if batter is diluted and stored for
longer than 24 hours.

WALNUTS

Available in shell and shelled. Shelled walnuts are
sold as halves and as pieces.

Pack:
By weight.

Kitchen Yields

1 cup halves consists of 60 pieces.
1 cup chopped weighs 4½ oz (126 g).
1 cup ground weighs 3½ oz (100 g).

Calories:
1 cup, or 4½ oz (126 g) chopped = 790 Calories.
1 cup, or 3½ oz (100 g) ground = 620 Calories.

WATER CHESTNUTS

Water chestnuts are available canned, fresh, and
as flour. In oriental cooking, several different
varieties are clearly distinguished. Fresh water
chestnuts are available only in ethnic markets.
The canned product is the accepted foodservice
standard.

CANNED WATER CHESTNUTS
Available sliced or whole.

Pack:

Whole:
Six #10 cans; twenty-four 10½-oz (300-g) cans.
There is no count.

Sliced:
Six #10 cans.
Other packs are available.

Kitchen Yields
One #10 can whole nuts weighs 35 oz (1 kg)
drained.
One 10½-oz (300-g) can whole nuts weighs 5 oz
(140 g) drained.
One #10 can sliced nuts weighs 40 oz (1.1 kg)
drained.

FRESH WATER CHESTNUTS
Brown bulbs with white interior.

Season:
Available year-round.

Pack:
10-lb lugs.

Size:
1 to 2 in (25 to 50 mm) across.

Kitchen Yields

Cleaning waste:
30 percent, by weight.

WATERCRESS

See Salad Greens.

WATER ICE

See Granite.

WATERMELON

See Melons.

WATER WEIGHTS

1 cup, or 8 fl oz (0.235 l) weighs 8.39 oz (0.235 kg).
1 pint, or 16 fl oz (0.47 l) weighs 16.78 oz (470 g).
1 qt, or 32 fl oz (0.94 l) weighs 33.57 oz (940 g).
1 gal, or 128 fl oz (3.8 l) weighs 135.71 oz (3.8 kg).

¼ l, or 8.5 fl oz weighs 8.9 oz (250 g).
½ l, or 17 fl oz weighs 17.85 oz (500 g).
1 l, or 34 fl. oz weighs 35.7 oz (1000 g).

WHEAT CAKES

See Griddle Cakes.

WEIGHT AND VOLUME EQUIVALENTS

WEIGHT EQUIVALENTS
Table W-1 lists common avoirdupois and metric weight equivalents.

VOLUME EQUIVALENTS
Table W-2 lists conversion factors for volume equivalents.

WHITE SAPOTA

Known also as *custard apple,* this tropical fruit can be eaten raw, or cooked. The skin is edible and should be light yellow when mature.

Season:
April to November.

Table W-1 Weight Equivalents

Avoirdupois Weight	Metric Equivalent
1 lb (16 oz)	453.6 g
1 oz	28.35 g
3½ oz	100.00 g
35.27 oz	1 kg (1,000 g)

Pack:
10-lb (4.5-kg) flats.

Count:
Varies. Average is the size of a large orange.

WILD BOAR

See Boar.

WILD RICE

Water grass seeds, still growing wild in Minnesota, Wisconsin, California, and Canada. The quality is determined by the number of broken kernels per 1 lb (450 g) and by the size of the kernels. Uniform kernel size is important, to ensure even cooking. There are no industry standards concerning kernel size or percentage of broken to whole kernels. The terms long grain, medium, and cracked blends are general references which can vary among shippers. Precooked wild rice has become available.

Table W-2 Volume Equivalents

Level Measure	Equivalent
1 gal (3.786 l)	4 qt (8 pints)
1 qt (0.946 l)	4 cups (2 pints)
1 pint (0.473 l)	2 cups (16 fl oz)
1 cup (0.237 l)	8 fl oz (½ pint, or 16 tb)
2 tb (0.028 ml)	1 fl oz
1 tb (0.015 ml)	3 tsp
1 l	1.05 qt (33.9 fl oz)
1 l	4 cups + 2 tb

Pack:
100-lb (45-kg) bags or boxes; 25-lb (11.3-kg) pails; six 5-lb (2.3-kg) boxes or tins; 1-lb (450-g) boxes or tins. Other packs are available.

Kitchen Yields
NOTE: The terms used below refer to 100 per cent wild rice and not to wild rice and brown rice blends. Long Grain blends require three times their own volume in liquid. Cooking time is 60 minutes. Medium grain blends and cracked blends require two and one-half times their own volume in liquid. Cooking time is 50 minutes. Yield is increased if product is soaked overnight. Soaking water should be used in cooking to preserve nutrients.

Serving size:
½ cup (0.11 l) cooked; 1 lb (450 g) produces 10 cups cooked product.

Calories:
½ cup, or 3 oz (85 g) cooked = 73 Calories.

WILD TURKEY

See Turkey.

WINE

Calories:
4 oz (0.11 l) dry wine = 100 Calories.
4 oz (0.11 l) sweet wine = 160 Calories.

WONTON WRAPPERS

See Chinese Foods.

Y

YAMS

See Sweet Potatoes and Yams.

YEAST

Yeast is available dry and fresh.
½ oz (14 g) fresh yeast is equivalent to 1 envelope dry yeast.
1 oz (28 g) fresh yeast is equivalent to 2 envelopes dry yeast.
Fresh yeast weighs twice as much as dry yeast; 1 lb (450 g) fresh yeast is equivalent to 8 oz (224 g) dry yeast.

Proofing Temperatures
Sweet dough: 95° to 98°F; humidity of 80% percent.

Bread dough: 80° to 82°F; humidity of 80% percent.
NOTE: Yeast dies at 138°F.

YOGURT
Fermented milk product available with varying fat content and with different fruit flavors.

Pack:
8-oz (224-g) and 16-oz (448-g) packages. Other packs are available.

Kitchen Yields

Serving size:
8 oz (224 g). Foodservice operators should only purchase individual 8-oz servings, which should then be served in the original container.

Calories:
8 oz (224 g) plain and fat-free = 110 Calories.
NOTE: Calorie count depends on fat content and fruit or flavor additives. Refer to package label for additional information.

YUCCA ROOT

A starchy root used in Central and South America. There are many varieties.

Season:
Available year-round.

Pack:
By weight.

Kitchen Yields

Peeling loss:
25 percent, by weight.

Z

ZUCCHINI

See Squash.

CREDITS

Abigail Kirsch Culinary Productions; Bedford, New York

Alaska Seafood Marketing Institute

Amendola, Joseph, *The Bakers Manual* (New York: Ahrens Publishing, 1960)

American Agri-Mushroom Business Enterprises; New York City

American Dairy Association

American Lamb Council

American Mushroom Institute

Apollo Foods, Inc.; Cleveland, Ohio

Bartolotta, A. C., Research Chef, Sexton & Co.; Elk Cove Village, Illinois

Batter Bake; Parsippany, New Jersey

Beatrice/Hunt Wesson, Inc.; Fullerton, California

Belgian Endive Marketing Board

Berelson Company; San Francisco, California

Berliner & Marx, Inc.

Blue Anchor, Inc., Seafood

Blue Diamond Almond Growers; Sacramento, California

Bruce Church, Inc., Produce

Bud of California

Bush Agricultural Resources; Jonesboro, Arkansas

Bush Brothers and Company; Dandridge, Tennessee

Butler, Kevin, Director of Purchasing, Hilton Hotels Corp.; New York City

Calavo Growers of California

California Apricot Advisory Board

California Artichoke Advisory Board

California Avocado Commission

California Fresh Market Tomato Advisory Board

California Iceberg Lettuce Commission

California Kiwi Fruit Commission

California Olive Industry; Fresno, California

California Pistachio Commission

California Prune Board

California Raisin Advisory Board

California Strawberry Advisory Board

California Table Grape Commission

California Tree Fruit Agreement

Carrer, Michael, Executive Chef, Helmsley Hotel, New York City

Carr's Classic Game

Castle and Cooke Foods

Castroville Artichoke People

Caviarteria, Inc.; New York City

Certified Angus Beef

Chiquita Brands, Inc.

Coco Lopez, USA; Columbus, Ohio

Consolidated Wild Rice Co.

Corrin Produce Sales, Inc.

Country Skillet Catfish Co.

Culinary Institute of America, *The Professional Chef* (Boston: CBI, 1979)

Czimer Foods, Inc.; Lockport, Illinois

Dahlen, Martha, and Phillipps, Karin, *A Popular Guide to Chinese Vegetables* (New York: Crown Publishers, 1983)

D'Artagnan, Inc.; Jersey City, New Jersey

Del Monte Fresh Fruit Co.

Dionne, René, Director of Purchasing, Johnson & Wales University; Providence, Rhode Island

Doherty, John, Executive Chef, The Waldorf Astoria; New York City

Dutch Valley Veal; South Holland, Illinois

Egg Nutrition Center; Washington, D.C.

Enfant Riant Escargots; Petaluma, California

Erman, Kurt, retired Executive Chef, The Waldorf Astoria; New York City

Fink Baking Corp.; Long Island City, New York

Fishery Products, Inc.; St. John's, Newfoundland, Canada

FLAV-R-PAC Frozen Foods

Florida Avocado Administrative Committee

Florida Celery Exchange

Florida Department of Citrus

Florida Lime and Avocado Administrative Committee

Florida Tomato Exchange

Food and Wines from France; New York City

Freshco, Inc.

Fresh Produce Foodservice Directory (Shawnee Mission, Kansas: Vance Publishing)

Fresh Western Marketing

Frieda's Finest/Produce

Friedrich, Frank, retired Chef Gardemanger, The Waldorf Astoria; New York City

Frionor Norwegian Frozen Fish, Ltd.; New Bedford, Massachusetts

Gamekeeper's Choice; Laburnum, Victoria, Australia

General Foods Corp.; White Plains, New York

Gilroy Farms, McCormick & Co., Inc.

Golden Dipt Co.; St. Louis, Missouri

Gourmet Fresh; Kennewick, Washington

Hazelnut Marketing Board; Tigard, Oregon

Idaho Potato Commission

International Apple Institute

Irongate Products Co.; New York City

Jac Creative Foods, Inc.; Los Angeles, California

J. R. Simplot Company

Kaufco Sales; West Nyack, New York

Kellogg's; Battle Creek, Michigan

King and Prince Seafood Corporation; Brunswick, Georgia

Kitchen Ready Foods; Great Neck, New York

Koegler, Jean, Executive Chef, Canteen Company, New York City

Kona Coffee Council

Kotschevar, Lendal H., *Quantity Food Purchasing* (New York: John Wiley & Sons, 1970)

Kronos Gyro Products; Astoria, New York

Lamb Weston; Portland, Oregon

Landreth Wild Rice Co.; San Antonio, Texas

Larsen Co.; Green Bay, Wisconsin

Levie, Albert, *The Meat Handbook* (Westport, Conn.: AVI Publishing, 1967)

Liberty Ramsey Imports; Carlstadt, New Jersey

Lo Presto, Butcher; New York City

Louisiana Crawfish Promotion and Research Board

Mann Packing Company, Inc.

Maple Leaf Farms; Milford, Indiana

Mash's, Inc., Meat Company

McQuail; Miami, Florida

Meat Buyers Guide, National Association of Meat Purveyors (Tucson, Ariz.: 1980)

Metropolis, George, Pastry Chef and Instructor, retired, Culinary Institute of America, Hyde Park, N.Y.

Michigan Apple Committee

Michigan Bean Commission

Michigan Blueberry Growers Association

Michigan Marketing Association

Michigan Plum Advisory Board

Mitsui Foods, Inc.; Hackensack, New Jersey

Muscovy Grove Duck Farm

Nabisco Brands, Inc.

National Association of Meat Purveyors, *Meat Buyers Guide* (Tucson, Ariz.: 1980)

National Onion Association; Greeley, Colorado

National Peach Council

National Pecan Marketing Council

National Pork Producers Council

National Restaurant Association, *Fresh Fruits Technical Bulletin*

National Turkey Federation; Reston, Virginia

New York Times; New York City

New Zealand Farm-Raised Venison Council

New Zealand Fishing Industry Board

New Zealand Kiwifruit Authority

New Zealand Lamb Company; Elmsford, New York

Nicolas, Jean, *American Fish and Shellfish* (Boston: CBI, 1981)

Noeth, Guenther, Banquet Service Director, Hotel Pierre; New York City

North American Blueberry Council

North Carolina Yam Commission, Inc.

North Star Foods, Inc.

North West Cherries; Yakima, Washington

Nova Scotia Food Products
Ocean Spray Cranberries, Inc.
Oregon, Washington, California Pear Bureau
Ore-Ida Foods, Inc.
Oscar Mayer Foodservice
Ottman Custom Processors, Inc.; Wilkinsonville, Massachusetts
Pacific International Rice Mills; Woodland, California
Pacific Pearl Seafoods-Wakefield; Bellevue, Washington
Papaya Administrative Committee
Pet Incorporated; St. Louis, Missouri
Pollio Dairy Products Corp.; Mineola, New York
Potato Board of Colorado
Reiner, Hermann, Executive Chef, Windows on the World and Inhilco, World Trade Center; New York City
Revson, Leslie, Executive Chef, Hotel Barbizon, New York City
Ritz, Willy, retired Pastry Chef, The Waldorf Astoria, New York City
RLB Food Distributers, West Caldwell, New Jersey
Salmon Institute
Schmidt, Arno, *Notes from the Chef's Desk* (Boston: CBI, 1977)
Seald-Sweet Growers, Inc.
S & H Organic Acres; Montgomery Creek, California
Singelton Seafood Company; Tampa, Florida

Sonnenschmidt, Fredric, and Nicolas, Jean, *Art of Gardemanger* (Boston: CBI, 1982)
Steinke, Klaus, formerly Banquet Service Manager, The Plaza, New York City
Sunkist Growers, Inc.
Sun World International, Inc.
Tarantino, Joseph, Pastry Chef and Instructor, New York Technical College; New York City
Texas Sweet Citrus Advertising, Inc.
Trombetti, Joseph, retired Executive Chef, The Plaza Hotel, New York City
Uncle Ben's, Inc.; Houston, Texas
Universal Frozen Foods; Twin Falls, Idaho
U.S. Department of Agriculture, "Food Buying Guide"
U.S. Department of Agriculture, "Fruits in Family Meals"
U.S. Department of Agriculture, "Nutrition: Food at Work for You"
U.S. Department of Agriculture, "Nutritive Value of Foods"
Virga's Pizza Crust Company; Bronx, New York
Virginia Dare Extract Company; Brooklyn, New York
Walker Foods; Springfield, New Jersey
Washington Asparagus Growers Association
Washington State Apple Commission
Washington State Fruit Commission
Washington State Potato Commission
Western Growers, Inc.
Wisconsin Milk Marketing Board

INDEX